Seoul

"All you've got to do is decide to go and the hardest part is over.

So go!"

TONY WHEELER, COFOUNDER – LONELY PLANET

THIS EDITION WRITTEN AND RESEARCHED BY

Trent Holden,
Simon Richmond

Contents

Plan Your Trip 4

Explore Seoul 44

Understand Seoul 155

Survival Guide 183

Seoul Maps 206

IZZET KERIBAR / GETTY IMAGES ©

WILL ROBB / GETTY IMAGES ©

(left) **Jongno-gu p48** Explore the area's mazelike streets

(above) **Gwangjang Market p122** Dine with locals at a food stall.

(right) **National Folk Museum of Korea p51** Learn about Korean history and culture.

WIBOWO RUSLI / GETTY IMAGES ©

Northern Seoul p124

Gwanghwamun & Jongno-gu p48

Myeong-dong & Jung-gu p71

Dongdaemun & Eastern Seoul p118

Western Seoul p84

Itaewon & Around p95

Gangnam & South of the Han River p106

Welcome to Seoul

Fashion- and technology-forward but also deeply traditional, this dynamic city mashes up temples, palaces, cutting-edge design and mountain trails, all to a nonstop K-Pop beat.

Historical Fragments

Gaze down on this sprawling metropolis of around 10 million people from atop any of Seoul's four guardian mountains and you'll sense the powerful *pungsu-jiri* (feng shui) that has long nurtured and protected the city. History clings tenaciously to the 'Miracle on the Han', a phoenix arisen from the ashes of the Korean War just over 60 years ago. So while Seoul has its eye clearly on the future, you'll also encounter fascinating fragments of the past in World Heritage–listed sites such as Jongmyo shrine, the alleys between the graceful *hanok* (traditional wooden homes) that cluster in Bukchon, and striding along the magnificent city walls.

Beyond the Walls

Public transport is brilliant, so there's no excuse for not stretching your travel horizons beyond the city limits. The fearsome Demilitarized Zone (DMZ), splitting South from North Korea, exerts a powerful attraction and is well worth visiting. Nearby is the charming arts and culture village of Heyri. To the west, Incheon is a fascinating port where the modern world came flooding into Korea at the end of the 19th century, while to the south is Suwon, home to impressive World Heritage–listed fortifications.

Twenty-Four-Hour City

Whatever you want, at any time of day or night, Seoul can provide. An early morning temple visit can lead to a palace tour followed by tea sipping in Bukchon and gallery-hopping in Samcheong-dong. *Soju* (a vodkalike drink) and snacks in a street tent bar will fuel you for shopping at the buzzing Dongdaemun or Namdaemun night markets, partying in Hongdae or Itaewon, or playing online games at a PC *bang* (internet gaming room). Follow this with steaming, soaking and snoozing in a *jjimjil-bang* (sauna and spa). By the time you look at your watch, it will be dawn again.

Design Matters

Over the last decade Seoul has worked hard to soften its industrial hard edges into an appealing urban ideal of parks, culture and design. Glass, concrete and steel are crafted into natural forms at the spectacular Dongdaemun Design Plaza & Park and the new City Hall. The popularity of the beautifully landscaped parks alongside the central Cheong-gye stream and the Han River has spurred on the creation of more green spaces and cycle routes. Join Seoulites enjoying time out shopping in stylish boutiques and drinking at cool cafes and convivial bars.

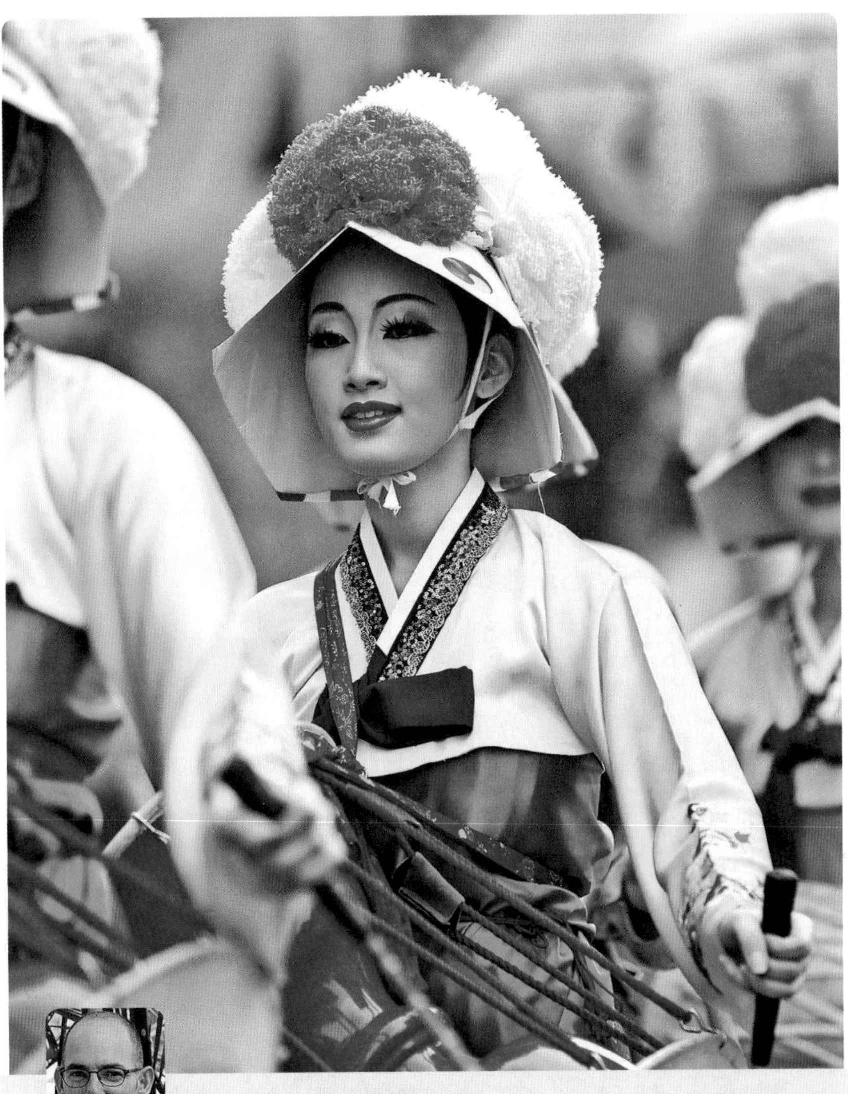

Why I Love Seoul

By Simon Richmond, Writer

Seoul is heaven for passionate foodies. Whether tucking into the snacks of commoners or the cuisine of kings, you just can't lose. A *hanjeongsik* (multicourse banquet) is a feast as much for the eyes as the tummy, as are the creations of chefs crafting neo-Korean dishes. Equally satisfying is scoffing down piping-hot, crispy *hotteok* (pancakes with sweet or savoury fillings) on a street corner, or delicious, fresh and fiery crab soup in Noryangjin Fish Market. And don't get me started on the wonderful universe of teas served in charming teahouses: this is where the soul of Seoul lies.

For more about our writers, see p232.

Top: Traditional drummers

Seoul's Top 10

1

Cheong-gye-cheon *(p56)*

1 A raised highway was demolished and the ground dug up to 'daylight' this long-buried stream. It transformed Seoul's centre, creating a riverside park and walking course that's a calm respite from the surrounding commercial hubbub. Public art is dotted along the banks and many events are held here, including a spectacular lantern festival in November, when thousands of glowing paper-and-paint sculptures are floated in the water. There's a museum where you can learn about the history of the Cheong-gye-cheon.

Gwanghwamun & Jongno-gu

Bukchon Hanok Village *(p53)*

2 In a city at the cutting edge of 21st-century technology, where apartment living is the norm, this neighbourhood stands as a testament to an age of craft when Seoulites lived in one-storey wooden *hanok* (traditional wooden homes), complete with graceful tiled roofs and internal courtyard gardens. Get lost wandering the labyrinthine streets, squished between two major palaces and rising up the foothills of Bukaksan. Take in the views and pause to pop into a cafe, art gallery, craft shop or small private museum along the way.

Gwanghwamun & Jongno-gu

JANE SWEENEY / JAI / CORBIS ©

2

RICHARD NEBESKY / GETTY IMAGES ©

Changdeokgung *(p52)*

3 The 'Palace of Illustrious Virtue' was built in the early 15th century as a secondary palace to Gyeongbokgung. These days this Unesco World Heritage–listed property exceeds it in beauty and grace – partly because so many of its buildings were actually lived in by royal-family members well into the 20th century. The most charming section is the Huwon, a 'secret garden' that is a royal horticultural idyll. Book well ahead to snag one of the limited tickets to view this special palace on the moonlight tours held during full-moon nights in the warm months.

Gwanghwamun & Jongno-gu

Gwangjang Market *(p122)*

4 This is one of Seoul's best markets. During the day, Gwangjang Market is known as a place for trading in secondhand clothes and fabrics. But it's at night that it really comes into its own, when some of its alleys fill up with vendors selling all manner of street eats. Stewed pig trotters and snouts, *gimbap* (rice, vegies and ham wrapped in rice and rolled in sheets of seaweed) and *bindaetteok* (plate-sized crispy pancakes of crushed mung beans and vegies fried on a skillet) are all washed down with copious amounts of *makgeolli* and *soju* (local liquors).

Dongdaemun & Eastern Seoul

Namsan & N Seoul Tower *(p73)*

5 Protected within a 109-hectare park and crowned by N Seoul Tower, one of Seoul's most distinctive architectural features, Namsan is the most central of the city's four guardian mountains. Locals actively patronise the park, keeping fit and taking in the cooler, sweeter air on hiking paths to the summit, including one that follows the line of the old Seoul city walls. The summit itself is highly commercial but still worth visiting; you won't just be marvelling at the view, but also at the multitude of inscribed padlocks that adorn the railings here – all signifying lovers' devotion.

Myeong-dong & Jung-gu

Lotus Lantern Festival *(p21)*

6 A week never passes in Seoul without some major festival or event. One of the most spectacular, that is well worth building your travel plans around, is the Lotus Lantern Festival, which happens in May in celebration of the Buddha's birthday. For weeks around this time, temples are strung with hundreds of rainbow-hued paper lanterns, a sight in itself. The highlight is a dazzling night-time parade that snakes its way through the city from Dongguk University to Jogye-sa, involving thousands of participants and every shape, size and colour of lantern. BELOW: JOGYE-SA (P55)

Month by Month

Hongdae *(p84)*

7 The area around Hongik University, Korea's leading art and design institution, has long acted as a magnet for young, independent and creatively minded Koreans. Hongdae is packed with quirky bars and cafes, jazzy boutiques, and cramped, smoky dance and live-music clubs where kids bop around to the latest K-Indie thrash bands and crooners. Come here to sample gourmet ice cream and artisan coffee, and pick up a cool craft souvenir at Saturday's Free Market. The vibe is infectious and has spilled over into neighbouring Sangsu-dong and Yeonnam-dong. RIGHT: HANDPAINTED LIGHTERS AT FREE MARKET (P94)

Western Seoul

7

The Demilitarized Zone *(p134)*

8 It's known as the Demilitarized Zone (DMZ). However, this 4km-wide, 250km-long heavily mined and guarded border, splitting a hostile North from South Korea is anything but. An entrenched symbol of the Cold War, the border has become a surreal tourist draw. The tension is most palpable in the Joint Security Area (JSA), the neutral space created after the 1953 Armistice for the holding of peace talks, which can only be visited on an organised tour. Observation points dotted along the DMZ also allow peeks into the secretive North. LEFT: FREEDOM BRIDGE (P135)

Day Trips from Seoul

Heyri *(p136)*

9 So peaceful and laid-back is the arty village of Heyri that it's hard to comprehend that less than 10km north is the heavily fortified border with North Korea. Conceived as a 'book village' connected to the nearby publishing centre of Paju Book City, this low-rise contemporary community is home to artists, writers, architects and other creative souls. There are scores of small art galleries, cafes, boutiques and quirky private collections turned into mini museums. With several pleasant, design-savvy places to stay, it makes for the perfect short break from Seoul, less than an hour away by express bus.

Day Trips from Seoul

10

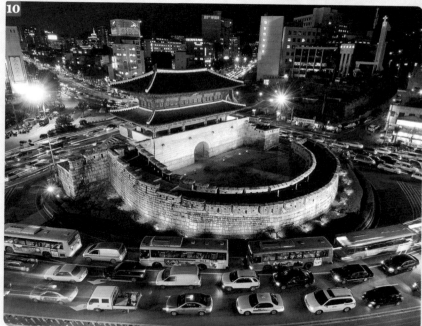

Dongdaemun *(p120)*

10 Historical and contemporary Seoul stand side by side in this eternally buzzing and sprawling market area. A facelift to Heunginjimun (aka Dongdaemun) has left the old east gate to the city looking grander than it has done in decades. Sections of the old city walls that the gate was once connected to have been uncovered and form part of the Dongdaemun History & Culture Park. Rising up behind this is the sleek, silvery form of the Zaha Hadid–designed Dongdaemun Design Plaza & Park, an architectural showstopper that could hardly be more 21st century in its conception.

Dongdaemun & Eastern Seoul

What's New

Contemporary Art Galleries

Samcheong-dong has consolidated its arty reputation with the opening of MMCA Seoul, a city-centre branch of the excellent contemporary-art gallery that has its main base at Gwacheon. But also prioritise a visit to the nearby Arario Museum in SPACE, a labyrinthine showcase for key works of Korean and international contemporary art by the likes of Korea's Lee Dongwook, Japan's Kohei Nawa and Britain's Tracey Emin. (p59)

City Hall

Head downstairs from the giant glass wave that looms over new City Hall to Citizens Hall for multimedia exhibitions, an archaeology museum and design shops. (p76)

Korea Furniture Museum

A hillside compound of traditional Korean buildings and gardens is the gorgeous frame for a top-notch collection of furniture showcasing local craft. (p126)

Lotte World Tower & Mall

The megamall is already open at the base of what will be Korea's tallest building with a 122nd-floor observatory. (p117)

Seochon

Scattered with *hanok* (traditional wooden homes), this neighbourhood immediately west of Gyeongbokgung is blossoming with trendy galleries, cafes and boutiques.

Dongjin Market

North of Hongdae, this Saturday craft and secondhand clothes market is surrounded by cafes, bars and casual eateries. (p94)

Insa-dong Maru

Track down Korean crafts, fashion and homewares at this slick shopping complex; in the basement gorge on the buffet feast at Bibigo Gyejeolbabsang. (p69)

Mullae Arts Village

Go on a street-art safari around the warren of small metalwork factories that is beginning to rub shoulders with artists' and design studios. (p88)

Craft Beer Bars

Spreading its reach from 'Craft Beer Valley' in Noksapyeong, the microbrew revolution continues to gain a head of steam with artisan beer-makers opening bars in Hongdae, Gangnam and beyond. (p102)

Makgeolli Revival

Traditional Korean alcoholic beverages such as the low-alcohol rice wine *makgeolli* come to the fore in new speciality bars and appreciation groups Makgeolli Makers and Makgeolli Mamas & Papas. (p166)

War & Women's Human Rights Museum

Learn the tragic history of sexual slavery across East Asia during WWII and of the ongoing problems women face in conflict zones. (p86)

Seoul City Wall Museum

Multimedia displays detail the history of Seoul's 14th-century city wall. There's also a model of Sungnyemun Gate made from Lego. (p121)

For more recommendations and reviews, see **lonelyplanet.com/south-korea/seoul**

Need to Know

For more information, see Survival Guide (p183)

Currency
Korean won (₩)

Languages
Korean and English

Visas
Australian, UK, US and most Western European citizens receive a 90-day entry permit on arrival.

Money
ATMs widely available. Credit cards accepted by most businesses, but some smaller food places and markets are cash only.

Mobile Phones
South Korea uses the CDMA digital standard; check compatibility with your phone provider. Phones can be hired at the airport and elsewhere.

Time
GMT/UTC plus nine hours. No daylight saving.

Tourist Information
Myeong-dong Tourist Information Center (☎02-778 0333; http://blog.naver.com/mdtic1129; 66, Eulji-ro, Jung-gu; ⌚9am-8pm; S Line 2 to Euljiro 1-ga, Exit 6) is centrally located.

Daily Costs

Budget: Less than ₩100,000
- Dorm bed: ₩20,000
- Street food: ₩1000–₩5000
- Local beer per bottle: ₩3000
- Hiking up Namsan: free
- Entry to National Museum of Korea: free
- Subway ticket: ₩1400

Midrange: ₩100,000–₩300,000
- *Hanok* guesthouse: ₩70,000
- Food walking tour: ₩60,000
- Entry to Gyeongbokgung: ₩3000
- *Galbi* (barbecued meat) meal: ₩50,000
- Theatre ticket: ₩40,000

Top End: More than ₩300,000
- Hotel: ₩200,000
- Royal Korean banquet: ₩70,000
- Scrub and massage at top-notch spa: ₩60,000
- Demilitarized Zone (DMZ) tour: ₩100,000

Advance Planning

Two months before Start learning *hangeul* (the Korean phonetic alphabet) and train for hiking up mountains. If visiting April to June, book for Moonlight Tours of Changdeokgung.

Three weeks before Plan itinerary, checking to see if there are any events or festivals you may be able to attend; book DMZ tour and templestay program.

One week before Make reservation at any top-end restaurants, buy tickets to any concerts you may want to attend.

Useful Websites

- **Visit Seoul** (www.visitseoul.net) The official government site to everything about the city.
- **Seoul** (http://magazine.seoulselection.com) Online version of the monthly magazine with its finger on the city's pulse.
- **Lonely Planet** (www.lonelyplanet.com/seoul) Destination information, hotel bookings, traveller forum and more.

WHEN TO GO

Spring and autumn are uniformly pleasant; summer is sweltering and muggy; and winters nasty and long. Typhoons are a possibility from late June to September.

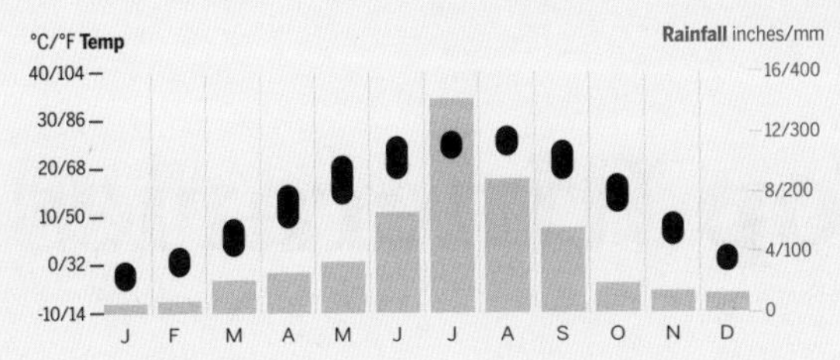

Arriving in Seoul

Incheon International Airport A'REX express trains to Seoul station ₩8000 (43 minutes); commuter trains ₩4250 (53 minutes). Bus to city-centre hotels from ₩9000 (one hour); taxi around ₩65,000.

Gimpo International Airport A'REX trains run to Seoul station (₩1300, 15 minutes) or take the subway (₩1450, 35 minutes). Both bus (from ₩5000) and taxi (around ₩35,000) will be slower – around 40 minutes to an hour, depending on traffic.

Seoul Station Long-distance trains arrive at this centrally located terminal; a taxi ride to most nearby hotels will be under ₩5000.

For much more on **arrival**, see p184

Getting Around

Buy a T-Money card (₩2500; http://eng.t-money.co.kr), which provides a ₩100 discount per trip on bus, subway, taxi and train fares.

- **Subway** The best way to get around, with an extensive network, frequent services and inexpensive fares.
- **Bus** Handy for routes around Namsan; less so for other places.
- **Taxi** Best for short trips; basic fare starts at ₩3000 for the first 2km.
- **Bicycle** Hire for pedaling along the Han River and through Olympic Park.
- **Car Hire** Useful only for long trips out of the city; budget from ₩80,000 per day.

For much more on **getting around**, see p186

Sleeping

There are plenty of budget guesthouses and five-star pamper palaces, but reserve well in advance especially if visiting during busy Asian travel seasons, such as Chinese New Year and Japan's Golden Week holidays (usually the end of April/early May). Rates at the cheaper places usually include the 10% government tax, but many midrange and top-end hotels quote without this amount. The top-end places also add another 10% for service.

Useful Websites

- **Korean Hotel Reservation Center** (www.khrc.com) Check for low rates on top-end hotels.
- **Best Guesthouse in Seoul** (www.guesthouseinseoul.org) Local guesthouses reviewed.
- **Lonely Planet** (www.lonelyplanet.com/seoul) Expert author reviews, user feedback, booking engine.

For much more on **sleeping**, see p145

SEOUL ADDRESSES

Korea's new address system consists of logically numbered houses on named streets – you'll notice numbered blue plaques on most buildings now and clear street signs in Korean and English. However, locals generally don't know the new street names, and old-style addresses are still used on some business cards and websites. To convert an old address to a new one go to http://eng.juso.go.kr/openEngPage.do.

For more on addresses, see p190.

Top Itineraries

Day One

Gwanghwamun & Jongno-gu (p48)

Start your tour of **Gyeongbokgung** at the palace's expertly restored main gate, Gwanghwamun, where you can watch the pageantry of the changing of the guard on the hour. Explore the winding streets of **Bukchon Hanok Village** and **Insa-dong**, pausing for refreshments at a cafe or teahouse in between browsing the equally ubiquitous art galleries and craft stores in these areas.

Lunch Dine cheaply at Tobang (p64) or in style at Min's Club (p66).

Gwanghwamun & Jongno-gu (p48)

Join the afternoon tour of **Changdeokgung**, which also includes the Huwon (Secret Garden). Explore the wooded grounds of the venerable shrine **Jongmyo**, housing the spirit tablets of the Joseon kings and queens.

Dinner Sample Korean street food at Gwangjang Market (p122).

Myeong-dong & Jung-gu (p71)

Take your seat at a fun nonverbal show such as **Nanta** or **Jump**. Be dazzled by the bright lights and retail overload of Myeong-dong and neighbouring **Namdaemun Market**, where the stalls stay open all night.

Day Two

Itaewon & Around (p95)

Survey centuries of Korean history and art by selectively dipping into the vast collection of the **National Museum of Korea**. Shuttle over to the west side of Yongsan-gu to enjoy the contemporary art and architecture at the splendid **Leeum Samsung Museum of Art**.

Lunch Tuck into southern American barbecue at Linus' BBQ (p100).

Myeong-dong & Jung-gu (p71)

Browse some of Itaewon's boutiques then, for a postlunch workout, hike up **Namsan** to **N Seoul Tower**. It's not a difficult climb, but if you don't have the energy then there's a cable car or a bus. It's very romantic watching the sunset from atop this central mountain as the night lights of Seoul flicker to life. Freshen up with a steam in the saunas and a soak in the tubs at the **Dragon Hill Spa & Resort**.

Dinner Savour delicious bibimbap at Mokmyeoksanbang (p78).

Itaewon & Around (p95)

Explore Itaewon after dinner for a fun night of hopping between cafes, bars and dance clubs.

WIBOWO RUSLI / GETTY IMAGES ©

Gyeongbokgung (p50)

ANGELO DESANTIS / GETTY IMAGES ©

Insa-dong (p59)

Day Three

Northern Seoul (p124)

Reflect on the struggles and sacrifices of Koreans to overcome colonialism and create a modern country at **Seodaemun Prison History Hall**. Afterwards, hike up nearby **Inwangsan** for fabulous views of the city, surreal rock formations and the other-worldly shamanistic rituals of **Inwangsan Guksadang**.

Lunch Fuel up on a Korean vegetarian feast at Deongjang Yesool (p130).

Northern Seoul (p124)

Keep on shadowing the **Seoul City Wall** down to Buam-dong and over **Bukaksan** and to Seongbuk-dong, a hike of around two hours. Catch your breath and rest your feet in the beautiful teahouse **Suyeon Sanbang**, and the equally serene surrounds of the temple **Gilsang-sa**.

Dinner Journey to Central Asia with lamb shashlik at Samarkand (p122).

Dongdaemun & Eastern Seoul (p118)

If your hiking legs haven't given out, it's only another hour or so following the City Wall over **Naksan** and down to Dongdaemun, where the night market will just be starting to crank up (alternatively take the subway). Admire the 21st-century architectural styling of **Dongdaemun Design Plaza & Park**, then trawl the market stalls for a new outfit.

Day Four

Western Seoul (p84)

Both contemporary art and panoramic views up and down the Han can be enjoyed at **63 Sky Art Gallery** on **Yeouido**. Hire a bicycle in Hangang Riverside Park and pedal out to **Seonyudo Park** on an island in the Han River.

Lunch Pick your seafood and have it cooked at Noryangjin Fish Market (p90).

Western Seoul (p84)

If you're interested in contemporary architecture, then **Ewha Womans University's** stunning entrance building and **KT&G SangsangMadang** in Hongdae are both worth seeing. Hongdae and neighbouring Sangsu-dong and Yeonnam-dong are brimming with hipster hang-outs; if it's Saturday you can shop for quirky, original craft souvenirs at the **Free Market** or **Dongjin Market**. A late-afternoon visit to the atmospheric Buddhist temple **Bongeun-sa** can segue nicely into browsing the boutiques of **Apgujeong**, **Cheongdam** or **Garosu-gil**.

Dinner Treat yourself to neo-Korean cuisine at Jungsik (p113).

Gangnam & South of the Han River (p106)

After dinner pitch up at the **Banpo Hangang Park** by 9pm to see the day's last floodlit flourish of the **Banpo Bridge Rainbow Fountain** off the Banpo Bridge.

If You Like...

Contemporary Architecture

Dongdaemun Design Plaza & Park Zaha Hadid's building is straight out of a sci-fi fantasy. (p120)

City Hall This giant glass wave is a reinterpretation of traditional Korean design. (p76)

Ewha Womans University Dominique Perrault's stunning main entrance dives six storeys underground. (p86)

Tangent Daniel Libeskind–designed building that's like a work of art. (p178)

Lotte World Tower & Mall Rising up to 123 floors, this super skyscraper is set to be the peninsula's tallest building. (p117)

Palaces

Changdeokgung The most attractive one, with a 'secret garden'. (p52)

Gyeongbokgung The biggest one, with extra museums and a changing of the guard. (p50)

Changgyeonggung The one with a beautiful pond and elegant greenhouse. (p127)

Deoksugung The one where Korea's last emperor lived and sipped coffee. (p75)

Unhyeongung The one where you can watch a traditional music performance on Fridays. (p60)

Major Museums

National Museum of Korean Contemporary History Walk through a visual record of the country's recent past. (p57)

National Museum of Korea Packed with national treasures spanning the centuries. (p97)

Dongdaemun Design Plaza & Park (p120)

Seoul Museum of History Learn how much the city has changed over the last century. (p57)

National Folk Museum of Korea Fascinating exhibits indoors and in the palace grounds. (p51)

War Memorial of Korea Masses of military-related displays and good exhibits on the Korean War. (p98)

Mountains, Hiking & City Wall

Bukaksan Start your circuit of the City Wall by hiking up the tallest of Seoul's four guardian mountains. (p132)

Naksan Heading east, the lowest of the guardian mountains with the arty neighbourhood of Ihwa-dong on its slopes. (p127)

Namsan The mountain at the heart of the city, criss-crossed with hiking trails and walking paths. (p73)

Inwangsan Climb up past weirdly eroded rocks and giant boulders for brilliant views. (p132)

Ansan One of the best spots to catch the sunrise, with a lower-level walking path. (p132)

Suwon Hike around the World Heritage–listed City Wall in this town south of Seoul. (p137)

Religious Buildings

Jogye-sa Home to Daeungjeon, the largest Buddhist temple building in Seoul. (p55)

Myeong-dong Catholic Cathedral Gothic-style cathedral with a vaulted ceiling and stained-glass windows. (p78)

Jeoldusan Martyrs' Shrine Memorial museum and church dedicated to Korea's Catholic martyrs and saints. (p86)

Inwangsan Guksadang Seoul's most famous shamanist shrine. (p130)

Bongeun-sa Join the Templelife program here every Thursday afternoon. (p110)

Gilsang-sa Former exclusive restaurant turned into a serene temple in the hills. (p129)

Sajikdan Stone altar in a tranquil park where devotees prayed for good harvests. (p59)

Traditional Architecture

Hanok Guesthouses The best way to experience a *hanok* (traditional wooden house) is to stay overnight in one. (p145)

Namsangol Hanok Village Five differing *yangban* (upper-class) houses are in this park at the foot of Namsan. (p77)

Korean Folk Village A gathering of some 260 thatched and tiled traditional buildings from around the country. (p138)

Bukchon Hanok Village Around 900 *hanok* make this Seoul's largest *hanok* neighbourhood. (p53)

Art Galleries

Seoul has scores of commercial art galleries and most offer free exhibitions. (p58)

Leeum Samsung Museum of Art Three top architect-designed buildings and a stunning collection of art from ancient to contemporary. (p99)

Arario Museum in SPACE Amazing contemporary art in a sleekly converted iconic 1970s building. (p59)

National Museum of Modern and Contemporary Art The best reason for making the trek out to Seoul Grand Park. (p112)

MMCA Seoul The new city-centre branch of the National Museum of Contemporary Art. (p59)

Seoul Museum of Art Good exhibitions in the former Supreme Court building. (p77)

For more top Seoul spots, see the following:

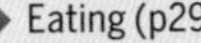

- Eating (p29)
- Drinking & Nightlife (p33)
- Entertainment (p36)
- Shopping (p38)
- Sports & Activities (p41)

Quirky Museums & Experiences

Lock Museum Exhibits locks as both lovely works of art and fearsome apparatuses, such as a medieval chastity belt. (p127)

Dragon Hill Spa & Resort Strip down and join relaxing Koreans for a communal sweat, steam and full-body scrub. (p105)

Seoul Yangnyeongsi Herb Medicine Museum Learn about your yin, yang and Sasang constitution. (p121)

Gwacheon National Science Museum Catch the hourly robot dance show performing Gangnam-style. (p112)

Samsung D'Light Techno-geek heaven offers a glimpse at the gadgets of tomorrow. (p112)

Modern Design Museum Fascinating private collection tracing the history of modern design in Korea. (p86)

Parks & Gardens

Olympic Park Home to a 1700-year-old earth fort and over 200 quirky sculptures. (p108)

Seoul Forest Expansive park by the Han River with wetlands and Sika deer. (p121)

Seonyudo Park Beautiful park and gardens on an island in the Han River. (p89)

Seonjeongneung Park housing the tombs of two Korean kings and one queen. (p110)

Month by Month

TOP EVENTS

Jongmyo Daeje, May

Lotus Lantern Festival (Yeon Deung Ho), May

Seoul Fringe Festival, August

Sajik Daeje, September

Seoul Lantern Festival, November

January

Wrap up well against very chilly weather as temperatures in Seoul can drop to below -10°C (14°F). It's a good time for trips to nearby ski resorts.

Seollal (Lunar New Year)

Seoul empties out as locals make the trip to their home town to visit relatives, honour ancestors and eat traditional foods over this three-day national festival. That said, there are a number of events for travellers in Seoul during this time, held at the major palaces as well as the Korean Folk Village, Namsangol Hanok Village and the National Folk Museum of Korea. For more information, see www.visitseoul.net or www.visitkorea.or.kr. Celebrations start on 8 February 2016, 28 January 2017 and 16 February 2018.

April

It can still be cold and wet in spring, so come prepared. Nature determines the exact timing, but early April is generally when parts of Seoul turn pink in a transient flurry of delicate cherry blossoms.

Festival Bom

Bom means 'spring' in Korean and that's when this citywide festival of the arts (www.festivalbom.org) occurs. Both local and international artists take part and performances range from dance and drama to music and installations.

Hangang Yeouido Spring Flower Festival

One of the best places to experience the blossoming trees and flowers is Yeouido (www.ydp.go.kr). Other good spots include Namsan and Ewha Womans University, and Jeongdok Public Library in Samcheong-dong.

Royal Wedding Ceremony of King Gojong and Empress Myeongseong

A re-enactment of the royal wedding ceremony of King Gojong, the last king of the Joseon dynasty, and Empress Myeongseong (Queen Min) is held on the third Saturday in April at Unhyeongung (www.unhyeongung.or.kr), where the original ceremony took place on 21 March 1866.

May

Buddha's birthday brings a kaleidoscope of light and colour, as rows of delicate paper lanterns, lit at dusk, are strung along

LUNAR CALENDAR

Local religious holidays and festivals, such as Seollal, follow the lunar calendar, while the rest follow the Gregorian (Western) calendar. Dates have been given for upcoming years.

the main thoroughfares and in temple courtyards.

Jongmyo Daeje

Held on the first Sunday of the month, this ceremony (www.jongmyo.net) honours Korea's royal ancestors. It involves a solemn costumed parade from Gyeongbokgung through downtown Seoul to the royal shrine at Jongmyo, where spectators can enjoy traditional music and an elaborate, all-day ritual.

Lotus Lantern Festival (Yeon Deung Ho)

Seoul's Buddhist temples, such as Jogye-sa and Bongeun-sa, are the focus of this celebration of Buddha's birthday (celebrated on 14 May 2016, 3 May 2017 and 22 May 2018). The weekend preceding the birthday, Seoul celebrates with a huge daytime street festival and evening lantern parade – the largest in South Korea; see www.llf.or.kr for details.

Seoul International Cartoon & Animation Festival (SICAF)

Half a million animation geeks pack auditoriums in Seoul each year to see why the city is an epicentre of animation (fans of *The Simpsons* have Korean artists to thank). See www.sicaf.org for details.

June

The hot weather and period before the rains of July mean this is a great time to enjoy Seoul's outdoors.

Korean Queer Festival

Seoul's LGBTIQ community emerges from the shadows for a series of citywide events, including a parade, street party and film festival. For details see www.kqcf.org.

Dano Festival

Held according to the lunar calendar (on 10 June in 2016), this festival features shamanist rituals and mask dances at several locales, including Namsangol Hanok Village and the National Folk Museum of Korea.

July

Pack heavy-duty rain gear and waterproof shoes, as this is when Seoul experiences a month of monsoonlike rains.

Bucheon International Fantastic Film Festival (BiFan)

Held in Bucheon, just outside of Seoul, BiFan (www.bifan.kr) is a feast of the best in movie sci-fi, fantasy and horror. Theatres are within walking distance of Songnae station (Line 1, towards Incheon).

August

The rain abates and is replaced by sweltering humidity. Cool off in Seoul's parks and public areas: there are free outdoor concerts most nights in Seoul Plaza and many free events held in the parks along the Han River.

Seoul Fringe Festival

One of Seoul's best performing-arts festivals (http://eng.seoulfringefestival.net), when local and international artists converge on the Hongdae area to flee the mainstream.

September

Apart from the following you can also catch a rerun of the royal wedding ceremony at Unhyeongung on the third Saturday of the month.

Sajik Daeje

Held at Sajikdan on the third Sunday of the month, the 'Great Rite for the Gods of Earth and Agriculture' is one of Seoul's most important ancestral rituals. The ceremonies, which include offerings of fresh meat and produce, are performed in traditional costumes to live music played by a court orchestra.

Chuseok

The Harvest Moon Festival is a major three-day holiday when families gather, eat crescent-shaped rice cakes and visit their ancestors' graves to make offerings of food and drink and perform *sebae* (a ritual bow). Begins 14 September in 2016, 3 October 2017 and 23 September in 2018.

Seoul Drum Festival

Focusing on Korea's fantastic percussive legacy, this three-day international event (www.seouldrum.go.kr) in Seoul Plaza brings together all kinds of ways to make a lot of noise.

October

Autumn is a great time to visit Seoul, particularly if you like hiking, as this is the season when the mountains run through a palate of rustic colours.

Korea International Art Fair (KIAF)

Held at COEX, KIAF (www.kiaf.org) is one of the region's top art fairs and a good opportunity to get a jump on the country's hot new artists.

Seoul International Fireworks Festival

Best viewed from Yeouido Hangang Park, this festival (www.hanwhafireworks.com/eng) sees dazzling fireworks displays staged by both Korean and international teams.

Asia Song Festival

This mega K-Pop event (www.asiasongfestival.com) at Jamsil Stadium includes performances by star *hallyu* (Korean Wave) bands and singers (meaning ones that have become popular outside of Korea), such as Girls' Generation and Super Junior.

November

Seoul Lantern Festival

Centred on the Cheong-gye-cheon, this festival (http://blog.naver.com/seoullantern) sees the stream-park illuminated by gigantic, fantastic lanterns made by master craftspeople.

(Top and bottom) Lotus Lantern Festival (p21), Cheong-gye-cheon (p56)

GLENN SUNDEEN - TIGERPAL / GETTY IMAGES ©

JANE SWEENEY / GETTY IMAGES ©

With Kids

Children are more than welcome in Seoul: this is a safe and family-friendly city with plenty of interesting museums (including several devoted to kids themselves), as well as parks, amusement parks and fun events that will appeal to all age groups.

K-Pop Rules

The best way to cut down on child grumbles in Seoul is to mix your sampling of traditional Korean culture with things that the kids are more likely to enjoy. Fortunately, thanks to the global appeal of local pop culture, the young ones are likely to be more au fait with contemporary Korean pop culture than you are! Be prepared to search out shops stocking Girls' Generation posters, DVDs of Korean TV soap operas such as *Boys Over Flowers*, or *manhwa* (Korean comics and graphic novels). Kyobo Bookshop (p68) is a good place to start.

Educational Experiences

Museums and other traditional culture centres don't need to be boring. The National Museum of Korea (p97) and the National Folk Museum (p51) have fun, hands-on children's sections, and the War Memorial of Korea (p98) has outdoor warplanes and tanks that make for a popular playground. Various events, some involving dressing up in traditional costumes or having a go at taekwondo happen at Namsangol Hanok Village (p77). Older kids and teenagers will likely want to visit places such as the Seoul Animation Center (p77) to learn more about local animated TV series and films, or Samsung D'Light (p112) to play with the latest digital technology. Nonverbal shows such as Nanta and Jump (p82) are great family entertainment.

Park & Animal Life

At the theme parks Lotte World (p109) and Everland (p138), family entertainment comes in megasized portions. Easier on the wallet are the scores of free open spaces that constitute Seoul's wealth of city-managed parks – places such as Seoul Forest (p121), Olympic Park (p108) and the string of bicycle-lane-connected parks that hug the Han River's banks (p87). Each summer six big outdoor-pool complexes open in the Han River parks, too.

Animal cafes, several of which are clustered in Hongdae (p92), are likely to appeal too – your kids can spend quality time with pet cats, dogs and even sheep.

Need to Know

Sleeping & Eating

Korean-style *ondol* rooms are ideal for families, as everyone sleeps on a *yo* (floor mattress) in the same space. Children are welcome in restaurants, but few places will have kids' menus; there's no shortage of the usual fast-food franchises if all else fails. High chairs are not common.

Babysitting

A few top hotels and residences can arrange babysitting services.

Festivals

On Children's Day (5 May) there are special events for kids across the city.

More Information

Lonely Planet's *Travel with Children* is good for general advice. **Korea 4 Expats.com** (www.korea4expats.com) has more child-related information on Seoul.

Like a Local

Prepare for Seoul's cultural divide. Bukchon and Seochon (both north of the Han River) are the city's historical heart, where courtly palace culture meets pre- and postcolonial commerce. South of the Han, nouveau riche Gangnam is stacked with top-end boutiques and expense-account restaurants and bars.

Round-the-Clock Shopping

Whichever side of the river they live on, Seoulites love (or is that live?) to shop. For all the city's headlong rush into the 21st century, sprawling all-night markets, such as those at Dongdaemun (p123) and Namdaemun (p74), confirm more traditional and time-worn images of Asian commerce. This impression is further reinforced by the bazaars devoted to herbal medicines at Seoul Yangnyeongsi (p123) and to antiques at Dapsimni (p123). A fascinating insight into local life can also be gleaned from what people sell off at flea markets, the biggest of which is the Seoul Folk Flea Market (p123). If the old and secondhand aren't to your taste, contemporary fashions and fads can be gauged on trips to mercantile hubs such as Myeong-dong, Apgujeong, Cheongdam and Garosu-gil.

Keeping Fit

Going hiking in and around Seoul can be a frightening business. This is not so much because of the precariousness of the mountain trails (quite the opposite – these are usually well marked and seldom short of small armies of hikers), but because you will almost certainly feel underdressed. Seoulites are super avid walkers and few would ever even think of venturing out without being kitted head to toe in the latest hi-tech and invariably brightly coloured gear. A trip to Dongdaemun Market or a shopping mall to purchase an outfit of local brands, such as Blackyak or the Redface, should have you breathing a little easier.

Hiking is not the only popular keep-fit pastime. The cycle lanes running alongside the Han River (p87) are also actively patronised, as are the free outdoor gyms located in many parks.

Bang-ing Around

The old expat playground of Itaewon has become a much more multicultural affair, appealing to worldly Koreans and their curious brethren. The adjacent areas of Hannam-dong, Haebangchon (aka HBC) and Gyeongridan have an equally, if not more, happening vibe.

However, to really take Seoul's relaxation pulse, a nocturnal visit to hip Hongdae and Daehangno – both major hubs for students and the young – is recommended. Here you'll encounter the highest concentrations of Seoul's various versions of the *bang*. Meaning 'room', *bang* come in the shape of karaoke rooms *(noraebang)*, private DVD screening rooms (DVD-*bang*) and online-game rooms (PC *bang*).

Finally, if you really want to sample local life, get naked! Stripping off and sweating at a *jjimjil-bang* (luxury sauna) is a very popular way for Seoulites to steam off their stresses.

For Free

You don't need a wallet packed with won to have an enjoyable time in Seoul. Many of the best things you can do – from hiking around the ancient city walls to enjoying the pageant of the changing of the guard at the palaces – cost nothing at all.

Architectural Treasures

Admission to most royal palaces is not costly and usually includes free guided tours. Additionally, it costs nothing to enjoy the changing of the guard ceremonies at Gyeongbokgung (p50), Deoksugung (p75) and the Bosingak bell tower pavilion (p62). Impressive religious architecture is freely on show at the Buddhist temples Jogye-sa (p55), Bongeun-sa (p110) and Gilsang-sa (p129). You can also view aristocratic *hanok* (traditional Korean one-storey wooden houses) for free at Namsangol Hanok Village (p77), or clusters of still-lived-in, more modest traditional homes in Bukchon, Seochon and Ikseon-dong (p61).

Those with more contemporary architectural tastes will want to get an eyeful of the sinuous lines of both Dongdaemun Design Plaza (p120) and the new City Hall (p76), as well as a host of stylish structures in Gangnam such as Daniel Libeskind's Tangent building (p178).

The Great Outdoors

Join the legions of locals who take full advantage of Seoul's mountainous topography. All four of the city's guardian mountains – Bukaksan, Naksan, Namsan and Inwangsan – have hiking routes; the really keen can summit them all by following the remains of Seoul's city walls. The panoramic city views are your reward for the effort.

The city government has also spent enormous sums to create pleasant waterside parks both along the Han River and in central Seoul, where the long-buried-over Cheong-gye-cheon (p56) now sparkles in the light of day. Seoul Forest (p121) is another major reforestation project, as is the creation of a beautiful landscaped park from an old water-filtration plant on the Han River island of Seonyudo (p89). For more about Seoul's hiking options, see p28.

Museums, Galleries & Street Art

The list of museums with no entrance fee is pretty extensive and includes the National Museum (p97), Seoul Museum of History (p57) and Seoul Museum of Art (p77). You don't need to be a buyer to drop by the scores of free art-gallery shows in areas such as Insa-dong and Samcheong-dong (p58). There are thousands of interesting outdoor sculptures scattered across Seoul, with over 200 of them alone in Olympic Park (p108). And for fun, inventive street art, wander the alleys of Ihwa-dong and Mullae Arts Village (p88).

Festivals & Events

Not a week goes by without a free festival or event happening somewhere in the city. Seoul's government often puts on free shows in Seoul Plaza (p76) in front of City Hall, and there's the spectacular lighting up of the fountain (p111) flowing off Banpo Bridge in the warmer months. There's no cost to join in the Sunday singalong service at the Yeouido Full Gospel Church (p88) – with a cast of tens of thousands – either.

Courses & Tours

Helping you know your hansik (Korean food) from your hanbok (traditional clothing), a variety of courses and tours will put you on the fast track to understanding Korean culture. Some are very popular, so they're worth booking well in advance, particularly the Koridoor Tours trip to the DMZ.

DEREK WINCHESTER / GETTY IMAGES ©

Sculpture at Templestay Information Center

Courses

Templestays & Meditation

Templestay (Map p212; ☎02-2013 2000; www.templestay.com; 56 Ujeongguk-ro, Jongno-gu; SLine 3 to Anguk, Exit 6) At the Templestay Information Center you can book overnight stay programs at beautiful temples in Seoul, including Bongeun-sa (p110), Jogye-sa (p55) and Gilsang-sa (p129), and around Korea. No attempt will be made to convert you to Buddhism during these inexpensive and relaxing programs, which are a brilliant way to learn a little about Korean Buddhism, meditation and crafts such as how to make paper lanterns and prayer beads.

International Seon Center (☎02-2260 3891; http://site.dongguk.edu/user/seoncenter eng/index.html; 30 Pildong-ro 1-gil, Jung-gu; SLine 3 to Dongguk University, Exit 6) Come here for English lectures on Buddhist teaching every Saturday, 2pm to 4pm, and for the Templelife program that runs every afternoon from 2pm to 5pm, which includes a chat with a monk over tea. You'll find the centre on the 2nd floor of the round theatre to the left of the campus inner gate (Hyehwamun).

Food, Drink & Culture

O'ngo (Map p212; ☎02-3446 1607; www.ongofood.com; 12 Samilde-ro 30-gil, Jongno-gu; tours from ₩57,000, courses from ₩65,000; SLine 1, 3 or 5 to Jongno 3-ga, Exit 5) Well-run cooking classes and food tours around the city are offered here. The beginners' class lasts two hours and you can choose a variety of different dishes to learn about, including *haemul pajeon* (seafood pancake), *sundubu* (soft tofu stew), *bulgogi* (marinated beef) and the many types of *kimchi*.

Delectable Travels (http://delectabletravels.com; full-day tour for 2 people US$600) Expert food guide Dan Grey, the go-to guy for visiting celebs and TV crews, runs full-day Ultimate Food Experiences around the city taking in a variety of markets and street food. Half-day tours are available on request.

Makgeolli Makers (www.facebook.com/makgeollimakers; Susubori Academy, 47 Kyonggidae-ro, Seodaemun-gu; course ₩45,000; SLine 2 or 5 to Chungjeongno, Exit 7) Becca Baldwin and Daniel Lenaghan, two well-qualified brewing instructors, offer these hands-on courses that provide all you need to know about *makgeolli* (a mildly alcoholic drink made from rice, water and *nuruk*, a wheat-based mix of yeasts, enzymes and moulds) and how to make it. The introductory

GREG THOMSON / GETTY IMAGES ©

Makgeolli (milky rice wine; p166)

courses run on a Sunday from 1pm to 4pm and you'll go home with your own batch of *makgeolli* ready to drink in about a week.

Gastro Tour Seoul (www.gastrotourseoul.com; tours from ₩90,000) Culinary and culture tours run by local Veronica Kang. Itineraries include tours around Insa-dong and Bukchon, Seoul's Little Tokyo in Ichon-dong, and a trip to a winery at Anseong in the Gyeonggi-do.

Yoo's Family (Map p212; 02-3673 0323; www.yoosfamily.com; 19 Yulgok-ro 10-gil, Jongno-gu; courses ₩20,000-65,000; S Line 3 to Anguk, Exit 4) Housed in a *hanok* (traditional Korean one-storey wooden house with a tiled roof), Yoo's Family's cooking courses cover making *kimchi* and *hotteok* (pancakes), as well as various other foods. You can also practice the tea ceremony, make prints from carved wooden blocks and dress up in *hanbok*. A minimum of two people is required.

Magpie Brewing Co. (Map p218; www.magpiebrewing.com; 6-15 Wausan-ro 19-gil, Mapo-gu; 5pm-2am Tue-Thu, 5pm-3am Fri, 2pm-3am Sat, 2pm-2am Sun; S Line 2 to Hongik University, Exit 9) To learn about craft beer brewing, check out the introductory courses run by Magpie.

Korean Language

YBM Sisa (Map p212; 02-2278 0509; http://kli.ybmedu.com; 104 Jong-ro, Jongno-gu; 6.30am-9pm Mon-Fri, 9am-4pm Sat & Sun; courses from ₩130,000; S Line 1, 3 or 5 to Jongno 3-ga, Exit 15) Korean classes (maximum size 10) for all ability levels cover grammar, writing and conversation. Private tuition (₩50,000 per hour for one person) can also be arranged here.

Yonsei University (Map p218; 02-2123 3465; www.yskli.com; 50 Yonsei-ro, Seodaemun-gu; S Line 2 to Sinchon, Exit 6) The university runs part- and full-time Korean language and culture classes for serious students.

Tours

Seoul City Tour Bus (Map p210; 02-777 6090; www.seoulcitybus.com; tours from adult/child ₩12,000/10,000; half-hourly 9am-7pm; S Line 5 to Gwanghwamun, Exit 6) Comfortable tour buses circuit top tourist attractions north of the Han River, allowing you to see a lot in a short time. Hop on and off anywhere along the two routes, one on a single-decker bus covering the palaces and sights in the downtown area, the other on a double-decker bus in a wider loop including Hongdae and Yeouido. Buy tickets on the bus, which can be caught outside Donghwa Duty Free Shop at Gwanghwamun. Check the website for details of night tours, which zigzag across the Han River so you can view the illuminated bridges, and for trips on the trolleylike buses.

Seoul City Walking Tours (02-6925 0777; http://dobo.visitseoul.net) Reserve three days in advance for one of 23 different free walking tours offered by the city in association with volunteer guides. Themes take you on tours around the palaces, Bukchon, Cheong-gye-cheon, Namsan fortress and City Hall.

Koridoor Tours (Map p224, C2; 02-794 2570; www.koridoor.co.kr; S Line 1 to Namyeong, Exit 2) Apart from running the very popular DMZ/JSA tour for the USO (United Service Organizations), this company also offers city tours; trips to out-of-town destinations, such as Suwon and Incheon; paragliding, scuba diving and deep-sea fishing tours; and ski trips to local resorts in the winter.

Royal Asiatic Society (www.raskb.com) Organises enlightening walking and bus tours to all parts of South Korea, usually on weekends; check the website for the schedule. Nonmembers are welcome to join. The reasonably priced tours are led by English-speakers who are experts in their field. The society also organises lectures several times a month in Seoul.

Viator.com (www.viator.com/Seoul/d973-ttd) Also check out the options here.

Hiking

With several mountains and hills within its boundaries, and even more a short journey away, Seoul is a fantastic place to plan some hiking. Trails are well marked and vary from relatively easy strolls of a few hours to a 10-day hiking challenge running 157km around the city.

Seoul City Walls

Initially built in 1396, Seoul's original **fortress wall** (http://seoulcitywall.seoul.go.kr) runs for 18.6km, connecting the peaks of Bukaksan (342m), Naksan (125m), Namsan (262m) and Inwangsan (338m), all north of the Han River. It was punctuated by four major gates and four subgates, of which six remain.

Over time parts of the wall were demolished, but in an effort to have the entire structure designated by Unesco as a World Heritage site, the city has been restoring some of the missing sections. At the time of writing some 70% (12.8km) is in place and it's relatively easy to follow a hiking route beside and, in several cases, atop the walls.

The circuit can be accomplished in a day, but is better split over two, should you prefer to take your time and do some sightseeing. Start at Heunginjimun (Dongdaemun), near to which is the Seoul City Wall Museum (p121), and walk in an anti-clockwise direction – this way you'll get the steepest section up and down Bukaksan done in the morning and could linger on Namsam later in the afternoon.

Namhan Sanseong Provincial Park

This park, 25km southeast of Seoul, is famous for its beautiful pine and oak forests, wild flowers and the World Heritage–listed remains of a fortress, parts of which date back to the 7th century. The most popular hiking route is a two-hour loop with sweeping panoramas. Or you can trek the entire fortress wall's perimeter in around seven hours. Be sure to mix up trails that lead in and out of the wall to change your views.

To get here, take subway Line 8 to Sanseong, then get a taxi or take bus 9 from Exit 2 of the station to the park's south gate, a total journey of around one hour from central Seoul.

Seoul Dulle-gil

More ambitious hikers can tackle part or all of the **Seoul Dulle-gil** (Seoul Trail; http://gil.seoul.go.kr) which runs for 157km around the city's outskirts. Each of the eight sections starts and finishes beside a subway station and goes over a mountain (sometimes two), through forests and parks and alongside streams.

Section 1 Suraksan and Bulamsan (18.6km, 8¾ hours; start S Dobongsan, finish S Taereung)

Section 2 Yongmasan (12.6km, 5¼ hours; start S Taereung, finish S Gwangnaru)

Section 3 Godeoksan and Iljasan (26.1km, nine hours; start S Gwangnaru, finish S Suseo)

Section 4 Daemosan and Umyeonsan (17.9km, eight hours; start S Suseo, finish S Sadang)

Section 5 Gwanaksan (12.7km, 5¾ hours; start S Sadang, finish S Seoksu)

Section 6 Anyangcheon stream (18km, 4½ hours; start S Seoksu, finish S Gayang)

Section 7 Bongsan and Aengbongsan (16.6km, 6¼ hours; start S Gayang, finish S Gubapal)

Section 8 Bukhansan (34.5km, 17 hours; start S Gubapal, finish S Dobongsan)

Bukhansan National Park

North of the city, Bukhansan National Park (p139) is studded with granite peaks which provide sweeping vistas, and is covered in pine and maple trees, gushing streams and remote temples.

CHRISTIAN OEY / GETTY IMAGES ©

Pork (*samgyeopsal*) barbecue (p164)

Eating

Sampling the varied and – to international travellers – generally unfamiliar delights of Korean cuisine is one of Seoul's great pleasures. Restaurants, cafes and street stalls are scattered throughout every neighbourhood with options to suit all budgets and tastes, from small, unpretentious joints serving healthy rice and vegetables, DIY beef or pork barbecue to the overflowing abundance and delicacy of a royal banquet.

What's Hot

While Korean food has been the darling of hipster food trends overseas for some years now, Seoul in turn has an obsession with international food. While crazes come and go, most are centred on world cuisine or what the latest K-Pop star was spotted eating last week. Fads can range from mile-long queues for churros, to pizza in a cone or gourmet popcorn flavoured with anything from white truffle to cookies-and-cream.

One current food trend is Seoul's infatuation with American cuisine, where Southern-style BBQ, pulled-pork sandwiches and Maine lobster rolls are all the rage.

Fusion food is another big hit, mixing traditional Korean flavours with contemporary dishes, from LA-style, food-truck *kimchi* tacos to high-end molecular fusion.

Restaurants

Most Korean-style restaurants offer a table-and-chairs option, but in some traditional places customers sit on floor cushions at low

NEED TO KNOW

For help decoding the menu, see p168.

Price Ranges

$	less than ₩10,000
$$	₩10,000–₩20,000
$$$	more than ₩20,000

Opening Hours

- **Restaurants and cafes** 11am to 11pm
- **Convenience stores** 24 hours

Reservations

For most places, it's unnecessary to book tables unless you want your own private room or are in a large group.

Guides & Blogs

- **ZenKimchi** (www.zenkimchi.com)
- **Seoul Eats** (www.seouleats.com)
- **Visit Seoul** (www.visitseoul.net)
- **Korea Taste** (www.koreataste.org)
- **Alien's Day Out** (www.aliensdayout.com)

Tipping & Service Charges

Not a Korean custom, and not expected.

tables. Few staff speak English, but most restaurants have some English on the menu.

In Seoul, eating out is a group activity. A number of Korean meals, such as *galbi* (beef ribs) or *jjimdak* (spicy chicken pieces with noodles), are not usually available for just one person.

On a Budget

Street stalls and *pojangmacha* (tent bars) are great options for inexpensive meals. Areas in Insa-dong, Myeong-dong and markets at Gwangjang, Namdaemun and Dongdaemun are the best spots to dig in with locals.

For eating on the go there's always convenience stores, with snack foods such as *gimbap* (rice wrapped in seaweed) or noodles for quick and easy meals; there's usually a small area with tables.

Vegetarians & Vegans

Though vegetarian and vegan travellers generally have a tough time in Korea, fortunately Seoul offers a much greater choice of

Namdaemun Market (p74)

meat- and dairy-free eating options. As well as Korean dishes such as bibimbap (usually rice, egg, meat and vegies with chilli sauce; order it without meat, or egg), a few tofu dishes and vegetable *pajeon* (savoury fried pancakes), you'll find several traditional restaurants that specialise in 100% vegetarian Buddhist temple food. There's also a growing number of Western-style vegetarian/vegan restaurants, plus international cuisine such as Indian and Middle Eastern.

The blogs **Alien's Day Out** (www.aliensdayout.com) and **Happy Cow** (www.happycow.net/asia/south_korea/seoul) are good resources for vegetarians looking for somewhere to dine. The food listings on **Visit Seoul** (www.visitseoul.net) are also very helpful.

Eating by Neighbourhood

- **Gwanghwamun & Jongno-gu** Insa-dong, Samcheong-dong and Bukchon are packed with places offering everything from street snacks to table-overflowing banquets. (p63)
- **Myeong-dong & Jung-gu** Fun street food; long-established traditional restaurants. (p78)
- **Western Seoul** The University districts are big on casual cafes and street eats. Seafood lovers shouldn't miss Noryangjin Fish Market. (p89)
- **Itaewon & Around** The best range of international restaurants that are used to dealing with expats. (p99)
- **Gangnam & South of the Han River** Expense-account restaurants in Apgujeong and Cheongdam. More casual hang-outs in Garosu-gil. (p113)

Above: Street-stall *tteokbokki* (rice cakes in a sweet sauce)

Right: *Ssambap* (assorted ingredients with rice and wraps)

SIMON RICHMOND / GETTY IMAGES ©

Lonely Planet's Top Choices

Jungsik (p113) Neo-Korean fine dining at affordable prices.

Noryangjin Fish Market (p90) Superfresh fish dinners at Korea's largest seafood market.

Congdu (p80) Subtle contemporary twists on Korean classics.

Samwon Garden (p113) The classic *galbi* experience.

Gwangjang Market (p122) Supertasty and cheap street food in a covered market.

Coreanos Kitchen (p113) Mexican-Korean-Texan taco-truck-style fusion.

Best by Budget

$

Tongin Market Box Lunch Cafe (p63) Old-school market arcade.

Tobang (p64) Great-value set Korean meals.

Myeong-dong Gyoja (p78) Hand-pulled noodle soup with dumplings.

Koong (p64) Kaeseong-style dumplings.

Namdaemun Market (p74) Fresh and tasty market dishes.

$$

Gogung (p65) Jeonju-style bibimbap rice dishes.

Seasons Table (p113) Good-value traditional Korean buffet.

Slobbie (p90) Slow down to enjoy honest, tasty Korean food.

$$$

Min's Club (p66) Elegant Korea-meets-Europe experience for food and surroundings.

Ogawa (p64) Upmarket sushi restaurant that won't break the bank.

GastroTong (p64) Sophisticated Swiss European cuisine.

N.Grill (p81) Incredible views and French cuisine cooked by a Michelin-starred chef.

Best by Cuisine

Traditional Korean

Korea House (p80) Traditional banquet and performance.

Hanmiri (p64) Modern take on traditional cuisine overlooking the Cheong-gye-cheon.

Gosang (p80) Buddhist temple dishes dating from Goryeo dynasty.

Jaha Sonmandoo (p130) Dumplings on the slopes of Bukaksan.

Tosokchon (p63) Ginseng-chicken stew that's worth the wait.

International

Linus' BBQ (p100) Alabama-style barbecue.

Ciuri Ciuri (p90) Savour Sicilian dishes in Hongdae.

Vatos (p99) Mexican street tacos with Korean flavours.

Samarkand (p122) Uzbekistan lamb shashlik and bread.

Menya Sandaime (p89) Slurp up delicious bowls of ramen.

Tuk Tuk Noodle Thai (p90) Uncompromising flavours at a top Thai restaurant.

Potala (p80) Authentic dishes from the Himalayan region.

Best for Vegetarians & Vegans

Balwoo Gongyang (p65) Buddhist vegetarian feasts overlooking Jogye-sa.

PLANT (p99) Vegan bakery and cafe in Itaewon.

Osegyehyang (p64) Insa-dong hideaway that keeps it vegan.

Rogpa Tea Stall (p63) Fair-trade Tibetan dishes in a charming teahouse.

Loving Hut (p90) Vegan haven in Sinchon.

Best Bakeries, Desserts & Cafes

Passion 5 (p99) Glitzy arcade with gourmet foods.

Seoureseo Duljjaero Jalhaneunjip (p64) Time travel to the '70s while enjoying red-bean porridge.

Fell & Cole (p90) Uniquely flavoured ice creams.

Suji's (p100) Proper breakfasts and home-baked goods.

Scoff (p130) Sweet British baked treats in Buam-dong.

Tartine (p101) American-style pies and desserts.

PHOTOGRAPH BY KANGHEEWAN / GETTY IMAGES ©

Street scene at night

Drinking & Nightlife

From quaintly rustic teahouses and coffee roasters to craft beer pubs and classy cocktail bars, Seoul offers an unbelievable number of places to relax over a drink. No-frills hof *(pubs) are common, and don't miss that quintessential Seoul nightlife experience:* soju *(local vodka) shots and snacks at a* pojangmacha *(street tent bar).*

Teahouses & Cafes

Korea's tea culture, which dates back centuries, can be appreciated in Seoul's many quaint and charming teahouses. These places major in herbal and fruit teas, many of which have medicinal properties, but it's also possible to sip quality green, black and other fermented teas.

In recent decades Koreans have taken to coffee in a big way. Properly brewed coffee is abundantly available, from the usual Western-style cafe chains to artisan third-wave roasters who treat their globally sourced, sometimes fair-trade beans with reverence.

You'll quickly suss out that a quality cup of tea or coffee in Seoul is not cheap, and is often the equivalent to what you can pay for a whole Korean meal. You're also paying for occupying the space, so don't feel bad about lingering all day over your drink. Many newer breeds of cafes and teahouses encourage you to do this by creating interesting environments packed with books, magazines, plants, art – even cats to cuddle or sheep to pet.

Drinking Trends

Makgeolli, a milky alcoholic brew made from unrefined fermented rice, long popular among the older generation, is catching on

NEED TO KNOW

Opening Hours

➡ **Bars** noon to 6am

➡ **Clubs** 10pm to 6am Wednesday to Sunday

How Much?

➡ **Local beer** ₩3000–₩5000

➡ **Craft beer** ₩5000–₩10,000

➡ **Cocktail** ₩6000–₩15,000

➡ **Coffee** ₩2500–₩6000

➡ **Tea** ₩6000–₩9000

Cover Charges

At clubs the entry charge of ₩10,000–₩30,000 usually includes a free drink.

Drinking Water

In restaurants and cafes you'll be presented with bottled or filtered water upon sitting down, which is safe to drink.

Drinking Etiquette

If out drinking with Koreans, always pour for your elders, never pour for yourself and use both hands to hold your glass when it's being filled.

with the young and trendy too. Seoul has several bars now where higher-quality styles of *makgeolli*, akin to the range of Japanese sake, are served and savoured.

Until recently beer *(maekju)* was the least exciting of all Korean alcohol; ubiquitous and cheap local brands, all lagers, include the equally bland Cass, Max and Hite. The craft beer revolution has well and truly hit Seoul though, with a growing number of microbreweries producing artisan ales to cater for locals' thirst for quality beer.

Bars

Drinking, and drinking heavily, is very much a part of Korean socialising, and an evening out can quickly turn into a blur of bar-hopping. Many a big night out starts and finishes in a *hof.* Inspired by German beer halls, the term generally means any watering hole that serves primarily draught Korean beer, with the requisite plate of fried chicken and other *anju* (snacks commonly eaten when drinking). Always check whether a bar requires you to buy a plate of *anju* before drinking; places that don't are called 'one-shot' bars.

If you're looking for something more sophisticated, there are plenty of craft beer bars, cocktail bars and quirky drinking dens in places such as Itaewon, Hongdae, Sinchon and Gangnam.

Tent Bars & Convenience Stores

Beloved by Seoulites are *pojangmacha* (tent bars). Usually shortened to *poja*, these humble blue-tarp shelters are scattered across the city's streets. *Poja* also serve food; if you've had plenty of *soju* you may feel brave enough to order *takbal* (chicken feet).

Poja are also cheap, but not as cheap as convenience stores, which are open 24 hours and often have places to sit, either inside or out, to drink your can of beer or bottle of *soju*. They're a popular hang-out in the evening with students and young expats.

Clubbing

Gangnam is home to Seoul's world-famous clubbing scene, but Itaewon and Hongdae have decent choices, too. Most clubs don't become busy until midnight and only start buzzing after 2am. Friday and Saturday nights have a real party atmosphere. Dress codes are generally not too strict.

LGBTIQ Scene

LGBTIQ-friendly areas of the city include Itaewon (mainly gay and transsexual/transvestite bars), Nagwon-dong near Insa-dong (gay bars) and Hongdae and Edae (mainly lesbian bars).

Drinking & Nightlife by Neighbourhood

➡ **Gwanghwamun & Jongno-gu** Teahouses and cafes in Insa-dong and Samcheong-dong, Bukchon and Tongui-dong; tent bars and gay bars in Nagwon-dong. (p66)

➡ **Western Seoul** Hongdae, Sangsu-dong and Yeonnam-dong for cool, youth-orientated bars, cafes, dance and live-music clubs. (p91)

➡ **Itaewon & Around** Expat-friendly bars and clubs; gay-friendly 'Homo Hill'; craft beers in Gyeongridan. (p101)

➡ **Gangnam & South of the Han River** Chic, pricey cocktails bars in Apgujeong and Cheongdam; mega clubs with top DJs. (p114)

➡ **Northern Seoul** Cool cafes and student bars around Daehangno; seek out charming cafes in Seongbuk-dong. (p131)

Lonely Planet's Top Choices

Suyeon Sanbang (p131) Charming teahouse in heritage *hanok* (traditional house) in the hills.

Sik Mool (p66) Sophisticated *hanok* cafe-bar in up-and-coming Ikseon-dong.

Mix & Malt (p131) Superb range of whiskies and cocktails in Daehangno.

Best Tea

Dawon (p66) Traditional teahouse in the heart of Insa-dong set around a spacious courtyard.

Cha Masineun Tteul (p67) Enjoy steamed pumpkin cake and lovely views.

Dalsaeneun Dalman Saenggak Handa (p67) Classic Insa-dong teashop hideaway.

Tea Therapy (p67) Brews for whatever ails you.

Best Coffee

Greenmile Coffee (p114) Roasts single-origin beans in the backstreets of Gangnam.

Steamers Coffee Factory (p115) Third-wave coffee-roasting champs.

Club Espresso (p132) Single-origin beans from around the world.

Anthracite (p91) Top independent coffee roaster and cafe in happening Sangsu.

Kopi Bangasgan (p67) Arty *hanok* cafe in Samcheong-dong.

Hakrim (p131) Little has changed here since the 1950s.

Best Cocktails & Wine

Southside Parlor (p101) Artisan cocktails by hipster mixologists.

Fox Wine Bistro (p92) Top selection of wines in Hongdae.

N.Grill (p81) Open-air bar with amazing views from N Seoul Tower.

Best Cafe-Bars

Café Sukkara (p91) Rustic lovely on the edge of Hongdae.

Ikdong Dabang (p67) Cool *hanok* conversion with art installations.

Sik Mool (p66) Sophisticated *hanok* cafe-bar in up-and-coming Ikseon-dong.

Ways of Seeing (p103) Designer cafe in the backstreets.

Best Microbrew Bars

Craftworks (p81) Responsible for kicking off Seoul's craft beer scene.

Magpie Brewing Co. (p91) One of Seoul's originals with branches in Gyeongridan and Hongdae.

Booth (p114) Another big player, with brewpubs across the city.

Pongdang (p114) Korean brewers who know their stuff.

Best Traditional Alcoholic Beverages

Damotori (p101) A cherished local, specialising in *makgeolli*.

Moon Jar (p115) Smart and rustic bar with a good menu.

Baekseju-maeul (p67) *Makgeolli* bar run by big brewer, Kooksoondang.

Story of the Blue Star (p67) Brass kettles full of *makgeolli* served in a dive-y hang-out.

Muldwinda (p81) Most stylish bar for sampling fine-grade *makgeolli*.

Wolhyang Casual joint for sampling *makgeolli* in Hongdae (p91) and Itaewon (p103).

Dallyeora Gaemi 1 (p131) A fun twist on a tent bar in Daehangno.

Best Clubbing

Club Octagon (p114) Gangnam club regarded as one of the world's best.

Cakeshop (p101) Fun-lovin', dive-y club in Itaewon.

Ellui (p114) Another famous Gangnam megaclub.

M2 (p92) Huge underground space for parties in Hongdae.

Best Gay & Lesbian Bars & Clubs

Barcode (p68) Cosy, convivial gay cocktail bar in Nagwon-dong.

Shortbus (p68) Spacious hang-out serving good cocktails.

Club MWG (p92) Grungy Hongdae club hosting regular LGBTIQ events.

Labris (p92) One of Seoul's few lesbian bars.

Queen (p104) Popular bar on Itaewon's Homo Hill.

Entertainment

Don't worry about the language barrier: Seoul's many performing-arts centres and theatres offer an intriguing and surprisingly accessible menu of traditional music, dance, drama, comedy, K-Pop and K-Indie bands.

Classical & Traditional

Seoul is the best place in Korea to enjoy traditional music and dance performances. Some shows may include half a dozen different dance and music styles. There's a broad range of international classical offerings too; top-class overseas orchestras and dance troupes frequently visit Seoul.

Live Music

From the glossy, manufactured K-Pop industry to the underground indie scene, Seoul offers a vibrant assortment of live music.

Hongdae is *the* place for Seoul's K-Indie scene. Here many great venues host nightly shows by local indie, punk, metal and hip-hop acts. Classy live-jazz venues can be found around the city too.

Bigger concerts by visiting superstars such as Lady Gaga are held in the Olympic Stadium (p117) or AX Korea. Touring bands and K-Pop acts often perform at the Gymnastic Stadium at Olympic Park (p108).

K-Pop fans can arrange tickets to be in the studio audience of TV progams; visit the **Korea Tourism Organization** (www.visitkorea.or.kr) site for details. The hologram performance at Klive (p123) is another option.

Bang Culture

Seoul is overflowing with *bang* – complexes of 'rooms' where you can make your own entertainment in a variety of ways, including playing computer games or watching DVDs. Most notable are *noraebang* (karaoke) rooms where you can sing along to well-known songs, including plenty with English lyrics.

Theatre & Cinema

Theatre, except for drama festivals, is usually performed in Korean: the very lively theatre scene in Daehangno is worth a visit despite this. Musicals and nonverbal performance shows, such as Nanta (p82), can be enjoyed even if you don't understand any Korean.

Non-Korean movies are screened in their original language with subtitles. Also, some cinemas screen Korean movies with English subtitles during nonpeak times; call ☎02-1330 for details.

Entertainment by Neighbourhood

- **Myeong-dong & Jung-gu** Nonverbal theatre is king here; see traditional shows at the Korea House and Namsangol Hanok Village. (p81)
- **Western Seoul** Hongdae is the hub of Seoul's vibrant indie-music scene; or see free movies at Cinemateque KOFA. (p93)
- **Gangnam & South of the Han River** Home to the Seoul Arts Center and LG Arts Center. (p115)
- **Northern Seoul** Daehangno is a performing-arts hub with scores of venues, big and small. (p131)

Lonely Planet's Top Choices

Nanta Theatre (p82) The first and the best of Seoul's wide selection of nonverbal shows.

National Theater of Korea (p81) Home to the national drama, *changgeuk* (Korean opera), orchestra and dance companies.

Korea House (p80) Intimate theatre for a quality variety show of traditional performing arts.

National Gugak Center (p115) Traditional Korean classical and folk music and dance.

Su Noraebang (p93) Karaoke in style in the heart of Hongdae.

Best for Theatre & Dance

Seoul Arts Center (p115) Opera, concert and recital performances.

Sejong Center for the Performing Arts (p68) Big musicals and intimate classical concerts are staged here.

LG Arts Center (p115) Slick theatre space hosting quality productions.

ArkoPAC (p131) Theatre company that specialises in dance performances.

Jeongdong Theater (p81) Modern traditional Korean theatre.

NEED TO KNOW

Tickets

- **Interpark** (http://ticket.interpark.com) Tickets for theatre, concerts and sporting events.
- **KTO Tourist Information Center** (p192) Sells daily discount tickets for shows.

Information

- **Korea Gig Guide** (www.koreagigguide.com)
- **Seoulist** (www.seoulistmag.com)
- **Groove Korea** (www.groovekorea.com)
- **10 Magazine** (www.10mag.com)

Best for K-Pop

Klive (p123) Hologram concert by hottest K-Pop stars.

K-Wave Experience (p111) Get the full K-Pop makeover and photo op.

K-Star Road (p111) Take a stroll down the 'Hallyuwood' Walk of Fame.

Seoul Global Cultural Center (p83) K-Pop dance classes to learn all the latest moves.

Best for K-Indie

FF (p93) Come early to hear local indie bands banging out their sets.

DGBD (p93) Standing room only at this legendary rock venue.

Club Ta (p93) Hub of Hongdae's ska and ska-punk scene.

Thunderhorse Tavern (p104) Dive-y Itaewon venue hosting local and expat bands.

Best for Movies

Cinemateque KOFA (p93) Free screenings of classic and contemporary Korean films.

Cinematheque/Seoul Arts Cinema (p68) A chance to catch local art-house films with subtitles.

Megabox COEX (p116) Cineplex with 17 cinemas and 4000 seats.

Best Arts Festivals

Seoul Performing Arts Festival (www.spaf.or.kr) Month-long event in September offering top-class local and international acts at ArkoPAC.

International Modern Dance Festival (www.modafe.org) Held in May and based at the Arko Art Center in Daehangno.

Seoul Fringe Festival (p21) Each August this performing-arts event takes over Hongdae.

Seoul International Dance Festival (www.sidance.org) Based at the Seoul Arts Center).

Best Mixed Events

Mudaeruk (p93) Electronica, films and art in the basement of the Lost Continent of Mu.

Café BBang (p93) Indie artists and bands as well as film, art exhibitions and parties.

Indie Art-Hall GONG (p93) All kinds of cool goings-on in part of a steel factory south of the Han.

SJ Kunsthalle (p115) Happening art and music space.

Best for Jazz

Club Evans (p93) Evergreen Hongdae jazz haunt.

All that Jazz (p104) Long-established, well-respected Itaewon venue.

Once in a Blue Moon (p116) Stylish bar with quality performers.

Jazz Story (p131) Live sets in a striking bar.

Seoul Jazz Festival (www.seouljazz.co.kr) Multiday event featuring world-class musos in May.

Shopping street, Myeong-dong (p82)

Shopping

Whether it's with traditional items such as hanbok *(traditional clothing) or* hanji *(handmade paper), art-and-design pieces, digital gizmos or K-Pop CDs, chances are slim that you'll leave Seoul empty-handed. Seoul's teeming markets, electronics emporiums, underground arcades, upmarket department stores and glitzy malls are all bursting at the seams with more goodies than Santa's sack.*

Always in Fashion

For clothing, shoes, accessories or fabrics you can't beat Dongdaemun Market or Myeong-dong, where you'll find plenty of local brands.

Outfits by hot local K-designers, such as Lie Sang Bong, Kathleen Kye, fleamadonna, Doii Lee and Misung Jung, are best sourced in major department stores or the boutiques of Myeong-dong, Apgujeong and Cheongdam.

For high-end fashion the ritzy Apgujeong Rodeo St in Gangnam district is a must. As well as local K-designers, all the big-name luxury brands such as Louis Vuitton, Gucci and Prada are here, and it's an experience that offers all the glamour and posturing fashionistas you'd find in LA's Beverly Hills; worth checking out even if you're not planning on buying.

Shirts or blouses made of lightweight, see-through *ramie* (cloth made from pounded bark) make for an unusual fashion gift; the quality is usually high, but as with naturally dyed *hanbok*, such clothes are pricey. Everyday *hanbok* is reasonably priced, but formal styles, made of colourful silk and intricately embroidered, are objects of wonder and cost a fortune.

Cosmetics are a big attraction for shoppers visiting Seoul. Myeong-dong is the best place to head, stacked with local cosmetic boutiques and chains selling top-quality, inexpensive skin and make-up products; many of which are organic. An item that proves particularly popular with locals and international visitors is BB (blemish balm) cream; a two-in-one moisturiser and make-up – made famous by its popularity with *hallyu* (Korean Wave) film and pop stars.

Antiques & Crafts

Souvenirs such as embroidery, patchwork wrapping cloths *(bojagi)*, handmade paper *(hanji)*, wooden masks, fans, carvings and lacquerware inlaid with mother-of-pearl *(najeon chilgi)* can be found at Insa-dong's craft shops. However, a better spot to pick up souvenirs is in the wholesale folk-arts market in Buildings C and D at Namdaemun Market (p74), which offers more affordable prices. Also here are kitchen and tableware stores where you can buy traditional stone bowls, plates, teacups and chopsticks, as well as cooking accessories.

More expensive items include pale green celadon pottery, reproduction Joseon-dynasty furniture and contemporary art from Seoul's multitude of commercial galleries.

Antique lovers should browse the Dapsimni arcades (p123), which specialise mainly in Joseon-era items such as pottery, Buddhist statues and furniture. Insa-dong and Itaewon also have plenty of antique stores that specialise in traditional artifacts. The Seoul Folk Flea Market (p123) is a lively spot to browse antiques, reproductions and collectables.

Food & Drink

The many types of Korean tea are a popular buy. Rice wines such as *makgeolli* and *baekseju*, and local liquors such as *soju*, are also good souvenirs. Ginseng, the wonder root, turns up everywhere. You can chew it, eat it, drink it or bathe in it to benefit from its health-giving properties.

Electronics & Digital Goods

While Seoul is home to some of the world's largest electronic companies such as Samsung and LG, don't come here expecting bargains on the latest gadgets. The Yongsan Electronics Market (p104), however, is a good spot to check out new-release digital goods, with many stalls crammed into several buildings. As well as the latest smartphones, it's also an excellent spot to pick up bargain-priced secondhand smartphones – all in very good working condition. If bargaining is not your thing, I'Park Mall (p105) also has a great range of electronic items at fixed prices.

NEED TO KNOW

Opening Hours

- **Shops** 10am to 9pm; some closed Sunday
- **Department Stores** 10am to 8pm
- **Markets** Times vary, but some stalls may stay open even on days when a market is generally closed.

Bargaining

Acceptable at markets and some shops. If you are buying more than one item, it's also OK to ask for a discount – use your judgement.

VAT Refunds

If you spend more than ₩30,000 at participating tax-free shops, you can receive a partial refund on some items (between 5% and 7%) of the 10% value added tax (VAT). Be sure to collect the special receipt. At Incheon International Airport go to a Customs Declaration Desk (near the check-in counters) *before* checking in your luggage, as the customs officer will want to see the items before stamping your receipt. After you go through immigration, show your stamped receipt at the refund desk to receive your refund.

Located within the building of Samsung's world headquarters, Samsung D'Light (p112) showcases all the new releases, plus exhibitions on technology and innovation.

Shopping by Neighbourhood

- **Gwanghwamun & Jongno-gu** Insa-dong and Samcheong-dong are packed with art galleries, traditional craft and antique shops and boutiques. Also look for similar in Seochon, west of the palace. (p68)
- **Myeong-dong & Jung-gu** Best for department stores, fashion outlets and cosmetics. All-night shopping at Namdaemun Market. (p82)
- **Western Seoul** Youthful fashion and culture are serviced in Hongdae and Yeonnam-dong. (p93)
- **Itaewon & Around** Itaewon is great for expat-sized clothing and shoes, and is developing a rep for boutiques. Near Yongsan station are tons of electronics vendors and a shopping mall. (p104)
- **Gangnam & South of the Han River** Luxe retail in Apgujeong and Cheongdam; more affordable boutiques in Garosu-gil; one-stop shopping at megamalls such as COEX and D Cube City. (p116)

Lonely Planet's Top Choices

Insa-dong Maru (p69) Slick showcase for local crafts, fashion and homewares.

KCDF Gallery (p69) Gorgeous design emporium embracing traditional crafts with a contemporary slant.

10 Corso Como Seoul (p116) Beautifully curated, high-fashion and lifestyle store in classy Cheongdam.

Namdaemun Market (p74) Haggle for bargains at this sprawling city-centre warren of stalls selling all life's essentials.

Shinsegae (p82) The 'Harrods' of Seoul is the city's classiest department store.

Best Markets

Namdaemun Market (p74) Korea's largest and most atmospheric market.

Gwangjang Market (p123) Most famous for food, but also has vintage clothing and textiles.

Dongdaemun Market (p123) Energetic 24-hour shopping and good market food.

Seoul Folk Flea Market (p123) Fantastic place to sift through trash and treasure.

Seoul Yangnyeongsi Herb Medicine Market (p123) Take in wonderful fragrances at Asia's largest herbal market.

Best Fashion

Doota (p123) Buzzing fashion mall with domestic brands, luxury designers and accessories.

10 Corso Como Seoul (p116) High-end fashion by international and local designers.

Lab 5 (p82) Good spot to seek out the latest in K-design.

Boon the Shop (p117) Designer boutiques and clothing in ritzy Apgujeong.

Gentle Monster (p94) Edgy shades and frames as worn by Korean stars.

Jilkyungyee (p69) Tastefully designed *hanbok* for both sexes.

Best for Design

Dongdaemun Design Plaza & Park (p120) Plenty of design shops, markets and exhibitions.

Market m* (p69) Wooden furniture, bags, storage and stationery from Korea and Japan.

Jonginamoo (p70) Traditional furniture and home decor.

Gallery Art Zone (p69) Contemporary Korean design from portable speakers to ceramics.

KT&G SangsangMadang (p86) The downstairs shop is a good spot for gifts.

Object Recycle (p94) Great selection of recycled and upcycled designer goods from across Korea.

Millimetre Milligram (p104) Designer accessories, furniture and art books.

Best for Books, CDs & DVDs

Seoul Selection (p69) Best choice of books and DVDs about Korea.

What the Book (p105) Good selection of novels, secondhand books and magazines.

Kyobo Bookshop (p68) Great range of English-language books, Korean CDs and stationery.

10 Corso Como Seoul (p116) Cool art and design books.

K-Wave Experience (p111) Has a decent stock of K-Wave CDs and DVDs.

Best Department Stores & Malls

COEX Mall (p116) A shiny, modern megamall that's Asia's largest underground shopping precinct.

Shinsegae (p82) Korea's first department store has local designers and a lovely roof garden.

Galleria (p116) Haute couture along Apgujeong Rodeo St.

Lotte Department Store (p82) Several branches across the city, including its original colossus shopping precinct.

Mecenatpolis Mall (p94) One of Seoul's newest and best-designed malls.

Hyundai Department Store (p116) Luxury brands by local and international designers.

Best for Electronics

Yongsan Electronics Market (p104) A complex of stores with the latest gadgets, as well as secondhand smartphones.

Samsung D'Light (p112) Displays the newest releases from this giant in technology.

I'Park Mall (p105) Department store selling an excellent selection of electronic goods

Best for Crafts & Souvenirs

Namdaemun Market (p74) Sprawling selection of traditional handicrafts at wholesale prices.

Ssamziegil (p70) Insa-dong complex for quirky fashion, accessories or souvenirs.

Free Market (p94) Weekly creative market in Hongdae.

Key (p93) Affordable, exclusive items, from jewellery to paintings.

Korea House (p80) Elegant selection of crafts.

JOHN W BANAGAN / GETTY IMAGES ©

Lotte World's indoor ice skating rink (p109)

Sports & Activities

Baseball and soccer are the major spectator sports in Seoul. As for activities, don't miss out on having a relaxing sweat and cleansing soak in a jjimjil-bang *(communal sauna and bathhouse). Hiking is popular year-round, while skiing and ice skating take over in winter.*

Spectator Sports

BASEBALL

Introduced in 1905 by American missionaries, baseball is Korea's favourite sport. There are three Seoul teams in the **Korean Baseball Organization** (KBO; http://eng.koreabaseball.com) and two of them – the Doosan Bears and the LG Twins – play at Jamsil Baseball Stadium at the Seoul Sports Complex (p117); the Nexen Heroes play at **Mokdong Stadium** (939 Anyangcheon-ro, Yangcheon-gu; S Line 5, Omokgyo, Exit 4). Matches take place from April to October (except for the summer break), and are well attended, with a lively boozy atmosphere and plenty of off-field entertainment. Games generally start at 6.30pm, with the occasional earlier start.

SOCCER

In the 12-team professional **K-League** (www.kleague.com/eng), FC Seoul plays from March to November in the World Cup Stadium (p94). Crowds are bigger and there's more atmosphere when the national team is playing at the stadium, cheered on by the Red Devil supporters.

TAEKWONDO

While not popular with locals as a spectator sport, those wanting to catch Korea's national martial art can head to Kukkiwon stadium (p117) to catch a tournament, training session or demonstration by some of its world's best exponents. Otherwise there are displays staged at Namsangol Hanok Village (p77) at 11am, 1pm and 4pm daily from May

NEED TO KNOW

Contacts & Information

- **Adventure Club** (www.adventurekorea.com) Contact for details of caving, rock climbing, white-water rafting, paintball games and other adventurous outdoor activities.
- **Seoul Hiking Group** (www.seoulhikinggroup.com) Heads off hiking at least once a week.
- **Korea4Expats.com** (www.korea4expats.com) Listings for community groups and different activities. Good info on cycling too.

Costs

- **Baseball/soccer tickets** ₩7000 to ₩20,000.
- **Jjimjil-bang** ₩7000 to ₩12,000 entry, depending on the level of facilities.

to November. Expect to see graceful movements, spectacular pine-board breaking and acrobatic high kicking. See www.taekwonseoul.kr for more information.

BASKETBALL

Seoul's Samsung Thunders and SK Knights play in the 10-team **Korean Basketball League** (KBL; www.kbl.or.kr) from October to April. Samsung Thunders play at Jamsil Arena at Seoul Sports Complex (p117), while the Knights are at Jamsil Students' Gymnasium in the Seoul Sports Complex.

SSIREUM

Ssireum is Korean-style wrestling, more like Mongolian wrestling than Japanese sumo. Competitions are held at Jangchung Gymnasium (p123) during Lunar New Year and Chuseok holidays.

Activities

TWENTY-FOUR-HOUR SPAS

The best *jjimjil-bang* (Korean spas) offer a variety of baths (maybe green tea or ginseng) and saunas (mugwort, pine or jade). The etiquette is to get fully naked for spas, hence men and women are always separate in the bath area. But saunas, napping rooms and other facilities may be mixed; in these areas wear the robes or shorts and T-shirts provided. Most spas are open 24 hours. The basic entry fee covers up to 12 hours of unlimited use of all the baths and saunas; treatments like body scrubs cost extra.

HIKING

See Hiking chapt(p28) for information.

TAEKWONDO COURSES

Namsangol Hanok Village arranges training courses for foreigners wanting a hands-on experience of Korea's national martial art; visit www.taekwonseoul.org for more info.

GOLF PRACTICE

Private golf courses are usually for members only, but there are driving ranges in top-end hotels and elsewhere including Gangnam.

CYCLING

Cycleways run along both sides of the Han River past sports fields and picnic areas. There are plenty of bike-hire stalls (₩3000 per hour, open 9am to 8.30pm March to November), as well as free rental close by the subways at Okso (Exit 4), Eungbong (Exit 1), Gongneung (Exit 4), Yeongdeungpo-gu Office (Exit 2), Sanggye (Exit 1), Gangbyeon (Exit 1) and Jamsil (Exit 2) – which can vary from two hours to all day. Bring your own padlock, and leave a driving licence or other ID.

SWIMMING

Outdoor pools open in July and August in the Han River parks.

WINTER SPORTS

From December to February a handful of ski resorts within easy reach of Seoul (an hour or less by bus) open. Many of the resorts closest to the city run free shuttle buses from Seoul's main stations, making it possible to do a day-long ski excursion and return to Seoul at night. If you'd like to stay overnight or for the weekend, travel-agency package deals are a good bet, as they include transport, accommodation, ski-equipment hire and lift passes. Check out **Bears Town Resort** (☎031 540 5000; www.bearstown.com), **Jisan Resort** (☎02-3442 0322, 031 638 8460; www.jisanresort.co.kr) or **Yangji Pine Resort** (☎02-744 2001, 031 338 2001; www.pineresort.com).

During the same months, skate under the stars at the magical, inexpensive ice-skating rink that appears on **Seoul Plaza** (서울광장 스케이트장; ☎for English 02-1330; www.seoulskate.or.kr; 110 Sejong-daero; per hr incl skate rental ₩1000; ⏲10am-10pm Sun-Thu, to 11pm Fri-Sat Dec-Feb; 👪; Ⓢ Line 1 or 2 to City Hall, Exit 5). Swimming pools along the Han River are also turned into skating rinks, as are the pools at the Grand Hyatt Seoul (p152) and **Banyan Tree Club & Spa** (☎02-2256 6677; www.banyantreeclub.net; 60 Jang Chang Dan-ro; ❄@📶🏊; Ⓢ Line 3 to Beotigogae, Exit 1). Lotte World's indoor ice-skating rink (p109) is open all year.

Lonely Planet's Top Choices

Cycle along the Han River (p87) Hire a bicycle and get some exercise on the lanes running either side of the Han.

Dragon Hill Spa & Resort (p105) The best of Seoul's inner-city *jjimjil-bang* experiences.

Bukaksan (p132) Hike alongside the old Seoul city wall.

Taekwondo Experience Program (p42) Join a practice session for this martial art at Namsangol Hanok Village.

Ice Skating on Seoul Plaza (p42) Enjoy this central outdoor rink set up each winter next to City Hall.

Watch a baseball game (p41) Head to Seoul Sports Complex and cheer along with the crowds.

Best for Hiking

Inwangsan (p132) Old city walls and shamanist shrines.

Ansan (p132) Level hiking trail, sunrise views.

Bukaksan (p132) Bring your passport as this is a high-security area.

Best Spas & Jjimjil-bang

Dragon Hill Spa & Resort (p105) Complex of pools, saunas and spas, including some infused with cedar or ginseng.

Silloam Sauna (p83) Range of spas to go with massage treatments.

Spa Lei (p117) Classy women-only spa in Gangnam.

Chunjiyun Spa (p83) Popular for its pinewood saunas and green-tea baths.

Itaewonland (p105) Local favourite with good-value treatments and spas.

Happy Day Spa (p151) A reasonably good 24-hour sauna and *jjimjil-bang* in the Marigold Hotel.

Best for Live Sports

Jamsil Baseball Stadium (p117) Enjoy an evening out at the ball game.

World Cup Stadium (p94) As well as soccer games there's a 24-hour sauna and gym here.

Jangchung Gymnasium (p123) Arena for *ssireum*.

Explore Seoul

SEOUL'S TOP SIGHTS

Statues at Bongeun-sa (p110)

Neighbourhoods at a Glance

❶ Gwanghwamun & Jongno-gu (p48)

The centuries-old heart of Seoul revolves around these once-regal quarters of palaces. Between Gyeongbokgung and Changdeokgung, Bukchon covers several smaller areas including Samcheong-dong and Gahoe-dong famous for its traditional *hanok* (wooden homes). Seochon is a popular area for wanderings between galleries, cafes and boutiques. South of Bukchon are the mazelike and touristy streets of Insa-dong, and the up-and-coming *hanok* area of Ikseon-dong.

❷ Myeong-dong & Jung-gu (p71)

Seoul's retail world bursts forth in the brightly lit, packed-to-the-gills and supreme-

ly noisy streets of Myeong-dong. This is Seoul's equivalent of London's Oxford St or New York's Fifth Ave, with the massive, 24-hour Namdaemun Market on hand just in case you need to exponentially add to your shopping options. Looming over the commercial frenzy are the peaceful and tree-clad slopes of Namsan, a great place for exercise and city views.

3 Western Seoul (p84)

Seoul's principal student quarter is home to Hongdae (around Hongik University), Edae (around Ewha Womans University) and Sinchon (between Yonsei and Sogang Universities). These are youthful, creative districts short on traditional sights, big on modern-day diversions and sybaritic entertainments. South of Hongdae across the Han River, the island of Yeouido has several places of interest, all easily visited if you hire a bike at its riverside or central park.

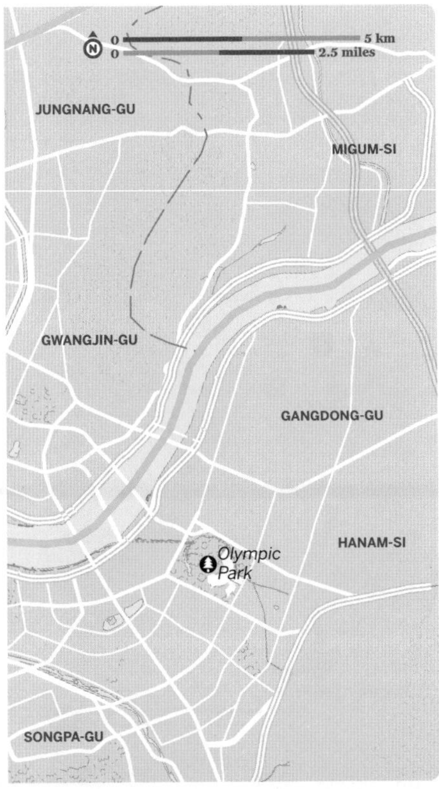

4 Itaewon & Around (p95)

The off-limits US army base is like a giant void around which Yongsan-gu's sights and attractions revolve. You'll surely be paying a visit or two to Itaewon to sample its eating, drinking and shopping possibilities. The adjacent areas of Hannam-dong, Haebang-chon (aka HBC) and Gyeongridan should be on your radar for the same reasons. The area has several major museums and a top resortlike *jjimjil-bang* (upmarket sauna).

5 Gangnam & South of the Han River (p106)

Gangnam (meaning south of the river) is a relatively newly built area with high-rise blocks bisected by broad highways. Expansive areas of greenery figure, too, in the shape of Olympic Park, the strip of recreation areas along the Han River, and, just outside the city limits, Seoul Grand Park. Luxury label boutiques are clustered in Apgujeong and Cheongdam. You'll also find several major performance-arts centres across the district.

6 Dongdaemun & Eastern Seoul (p118)

The sprawling, high-rise, 24-hour shopping experience that is Dongdaemun is the largest of several markets east of the city. You can shop for clothing here, and flea-market goods, antiques and herbal medicines further east. Dramatic contemporary architecture is provided by Dongdaemun Plaza & Park, while a stroll along a quieter section of the Cheong-gye-cheon is a pleasant way to reconvene with nature.

7 Northern Seoul (p124)

Some of Seoul's most charming neighbourhoods are clustered on three of the city's guardian mountains. Downhill from Naksan you'll find the student and performing-arts hub of Daehangno. Moving anticlockwise across to Bukaksan first comes Seongbuk-dong then Buam-dong, quietly affluent residential districts. The slopes of Inwangsan are home to the city's most famous shamanist shrine and there's a good park dedicated to the country's independence at Seodaemun.

Gwanghwamun & Jongno-gu

GWANGHWAMUN | INSA-DONG | BUKCHON | SAMCHEONG-DONG

Neighbourhood Top Five

1. Admire the scale and artistry of **Gyeongbokgung** (p50), the largest of Seoul's palaces, fronted by the grand gateway Gwanghwamun, where you can watch the changing of the guard.
2. Discover Huwon, the serene traditional garden secreted behind **Changdeokgung** (p52).
3. Get lost in picturesque **Bukchon Hanok Village** (p53), the city's densest cluster of traditional-style homes.
4. Learn about Buddhism at **Jogye-sa** (p55), one of Seoul's most active temples and epicentre of the spectacular Lotus Lantern Festival in May.
5. Browse the impressive collection of contemporary art at the **Arario Museum in SPACE** (p59).

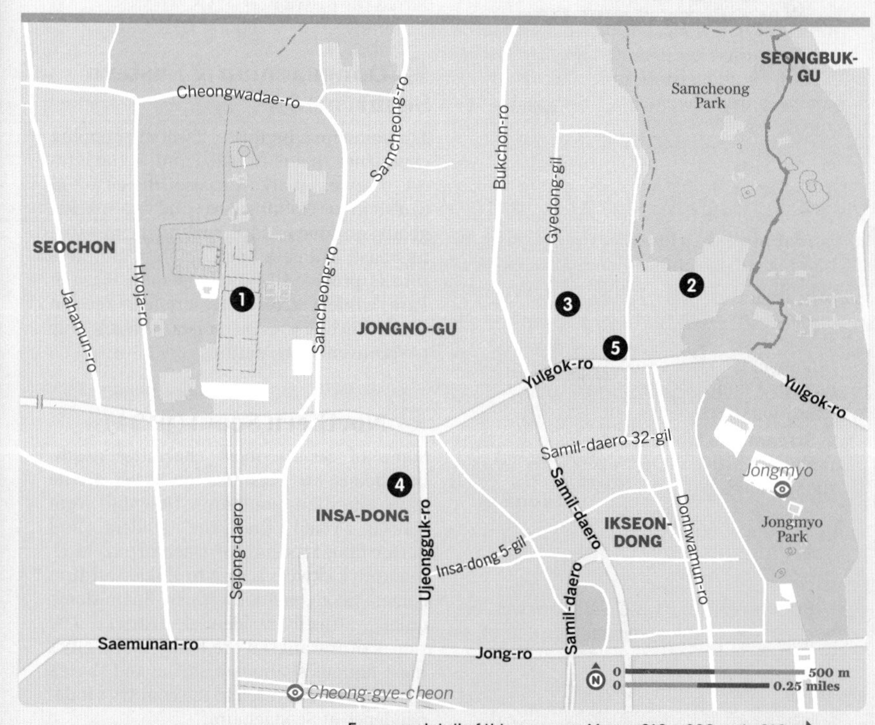

For more detail of this area, see Maps p210, p208 and p212

Explore: Gwanghwamun & Jongno-gu

Although their size and splendour have been greatly reduced from their heyday in the 18th century, Seoul's royal palace compounds, in the district of Jongno-gu, provide a glimpse of what it was like to live at the powerful heart of the old city. The area is also referred to as Gwanghwamun after the majestic gate to the main palace of Gyeongbokgung and the elongated square in front of it.

Save for the odd painted screen and altar, the large palace buildings are mostly empty, allowing you to appreciate the Confucian ideals of frugality, simplicity and separation of the sexes in the architecture as well as the gardens.

Between Gyeongbokgung and Changdeokgung, stroll around Bukchon ('north village'), which covers several smaller areas including Samcheong-dong and Gahoe-dong, famous for its traditional houses. Centuries ago this is where the *yangban* (aristocrats) lived but most estates were divided into plots in the early 20th century to create the smaller *hanok* (wooden houses) you can now view around Gahoe-dong. West of Gyeongbokgung smaller clusters of *hanok* can be found in Seochon ('west village'), an increasingly trendy area of Seoul.

South of Bukchon are the equally dense and mazelike streets of Insa-dong, one of Seoul's most tourist-friendly areas, packed with craft shops, galleries, traditional teahouses and restaurants, and Ikseon-dong, another compact area of *hanok* beginning to blossom with bars and cafes.

Local Life

- **Teatime** Take a breather from sightseeing over a beverage in one of Insa-dong, Bukchon or Seochon's charming traditional teahouses or contemporary cafes.
- **Jongmyo Square** The park in front of this venerable shrine (p54) is a daily gathering spot for Seoul's senior set who come to natter, play board games such as *baduk* and *janggi* and sometimes dance to *trot* (traditional electro-pop music).
- **Streamside Wanders** Stroll along the landscaped paths either side of the Cheong-gye-cheon (p56); if the weather's fine, cool your heels in the stream.

Getting There & Away

- **Subway** Lines 1, 3 and 5 all have stations in this area with Anguk being the best for Insa-dong and Bukchon.
- **Tour Bus** The Seoul City Tour Bus has stops around the palaces and Insa-dong.

Lonely Planet's Top Tip

If you plan to visit all four of Seoul's palaces – Gyeongbokgung, Changdeokgung, Changgyeonggung and Deoksugung – and the shrine Jongmyo, you can save some money by buying a combined ticket (₩10,000) valid for up to a month. The ticket is sold at each of the palaces and also covers entry to Huwon at Changdeokgung.

Best Places to Eat

- Rogpa Tea Stall (p63)
- Balwoo Gongyang (p65)
- Ogawa (p64)

For reviews, see p63

Best Places to Drink

- Sik Mool (p66)
- Dawon (p66)
- Story of the Blue Star (p67)

For reviews, see p66

Best Places to Shop

- KCDF Gallery (p69)
- Insa-dong Maru (p69)
- Kyobo Bookshop (p68)

For reviews, see p68

TOP SIGHT
GYEONGBOKGUNG

LIGHT OF PEACE / GETTY IMAGES ©

Like a phoenix, Seoul's premier palace has risen several times from the ashes of destruction. Hordes of tourists have replaced the thousands of government officials, scholars, eunuchs, concubines, soldiers and servants who once lived here. With its grand buildings, changing-of-the-guard ceremonies and several museums, you should set aside at least half a day to see it all.

Palace History

Originally built by King Taejo in 1395, Gyeongbokgung served as the principal royal residence until 1592, when it was burnt down during the Japanese invasion. It lay in ruins for nearly 300 years until Heungseon Daewongun, regent and father of King Gojong, started to rebuild it in 1865. Gojong moved in during 1868, but the expensive rebuilding project bankrupted the government.

During Japanese colonial rule, the front section of the palace was again destroyed in order to build the enormous Japanese Government General Building. This was itself demolished in the 1990s to enable Gwanghwamun to be rebuilt to how you see it today.

Palace Layout

The palace's impressive main gate, **Gwanghwamun**, restored in 2010, is flanked by stone carvings of *haechi*, mythical lionlike creatures traditionally set to protect the palace against fire; they never really did work and, appearances to the contrary, are superfluous today as the gate is now a painted concrete rather than wood structure.

Moving across the palace's broad front courtyard, you pass through a second gate **Heungnyemun**, and over a small artificial stream (for good feng shui a palace should have

DON'T MISS

- Gwanghwamun
- Geunjeongjeon
- Gyeonghoeru
- National Folk Museum of Korea
- National Palace Museum of Korea

PRACTICALITIES

- 경복궁, Palace of Shining Happiness
- Map p210
- www.royalpalace.go.kr/html/eng
- adult/child ₩3000/1500
- 9am-6.30pm Wed-Mon Jun-Aug, to 6pm Mar-May, Sep & Oct, to 5pm Nov-Feb
- S Line 3 to Gyeongbokgung, Exit 5

water in front and a mountain to the rear, which in this case is Bukaksan) to face the ornate two-storey **Geunjeongjeon**. In this impressive throne hall kings were crowned, met foreign envoys and conducted affairs of state.

West of Geunjeongjeon is **Gyeonghoeru**, a large pavilion resting on 48 pillars and overlooking an artificial lake with two small islands. State banquets were held inside and royals went boating on the pond.

Living Quarters & Gardens

A series of smaller meeting halls precede the king's living quarters, **Gangyeongjeon**, behind which are **Gyotaejeon**, those of the queen. Next you'll come to the terraced garden, **Amisan**; the red-brick chimneys decorated with longevity symbols on the garden's top terrace were used to release smoke from the palace's *ondol* (underfloor heating) system.

Symbolically located on the eastern side of the grounds (where the sun rises) is **Donggung**, the living quarters for the crown prince. To the rear, King Gojong built more halls for his own personal use and an ornamental pond with **Hyangwonjeong**, an attractive hexagonal pavilion on an island.

Museums Within the Palace

The **National Palace Museum of Korea** (국립고궁박물관; Map p210; 02-3701 7500; www.gogung.go.kr; 12 Hyoja-ro, Jongno-gu; 9am-5pm Tue-Fri, to 6pm Sat & Sun; S Line 3 to Gyeongbukgong, Exit 5) FREE, to the left just inside Gwanghwamun, has royal artefacts that highlight the wonderful artistic skills of the Joseon era: royal seals, illustrations of court ceremonies, and the gold-embroidered *hanbok* (traditional clothing) and exquisite hairpins worn by the queens and princesses. Note this museum closes on a different day to the palace.

In a separate section in the northeast of the grounds is the excellent **National Folk Museum of Korea** (국립민속박물관; Map p210; 02-3704 3114; www.nfm.go.kr; 37 Samcheong-ro, Jongno-gu; 9am-6pm Wed-Mon Mar-Oct, to 5pm Wed-Mon Nov-Feb; S Line 3 to Anguk, Exit 1) FREE. It has three main exhibition halls covering the history of the Korean people, the agricultural way of life and the life of *yangban* (aristocrats) during the Joseon era. Among the many interesting exhibits is an amazingly colourful funeral bier – these were used to give the deceased a great send-off.

On the approach to the museum is an **open-air exhibition** of historical buildings and structures, including a street of buildings styled as they would have been in the early 20th century. Also here is the separate **National Children's Museum** (02-3704 4540; www.kidsnfm.go.kr/eng; 37 Samcheong-ro, Jongno-gu; S Line 3 to Anguk, Exit 1) FREE and play area.

QUEEN MIN'S ASSASSINATION

In the early hours of 8 October 1895, Gyeongbokgung was the scene of a dramatic moment in Korean history. Japanese assassins broke into the palace and murdered Empress Myeongseong (Queen Min), one of the most powerful figures at that time in Korea. She was targeted because of her attempts to modernise Korea and protect its independence. Later 56 individuals were arrested but not one was convicted for the murder.

An audio commentary and a free guided tour (in English at 11am, 1.30pm and 3.30pm) are available to learn more about the palace. At the National Folk Museum of Korea the English guided tours start at 10.30am and 2.30pm, while at the National Palace Museum of Korea, the tour is at 3pm. Changing of the guard ceremonies beside Gwanghwamun occur every hour, on the hour between 10am and 4pm.

TOP SIGHT
CHANGDEOKGUNG

The most beautiful of Seoul's four main palaces, World Heritage–listed Changdeokgung was originally built in the early 15th century as a secondary palace to Gyeongbokgung. Following the destruction of both palaces during the Japanese invasion in the 1590s, Changdeokgung was rebuilt and became the primary royal residence until 1872. It remained in use well into the 20th century.

Visiting the Palace

You must join a guided tour to look around Changdeokgung. English tours run at 10.30am and 2.30pm; if you don't care about the commentary then there are Korean tours on the hour. To see the palace's lovely **Huwon** (Secret Garden) section, join tours that run at 11.30am and 1.30pm, with an extra 3.30pm tour March to October. Book online or come early as the Huwon tours are restricted to 50 people at a time.

Also well worth joining are the monthly **Moonlight Tours** (April to June only), limited to 100 people and costing ₩30,000. Tickets can be bought online from **Interpark** (http://ticket.interpark.com); look under 'Exhibitions/Sports' and book well in advance as it's very popular.

DON'T MISS

- Huwon
- Injeongjeon
- Nakseonjae
- Ongnyucheon

PRACTICALITIES

- 창덕궁
- Map p208
- http://eng.cdg.go.kr/main/main.htm
- 99 Yulgok-ro, Jongno-gu
- adult/child ₩3000/1500, plus Huwon ₩8000/4000
- S Line 3 to Anguk, Exit 3

Palace Layout

Enter through the imposing gate, **Donhwamun**, dating from 1608, turn right and cross over the stone bridge (built in 1414) – note the guardian animals carved on its sides. On the left is the beautiful main palace building, **Injeongjeon**. It sits in harmony with the paved courtyard, the open corridors and the trees behind it.

Next door are the government office buildings, including one with a blue-tiled roof. Further on are the private living quarters of the royal family. Peering inside the partially furnished rooms, you can feel what these Joseon palaces were like in their heyday – a bustling beehive buzzing round the king, full of gossip, intrigue and whispering.

Round the back is a terraced garden with decorative *ondol* chimneys. Over on the right is something completely different – **Nakseonjae**, built by King Heonjong (r 1834–49) in an austere Confucian style using unpainted wood. Royal descendants lived here until 1989.

The Secret Garden

Walk through the dense woodland and suddenly you come across a serene glade. The **Huwon** is a beautiful vista of pavilions on the edge of a square lily pond, with other halls and a two-storey library. The board out the front, written by King Jeongjo, means 'Gather the Universe'. Joseon kings relaxed, studied and wrote poems in this tranquil setting.

Further on are a couple more ponds and **Yeongyeongdang**, originally built in 1828 as a place for the crown prince to study. **Ongnyucheon** is a brook at the back of the garden where there's a huge rock, **Soyoam**, with three Chinese characters inscribed on it by King Injo in 1636 – *ong-nyu-cheon,* which means 'jade flowing stream' – and a poem composed in Chinese characters by King Sukjong in 1690.

TOP SIGHT
BUKCHON HANOK VILLAGE

Bukchon (North Village), covering the area between Gyeongbokgung and Changdeokgung, is home to around 900 *hanok*, Seoul's largest concentration of these traditional Korean homes. Although super-touristy in parts, it's a pleasure to aimlessly wander and get lost in the streets here, admiring the buildings' patterned walls and tiled roofs contrasting with the modern city in the distance.

DON'T MISS

- Bukchon Traditional Culture Center
- Simsimheon
- Gahoe Minhwa Workshop
- Dong-Lim Knot Workshop

PRACTICALITIES

- 북촌한옥마을
- Map p208
- http://bukchon.seoul.go.kr
- S Line 3 to Anguk, Exit 3

Bukchon Information

To find out more about area head first to the **Bukchon Traditional Culture Center** (북촌문화센터; Map p208; ☎02-2171 2459; http://bukchon.seoul.go.kr/eng/exp/center1_1.jsp; 37 Gyedong-gil, Jongno-gu; ⏲9am-6pm Mon-Sat) FREE, which has a small exhibition about *hanok* and is housed, appropriately enough, in a *hanok*.

With three days' advance notice you can arrange a free guided tour of the area with a volunteer from Seoul City Walking Tours (p27). Free maps and leaflets about the area can also be picked up from **Bukchon Tourist Information Center** (Map p208; cnr Bukchon-ro & Bukchon-ro 4-gil).

Note that massed tour groups swamp Bukchon every weekend, particularly during the middle hours of the day; avoid the crowds by visiting early in the morning or later in the evening.

Inside the Hanok

Given the throng of tourists and the number of *hanok* that now house commercial businesses, it's easy to overlook the fact that this region was once a residential area and still remains so in parts.

For a critical take on the contemporary history and development of Bukchon see www.kahoidong.com. The site is run by David Kilburn, who lives with his wife in one of the most traditional of *hanok* in Gahoe-dong, the most picturesque – and thus busiest – part of Bukchon.

Despite being zoned as a residential area, several *hanok* here are open to the public. **Simsimheon** (심심헌; Map p208; ☎02-763 3393; www.simsimheon.com; 47 Bukchon-ro 11-gil, Jongno-gu; admission ₩15,000; ⏲9am-6.30pm Mon-Sat; S Line 3 to Anguk, Exit 2), meaning 'House Where the Heart is Found' is a modern *hanok* rebuilt using traditional methods on the site of two older ones. Entry includes tea, which is sipped overlooking the internal garden.

Craft & Art Museums & Workshops

There are several places in Bukchon where you can learn about the traditional crafts still practised in this area or view private collections of arts and crafts.

Housing a large collection of amulets and folk paintings, **Gahoe Minhwa Workshop** (가회민화공방; Map p208; ☎02-741 0466; www.gahoemuseum.org; 17 Bukchon-ro 8-gil; adult/child ₩2000/1000; ⏲10.30am-6pm Tue-Sun; S Line 3 to Anguk, Exit 2) is a combined house museum and cultural centre that also offers classes teaching traditional painting, which can be done as a print or on a T-shirt. Enter the *hanok* housing the **Dong-Lim Knot Workshop** (Map p208; www.shimyoungmi.com; 10 Bukchon-ro 12-gil; classes from ₩1000; ⏲10am-6pm Tue-Sun; S Line 3 to Anguk, Exit 2) to find out about traditional knotting techniques and to attend classes on how to make tassels, jewellery and other ornaments from threads.

JANE SWEENEY / GETTY IMAGES ©

TOP SIGHT
JONGMYO

Surrounded by dense woodland, World Heritage–listed Jongmyo houses the 'spirit tablets' of the Joseon kings and queens and some of their most loyal government officials. Their spirits are believed to reside in a special hole bored into the wooden tablets.

Shrine Layout

Near the entrance to Jongmyo are two ponds, both square (representing earth) with a round island (representing the heavens). In the middle of the main path you'll notice triple stone paths; one is for the king, the other for the crown prince and the raised middle section for the spirits.

The stately main shrine, **Jeongjeon**, constructed in 1395, is fronted by a large stone-flagged courtyard. Inside are 49 royal spirit tablets in 19 small windowless rooms which are usually locked.

On the right-hand side of the main entrance is **Gongsindang**, which houses the spirit tablets of 83 meritorious subjects. They served their kings well and were rewarded with their spirit tablets sharing the royal compound – the highest honour they could hope for. On the left side are shrines to Chilsa, the seven gods who aid kings.

The smaller shrine, **Yeongnyeongjeon** (Hall of Eternal Peace), built in 1421, has 34 spirit tablets of lesser kings in six rooms. These include four ancestors of King Taejo (the founder of the Joseon dynasty) who were made kings posthumously. Behind this building a footbridge leads over to Changgyeonggung (p127).

Jongmyo Daeje

On the first Sunday in May the Yi clan, descendants of the Joseon kings, enact this ceremony, making lavish offerings of food and drink to the spirits of their royal ancestors. Starting at 11.30am with a procession from Gwanghwamun Sq to the shrine, the ceremony culminates seven hours later at the main shrine Jeongjeon.

DON'T MISS

- Jeongjeon
- Gonsindang
- Yeongnyeongjeon

PRACTICALITIES

- 종묘
- Map p212
- 02-765 0195
- http://jm.cha.go.kr
- 157 Jong-ro, Jongno-gu
- adult/child ₩1000/500
- 9am-5pm Wed-Mon Mar-Oct, to 4.30pm Wed-Mon Nov-Feb
- Line 1, 3 or 5 to Jongno 3-ga, Exit 11

TOP SIGHT
JOGYE-SA

The headquarters of the Jogye Order of Korean Buddhism has the largest hall of worship in Seoul, decorated with murals from Buddha's life and carved floral latticework doors. The temple compound, always a hive of activity, really comes alive during the city's spectacular Lotus Lantern Festival (p21) celebrating Buddha's birthday in May, and is a great place to learn a little about Buddhist practice.

DON'T MISS

- Daeungjeon
- Beomjongru
- Temple Life program

PRACTICALITIES

- 조계사
- Map p212
- 02-768 8600
- www.jogyesa.kr/user/english
- 55-Ujeongguk-ro, Jongno-gu
- 24hr
- Line 3 to Anguk, Exit 6

Daeungjeon

Inside Daeungjeon (대웅전; Worship Hall) at Jogye-sa are three giant gilded Buddha statues: on the left is Amitabha, Buddha of the Western Paradise; in the centre is the historical Buddha, who lived in India and achieved enlightenment; on the right is the Bhaisaiya or Medicine Buddha, with a medicine bowl in his hand. The small 15th-century Buddha in the glass case was the main Buddha statue before he was replaced by the much larger ones in 2006. On the right-hand side is a guardian altar with lots of fierce-looking guardians in the painting behind, and on the left side is the altar used for memorial services.

Believers who enter the temple bow three times, touching their forehead to the ground – once for Buddha, once for the *dharma* (teaching) and once for the *sangha* (monks), 20 of whom serve in this temple.

Around the Compound

Behind Daeungjeon is the modern **Geuknakjeon** (Paradise Hall) dedicated to Amitabha Buddha; funeral services, *dharma* talks and other prayer services are held here.

On the left side of the compound is the octagonal 10-storey **stupa** in which is enshrined a relic of Buddha brought to Korea in 1913 by a Sri Lankan monk.

Beomjongru (Brahma Bell Pavilion) houses a drum to summon earthbound animals, a wooden fish-shaped gong to summon aquatic beings, a metal cloud-shaped gong to summon birds and a large bronze bell to summon underground creatures. The bell is rung 28 times at 4am and 33 times at 6pm.

Also within the grounds is the **Central Buddhist Museum** (Map p212; 02-2011 1960; 9am-6pm Tue-Sun) FREE displaying regularly changing exhibitions relating to the religion. Attached to the museum is a tea shop and gift shop.

Temple Life Programs

Near the main entrance, the **Information Center for Foreigners** (Map p212; 02-732 5292; 10am-5pm) is staffed by English-speaking guides. Drop by here to make a booking for the **Temple Life program** (₩30,000; 1pm Sat, 3 hrs), which includes a temple tour, meditation practice, lotus-lantern and prayer-bead making, woodblock printing, painting and a tea ceremony. An overnight templestay can also be arranged here.

To find out more about Buddhism or book a Templestay program elsewhere in Seoul or Korea, the Templestay Information Center (p26) is just across the street from Jogye-sa. Along the street you'll also find many shops selling monks' robes, prayer beads, lanterns and the like.

TOP SIGHT
CHEONG-GYE-CHEON

This revitalised stream with its walkways, footbridges, waterfalls and public artworks is a hit with Seoulites who come to escape the urban hubbub and, in summer, dangle their feet in the water.

Urban Renewal

A raised highway was torn down and roads removed in a US$384-million urban-renewal project to 'daylight' the Cheong-gye-cheon, a stream that used to run through northern Seoul's centre, out to the Han River. The water that now flows for 5.8km down this beautifully landscaped oasis is actually pumped in at great expense from elsewhere, inciting the ire of environmentalists.

Public Art

Cheong-gye Plaza (Map p210) marks the start of the stream and is the setting for various public events. It's spiked with the giant pink-and-blue sculpture by Claes Oldenburg and Coosje van Bruggen entitled **Spring** (Map p210).

Between the Gwang-gyo and Jangton-gyo bridges is a 192m wall **mural** of painted tiles depicting King Jeongjo visiting his father's tomb in Hwaseong (Suwon) in 1785. Continue on past Dongdaemun and you'll eventually reach the Cheonggyecheon Museum (p121).

Seoul Lantern Festival

Centred along the Cheong-gye-cheon in November, **Seoul Lantern Festival** (http://blog.naver.com/seoullantern) sees the stream park illuminated by gigantic fantastic lanterns made by master craftspeople.

DON'T MISS

- Cheong-gye Plaza
- Mural of King Jeongjo's royal parade
- Walking beside the stream

PRACTICALITIES

- 청계천
- Map p210
- www.cheonggyecheon.or.kr
- 110 Sejong-daero, Jung-gu
- S Line 5 to Gwanghwamun, Exit 5

SIGHTS

Gwanghwamun & Around

GYEONGBOKGUNG PALACE

See p50.

DAELIM CONTEMPORARY ART MUSEUM GALLERY

Map p210 (02-720 0667; www.daelimmuseum.org; 21 Jahamun-ro 4-gil, Jongno-gu; 10am-6pm Tue, Wed, Fri, Sun, to 8pm Thu & Sat; ; S Line 3 to Gyeongbokgung, Exit 5) Daelim specialises in exhibitions on photography, design and fashion. The building, which was originally a family house, was remodelled by French architect Vincent Cornu and has a lovely garden to the rear and a cheap cafe and events hall in a separate building to the right of the main gallery. Admission charge varies with exhibitions.

GWANGHWAMUN SQUARE SQUARE

Map p210 (광화문광장; Sejong-daero, Jongno-gu; S Line 5 to Gwanghwamun, Exit 4) Upgraded in recent years, this broad, elongated square provides a grand approach to Gyeongbukgong and is used for various events (as well as protests). Giant statues celebrate two national heroes: **Admiral Yi Sun-sin** (Map p210), 1545–98, who stands atop a plinth at the square's southern end; and **King Sejong** (Map p210), 1397–1450, who sits regally on a throne in the middle of the square. An entrance at the base of the King Sejong statue leads down to an **underground exhibition** (10.30am-10pm Tue-Sun) FREE with sections on both the men.

King Sejong is revered as a scholar king of unmatched abilities. Admiral Yi Sun-sin designed new types of metal-clad warships called *geobukseon* (turtle boats), and used them to help achieve a series of stunning victories over the much larger Japanese navy that attacked Korea at the end of the 16th century.

CHEONG-GYE-CHEON STREAM

See p56.

NATIONAL MUSEUM OF KOREAN CONTEMPORARY HISTORY MUSEUM

Map p210 (02-3703 9200; www.much.go.kr; 198 Sejong-daero, Jongno-gu; 9am-6pm Tue, Thu, Fri & Sun, to 9pm Wed & Sat; S Line 5 to Gwanghwamun, Exit 2) FREE The last century has been a tumultuous time for Korea, the key moments of which are memorialised and celebrated in this museum charting the highs and lows of that journey. The displays are modern, multilingual and engaging, as well as proof of how far the country has come in the decades since its almost total destruction during the Korean War.

Head to the roof garden for a great view of Gyeongbokgung and Gwanghwamun Sq.

SEJONG GALLERY GALLERY

Map p210 (02-399 1111; www.sejongpac.or.kr; 175 Sejong-daero, Jongno-gu; 10am-5pm; S Line 5 to Gwanghwamun, Exit 8) FREE The regularly changing exhibitions at the gallery in the Sejong Center are generally worth a look for an insight into what's going on in the local contemporary-art scene. The **sculpture garden** behind the complex is also a pleasant place to hang out with some interesting pieces.

HAMMERING MAN STATUE

Map p210 (Saemunan-ro, Jongno-gu; S Line 5 to Gwanghwamun, Exit 6) Constructed from 50 tonnes of steel by American artist Jonathan Borofsky, this 22m-tall superman of a blacksmith has been silently hammering away in Seoul since 2002. The statue provokes thoughts about work: is it just a meaningless ritual that dominates our lives?

SEOUL MUSEUM OF HISTORY MUSEUM

Map p210 (서울역사박물관; 02-724 0114; www.museum.seoul.kr; 55 Saemunan-ro, Jongno-gu; 9am-8pm Tue-Fri, to 7pm Sat & Sun; S Line 5 to Gwanghwamun, Exit 7) FREE To gain an appreciation of the total transformation of Seoul down the centuries, visit this fascinating museum which charts the city's history since the dawn of the Joseon dynasty. Outside is one of the old tram cars that used to run in the city in the 1930s as well as a section of the old Gwanghwamun gate. Inside there's a massive scale model of the city you can walk around as well as donated exhibitions of crafts and photographs.

There may be charges for special exhibitions. Classical music concerts are sometimes staged here.

GYEONGHUIGUNG PALACE

Map p210 (경희궁, Palace of Shining Celebration; 02-724 0274; 55 Saemunan-ro, Jongno-gu; 9am-6pm Tue-Sun; S Line 5 to Gwanghwamun, Exit 1) FREE The Palace of Shining Celebration, completed in 1623, used to consist of a warren of courtyards, buildings, walls

GALLERIES GALORE

Seoul's eclectic contemporary-art scene is clustered either side of Gyeongbukgong, in Samcheong-dong, Tongui-dong and Insa-dong. The many commercial galleries here put on regularly changing shows of both local and international artists, which unless otherwise mentioned are free to browse. Useful resources include the free monthly art magazine *ArtnMap* (www.artnmap.com) and *Seoul Art Guide* (in Korean).

Samcheong-dong

Artsonje Center (Map p208; ☎02-733 8945; www.artsonje.org/asc; 87 Yulgok-ro 3-gil; adult/child ₩3000/1000; ⏰11am-7pm Tue-Sun; Ⓢ Line 3 to Anguk, Exit 1) Founded in 1998, Artsonje supports experimental art, runs workshops and has lectures as well as an annual Open Call for new works. Also here is a cafe and art-house cinema. It is also the Seoul outpost for the fascinating **Real DMZ Project** (http://realdmz.org), an annual show with artworks based on research carried out in the Demilitarized Zone (DMZ).

Gallery Hyundai (Map p210; ☎02-287 3500; www.galleryhyundai.com; 8 Samcheong-ro; ⏰10am-6pm; Ⓢ Line 3 to Anguk, Exit 1) The trailblazer for Korea's contemporary commercial-gallery scene, Hyundai has been going strong since 1970 and represents some of the giants of the scene, including Lee Joong-seop and Paik Nam June. As well as this exhibition space it has another branch nearby at 14 Samcheong-ro.

Hakgojae (Map p208; ☎02-720 1524; www.hakgojae.com; 50 Samcheong-ro; ⏰10am-7pm Tue-Sat, to 6pm Sun; Ⓢ Line 3 to Anguk, Exit 1) This elegant gallery is easily spotted by the robot sculpture on the roof of its modern section. Entry is via the converted *hanok* building which neatly symbolises the gallery's aim 'to review the old to learn the new'.

Kukje (Map p208; ☎02-735 8441; www.kukjegallery.com; 54 Samcheong-ro; ⏰10am-6pm Mon-Sat, to 5pm Sun; Ⓢ Line 3 to Anguk, Exit 1) Kukje's two main gallery spaces are found off the main road, behind their restaurant building which has the running woman sculpture by Jonathan Borofsky on its roof. It's a leading venue for international artists to exhibit, with the likes of Damien Hirst, Anish Kapoor and Bill Viola all having shows here.

Tongui-dong

Jean Art Gallery (Map p210; ☎02-738 7570; www.jeanart.net; 25 Hyoja-ro; ⏰10am-6pm Tue-Fri, to 5pm Sat & Sun; Ⓢ Line 3 to Gyeongbokgung, Exit 3 or 4) Pioneer of the Tongui-dong gallery scene and specialising in representing contemporary Korean and Japanese artists, such as Naru Yoshitomo and Yayoi Kusama; one of Yayoi's 2m-tall dotted pumpkin sculptures stands in a courtyard outside one of the gallery's buildings.

Artside (Map p210; ☎02-725 1020; www.artside.org; 15 Jahamun-ro 6-gil; ⏰10am-6.30pm Tue-Sun; Ⓢ Line 3 to Gyeongbokgung, Exit 3 or 4) Since 1999, Artside has taken a leading role in artistic exchange between Korea and China by regularly staging exhibits by contemporary Chinese artists such as Zhang Xiaogang.

Gallery Simon (Map p210; ☎02-549 3031; http://gallerysimon.com; 20, Jahamun-ro 6-gil; ⏰10am-6.30pm Tue-Sun; Ⓢ Line 3 to Gyeongbokgung, Exit 3 or 4) Exhibitions include sculptures and interesting installations. Has a chic top-floor cafe with views over *hanok* roofs.

Ryugaheon (류가헌; Map p210; ☎02-720 2010; www.ryugaheon.com; 10-3 Hyoja-ro 7-gil; ⏰10.30am-6.30pm Tue-Sun; Ⓢ Line 3 to Gyeongbokgung, Exit 5) Based in a restored *hanok*, Ryugaheon specialises in photography exhibitions, but you may also see other types of art here such as canvases of embroidered flowers. There are two display spaces and a small library of art books you're welcome to browse.

Insa-dong

Hwabong Gallery (Map p212; ☎02-737 0057; www.hwabong.com; 10 Insa-dong 7-gil; ⏰10am-7pm; Ⓢ Line 3 to Anguk, Exit 6) Cutting-edge Korean art is usually on show in this basement space alongside permanent displays of the smallest book in the world (no more than a dot), and the largest book.

Sun Art Center (Map p212; ☎02-734 0458; www.sungallery.co.kr; 8 Insa-dong 5-gil; ⏰10am-6pm Tue-Sun; Ⓢ Line 3 to Anguk, Exit 6) One of Seoul's longest running commercial-art galleries, in business since 1977, Sun Art specialises in early-20th-century Korean art.

and gates spread over a large area. But it was destroyed during the Japanese annexation and a Japanese school was established here. Only the main audience hall, **Sungjeongjeon**, and the smaller official **hall** behind it along with a few paved courtyards and corridors have been restored.

The impressive entrance gate, **Heunghwamun** (Map p210), has toured around Seoul, and was moved to its present site in 1988. To the left before you reach the palace buildings is the **SeMA Gyeonghuigung Museum of Art** (Map p210; ☎02-723 2491; http://sema.seoul.go.kr/global/eindex.jsp; 45 Saemunan-ro, Jongno-gu; ⏲10am-6pm Tue-Sun; Ⓢ Line 5 to Gwanghwamun, Exit 1) FREE, hosting regularly changing art exhibitions of a variable quality and interest.

SAJIKDAN SHRINE

Map p210 (사직단; www.jongno.go.kr; Sajik Park, 89 Sajik-ro, Jongno-gu; Ⓢ Line 3 to Gyeongbokgung, Exit 5) FREE This impressive stone altar in a tranquil park surrounded by low stone walls and ornate wooden gates dates back to 1395 and King Taejo, founder of the Joseon dynasty. It was used to pray to the gods for good harvests.

CHEONGWADAE SARANGCHAE EXHIBITION

Map p210 (청와대 사랑채; www.cwdsarangchae.kr; 45 Hyoja-ro 13-gil, Jongno-gu; ⏲9am-6pm Tue-Sun; Ⓢ Line 3 to Gyeongbokgung, Exit 4) FREE Much more interesting than the tour of Cheongwadae itself is this exhibition hall opposite the exit from the presidential compound. Inside are displays promoting Korea and Seoul as well as the work of past presidents and some of the gifts they have been given by international visitors. It's all very nicely put together and in one section you have a photo op with a digitised image of the president on Cheongwadae's front lawn.

There's also a pleasant cafe next to which **cooking classes** are run for overseas tourists (₩10,000, for groups of 10 or more); make a reservation through the website.

CHEONGWADAE HISTORIC BUILDING

Map p210 (청와대, Blue House; ☎02-737 5800; www.president.go.kr; 1 Cheongwadae-ro, Jongno-gu; ⏲tours 10am, 11am, 2pm & 3pm Tue-Sat; Ⓢ Line 3 to Gyeongbokgung, Exit 5) FREE Security is so tight around the Blue House (so called because of its blue tiled roof) at the base of Bukaksan that even innocently walking past the presidential residence is likely to get you stopped and questioned by mirror-glassed special agents. However, it is possible to see inside if you join a free 40-minute tour which must be prebooked online, but is not really worth the hassle involved.

Bring your passport and join the tour at the ticket booth in Gyeongbokgung's car park. A tour bus then takes you the short distance from the car park to Cheongwadae's public entrance. On arrival you'll be shown a five-minute film then whisked around the palatial grounds, which are nice enough.

⊙ Insa-dong, Bukchon & Samcheong-dong

CHANGDEOKGUNG PALACE

See p52.

BUKCHON HANOK VILLAGE AREA

See p53.

ARARIO MUSEUM IN SPACE MUSEUM

Map p208 (☎02-736 5700; www.arariomuseum.org; 83 Yulgok-ro, Jongno-gu, adult/child/youth ₩10,000/4000/6000; ⏲10am-7pm; Ⓢ Line 3 to Anguk, Exit 3) Korean business magnate and contemporary-art collector Kam Chang-il has found the perfect home for jewels from his collection at this ivy-clad brick building that's considered a seminal piece of early 1970s architecture. The building's compact, low-ceilinged rooms and labyrinthine layout fit the conceptual pieces, by the likes of Nam Jun Paik, Koo Kang, Lee Ufan, Tracey Emin, Damien Hirst and Sam Taylor Johnson, like a glove – you never know what artistic wonder lies around the next corner.

Also part of the building are a *hanok* and a five-storey glass annexe (added in 1997); both are used as cafes and restaurants.

MMCA SEOUL MUSEUM

Map p208 (☎02-3701 9500; www.mmca.go.kr; 30 Samcheong-ro, Jongno-gu; admission ₩4000; ⏲10am-6pm Tue, Thu, Fri & Sun, to 9pm Wed & Sat; Ⓢ Line 3 to Anguk, Exit 1) Combining architectural elements from several centuries of Seoul's history, this new branch of the city's premier contemporary-art museum is a work in progress. The melding of spacious new gallery buildings with the artdeco buildings of the former Defense Security Command is impressive but at the time of writing the facility had yet to get a director (because this a politically sensitive appointment) and its shows have met with muted critical reaction. Nonetheless, it's well worth a visit.

In a garden to the rear of the main gallery buildings you'll find the restored **Jongchinbu** (the office of royal genealogy during the Joseon dynasty) restored to its original site after a spell spent up the road next to Jeongdok Library. This traditional structure is a nice contrast to Park Ki Won's *Flash Wall,* a set of wire-wool candyfloss gateways also in the garden.

A free shuttle bus runs four times a day between the other branches of the MCCA in Gwacheon and Deoksugung.

ANOTHER WAY OF SEEING — GALLERY

Map p208 (우리들의 눈; ☎02-733 1996; http://artblind.or.kr; 19 Bukchon-ro 5na-gil, Jongno-gu; ⏲10am-6pm Tue-Sun; Ⓢ Line 3 to Anguk, Exit 1) Running a program to support art education and activities for the blind, Another Way of Seeing is a gallery where the thought-provoking exhibitions frequently play on senses other than sight, such as smell, touch and sound.

UNHYEONGUNG — PALACE

Map p212 (운현궁; Cloud Hanging over the Valley Palace; ☎02-766 9090; www.unhyeongung.or.kr; 464 Samil-daero, Jongno-gu; adult/child ₩700/300; ⏲9am-7pm Tue-Sun Apr-Oct, to 6pm Tue-Sun Nov-Mar; Ⓢ Line 3 to Anguk, Exit 4) This palace has a modest, natural-wood design reflecting the austere tastes of Heungseon Daewongun (1820–98), King Gojong's stern and conservative father. Rooms are furnished and mannequins display the dress styles of the time. It's also possible to try on *hanbok* (₩1000), and various artistic events are staged here throughout the year including traditional **music and dance concerts**, usually on Friday at noon.

Heungseon Daewongun's policies included massacring Korean Catholics, excluding foreigners from Korea, closing Confucian schools and rebuilding Gyeongbokgung. Gojong was born and raised here until 1863 when he ascended the throne aged 12 with his father acting as regent.

JONGMYO — SHRINE

See p54.

CHEONDOGYO TEMPLE — TEMPLE

Map p212 (천도교 중앙대교당; ☎02-732 3956; www.chondogyo.or.kr; 11-4 Insa-dong 10-gil, Jongno-gu; ⏲9am-6pm; Ⓢ Line 3 to Anguk, Exit 6) Cheondogyo means 'Religion of the Heavenly Way', and this temple is the hall of worship for a home-grown faith containing Buddhist, Confucian and Christian elements that gathered momentum in the 1860s. Designed by a Japanese architect and completed in 1921, this is a handsome baroque-style, red-brick and stone building with a tower. Inside, the wood panelling, lines of chairs and plain decoration create an impression of a lecture theatre, although there are stained-glass windows.

Cheondogyo members were key figures in the Donghak rebellion and the independence movements opposed to Japanese rule. The founder, Great Master Suun (1824–64), was executed for being a radical reformer. Followers believe that God is within everyone. Services are held every Sunday at 11am.

SOOL GALLERY — CULTURAL CENTRE

Map p212 (전통주 갤러리; ☎02-739 6220; www.facebook.com/thesoolgallery; KDCF, 8 Insa-dong 11-gil, Jongno-gu; ⏲10am-6pm Tue-Sun; Ⓢ Line 3 to Anguk, Exit 6) FREE In the basement of the KCDF building, this small exhibition with some English explanations will clue you into the various types of Korean alcohol, such as *makgeolli* (milky rice wine), *soju* (local vodka) and *yakju* (medicinal alcohol). If you book ahead for the so-so tour, you at least get to sample four type of the tipples at the end.

MOKIN MUSEUM — MUSEUM

Map p212 (목인박물관; ☎02-722 5066; www.mokinmuseum.com; 20 Insa-dong 11-gil, Jongno-gu; adult/child ₩5000/3000; ⏲10am-6pm Tue-Sun; Ⓢ Line 3 to Anguk, Exit 6) *Mokin* are carved and painted wooden figures and decorative motifs that were used to decorate *sangyeo* (funeral carriages). Carved by craftspeople, they are a unique folk art drenched in Buddhist and shamanist beliefs, and this small private museum includes some prime examples. You'll also find carvings from other parts of Asia here and a roof garden.

Among *mokin,* flowers represent wealth and yearning for a perfect world, while birds represent messengers from this world to the next, fish symbolise life and learning (as they never close their eyes), and tigers and goblins scare evil spirits away.

JOGYE-SA — TEMPLE

See p55.

TAPGOL PARK — PARK

Map p212 (탑골공원; 99 Jong-ro, Jongno-gu; ⏲6am-8pm; Ⓢ Line 1 or 5 to Jongno 3-ga, Exit 1 or 5) Seoul's first modern-style park, opened in 1897, stands on the precincts of Wongak-sa,

Neighbourhood Walk
Bukchon Views

START ANGUK STATION, EXIT 3
END ANGUK STATION, EXIT 1
LENGTH 3KM; TWO HOURS

Take in views across Bukchon's tiled *hanok* roofs on this walk around the area between Gyeongbokgung and Changdeokgung. Don't worry if you get a little lost in the maze of streets – that's part of the pleasure. This walk is best done in the early morning or early evening (or even on a moonlit night) to avoid the daytime crowds.

From the **1 Anguk station subway exit** turn left at the first junction and walk 200m to **2 Bukchon Traditional Culture Center** (p53), where you can learn about the area's architecture. Continue to head north up Gyedong-gil, an attractive street lined with cafes, boutiques and *hanok* guesthouses; at the T-junction at the top of the hill is the entrance to **3 Choong Ang High School**, an attractive early-20th-century educational complex that featured as a location in the hit Korean TV drama *Winter Sonata*.

Wind your way back downhill from here past the **4 Gahoe Minhwa Workshop** (p53) and the **5 Dong-Lim Knot Workshop** (p53) to emerge on the major road Bukchon-ro. Cross over and locate the start of **6 Bukchon-ro 11-gil**; follow this narrow street uphill towards the parallel set of picturesque streets lined with *hanok* in Gahoe-dong. To see inside one of the *hanok* pause at **7 Simsimheon** (p53).

Turn left and go a few blocks west to Bukchon-ro 5na-gil; just to the right is a **8 viewing spot** across Samcheong-dong. Head south down the hill, perhaps pausing for tea at **9 Cha Masineun Tteul** (p67). Further downhill is **10 Another Way of Seeing** (p60), an art gallery with interesting exhibitions by the vision impaired.

Turn left after the **11 World Jewellery Museum** and then right at the junction; on the corner by another tourist information booth, walk up to **12 Jeongdok Public Library**, where the small, quiet park in front of the building is a prime spot for viewing cherry blossoms in spring and the yellowing leaves of ginkgo trees in autumn.

Return to the subway station via Yunposeon-gil.

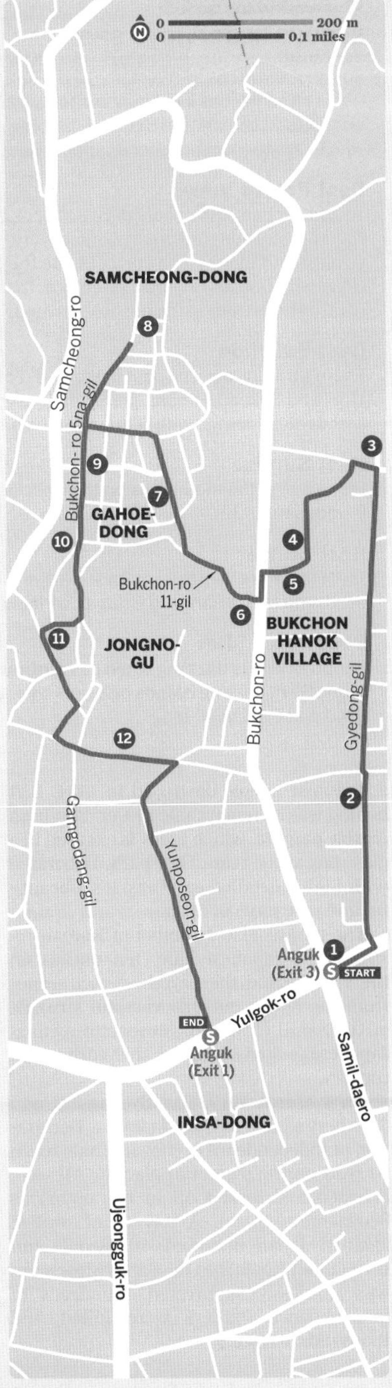

LOCAL KNOWLEDGE

SEOUL'S BEST PHOTO SPOTS

Editor of the monthly magazine *Seoul* and author of guidebooks to Seoul and Korea, Robert Koehler has lived in Korea for over 18 years. He also regularly posts stunning photographic images of Seoul on his blog at http://rjkoehler.tumblr.com. He shared with us his top locations for snapping Seoul in her best light.

Best Palace Views

You can get amazing shots of Gyeongbokgung (p50) from the roof garden of the National Museum of Korean Contemporary History (p57). Also, it may seem a bit strange, but there's a balcony outside the cafe on the 5th floor of Seoul National University Cancer Hospital, directly across from the entrance of Changgyeonggung (p127) and providing the best view over it.

Best Bukchon

There's a small parking spot in the midst of Gahoe-dong, on the corner of Bukchon-ro 11-gil and Bukchon-ro 5na-gil. From here you can get the classic old and new Seoul architecture combo with Namsan in the background.

Best Sunrise

Climb one of the mountains on the west side of the city – either Ansan (p132) or Inwangsan (p132).

Best Sunset

Try Noeul Park, aka Sunset Park, part of World Cup Park (p88), or near the cafe on the north end of the Hangang Bridge overlooking Yeouido.

Best Night Shot

Banpo Bridge is dazzling when its **rainbow fountain** (p111) is in action. The nearby Some Sevit floating islands also look their best when illuminated. **Namsan** (p73) is a good place to shoot, too.

a Buddhist temple destroyed in 1504. Left behind was its remarkable 10-tier, 12m-high marble **pagoda**, which today is encased in a glass box at the rear of the park. Decorated with highly detailed carvings, it's a beautiful and rare piece of art.

The park is also a symbol of Korean resistance to Japanese rule. Ten murals on the wall behind the pagoda depict scenes from the heroic but unsuccessful struggle of the Samil (1 March) Movement against Japanese colonisation in the early 20th century.

On 1 March 1919, Son Byeong-hui and 32 others signed and read aloud a Declaration of Independence (a copy in English can be read on the memorial plaque). All were arrested and locked up in the notorious Seodaemun Prison. A torrent of protest against Japan followed in Seoul and throughout Korea, but the Samil Movement was ruthlessly suppressed. Hundreds of independence fighters were killed and thousands arrested.

BOSINGAK BELL TOWER

Map p212 (보신각; 54 Jong-ro, Jongno-gu; S Line 1 to Jonggak, Exit 4) Contrasting with the modern **Jongno Tower** (Map p212; 51 Jung-ro, Jongno-gu; S Line 1, 3 or 5 to Jonggak, Exit 3) opposite, this ornate pavilion houses a recent copy of the city bell – the original, forged in 1468, is in the garden of the National Museum of Korea. Costumed guards patrol around the bell and ring it 12 times at noon (the ceremony runs from 11am to 12.20pm Tuesday to Sunday).

In the past the great bell was struck 28 times every night at 10pm to ask the heavens for a peaceful night and to signal the closure of the gates and the start of the nightly curfew. To signal the start of the new day it was struck 33 times for the 33 Buddhist heavens at 4am, after which the gates were reopened. It also sounded when fire broke out, as often happened with so many wooden and thatched buildings.

EATING

Gwanghwamun & Around

★ROGPA TEA STALL VEGETARIAN $

Map p210 (사직동, 그 가게; http://blog.naver.com/rogpashop; 16 Sajik-ro 9-gil, Jongno-gu, noon-8pm Tue-Sun; mains ₩6000-8000; ; Line 3 to Gyeongbokgung, Exit 1) You'll feel whisked to the Himalayas at this charming fair-trade cafe that raises awareness about the Tibetans' situation (Rogpa is Tibetan for friend and helper). Everything is vegetarian and freshly made, beautifully presented and rather delicious. Dig into a mild curry followed by a sweet *dosa* (crispy lentil pancake) and chai made with soy milk.

Staff also run the shop next door selling handicrafts made by Tibetans exiled in India.

★TONGIN MARKET BOX LUNCH CAFE KOREAN $

Map p210 (통인시장; http://tonginmarket.co.kr; 18 Jahamun-ro 15-gl, Jongno-gu; meals ₩5000; 11am-4pm Tue-Sun; Line 3 to Gyeongbokgung, Exit 2) For a fun lunch, buy 10 brass coins (₩5000) at the cafe about halfway along this old-school covered market. You'll be given a plastic tray with which you can then go shopping in the market. Exchange your coins for dishes such as savoury pancakes, *gimbap* (seaweed-covered rice rolls) and *tteokbokki* (spicy rice-cake stew).

You can buy more coins, if needed, and use them (or cash) to pay for rice and soup (₩1000 each, *kimchi* is free) at the cafe.

JOSEON GIMBAP KOREAN $

Map p208 (조선김밥; 78 Yulgok-ro 1-gil, Jongno-gu; gimbap ₩3500; 11am-2.30pm & 4.30-7.30pm Mon-Sat; Line 3 to Anguk, Exit 1) Behind the new contemporary-art museum, this quirky, tiny place has astro turf in the front seating area where you get a ringside seat on the jumbo *gimbap* being made. These whoppers come with a range of side dishes, making it one of the best value feeds in the city.

POTATO PASSION INTERNATIONAL $

Map p210 (열정감자; www.facebook.com/sellourpassion; 30 Jahamun-ro 1-gil, Jongno-gu; fried food from ₩3500; 4pm-1am Mon-Fri, 11.30am-1am Sat & Sun; Line 3 to Gyeongbokgung, Exit 4) Proving it's not what you do but how you do it, the keen young guys behind this tent-bar operation aim to give the humble chip and fried chicken a stylish Seoul makeover. There's a selection of sauces and sweet-potato chips as an alternative. Wash it all down with watery Max beer served in Pyrex measuring jugs.

TOSOKCHON KOREAN $$

Map p210 (토속촌; 02-737 7444; 5 Jahamun-ro 5-gil, Jongno-gu; mains ₩15,000-22,000; 10am-10pm; ; Line 3 to Gyeongbokgung, Exit 2) Spread over a series of *hanok*, Tosokchon is so famous for its *samgyetang* (ginseng chicken soup) that there is always a long queue waiting to get in, particularly at weekends. Try the black-chicken version which uses the silkie breed with naturally black flesh and bones.

EURO GOURMET CAFE, DELI $$

Map p210 (www.eurogourmet.co.kr; cnr Jahamun-ro 10-gil, Jongno-gu; mains ₩9000-35,000; 10am-10pm; ; Line 3 to Gyeongbokgung, Exit 3) Little sibling to neighbouring GastroTong is this delightful Euro-style deli-cafe specialising in sandwiches, pasta and baguette-style pizza made with premium ingredients.

OKITCHEN ITALIAN $$

Map p210 (02-772 6420; www.okitchen.us; B1 The-K Twin Tower, 50 Jong-ro 1-gil, Jongno-gu; mains ₩17,000-19,000; noon-3pm & 6-9pm; ; Line 5 to Gwanghwamun, Exit 2) Friendly service and set two-course menus (starting at ₩24,000) that balance price with quality make this a good option for a quality Italian meal which covers a good range of pasta dishes, antipasti and nice desserts. Chatty proprietor, Yonaguni Susumu hails from Okinawa and used to live in New York with his Korean food-stylist wife.

SONG'S KITCHEN KOREAN $$

Map p210 (02-725 1713; 35-3 Pirundae-ro, Jongno-gu; mains ₩10,000-25,000; 11.30am-11pm Tue-Sun; Line 3 to Gyeongbokgung, Exit 2) In an artfully styled *hanok*, interesting dishes to share are offered (such as *tteokbokki* served in a carved-out squash), alongside Western cuisine including pizza and fried-rice filled omelettes. There's a good wine and drinks list, making it a pleasant spot to linger in the evening.

★OGAWA JAPANESE $$$

Map p210 (오가와; ☎02-735 1001; 19 Saemunan-ro 5-gil, Jongno-gu; set menu lunch/dinner ₩40,000/60,000; ⏲noon-2pm & 5-8.30pm Mon-Sat; Ⓢ Line 5 to Gwanghwamun, Exit 1) In the basement of the Royal Building, Ogawa's expert chefs craft sushi, piece by piece, and serve it directly over the kitchen counter – in the best Japanese style (although this is still sushi with Korean twists). Extra dishes, such as noodles and abalone porridge, mean you certainly won't leave hungry. Booking is essential as space is limited.

★GASTROTONG SWISS, EUROPEAN $$$

Map p210 (☎02-730 4162; www.gastrotong.co.kr; 1-36 Jahamun-ro 6-gil; set course lunch/dinner from ₩30,000/50,000; ⏲noon-3pm & 6-8.30pm; 📶📖; Ⓢ Line 3 to Gyeongbokgung, Exit 3) Swiss-German chef Roland Hinni and his wife Yong-Shin run this charming gourmet restaurant that blends sophistication with traditional European cooking. The set lunches are splendid deals, including appetiser, soup or salad, dessert and drinks as well as a wide choice of main courses. It's small so booking is essential.

HANMIRI KOREAN $$$

Map p210 (한미리; ☎02-757 5707; www.hanmiri.co.kr; 2nd fl, Premier Place, 8 Cheonggyecheon-ro, Jongno-gu; lunch/dinner from ₩30,000/50,000; ⏲noon-3pm & 6-10pm; 📖; Ⓢ Line 5 to Gwanghwamun, Exit 5) Sit on chairs at tables for this modern take on royal cuisine; book a table with windows overlooking the Cheong-gyecheon. It's gourmet and foreigner friendly. There's another branch in Gangnam.

Insa-dong, Bukchon & Samcheong-dong

★TOBANG KOREAN $

Map p212 (토방; ☎02-735 8156; 50-1 Insa-dong-gil, Jongno-gu; meals ₩6000; ⏲11.30am-9pm; Ⓢ Line 3 to Anguk, Exit 6) A white sign with two Chinese characters above a doorway leads the way to this excellent-value eatery, where you sit on floor cushions under paper lanterns. Order spicy stews *sundubu jjigae* or *doenjang jjigae* for some Korean home-cooking flavour and excellent side dishes that include bean sprouts, cuttlefish, raw crab in red-pepper sauce, soup and rice.

★KOONG DUMPLINGS $

Map p212 (궁; ☎02-733 9240; www.koong.co.kr; 11-3 Insa-dong 10-gil, Jongno-gu; dumplings ₩10,000; ⏲11.30am-9.30pm; Ⓢ Line 3 to Anguk, Exit 6) Koong's traditional Kaeseong-style dumplings are legendary and more than a mouthful. Only order one portion, unless you're super hungry, or enjoy them in a flavourful soup along with chewy balls of rice cake.

WOOD AND BRICK BAKERY $

Map p226 (☎02-747 1592; www.woodnbrick.com; 3 Bukchon-ro 5-gil, Jongno-gu; baked goods ₩5000-10,000; ⏲cafe 8am-10pm, restaurant noon-10pm; Ⓢ Line 3 to Anguk, Exit 2) The terrace seating at this combined bakery cafe and restaurant is a great spot from which to watch the comings and goings of Bukchon. The baked goods, sandwiches and European-deli-style eats are top notch.

OSEGYEHYANG VEGAN $

Map p212 (오세계향; ☎02-735 7171; www.go5.co.kr; 14-5 Insa-dong 12-gil, Jongno-gu; meals from ₩7000; ⏲noon-3pm & 4.30-9pm; 🖉; Ⓢ Line 3 to Anguk, Exit 6) Run by members of a Taiwanese religious sect, the vegetarian food here combines all sorts of mixtures and flavours. The barbecue-meat-substitute dish is flavoursome.

JILSIRU TTEOK CAFÉ DESSERT $

Map p212 (질시루 떡 카페; www.kfr.or.kr; 71 Donhwamun-ro, Jongno-gu; tteok/set ₩1500/6000; ⏲8am-9pm Mon-Sat, to 8pm Sun; Ⓢ Line 1, 3 or 5 to Jongno 3-ga, Exit 6) At this cafe on the ground floor of the Institute of Traditional Korean Food, you can choose from soft, delicately flavoured handmade gourmet rice cakes *(tteok)* with all sorts of flavours including citron or coffee.

Upstairs is the **Tteok Museum** (떡박물관; ☎02-741 5411; www.tkmuseum.or.kr/eng/index.htm; adult/youth ₩3000/2000; ⏲10am-5pm Mon-Sat, from noon Sun) where you can learn more about these Korean sweets.

SEOURESEO DULJJAERO JALHANEUNJIP DESSERT $

(서울서둘째로잘하는집; ☎02-734 5302; 122-1 Samcheong-ro, Jongno-gu; desserts ₩5000; ⏲11am-10pm Tue-Sun; Ⓢ Line 3 to Anguk, Exit 1) Little has changed at 'Second Best Place in Seoul', a tiny tea and dessert cafe, since it opened in 1976. Apart from the medicinal teas, it serves wonderful thick *danpatjuk* (red-bean porridge with ginseng, chestnut and peanuts).

★GOGUNG KOREAN $$

Map p212 (고궁; ☎02-736 3211; www.gogung.co.kr; 44 Insa-dong-gil, Jongno-gu; meals from ₩8000-12,000; ⏰11am-10pm; Ⓢ Line 3 to Anguk, Exit 6) In the basement of Ssamziegil is this smart and stylish restaurant, specialising in Jeonju (capital of Jeollabuk Province) bibimbap, which is fresh and garnished with nuts, but contains raw minced beef. The *dolsot* bibimbap is served in a stone hotpot. Both come with side dishes. Also try the *moju*, a sweet, cinnamon home-brew drink.

TEA MUSEUM INTERNATIONAL $$

Map p208 (☎02-747 4587; www.facebook.com/TeaMuseum; 61 Changdeokgung-gil, Jongno-gu; mains ₩15,000-50,000; ⏰11am-8.30pm; 📶📄; Ⓢ Line 3 to Anguk, Exit 3) Organic produce and unusual recipes for Seoul, such as Jerusalem artichoke ravioli and Provençale-style lamb chop, mark out this elegant cafe, restaurant and gallery along with its lush front garden and views across to the neighbouring palace. It also sells its own range of black and herbal teas and infusions that can be sampled with freshly made cakes.

BIBIGO GYEJEOLBABSANG KOREAN $$

Map p212 (비비고 계절밥상; ☎02-2223 2551; B1 Insa-dong Maru, 35-4 6 Insa-dong-gil, Jongno-gu; buffet lunch Mon-Fri ₩13,900, Sat & Sun ₩22,900, dinner ₩22,900; ⏰10.30am-10.30pm; Ⓢ Line 3 to Anguk, Exit 6) There's usually a line for 'Season's Table', a good-value *hansik* (Korean food) buffet in the basement of Insa-dong Maru. A wide range of dishes are temptingly laid out and include items such as hot-stone bibimbap which you need to order with one of the chits on your table. Desserts and some drinks are included.

2046 PANSTEAK STEAK $$

Map p208 (☎070-4686 9198; 20 Bukchon-ro 4-gil, Jongno-gu; mains from ₩14,000; ⏰11.30am-9pm Mon-Sat, to 8pm Sun; 📄; Ⓢ Line 3 to Anguk, Exit 2) Sometimes you just need a nicely cooked piece of meat – 2046 Pansteak serves up just that, still sizzling on an iron skillet along with spinach, a choice of two sauces and other garnishes. It's not too pricey and has a relaxed, youthful environment.

JIRISAN KOREAN $$

Map p212 (지리산; ☎02-723 4696; 30 Insa-dong 14-gil, Jongno-gu; meals from ₩10,000; ⏰noon-10pm; Ⓢ Line 3 to Anguk, Exit 6) A great place to try *dolsotbap* (hotpot rice, ₩10,000) in an authentic atmosphere. Various ingredients are added to the rice, and you mix it all up in a separate bowl with the sauces and side dishes – a do-it-yourself bibimbap.

Pour the weak burnt-rice tea from the kettle into the stone pot and put the lid on, then drink it at the end of the meal.

JONGNO SARANGGA KOREAN $$

Map p210 (종로사랑가; ☎02-730 7754; 78 Sambong-ro, Jongno-gu; meals ₩6000-13,000; ⏰11.30am-10pm; 📄; Ⓢ Line 1 to Jonggak, Exit 2) One of this convivial restaurant's specialities is *neobiani*, a flavoursome beef patty the size of a small pizza. Meant for sharing, it comes with a mass of side dishes amounting to a feast.

DEJANGJANGI HWADEOGPIJAJIP PIZZA $$

Map p208 (대장장이 화덕피자집; ☎02-765 4298; 3 Bukchon-ro 11-gil, Jongno-gu; pizzas ₩14,000-20,000; ⏰noon-10pm; 📶📄; Ⓢ Line 3 to Anguk, Exit 2) *Daijangjangi* means 'blacksmith' and that is exactly what the owner Lee Jae-Sung is. Some of his metal creations adorn the quirky interior of this *hanok* turned pizzeria. The pizza is authentic and the service friendly.

SOLMOE-MAEUL KOREAN $$

Map p208 (솔뫼마을; ☎02-720 0995; 100-1 Samcheong-ro, Jongno-gu; mains ₩8000-15,000; ⏰11.30am-10pm; 📄; Ⓢ Line 3 to Anguk, Exit 1) Sit on the floor or on chairs on the narrow balcony to enjoy an excellent multicourse meal for ₩28,000 that includes *bulgogi* (cooked slices of beef). The *gujeolpan* (a royal court dish) is a speciality with pink radish wraps, as is the *pajeon* (savoury pancakes) and the sprouty version of bibimbap.

★BALWOO GONGYANG VEGETARIAN $$$

Map p212 (발우공양; ☎02-2031 2081; www.balwoogongyang.or.kr; 5th fl, Templestay Information Center, 56 Ujeongguk-ro, Jongno-gu; lunch/dinner from ₩27,500/39,600; ⏰11.40am-3pm & 6-8.50pm; ✎; Ⓢ Line 3 to Anguk, Exit 6) Reserve three days in advance for the delicate temple-style cuisine served here. Take your time to fully savour the subtle flavours and different textures of the vegetarian dishes, which range from rice porridge and delicate salads to dumplings and fried shitake mushrooms and mugwort in a sweet-and-sour sauce.

For less fancy vegetarian food **Balwoo Gongyang Kong** on the building's 2nd floor offers a buffet (₩8000) or simple noodle and rice dishes for around ₩4000.

★**MIN'S CLUB** FUSION $$$

Map p212 (민가다헌; ☎02-733 2966; www.minsclub.co.kr; 23-9 Insa-dong 10-gil, Jongno-gu; set course lunch/dinner from ₩32,000/70,000; ⊙noon-2.30pm & 6-9.30pm; 📵; Ⓢ Line 3 to Anguk, Exit 6) Old-world architecture meets new-world cuisine in this classy restaurant housed in a beautifully restored turn-of-the-20th-century *hanok*, said to be the first in Seoul to incorporate Western features such as en suite bathrooms. The European-Korean meals (more European than Korean) are beautifully presented and there's an extensive wine selection.

DRINKING & NIGHTLIFE

Gwanghwamun & Around

★**DAEO SOCHOM** CAFE

Map p210 (대오서점; ☎010-570 1349; 55 Jahamun-ro 7-gil, Jongno-gu; ⊙noon-8pm Tue-Sun; Ⓢ Line 3 to Gyeongbokgung, Exit 2) Opened as a bookshop in 1951 by Mrs Kwong and her husband Mr Cho, this charming cafe is still run by the same family and oozes bygone-days atmosphere with lots of memorabilia and quirky decor. Entry is ₩5000, which gets you a choice of drink.

ET M'AMIE TEAHOUSE

Map p210 (36 Jahamun-ro, Jongno-gu; ⊙noon-10.30pm Mon-Fri, from 1pm Sat & Sun; Ⓢ Line 3 to Gyeongbokgung, Exit 5) A rabbit poking its head from a lampshade, attractive print wallpaper, curtains and upholstery add to the charm of this *salon de thé* (tearoom) serving Mariage Frères teas and home-baked goodies. Treat yourself to its afternoon tea tray for ₩24,000 for two.

MK2 CAFE

Map p210 (17 Jahamun-ro 10-gil, Jongno-gu; ⊙11am-11pm; 📶; Ⓢ Line 3 to Gyeongbokgung, Exit 5) The name indicates the style of this cafe, which is tastefully furnished with mid-century-modern pieces. It's a good spot for coffee and snacks while exploring Seochon.

HOPSCOTCH BAR

Map p210 (☎02-722 0145; www.hopscotch.co.kr; 14-1 Hyoja-ro 7-gil, Jongno-gu; ⊙5pm-1am Mon-Fri, 11.30am-9pm Sat & Sun; Ⓢ Line 3 to Gyeongbokgung, Exit 4) The prime appeal of this gastropub is its location in a converted *hanok*, which makes for a cosy spot to sample its range of local and international microbrews. The US comfort food is very tasty but served in small portions and on the pricey side.

Insa-dong, Bukchon & Samcheong-dong

★**SIK MOOL** BAR

Map p212 (식물; ☎02-747 4858; 46-1 Donhwamun-ro 11-gil, Jongno-gu; ⊙11am-midnight; Ⓢ Line 1, 3 or 5 to Jongno 3-ga, Exit 6) Four *hanok* were creatively combined to create this chic designer cafe-bar that blends old and new Seoul. Clay tile walls, Soviet-era propaganda posters, mismatched modern furniture and contemporary art surround a young crowd sipping cocktails, coffee and wine and nibbling on house-made pizza.

★**DAWON** TEAHOUSE

Map p212 (다원; ☎02-730 6305; 11-4 Insa-dong 10-gil, Jongno-gu; teas ₩7000; ⊙10.30am-10.30pm; Ⓢ Line 3 to Anguk, Exit 6) The perfect place to unwind under the shady fruit trees in a courtyard with flickering candles. In colder weather sit indoors in *hanok* rooms decorated with scribbles or in the garden pavilion. The teas are superb, especially *omijacha hwachae* (fruit and five-flavour berry punch), a summer drink.

Small exhibition spaces surround the courtyard.

★**BREW 3.14** BAR

Map p212 (☎070-4178 3014; www.facebook.com/brew314; 39 Donhwamun-ro 11-gil, Jongno-gu; ⊙4pm-midnight; Ⓢ Line 1, 3 or 5 to Jongno 3-ga, Exit 6) Along with sibling operation Brew 3.15 across the road, Brew 3.14 has carved a name for itself with its great selection of local craft beers, delicious pizza (which they call by the American name 'pie') and moreish fried chicken. Both bars are quiet, convivial places to hang out over pints and eats.

★STORY OF THE BLUE STAR BAR

Map p212 (푸른별 주막; ☎02-734 3095; 17-1 Insa-dong 16-gil, Jongno-gu; ⏰3pm-midnight; Ⓢ Line 3 to Anguk, Exit 6) Owned by a stage actor, this rustic hang-out, plastered with posters, is an atmospheric place to sample *makgeolli* rice wine served out of brass kettles into brass bowls. Flavours include mulberry leaf, green tea and taro. Order slices of its homemade organic tofu and *kimchi* to eat as you drink.

TEA THERAPY TEAHOUSE

Map p208 (☎02-730 7507; http://teatherapy.com; 74 Yunposun-gil, Jongno-gu; ⏰10am-10pm; 📶; Ⓢ Line 3 to Anguk, Exit 2) Teas and herbal infusions for whatever ails you. Ask for the handy chart in English to aid you in your decisions from the wide range of concoctions available (also sold packaged for takeaway). It's a retro-stylish kind of place with free foot baths outside the front door.

IKDONG DABANG BAR

Map p212 (익동다방; ☎070-8690 2759; www.facebook.com/ikdongdabang; 17-19 Supyo-ro 28-gil, Jongno-gu; ⏰11am-11pm; Ⓢ Line 1, 3 or 5 to Jongno 3-ga, Exit 6) More evidence of the evolution of Ikseon-dong's cluster of *hanok* into cool cafe-bars and guesthouses is this arty *dabang* (an old Korean name for a cafe). Look for the bright yellow-and-blue, painted-steel-frame sculpture that leads into a courtyard sometimes used for musical performances.

KOPI BANGASGAN CAFE

Map p208 (커피 방앗간; 118-11 Bukchon-ro 5ga-gil, Jongno-gu; ⏰8.30am-10.30pm; Ⓢ Line 3 to Anguk, Exit 1) Based in a *hanok*, 'Coffee Mill' is a charming spot decorated with retro pieces and the quirky, colourful artworks of owner Lee Gyeong-hwan, whom you're likely to spot painting at the counter. Apart from various coffees it also serves waffles.

CHA MASINEUN TTEUL TEAHOUSE

Map p208 (차마시는뜰; 26 Bukchon-ro 11na-gil, Jongno-gu; ⏰10.30am-10pm; Ⓢ Line 3 to Anguk, Exit 1) Overlooking Samcheong-dong and Gwanghwamun is this lovely *hanok* with low tables arranged around a courtyard. It serves traditional teas and a delicious bright-yellow pumpkin rice cake that is served fresh from the steamer.

BAEKSEJU-MAEUL BAR

Map p212 (백세주마을; ☎02-720 0055; www.ksdb.co.kr; 10 Ujeongguk-ro 2-gil, Jongno-gu; ⏰5pm-1am; Ⓢ Line 2 to Jonggak, Exit 4) From the floor seating area there's a dress-circle view of the Bosingak pavilion. See the website's English pages to learn more about the excellent range of traditional rice wines available at this drinking and dining outlet for brewer Kooksoondang.

CAFFE THEMSELVES CAFE

(www.caffethemselves.com; 388 Samil-daero, Jongno-gu; coffee ₩5500; ⏰10am-10pm; 📶; Ⓢ Line 1 to Jonggak, Exit 12) A worthy stop for those who take their coffee seriously, here baristas know how to do a decent single-origin espresso, slow drip or cold brew. They roast their own beans, which they sell by the bag, as well as having ready-made samples to try.

DALSAENEUN DALMAN SAENGGAK HANDA TEAHOUSE

Map p212 (달새는 달만 생각한다; ☎02-720 6229; 14-3 Insa-dong 12-gil, Jongno-gu; teas ₩7000-9000; ⏰10am-11pm; Ⓢ Line 3 to Anguk, Exit 6) 'Moon Bird Thinks Only of the Moon' is packed with plants and rustic artefacts. Birdsong, soothing music and trickling water add to the atmosphere. Huddle in a cubicle and savour one of the teas, which include *gamnipcha* (persimmon-leaf tea). *Saenggangcha* (ginger tea) is peppery but sweet.

BEAUTIFUL TEA MUSEUM TEAHOUSE

Map p212 (☎02-735 6678; www.tmuseum.co.kr; 19-11 Insa-dong-gil, Jongno-gu; ⏰10.30am-10pm; Ⓢ Line 3 to Anguk, Exit 6) As well as Korean teas you can sip teas from around the world in the pleasant covered courtyard of this modern *hanok*. Loose-leaf teas and tea-making sets and implements are also sold here and there's an exhibition area.

CAFÉ YEON CAFE, BAR

Map p208 (www.facebook.com/cafeyeon; 84-3 Samcheong-ro, Jongno-gu; ⏰noon-11pm; Ⓢ Line 3 to Anguk, Exit 1) The *hanok* goes global at this charming 'traveller's hang-out' decorated with colourful cushions, photos and Snoopy items. As well as beer and cocktails it also serves soft drinks and snacks.

LOCAL KNOWLEDGE

NAGWON-DONG GAY BARS

Itaewon's 'Homo Hill' is not the only place in Seoul with gay bars. Far more popular with Korean *iban* (the local word for gays) are the scores of GLBT-run bars around Jongno 3-ga subway station. However, not all are welcoming of foreigners, and others will expect patrons to pay a hefty cover charge for *anju* (snacks).

Alternatively, the outdoor *pojangmacha* food stalls around Jongno 3-ga where you can sink cheap bear, *soju* (local vodka) and snacks are prime hangouts for the gay community.

'One-shot bars' are places where you can drink without a cover charge.

Barcode (Map p212; 41-1 Donhwamun-ro, Jongno-gu; ⏲7pm-4am; Ⓢ Lines 1, 3 & 5 to Jongno 3-ga, Exit 3) Run by friendly English-speaking Kim Hyoung-Jin, this stylish one-shot bar is on the 2nd floor – look for the English sign as you come out of the subway.

Shortbus (Map p212; korea-shortbus.wix.com/shortbus; 45 Donhwamun-ro, Jongno-gu; ⏲7pm-5am; Ⓢ Line 1, 3 or 5 to Jongno 3-ga, Exit 3) This wine-and-cocktail, one-shot bar is appealing, spacious and the bar tenders mix a mean mojito. It's on the 3rd floor with an English sign.

TOP CLOUD WINE BAR

Map p212 (탑 클라우드; ☎02-2198 3300; www.topcloud.co.kr; 33rd fl, Jongno Tower, 51 Jong-ro, Jongno-gu; ⏲noon-midnight; Ⓢ Line 1, 3 or 5 to Jonggak, Exit 3) Pricey drinks, including a good selection of wine, come with knockout views from the enormous windows at this restaurant and bar perched 33 floors above downtown Seoul. Live jazz runs from 7pm each night, but if you're coming just for a drink show up after 8.30pm when the dinnertime buffet (₩59,000) finishes.

☆ ENTERTAINMENT

SEJONG CENTER FOR THE PERFORMING ARTS THEATRE

Map p210 (세종문화회관; ☎02-399 1114; www.sejongpac.or.kr; 175 Sejong-daero, Jongno-gu; Ⓢ Line 5 to Gwanghwamun, Exit 1 or 8) One of Seoul's leading arts complexes with several performance and exhibition spaces puts on major drama, music and art shows – everything from large-scale musicals to fusion *gugak* (traditional Korean music) and chamber orchestras.

BIBAP PERFORMING ARTS

(☎02-766 0815; www.bibap.co.kr; 386, Samil-daero, Jongno-gu; tickets from ₩40,000; ⏲8pm Mon, 5pm & 8pm Tue-Sat, 3pm & 6pm Sun; Ⓢ Line 1 to Jonggak, Exit 12) A theatre production that involves a comedic *Iron Chef*–style contest which stirs beatbox and a cappella into the mix.

CINEMATHEQUE/ SEOUL ARTS CINEMA CINEMA

Map p212 (☎02-741 9782; www.cinematheque.seoul.kr; 4th fl, Nagwon Arcade, 428, Samil-daero, Jongno-gu; tickets ₩5000; Ⓢ Line 1, 3 or 5 to Jongno 3-ga, Exit 5) Catch independent and foreign films (with subtitles in Korean) at this arts cinema where you'll also find Hollywood golden oldies screening at the Silver Cinema. Some Korean films may have English subtitles but it's best to check first. Various film festivals and retrospectives are held here including the **LGBT Film Festival** (www.selff.org) in June.

SHOPPING

Gwanghwamun & Around

★KYOBO BOOKSHOP BOOKS, MUSIC

Map p210 (☎02-3973 5100; www.kyobobook.co.kr; B1, Kyobo Bldg, 1 Jong-ro, Jongno-gu; ⏲9.30am-10pm; Ⓢ Line 5 to Gwanghwamun, Exit 4) Kyobo's flagship branch sells a wide range of English-language books and magazines (you'll find them on the left from the main entrance), as well as stationery, gifts, electronics and CDs and DVDs in its excellent **Hottracks** (www.hottracks.co.kr) section.

SEOUL SELECTION BOOKS, DVDS

Map p210 (☎02-734 9565; www.seoulselection.co.kr; 6 Samcheong-ro, Jongno-gu; ⏰9.30am-6.30pm Mon-Fri, 1-6pm Sat; Ⓢ Line 3 to Anguk, Exit 1) Staff speak English here and can recommend titles published by Seoul Selection as well as a wide range of other publishers' books on Korean culture in English, along with Korean CDs and Korean movies and drama series on DVD (with English subtitles). The website has an excellent monthly newsletter about what's on in Seoul.

Ask staff about English-language walking tours of Bukchon that run on Saturday (₩30,000).

MARKET M* HOMEWARES

Map p210 (www.market-m.co.kr; 5 Jahamun-ro 13-gil, Jongno-gu; ⏰11am-6.30 Mon-Fri, 12.30-6.30pm Sat & Sun; Ⓢ Line 3 to Gyeongbokgung, Exit 2) Enjoy a free cup of coffee while browsing this compact, upmarket version of Ikea, selling well-designed, simple wooden furniture and other products such as bags, storage and stationery from Korea and Japan. Look for the delightful waxed-paper bags by Japanese brand Siwa.

YUIMARU GIFTS

Map p210 (유이마루; ☎02-3446 4603; www.yuimaru.co.kr; 3 Sajik-ro 9ga-gil, Jongno-gu; ⏰noon-6.30pm Mon-Fri, to 6pm Sat & Sun; Ⓢ Line 3 to Gyeongbokgung, Exit 1) The black cat Curo is the superstar character in hundreds of costumes and disguises – everything from Darth Vader to Marylin Monroe – at this creative stationery and gifts store. Her multiple personalities appear printed on cards, stickers, bags and T-shirts.

MONO COLLECTION TRADITIONAL FABRICS

Map p210 (www.monocollection.com; 17 Jahamun-ro 10-gil, Jongno-gu; ⏰9.30am-6.30pm Mon-Fri; Ⓢ Line 3 to Gyeongbokgung, Exit 5) Chang Eung Bong creates and sources exquisite fabrics used for fashion and soft furnishings, including gorgeous quilts, pillows and contemporary spins on *hanbok*. Browse the collection in the studio above MK2 cafe.

SEJONG ART MARKET SOSO MARKET

Map p210 (www.sejongpac.or.kr/eng; 175 Sejong-daero, Jongno-gu; ⏰noon-6pm, 1st & 3rd Sat May-Oct; Ⓢ Line 5 to Gwanghwamun, Exits 1 or 8) The attractive sculpture garden behind the Sejong Center is the location of this spring-to-early-autumn, twice-monthly market where you can buy a wide variety of works from up-and-coming artists and designers.

Insa-dong, Bukchon & Samcheong-dong

★ **KCDF GALLERY** CRAFTS

Map p212 (☎02-793 9041; www.kcdf.kr; 8 Insa-dong 11-gil, Jongno-gu; ⏰10am-7pm; Ⓢ Line 3 to Anguk, Exit 6) The Korean Craft and Design Foundation's gallery has a shop on the ground floor showcasing some of the finest locally made products, including woodwork, pottery and jewellery. It's the ideal place to find a unique, sophisticated gift or souvenir.

★ **INSA-DONG MARU** CRAFTS

Map p212 (☎02-2223 2500; www.insadongmaru.co.kr; 35-4 6 Insa-dong-gil, Jongno-gu; ⏰10.30am-8.30pm Sun-Fri, to 9pm Sat; Ⓢ Line 3 to Anguk, Exit 6) Around 60 different Korean designer shops selling crafts, fashion and homewares are gathered at this slick, new complex spread over several levels around a central rest area where there's a piano available for impromptu concerts by passers by.

Shops to look out for here include the monochrome accessories of **4T** (www.4ourt.co.kr) and the handmade shoes of **Le Cordonnier** (www.ucnehandworks.co), where the master cobbler Yun Hongsik shares a space with his watch-designer daughter's brand, **Metal et Linnen** (www.metaletlinnen.com).

GALLERY ART ZONE SOUVENIRS

Map p208 (www.mmca.go.kr; MMCA Seoul, 30 Samcheong-ro, Jongno-gu; ⏰10am-6pm Tue, Thu, Fri & Sun, to 9pm Wed & Sat; Ⓢ Line 3 to Anguk, Exit 1) For consumers of contemporary Korean art and design these five gallery spaces at the MMCA showcase some of the best of what's on offer from fashion and electronic goods to ceramics and stationery.

JILKYUNGYEE FASHION

Map p208 (질경이; ☎02-732 5606; www.jilkyungyee.co.kr; 88 Samcheong-ro, Jongno-gu; Ⓢ Line 3 to Anguk, Exit 1) Lee Ki-Yeon trained as an artist in the late 1970s when she became interested in natural dyeing and traditional Korean fashion. She went on to establish this fashion brand selling tastefully designed *hanbok*, everyday and special-occasion clothing for both sexes.

The styles are easy to wear and are often more contemporary in their design than you'll find elswhere.

SSAMZIEGIL HANDICRAFTS

Map p212 (www.ssamzigil.com; 42 Insa-dong-gil, Jongno-gu; ⌚10.30am-8.30pm; Ⓢ Line 3 to Anguk, Exit 6) An arty four-storey complex built around a courtyard that's a popular stop for one-off clothing, accessories or household goods.

In the basement look for **Cerawork** (Map p212; www.cerawork.co.kr; B1 Ssamziegil; ⌚10.30am-8.30pm), where you can paint your own design onto pottery for a unique souvenir.

DOLSILNAI FASHION

Map p212 (돌실나이; ☎02-737 2232; www.dolsilnai.co.kr; 35 Insa-dong-gil, Jongno-gu; ⌚10.30am-8pm; Ⓢ Line 3 to Anguk, Exit 6) Come here for beautifully designed, casual *hanbok* (traditional Korean clothing) made from natural fabrics in a variety of soft natural and pastel colours. There's always a selection of garments for men and women that are discounted.

There are also branches in Sinchon and Daehangno.

JONGINAMOO HOMEWARES

Map p208 (종이나무; http://jonginamoo.com; 3 Bukchon-ro 5-gil, Jongno-gu; ⌚10am-10pm Mon-Sat, from noon Sun; Ⓢ Line 3 to Anguk, Exit 2) Selling beautiful traditional-styled furniture and decorative pieces for your home-including a variety of lamps with shades made of *hanji* (handmade paper).

O'SULLOC TEA SHOP

Map p212 (www.osulloc.com; 45-1 Insa-dong-gil, Jongno-gu; ⌚10am-10pm; Ⓢ Line 3 to Anguk, Exit 6) A variety of nicely packaged teas grown at the company's plantations on Jeju-do (Jeju Island) as well as tea-making implements are on offer here. A cafe upstairs serves up the mainly green teas in all sorts of drinkable and edible ways and there's a premium tasting lounge on the top floor.

There are several other branches around Seoul.

KUKJAE EMBROIDERY HANDICRAFTS

Map p212 (☎02-732 0830; www.suyeh.co.kr; 41 Insa-dong-gil, Jongno-gu; ⌚10am-8.30pm; Ⓢ Line 3 to Anguk, Exit 6) Exquisite traditional embroidery pieces, including handbags, cushions and pillows, from Kukjae have often been presented as official gifts by Korean presidents to visiting dignitaries. You'll also find *bojagi* patchwork cloths here used for gift wrapping or display.

MIK JEWELLERY

Map p208 (www.m-mik.com; 117 Gyedong-gil, Jongno-gu; ⌚10am-6pm Wed-Mon; Ⓢ Line 3 to Anguk, Exit 3) You're likely to find Lim Dong Wook, the designer of these original unisex shirt-button covers at this, his atelier and showroom. These pieces of jewellery are a neat replacement for a tie or brooch and range in price from ₩20,000 for simple designs to ₩268,000 for ones made from silver.

YIDO HOMEWARES

Map p208 (www.yido.kr; 191 Changdeokgung-gil, Jongno-gu; ⌚10am-7pm; Ⓢ Line 3 to Anguk, Exit 2) Tastefully designed, natural glazed pottery for daily and decorative use are artfully displayed on the ground floor of this complex that includes a gallery, basement cafe and academy where you can learn to throw or hand mould pots.

NAKWON MUSICAL INSTRUMENTS ARCADE MUSIC

Map p212 (http://enakwon.com/main; 428 Samil-daero, Jongno-gu; ⌚10am-7.30pm Mon-Sat; Ⓢ Line 1, 3 or 5 to Jongno 3-ga, Exit 5) Want a pink guitar or an orange banjo? Browse the vast variety of musical instruments and equipment of all kinds spread mainly over the 2nd and 3rd floors of this large arcade in a dazzling maze of shops.

Myeong-dong & Jung-gu

Neighbourhood Top Five

❶ Climb or ride the cable car up **Namsan**, topped by **N Seoul Tower** (p73); the 262m central-city peak is a leafy retreat from Myeong-dong's commercial throng.

❷ Haggle day and night with the vendors at the mammoth **Namdaemun Market** (p74).

❸ Learn about traditional Korean houses and culture at **Namsangol Hanok Village** (p77).

❹ Go shopping crazy on the packed, neon-festooned streets of **Myeong-dong** (p82).

❺ Enjoy the changing of the guard outside **Deoksugung** (p75) and wander the pleasant palace grounds.

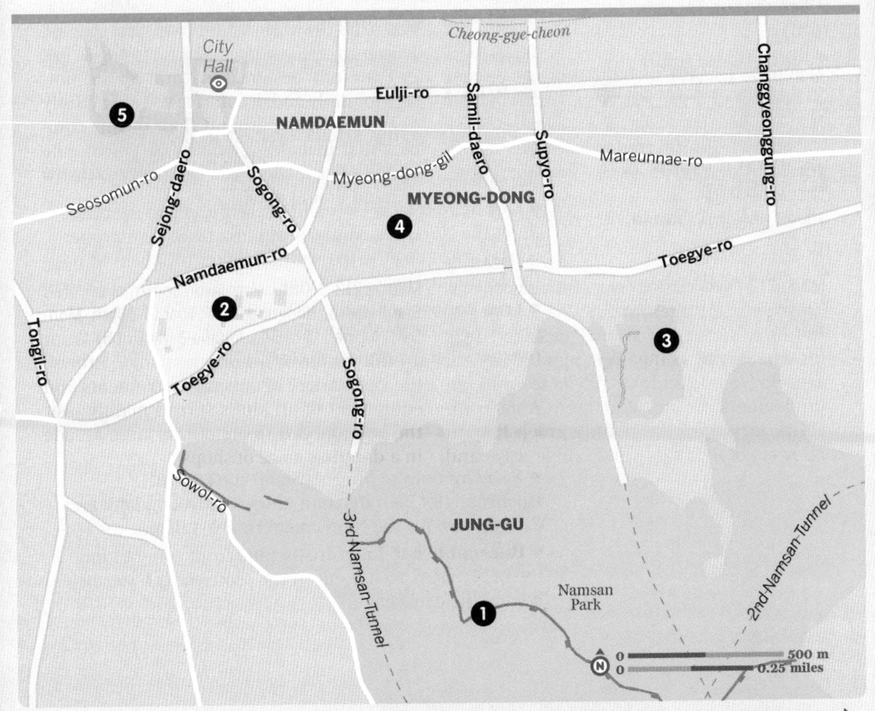

For more detail of this area see Map p216

Lonely Planet's Top Tip

On the roof of the original Shinsegae building is Trinity Garden, dotted with sculptures by Henry Moore, Joan Miró and Jeff Koons among others; there's a cafe or you could enjoy a picnic of goodies bought from the department store's food hall.

Best Places to Eat

- Gosang (p80)
- Congdu (p80)
- Chung-jeong-gak (p78)

For reviews, see p78

Best Entertainment

- Nanta Theatre (p82)
- Jeongdong Theater (p81)
- Korea House (p80)

For reviews, see p81 

Best Places to Shop

- Namdaemun Market (p74)
- Shinsegae (p82)
- Lotte Department Store (p82)

For reviews, see p82

Explore: Myeong-dong & Jung-gu

Branding itself the city's belly button, Jung-gu (www.junggu.seoul.kr) stretches from the southern city gate of Sungnyemun and round-the-clock Namdaemun Market towards the eastern gate of Heunginjimun. Dominating the district's heart is the youth-fashion shopping area of Myeong-dong. Myeong means 'light' – apt for an area where Seoul's commercial razzle-dazzle reaches its apogee.

Myeong-dong's streets and alleyways are invariably teeming with shoppers. Masses of boutiques cater to every youthful style tribe, along with plenty of cafes, restaurants and high-rise shopping malls. Japanese visitors in particular adore it and you'll often hear shop and stall vendors address the crowd in that language. The mass of humanity, noise and visual stimulation can become overwhelming, but don't let that put you off spending some time soaking up the electric atmosphere and indulging in retail therapy.

Tranquillity can be regained on nearby Namsan, downtown Seoul's green lung, its hiking trails, parkland and old City Wall newly spruced up. Also providing a change of pace is the area to the west of Seoul Plaza and City Hall. Here you'll find Deoksugung, a lovely palace around which early missionaries built Seoul's first churches and schools, and where foreign legations were based; many old buildings have been preserved.

Local Life

- **Sunday worship** Attend a service at the historic Myeong-dong Catholic Cathedral (p78) or the Romanesque-style Anglican Church.
- **Get fit** Join locals stretching their legs and keeping fit on the Northern Namsan walking trail; for a proper workout drop by the free outdoor gym (p73) behind the National Theater of Korea.
- **Free concerts** From mid-May to the end of August grassy Seoul Plaza (p76), fronting the City Hall, has free performances most nights.

Getting There & Away

- **Subway** Line 4 connects Seoul station with Hoehyeon (for Namdaemun Market), Myeongdong and Chungmuro for the Namsangol Hanok Village.
- **Bus/cable car** Taxis are banned from going to the top of Namsan, so use one of the ecofriendly buses or hop on the cable car.

TOP SIGHT
NAMSAN & N SEOUL TOWER

Beloved by locals as a place for exercise, peaceful contemplation and hanging out with loved ones, Namsan (남산) was a sacred shamanistic spot when the Joseon ruler Taejo ordered the construction of a fortress wall across this and Seoul's three other guardian mountains. The mountain is protected within a 109-hectare park and crowned by one of the city's most iconic features: N Seoul Tower.

DON'T MISS

- N Seoul Tower
- Bongsudae
- City Wall
- Northern Namsan Circuit

PRACTICALITIES

- Map p216
- www.nseoultower.com
- adult/child ₩9000/7000
- ⏲10am-11pm
- 🚌shuttle buses 2, 3, 5

N Seoul Tower

The iconic N Seoul tower (236m), the geographical centre of Seoul, sits atop the city's guardian mountain. The panoramic views of the metropolis from its observation deck are immense. Come at sunset and you can watch the city morph into a galaxy of twinkling stars. The tower has become a hot date spot with the railings around it festooned with locks inscribed with lovers' names.

Walking up Namsan isn't difficult, but riding the **cable car** (Map p216; one-way/return adult ₩6000/8500, child ₩3000/5500; ⏲10am-11pm; Ⓢ Line 4 to Myeongdong, Exit 3) is popular for more good views. Shuttle buses run from 7.30am to 11.30pm from various subway stations around the mountain.

Historic Structures

Sections of the original **City Wall** still snake across Namsan; near the summit you can also see the **Bongsudae** (Signal Beacons), a communications system used for 500 years to notify the central government of urgent political and military information. A traditional lighting ceremony is held here between 3pm and 4pm Tuesday to Sunday.

In the 1920s the Japanese built a Shinto shrine on the mountain, removing the shamanist prayer hall Guksadang from Namsan's summit in the process (it was rebuilt on Inwangsan).

Northern Namsan Circuit

Over the last few years the city has been restoring parts of the City Wall and parks and trails on the mountain. Along the Namsan Northern Circuit, a pedestrian path that snakes for 3km from the lower cable-car station to the National Theater, you'll find the beautifully ornate and peaceful **Waryongmyo** (Map p216; ⏲8am-4pm). Built in 1862, this Buddhist/Taoist/shamanist shrine is dedicated to Zhuge Liang (AD 181–234), a Chinese statesman and general.

Further along is the archery practice ground for the **Korea Whal Culture Association** (Map p216; www.korea-bow.or.kr; 20 arrows ₩2100, 1½hr lesson ₩5000; ⏲9am-6pm) where you can practice firing arrows; lessons are 10am Saturday. Nearby is an **outdoor gym** (Map p216) FREE with proper weights and equipment.

Southern Namsan Circuit

The Southern Namsan Circuit has a pedestrian path and a road used by buses. It cuts through the old City Wall. Accessed from the Southern Namsan Circuit or via a pedestrian bridge over the road from near the Grand Hyatt is the **Namsan Outdoor Botanical Garden**. Paths lead from here through more wooded sections of Namsan Park where you'll find a firefly habitat.

PHOTOGRAPH BY KANGHEEWAN / GETTY IMAGES ©

TOP SIGHT
NAMDAEMUN MARKET & AROUND

At this sprawling market you can find pretty much anything – from food and flowers to spectacles and camera equipment. It can be a confusing place; get your bearings from the numbered gates on the periphery. Its tourist information centre (Map p216) has a good map.

What's on Sale

Haggling is the mode of business. Different sections have different opening hours and some shops open on Sunday, although that's not the best time to visit. One of Seoul's best places for Korean souvenirs is the wholesale handicrafts section in the upper floors of **Joongang Building C and D** (Gate 2; ⌚7am-6pm Mon-Fri, to 2pm Sat), with good discounts on the same items you'll find in Insa-dong. Also here is traditional Korean cookware. Other shops include **Samho Woojoo** (Map p216; Gate 3; ⌚7am-5pm Mon-Sat), with a jaw-dropping amount of fashion jewellery, and **camera shops** near Gate 1.

Dining Options

Small stalls selling *sujebi* (dough and shellfish soup), homemade *kalguksu* noodles and bibimbap for around ₩5000 are clustered on **Kalguksu Alley** near Gate 5. **Haejangguk Alley**, between Gates 2 and 3, is also good for Korean eateries. Next to Gate 2 is a great stall selling vegie *hotteok* (deep-fried pancakes) for ₩1000 and toasted sandwiches (₩1700).

Sungnyemun

Also known as Namdaemun (남대문), meaning 'Great South Gate', Seoul's picturesque **Sungnyemun** (www.sungnyemun.or.kr; ⌚9am-6pm Tue-Sun) FREE is one of the capital's four main gates built in the 14th century. Its arched entrance, topped by a double-storey pavilion, is accessed by pedestrian crossing from Gate 1. It's been reconstructed a number times over the years following damage under Japanese occupation and during the Korean War, and most recently after an arson attack in 2008 – a painstaking process that took four years.

DON'T MISS

- Joongang Building C&D
- Sungnyemun
- Kalguksu and Haejangguk food alleys

PRACTICALITIES

- 남대문시장
- Map p216
- www.namdaemunmarket.co.kr
- 21 Namdaemunsijang 4-gil, Jung-gu
- ⌚24hr
- S Line 4 to Hoehyeon, Exit 5

TOP SIGHT DEOKSUGUNG

One of Seoul's five grand palaces built during the Joseon dynasty, Deoksugung is the only one you can visit in the evening and see the buildings illuminated. It first served as a palace in 1593 and is a fascinating mix of traditional Korean and Western-style neoclassical structures.

Palace History

Deoksugung became a palace in 1593 when King Seonjo moved in after all of Seoul's other palaces were destroyed during the Japanese invasion. Despite two kings being crowned here, it was a secondary palace from 1615 until 1897, when Emperor Gojong took up residence so he could be close to where foreign legations were concentrated in the city at the time. Forced by the Japanese to abdicate 10 years later, Gojong carried on living here in some style until he died in 1919.

Palace Buildings

Deoksugung is a potpourri of contrasting architectural styles. **Junghwajeon**, the palace's main throne hall, was used for ceremonial occasions such as coronations, and is adorned with dragons and has golden window frames.

Behind it is the grand neoclassical-style **Seokjojeon**, designed by British architect GR Harding and completed in 1910. Today it houses the **Daehan Empire History Museum** (02-751 0753; www.deoksugung.go.kr; Deoksugung, 99 Sejong-daero, Jung-gu; 9.30am-5pm Tue-Sun; S Line 1 or 2 to City Hall, Exit 2) FREE, which displays the mansion's opulent interior. You can only visit as part of a 45-minute tour, best booked online (though it's not in English), or otherwise chance your luck upon arrival; tours depart approximately every half hour until 5pm. The equally grand western wing was designed by a Japanese architect in 1938. It's now the **MMCA Deoksugung** (National Museum of Modern & Contemporary Art; Map p216; www.mmca.go.kr; Deoksugung, 99 Sejong-daero, Jung-gu; 10am-7pm Tue-Thu, to 9pm Fri-Sun; S Line 1 or 2 to City Hall, Exit 2), with a collection of permanent and temporary contemporary art.

Behind Gojong's living quarters, **Hamnyeongjeon**, is the interesting fusion-style pavilion **Jeonggwanheon**, designed by Russian architect Aleksey Seredin-Sabatin as a place for the emperor to savour coffee and entertain guests. Gojong developed a taste for the beverage while holed up for a year in the Russian legation following the assassination of Queen Min. The pavilion's pillars, a verandah and metal railings are decorated with deer and bats – both auspicious creatures.

Daily Events

The **changing of the guard** is an impressive ceremony involving 50 participants, who dress up as Joseon-era soldiers and bandsmen. It happens at the Daehanmun main gate three times a day at 11am, 2pm and 3.30pm Tuesday to Sunday.

Free **guided tours** of the palace (in English) take place at 10.30am and 1.30pm Tuesday to Friday, and at 1.30pm on weekends. Otherwise you can pick up a detailed guide for ₩500.

DON'T MISS

- Changing of the Guard
- Jeonggwanheon
- Junghwajeon
- Seokjojeon

PRACTICALITIES

- 덕수궁, Palace of Virtuous Longevity
- Map p216
- www.deoksugung.go.kr
- 99 Sejong-daero, Jung-gu
- adult/child/under 7yr ₩1000/500/free
- 9am-9pm Tue-Sun
- S Line 1 or 2 to City Hall, Exit 2

TOP SIGHT CITY HALL

Looking like a tsunami made of glass and steel, the City Hall was completely redeveloped in 2013. It is a modern reinterpretation of traditional Korean design; the cresting wave providing shade (like eaves found on palaces and temple roofs) over the handsome old City Hall which was built from stone in 1926.

City Hall

As well as admiring its striking glassed wave facade, head inside to check out City Hall's lobby with its vertical garden comprising 65,000 plants; formerly the world's largest in the 2013 *Guiness Book of Records*. Head up to its 8th floor **Sky Plaza Gallery** for photo and art exhibitions.

Seoul Metropolitan Library

Opened in 2012, the **Seoul Metropolitan Library** (http://lib.seoul.go.kr; ⏲9am-9pm) is within the original City Hall Reniassance-style building constructed in 1926 that's fronted by a clock. As well as a public library, there's photography exhibitions relating to Seoul's history. At the main desk you can pick up a self-guided tour with map, or book online at www.visitseoul for English-speaking tours at 10am Tuesday to Friday, and 10.30am and 3pm Saturday, plus 10.30am and 2.30pm Sunday.

Citizens Hall

Head down to City Hall's basement to reach **Citizens Hall** (☎02-739 7733; www.seoulcitizenshall.kr; Basement, City Hall; ⏲9am-9pm Tue-Sun) FREE, a multipurpose space with an interesting mix of multimedia art exhibitions, design shops and a fair-trade cafe. There's also a 21st-century version of Speakers Corner and Media Wall where locals can express their views. Pick up a map and guide from the information desk.

Also here is the **Gungisi Relics Exhibition Hall** (www.seoulcitizenshall.kr; Basement, City Hall; ⏲9am-9pm Tue-Sun) FREE, a glassed-in archaeological site displaying items dating from the Joseon dynasty unearthed during excavation of the complex. It was the site of an armoury, so items include arrowheads and various firearms.

Seoul Plaza

Fronting City Hall, grassy **Seoul Plaza** has been a gathering spot for the masses from democracy protests to major events such as the 2002 World Cup. It's also the scene for events and free performances most nights during the summer, as well as an outdoor ice-skating rink for a couple of months each winter.

DON'T MISS

- ➡ Citizens Hall
- ➡ Seoul Plaza
- ➡ Seoul Metropolitan Library

PRACTICALITIES

- ➡ 서울시청사
- ➡ Map p216
- ➡ english.seoul.go.kr
- ➡ 110 Sejong-daero, Jung-gu
- ➡ ⏲7.30am-6pm Mon-Fri, from 9am Sat & Sun
- ➡ Ⓢ Line 1 or 2 to City Hall, Exit 5

SIGHTS

DEOKSUGUNG PALACE

See p75.

CITY HALL ARCHITECTURE

See p76.

SEOUL MUSEUM OF ART GALLERY

Map p216 (서울시립미술관, SEMA; ☎02-2124 8800; www.sema.seoul.go.kr/; 61 Deoksugung-gil, Jung-gu; ⏰10am-8pm Tue-Fri, to 7pm Sat & Sun; Ⓢ Line 1 or 2 to City Hall, Exit 2) FREE Hosting world-class exhibitions that are always worth a visit, this museum has ultra-modern, bright galleries inside the handsome brick-and-stone facade of the 1928 Supreme Court building. For some special exhibitions an entrance fee is charged.

PLATEAU GALLERY

Map p216 (www.plateau.or.kr; 150 Taepyeong-no 2-ga, Jung-gu; adult/child ₩3000/2000; ⏰10am-6pm Tue-Sun; Ⓢ Line 1 or 2 to City Hall, Exit 8) Sponsored by Samsung, and formerly known as the Rodin Gallery, this unusual glass pavilion was built to house castings of two monumental sculptures by Auguste Rodin: *The Gates of Hell* and *The Burgers of Calais*. Changing contemporary-art exhibitions are staged in two additional gallery spaces.

NAMDAEMUN MARKET MARKET

See p74.

SKYGARDEN PARK

Map p216 (Seoul station; Ⓢ Line 1 or 4 to Seoul station, Exit 2) Earmarked for completion by the end of 2017, Seoul's Skygarden is proposed to be what the High Line is to New York, an elevated urban park in the heart of the city. It will run along an abandoned stretch of highway overpass near Seoul station.

CULTURE STATION SEOUL 284 ARCHITECTURE, GALLERY

Map p216 (www.seoul284.org; 426 Cheongpa-ro, Jung-gu; ⏰10am-7pm Tue-Sun; Ⓢ Line 1 or 4 to Seoul station, Exit 2) FREE This grand 1925 building with a domed roof has been beautifully restored inside and out and made into a cultural-arts space staging a variety of events. The number 284 refers to the station's historic site number.

AHN JUNG-GEUN MEMORIAL HALL MUSEUM

Map p216 (☎02-3789 1016; www.patriot.or.kr; 471-2 Namdaemun-ro 5-ga, Jung-gu; ⏰10am-6pm Tue-Sun, to 5pm Nov-Feb; Ⓢ Line 1 to Seoul station, Exit 9-1) FREE In a striking contemporary building on the west flank of Namsan, this well-presented museum is dedicated to Korean independence fighter Ahn Jung-guen. Ahn assassinated Ito Hirobumi, the Japanese governor-general of Korea, in 1909 at Harbin station in Japanese-controlled Manchuria, a crime he paid for with his life.

N SEOUL TOWER & NAMSAN TOWER

See p73.

NAMSANGOL HANOK VILLAGE CULTURAL CENTRE

Map p216 (남산골한옥마을; ☎02-2264 4412; 28 Toegye-ro 34-gil, Jung-gu; ⏰9am-9pm Wed-Mon Apr-Oct, to 8pm Wed-Mon Nov-Mar, office 10am-5pm; Ⓢ Line 3 or 4 to Chungmuro, Exit 4) FREE Located in a park at the foot of Namsan, this peaceful village is a wonderful spot to encounter traditional Korean culture. It features five differing *yangban* (upper class) houses from the Joseon era, all relocated here from different parts of Seoul. Also here is **Seoul Namsan Gugakdang** (☎02-2261 0512; tickets from ₩20,000; ⏰closed Tue), where traditional music and concerts are staged most evenings.

On the right of the entrance gate is an office that provides free hour-long guided tours around the village at 10.30am, noon, 2pm and 3.30pm.

Here you can also partake in cultural programs, including wearing *hanbok* (traditional costumes), calligraphy, making *hanji* (traditional paper), kites and masks, and sipping traditional teas at **Davansa Teahouse** (Map p216; Namsangol Hanok Village, 28 Toegye-ro 34-gil, Jung-gu; ⏰10am-6pm; Ⓢ Line 3 or 4 to Chungmuro, Exit 4).

From May to November, displays of the traditional Korean martial art **taekwondo** are staged daily in the village at 11am, 1pm and 4pm.

Also of note is the circular sci-fi-looking **time capsule** with everyday items buried in 1994 to mark Seoul's 600th anniversary. It's not to be opened until the year 2394!

SEOUL ANIMATION CENTER MUSEUM

Map p216 (서울애니메이션센터; www.ani.seoul.kr; 126 Sopa-ro, Jung-gu; ⏰9am-5.50pm Tue-Sun; Ⓢ Line 4 to Myeongdong, Exit 1 or 3) FREE Up the hill on the way to the cable car you'll find this museum and cinema devoted to cartoons and animation from Korea and beyond.

MYEONG-DONG CATHOLIC CATHEDRAL
CHURCH

Map p216 (명동성당; ☎02-774 1784; www.mdsd.or.kr; 74 Myeong-dong-gil, Jung-gu; S Line 4 to Myeongdong, Exit 6) FREE Go inside this elegant, red- and grey-brick Gothic-style cathedral, consecrated in 1898, to admire the vaulted ceiling and stained-glass windows. The cathedral provided a sanctuary for student and trade-union protestors during military rule, becoming a national symbol of democracy and human rights. Its sleek, modern plaza entrance adds an intriguing 21st-century touch with designer shops and cafes.

BANK OF KOREA MONEY MUSEUM
MUSEUM

Map p216 (☎02-759 4881; www.museum.bok.or.kr; 39 Namdaemun-ro, Jung-gu; ⏲10am-5pm Tue-Sun; 👪; S Line 4 to Hoehyeon, Exit 7) FREE Built in 1912, and an outstanding example of Japanese colonial architecture, the old Bank of Korea now houses a reasonably interesting exhibition on the history of local and foreign currency. There are plenty of interactive displays for kids, such as being able to press your own coin or test for counterfeit notes.

AGRICULTURE MUSEUM
MUSEUM

Map p216 (농업박물관; ☎02-2080 5727; 16 Saemunan-ro, Jung-gu; ⏲9.30am-6pm Tue-Sun; S Line 5 to Seodaemun, Exit 5) FREE Much more interesting than it sounds, this museum has imaginative displays that relate to the history and practice of farming on the Korean peninsula through the dynasties. Upstairs covers general aspects of traditional life in rural Korea.

EATING

There's an excellent choice of street food cooked up by vendors within Myeong-dong's shopping district.

★MYEONG-DONG GYOJA
NOODLES $

Map p216 (명동교자; www.mdkj.co.kr; 29 Myeongdong 10-gil, Jung-gu; noodles ₩8000; ⏲10.30am-9.30pm; 📋; S Line 4 to Myeongdong, Exit 8) The special *kalguksu* (noodles in a meat, dumpling and vegetable broth) is famous, so it's busy, busy, busy. Fortunately it has multiple levels and a nearby branch to meet the demand.

MOKMYEOKSANBANG
KOREAN $

Map p216 (목멱산방; Northern Namsan Circuit, Jung-gu; mains ₩8000-10,000; ⏲11.30am-8pm; 📋; S Line 4 to Myeongdong, Exit 3) Order and pay at the till, then pick up delicious and beautifully presented bibimbap from the kitchen when your electronic buzzer rings. The traditional wooden house in which the restaurant is based is named after the ancient name for Namsan (Mokmyeok); it also serves Korean teas and *makgeolli* (rice wine) in brass kettles.

SINSEON SEOLNONGTANG
KOREAN $

Map p216 (신선설농탕; www.kood.co.kr; 3-1 Myeongdong 10-gil, Jung-gu; meals ₩7000-11,000; ⏲24hr; 📋; S Line 4 to Myeongdong, Exit 7) *Mandu* (dumplings), tofu or ginseng can be added to the beef-broth dishes served at this inexpensive chain, but purists will want to stick to the traditional version.

A PERSON
MEXICAN $

Map p216 (Taepyeong-ro 2-ga 366-1; burritos from ₩6500; ⏲4.30pm-1am; 📶📋; S Line 1 or 2 to City Hall, Exit 2) A cool little spot with stencil art and comic-book-themed murals on its walls, this basement den does tasty pork belly and shrimp burritos, matched perfectly with Korean craft beers.

WANGBIJIP
KOREAN $$

Map p216 (왕비집; www.wangbijib.com; 2nd fl, 34-1 Myeongdong 1-ga, Jung-gu; mains from ₩12,000; ⏲11.30am-11pm; S Line 4 to Myeongdong, Exit 8) Head upstairs to this tasteful Korean restaurant popular for grilled meats and other traditional dishes such as *samgyetang* (chicken stuffed with ginseng) and bibimbap.

CHUNG-JEONG-GAK
ITALIAN $$

(충정각; ☎02-313 0424; Chungjeong-ro, Seodaemun-gu; mains from ₩15,000, set menu from ₩22,000; ⏲11am-10pm Mon-Sat; 📶📋; S Line 2 or 5 to Chungjeongno, Exit 9) Housed in an attractive red-brick, Western-style building from around 1910 with white-wood wraparound verandah, this restaurant is a fragment of Seoul's past. The Italian food is delicious, and as it's across from Nanta Theatre (p82) it's a good spot for pre- or post-show meal. Inside it also has an art gallery. From the subway exit turn right and it's on your right.

BAEKJE SAMGYETANG
KOREAN $$

Map p216 (백제삼계탕; 50-11 Myeongdong 2-ga; mains from ₩15,000; ⏲9am-10pm; 📋; S Line 4

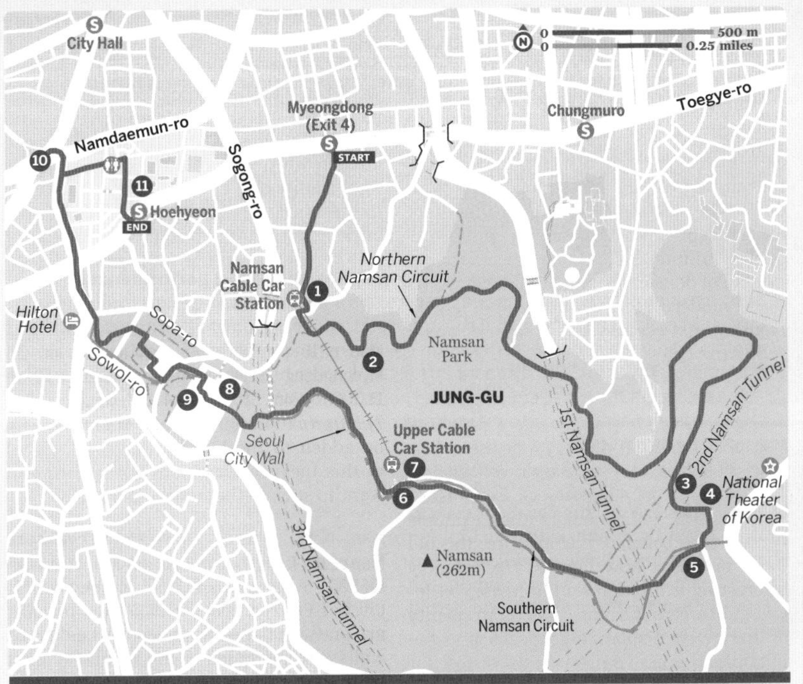

Neighbourhood Walk
Namsan Circuit

START MYEONGDONG STATION, EXIT 4
END HOEHYEON STATION
LENGTH 6KM; THREE HOURS

Following pedestrian pathways and parts of the Seoul City Wall, this hike takes you around and over Namsan, providing sweeping city views along the way and a chance to enjoy the mountain's greenery and fresh air. It's best done early in the morning, but leafy trees do provide some shade most of the way. From the subway exit walk up to the 1 **cable car station**; just before you reach here you'll see steps leading up the mountainside to the pedestrian-only Northern Namsan Circuit.

Walk left for five minutes, and pause to look around the shrine 2 **Waryongmyo** (p73), before following the road as it undulates gently around the mountain, past routes down to Namsangol Hanok Village and Dongguk University, until you reach the 3 **outdoor gym** (p73), uphill from the National Theater of Korea.

You can cut out the next bit by hopping on one of the buses that go to the peak from the 4 **bus stop** near here. Otherwise, turn right at the start of the Southern Namsan Circuit road and you'll soon see the 5 **City Wall**. A steep set of steps shadows the wall for part of the way to the summit; at the fork continue on the steps over the wall and follow the path to 6 **N Seoul Tower** (p73) and the 7 **Bongsudae** (Signal Beacons; p73).

Grab some refreshments to enjoy at the geological centre of Seoul, before picking up the City Wall trail down to pretty 8 **Joongang Park**. On the left is 9 **Ahn Jung-geun Memorial Hall** (p77).

The park continues over a road tunnel down towards the Hilton Hotel with reconstructed sections of the wall. Finish up taking a look at the reconstruction of 10 **Sungnyemun** (p74), then browsing 11 **Namdaemun Market** (p74).

KOREA HOUSE

Scoring a hat trick for high-quality food, entertainment and shopping is **Korea House** (한국의집; Map p216; ☎02-2266 9101; www.koreahouse.or.kr; 10 Toegye-ro 36-gil, Jung-gu; set menu lunch/dinner ₩45,000/68,200, performances ₩50,000; ⏲lunch noon-2pm Mon-Fri, dinner 5-6.30pm & 7-8.30pm, performances 6.30pm & 8.30pm, shop 10am-8pm; S Line 3 or 4 to Chungmuro, Exit 3). A dozen dainty, artistic courses make up the royal banquet. The *hanok* (traditional wooden house), the *hanbok*-clad waitresses, the *gayageum* (zither) music and the platters and boxes the food is served in are all part of the experience.

The intimate theatre stages two, hour-long **dance and music performances**. Put on by a troupe of top musicians and dancers, the shows have some English commentary on a screen. The show includes elegant court dances, *pansori* (a type of opera), a spiritual shamanist dance, *samullori* (a folk dance) and *samgomu* (acrobatic female drummers). There's a 30% discount on tickets if you're here for dinner.

Rounding out the experience is Korea House's **shop** which stocks quality design goods, traditional crafts and books, including *Eumsik Dimibang*, a Joseon-era cookbook dating from 1670.

to Myeongdong, Exit 6) This 2nd-floor restaurant, marked by a sign with red Chinese characters, offers reliable *samgyetang*. Put salt and pepper into the saucer and dip the pieces of chicken into it. Drink the herbal soup at the end.

SOO:P COFFEE FLOWER — CAFE $$

Map p216 (www.soopcoffeeflower.com; 97 Sogong-ro, Jung-gu; coffee ₩2500, sandwiches ₩8000; ⏲11am-10pm Mon-Sat; 📶📖; S Line 1 or 2 to City Hall, Exit 7) A slice of arty Hongdae in downtown Seoul, this earthy light-filled cafe is filled with pot plants and makes a great spot for a light meal such as gourmet sandwiches, organic vegie bibimbap and homemade cakes. They also do a good coffee.

GOGUNG — KOREAN $$

Map p216 (고궁; www.gogung.co.kr; 37 Myeongdong 8ga-gil, Jung-gu; mains from ₩11,000; ⏲9am-10pm; 📶🖋📖; S Line 4 to Myeongdong, Exit 10) An atmospheric restaurant that specialises in authentic Jeonju bibimbap, among other varieties, accompanied by live traditional Korean music.

POTALA — TIBETAN, INDIAN $$

Map p216 (www.potala.co.kr; 4th fl, 32-14 Myeongdong 2-ga, Jung-gu; mains ₩9,000-20,000; ⏲11am-11pm; 🖋; S Line 4 to Myeongdong, Exit 8) Books about Tibet and colourful crafts and pictures adorn this restaurant where you can sample the cuisine of the high Himalaya plateau, including *momo* (dumplings) cooked by Nepali chefs. While not exclusively vegetarian, there are plenty of vegie options.

HADONGKWAN — KOREAN $$

Map p216 (하동관; www.hadongkwan.com; Myeongdong 1-ga, Jung-gu; soup ₩12,000-15,000; ⏲7am-4pm; S Line 4 to Myeongdong, Exit 8) In business since 1935, this popular pit stop's big bowls of wholesome beef broth and rice come either in the regular version with slices of meat or the more expensive one with added tripe. Add salt and masses of sliced spring onions to taste.

★CONGDU — KOREAN $$$

Map p216 (www.congdu.com; 116-1 Deoksugung-gil, Jung-gu; mains from ₩29,800, set-course lunch/dinner from ₩36,800/58,800; ⏲11.30am-1.50pm & 5.30-8.30pm; 📖; S Line 5 to Gwanghwamun, Exit 6) Feast on elegantly presented, contemporary twists on Korean classics, such as pine-nut soup with soy milk *espuma* (foam) or raw blue crab, at this serene restaurant tucked away behind the British Embassy. The main dining room becomes an open roof terrace in good weather.

★GOSANG — KOREAN $$$

Map p216 (고상; ☎02-6030 8955; www.barugosang.com; 67 Suha-dong, Jung-gu; lunch/dinner set course ₩39,900/50,000; ⏲11.30am-3.30pm & 5.30-10pm; 🖋; S Line 2 to Euljiro 1-ga, Exit 4) One worth dressing up for, this classy restaurant specialises in vegetarian temple dishes that date from the Goryeo dynsasty. It's all set-course, traditional-style banquets here, and there's also a meat option. It's in a posh food court in the basement of the Center 1 Building.

★N.GRILL INTERNATIONAL **$$$**

Map p216 (☎02-3455 9297; www.nseoultower.co.kr; N Seoul Tower, Namsan; lunch/dinner from ₩55,000/95,000; ⊙11am-3pm & 5-11pm; Ⓢ Line 4 to Myeongdong, Exit 3 then cable car) Led by Michelin-starred British chef Duncan Robertson, this upmarket revolving restaurant sits uptop the iconic N Seoul Tower (p73). Views are amazing, as is its French-style cooking mixed with Korean influences. Reservations are essential. Downstairs, the open-air N Terrace is a good spot for a cocktail with a view.

CHEOLCHEOL BOKJIP SEAFOOD **$$$**

Map p216 (철철 복집; ☎02-776 2418; 29 Eulji-ro 3-gil, Jung-gu; mains from ₩27,000; ⊙11am-10pm; Ⓢ Line 2 to Euljiro 1-ga, Exit 2) A good place for adventurous diners to tick off pufferfish from their list, this local eatery is known for its *bulgogi* pufferfish barbecued in front of you. There's also pufferfish *bokguk* (soup), all freshly, and expertly, prepared.

PIERRE GAGNAIRE À SÉOUL FRENCH **$$$**

Map p216 (☎02-317 7181; www.pierregagnaire.co.kr; 35th fl, New Wing Lotte Hotel, 30 Eulji-ro, Jung-gu; 3-course mains from ₩85,000; ⊙noon-3pm & 6-10pm; Ⓢ Line 2 to Euljiro 1-ga, Exit 8) Michelin-starred chef Pierre Gagnaire's Seoul restaurant is an epicurean and wallet-hammering experience; alternatively, drop by the attached glam-to-the-max bar specialising in vodka and Champagne. You'll need to reserve a month in advance.

DRINKING & NIGHTLIFE

★MULDWINDA BAR

(물뒨다; ☎02-392 4200; www.facebook.com/muldwindakr; 43 Kyonggidae-ro, Seodaemun-gu; Ⓢ Line 2 or 5 to Chungjeongno, Exit 7) Seoul's most sophisticated *makgeolli* bar is a place for connoisseurs of Korean liquors and those who'd like to learn a bit more about the depths and breadths of local tipples. Set up by graduates from the nearby Susubori Academy (where you can learn how to make *makgeolli*), it serves good food and is decorated with class.

CRAFTWORKS MICROBREWERY

Map p216 (www.craftworkstaphouse.com/downtown; Pine Avenue Mall, 100 Eulji-ro, Jung-gu; Ⓢ Line 2 or 3 to Euljiro 3-ga, Exit 12) Hidden away in an underground mall in Seoul's downtown business district, this branch of Craftworks microbrew pub is a good spot to take a break with an excellent choice of craft beers.

WALKABOUT BAR

Map p216 (http://blog.naver.com/walkaboutnu; 49 Toegye-ro 20-gil, Jung-gu; ⊙10am-midnight Mon-Sat, 2-10pm Sun; ; Ⓢ Line 4 to Myeongdong, Exit 3) Among Myeong-dong's backpacker enclave leading up to Namsan, this travel-themed bar is run by a couple of young travel nuts who serve Korean craft beers on tap.

COFFEE LIBRE CAFE

Map p216 (www.coffeelibre.kr; Myeong-dong Cathedral, 74 Myeong-dong-gil, Jung-gu; ⊙9am-9pm; Ⓢ Line 4 to Myeongdong, Exit 4) A tiny branch of this speciality coffee roaster with a somewhat bizarre location within the Myeong-dong Cathedral complex, but makes for a good pit stop to refuel on single-origin pour overs, AeroPress or espressos.

CAFE THE STORY CAFE

Map p216 (Namsan; ⊙8am-7pm Mon-Fri, 9am-3pm Sat; ; Ⓢ Line 4 to Myeongdong, Exit 1) Myeong-dong isn't short on chain cafes, but for something with more individual character, hike up to this hidden gem on the lower slope of Namsan next to Literature House.

CAT CAFE CAFE

Map p216 (www.godabang.com; 6th fl, 51-14 Myeongdong 2-ga, Jung-gu; adult/child incl drink ₩8000/5000; ⊙1-10pm Mon-Fri, noon-10pm Sat & Sun; Ⓢ Line 4 to Myeongdong, Exit 6) One of Seoul's growing legion of pet-themed cafes, here you sip a hot drink while cuddling a number of prized-looking cats.

ENTERTAINMENT

★JEONGDONG THEATER THEATRE

Map p216 (☎02-751 1500; www.jeongdong.or.kr; 43 Jeongdong-gil, Jung-gu; tickets ₩30,000-40,000; ⊙4pm & 8pm Tue-Sun; Ⓢ Line 1 or 2 to City Hall, Exit 2) Most famous for its critically acclaimed musical *Miso,* this theatre company also produces a number of traditional nonverbal musicals.

★NATIONAL THEATER OF KOREA THEATRE

Map p216 (☎02-2280 4122; www.ntok.go.kr; 59 Jangchungdan-ro, Jung-gu; Ⓢ Line 3 to Dongguk University, Exit 6) The several venues here are home to the national drama, *changgeuk*

SEOUL SHOWTIME

Recommended production shows include **Jump** (Map p216; ☎02-722 3995; www.hijump.co.kr; 22 Jeong-dong, Jung-gu; tickets from ₩40,000; ⏲4pm Mon, 4pm & 8pm Tue-Sat, 3pm & 6pm Sun; Ⓢ Line 5 to Gwanghwamun, Exit 6), featuring a wacky Korean family all crazy about martial arts, and Bibap (p68), a comedic *Iron Chef*–style contest.

Running for over 15 years, with no end in sight, **Nanta Theatre** (눈스퀘어; Map p216; ☎02-739 8288; www.nanta.co.kr; 3rd fl, Unesco Bldg, 26 Myeongdong-gil, Jung-gu; tickets ₩40,000-60,000; ⏲2pm, 5pm & 8pm; Ⓢ Line 4 to Myeongdong, Exit 6) is Korea's most successful nonverbal performance. Set in a kitchen, this high-octane, 90-minute show mixes magic tricks, *samulnori* folk music, drumming, kitchen utensils, comedy, dance, martial arts and audience participation. It's top-class entertainment that has been a hit wherever it plays. There's another venue in **Chungjeongo** (☎02-739 8288; www.nanta.co.kr; 476 Chungjeongno 3-ga, Seodaemungu; tickets ₩40,000-60,000; ⏲shows 5pm & 8pm; Ⓢ Line 5 to Chungjeongo, Exit 7).

(Korean opera), orchestra and dance companies. Free concerts and movies are put on in summer at the outdoor stage. Walk 10 minutes here or hop on bus 2 at the stop behind Exit 6 of the subway.

MYEONGDONG THEATER — THEATRE

Map p216 (☎02-727 0951; www.mdtheater.or.kr; 35 Myeongdong-gil, Jung-gu; ⏲7.30pm; Ⓢ Line 2 to Euljiro 1-ga, Exit 6) Dating back to the 1930s, this attractive downtown theatre was resurrected in 2011 and hosts quality productions from modern Korean classics to Shakespeare, all with English subtitles.

SHOPPING

The largest market in Korea is Myeongdong's Namdaemun Market (p74).

★SHINSEGAE — DEPARTMENT STORE

Map p216 (신세계백화점; ☎02-2026 9000; www.shinsegae.com; 63 Sogong-ro, Jung-gu; ⏲10.30am-8pm; Ⓢ Line 4 to Hoehyeon, Exit 7) Wrap yourself in luxury inside the Seoul equivalent of Harrods. It's split over two buildings, the older part based in a gorgeous 1930 colonial building that was Seoul's first department store, Mitsukoshi. Check out local designer fashion labels and the opulent supermarket in the basement with a food court; another food court is up on the 11th floor of the building with an attached roof garden to relax in.

LOTTE DEPARTMENT STORE — DEPARTMENT STORE

Map p216 (롯데백화점; ☎02-771 2500; http://store.lotteshopping.com; 81 Namdaemun-ro, Jung-gu; ⏲10.30am-8pm; Ⓢ Line 2 to Euljiro 1-ga, Exit 8) Retail behemoth Lotte spreads its tentacles across four buildings: the main department store, Lotte Young Plaza, Lotte Avenuel and a duty-free shop. Also here is a multiplex cinema, restaurants and hotel.

LAB 5 — FASHION

Map p216 (Level 5, Noon Sq, Myeongdong 2-ga, Jung-gu; Ⓢ Line 2 to Euljiro 1-ga, Exit 6) No need to root around Dongdaemun Market for the latest hot K-designers, with this store showcasing the designs of 100 rising stars including participants of *Project Runway Korea*.

PRIMERA — ACCESSORIES

Map p216 (www.primera.co.kr; 22 Myeongdong 4-gil, Jung-gu; ⏲10am-10pm; Ⓢ Line 4 to Myeongdong, Exit 5) The flagship store of this Korean cosmetics store specialises in organic skin products and essential oils using germinated sprouts.

ÅLAND — FASHION

Map p216 (www.a-land.co.kr; 30 Myeongdong 6-gil, Jung-gu; ⏲10.30am-10.30pm; Ⓢ Line 4 to Myeongdong, Exit 6) Spread over three levels, this multilabel boutique mixes up vintage and garage-sale items with new designer pieces to wear and decorate your home with. For menswear head to the building across the street.

MIGLIORE MALL — FASHION

Map p216 (밀리오레 명동점; ☎02-2124 0005; www.migliore.co.kr; 115 Toegye-ro, Jung-gu; ⏲11am-11.30pm Tue-Sun; Ⓢ Line 4 to Myeongdong, Exit 6) Always teeming with young trendsetters, this high-rise mall is packed with small fashion shops.

SPORTS & ACTIVITIES

★SEOUL GLOBAL CULTURAL CENTER CULTURAL TOUR

Map p216 (☎02-3789 7961; www.seoulcultural center.com; 5th fl, M-Plaza Bldg, 27 Myeongdong 8-gil, Jung-gu; ⊙10.30am-7.30pm; Ⓢ Line 4 to Myeongdong, Exit 6) Set up to promote Korean culture to foreigners, this centre offers classes in anything from *hanji* craft, painting and calligraphy to Korean film screenings, photo ops wearing traditional clothing or K-Pop dance lessons (₩5000, 1½ hours). Most activities are free; visit the website for schedules and events.

KIMCHI ACADEMY HOUSE COOKING COURSE

Map p216 (☎02-318 7051; kimchischool@naver.com; 4th fl Gyeongdo Bldg, 19 Myeongdong 8-gil, Jung-gu; 1hr class ₩30,000; Ⓢ Line 4 to Myeongdong, Exit 6) Learn how to make *kimchi* while wearing *hanbok*.

SILLOAM SAUNA JJIMJIL-BANG

Map p216 (실로암사우나찜질방; ☎02-364 3944; www.silloamsauna.com; 128-104 Jungnim-dong, Jung-gu; sauna adult/child before 8pm ₩8000/6000; sauna & jjimjil-bang ₩10,000/7000; ⊙24hr; Ⓢ Line 1 or 4 to Seoul station, Exit 1) Across the street from Seoul station, this spick-and-span foreigner-friendly *jjimjil-bang* (Korean spa) has a wide range of baths and sauna rooms. It's also a shoestringer sleeping option if you need a place to stay for a night.

CHUNJIYUN SPA SPA

Map p216 (☎02-318 8011; http://seoulesthe.com; Myeong-dong; admission ₩20,000; ⊙9am-midnight; Ⓢ Line 4 to Myeongdong, Exit 8) This spa offers a good choice for women such as a pinewood, jade and clay sauna as well as green tea, ginseng and mugwort hot baths. Men on the other hand only get to use the stock-standard spas. It's in the basement a few doors up from Gogung restaurant.

Western Seoul

HONGDAE & AROUND | YEOUIDO & AROUND

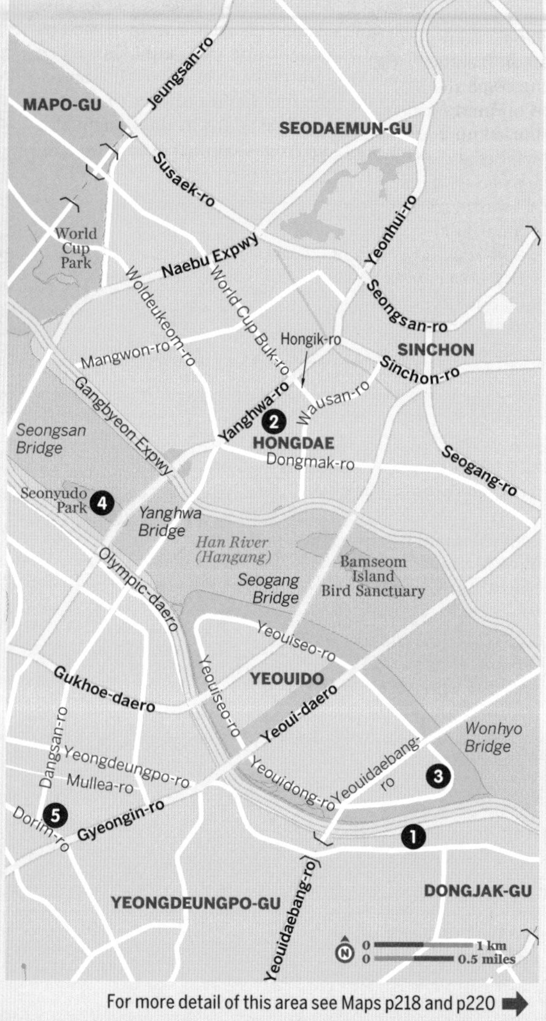

For more detail of this area see Maps p218 and p220

Neighbourhood Top Five

❶ Shop at **Noryangjin Fish Market** (p90), Korea's largest seafood market, where you can buy everything from king crabs to sea cucumbers, and have it cooked up on the spot.

❷ Hit **Hongdae** (p91) for its buzzing nightlife where you can dance the night away or groove to the latest K-Indie band.

❸ Enjoy the view and surrounding art at the top of **63 Square** (p88).

❹ Hire a bike on Yeouido and cycle along the Han River to **Seonyudo Park** (p89).

❺ Explore **Mullae Arts Village** (p88), where artists rub shoulders with metalworking factories.

Explore Western Seoul

The areas of Hongdae (around Hongik University), Edae (around Ewha Womans University) and Sinchon (between Yonsei and Sogang Universities) are all packed with places for students to be diverted from their studies. Hongik is Korea's leading art and design institution, so this is a particularly fertile patch for chaotic creativity and unbridled hedonism; it's also the epicentre for the K-Indie scene, with scores of live-music clubs and dance spots. Up the road, French architect Dominique Perrault's stunning redesign of the Ewha campus centre has put that area on the archi-tour map.

Major retailers have moved into Hongdae, pushing up rents and pushing out smaller, independent boutiques, cafes and bars to nearby areas such as Sangsu-dong and Yeonnam-dong. The latter is Seoul's latest hip 'hood, benefiting from a new park on its southern flank, a section of what will eventually become the 6.3km-long Gyeongui Line Forest Trail built on land formerly used for a railway line that has been buried underground.

Yeouido, a 3km-long and 2km-wide island on the southern side of the Han River, is home to skyscrapers housing media, finance and insurance companies, as well as the National Assembly and stock-exchange buildings. Attractions here include Yeouido Park and Yeouido Hangang Riverside Park, both lovely places to relax or go for a bike ride, and the observation deck of 63 Square, providing a bird's-eye view of the city. Nearby is the brand-new complex of Noryangjin, Seoul's premier fish market.

Local Life

- **Worship** Join in the singing with a 15,000-plus congregation at Sunday services at Yeouido Full Gospel Church (p88).
- **Markets** Shop for handmade souvenirs and listen to local musicians at Hongdae's Free Market (p94), in the park opposite Hongik University, or Yeonnam-dong's Dongjin Market (p94).
- **Blossoms** Yeouido is gorgeous in mid-April when the island's many cherry trees blossom; at its peak they're lit up at night and seemingly the whole of Seoul decamps here.

Getting There & Away

- **Subway** The best way to get to all these areas; Hongik University also has a stop on the A'REX Line from Incheon International Airport.
- **Bicycle** Hire them on Yeouido; they are the best way to get around the island and across the north side of the Han River where there are also cycle lanes.

Lonely Planet's Top Tip

For details on the latest gigs in Hongdae (and elsewhere) check out **Do Indie** (www.doindie.co.kr/en), then book tickets at **XIndie Ticket Lounge** (Map p218; ☎02-322 2218; www.ticketlounge.co.kr; Eoulmadang-ro, Mapo-gu; ⏰1-9pm Tue-Sun; Ⓢ Line 6 to Sangsu, Exit 1).

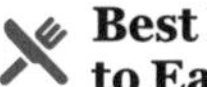

Best Places to Eat

- Noryangjin Fish Market (p90)
- Menya Sandaime (p89)
- Tuk Tuk Noodle Thai (p90)

For reviews, see p89 ➡

Best Places to Drink

- Anthracite (p91)
- Café Sukkara (p91)
- Wolhyang (p91)

For reviews, see p91 ➡

Best Places for Live Music

- Mudaeruk (p93)
- Club Evans (p93)
- FF (p93)

For reviews, see p93 ➡

SIGHTS

Hongdae & Around

JEOLDUSAN MARTYRS' SHRINE MUSEUM

(절두산 순교성지; ☎02-3142 4434; www.jeoldusan.or.kr; 6 Tojeong-ro, Mapo-gu; museum by donation; ⊙shrine 24hr, museum 9.30am-5pm Tue-Sun; Ⓢ Line 2 or 6 to Hapjeong, Exit 7) Jeoldusan means 'Beheading Hill' – this is where up to 2000 Korean Catholics were executed in 1866 following a royal decree, most thrown off the high cliff here into the Han River. Next to the chapel (where Mass is held daily at 10am and 3pm), the museum includes some of the grizzly wooden torture equipment used on the Catholic martyrs, 27 of whom have been made saints. There are also books, diaries and relics of the Catholic converts.

Various statues and monuments are dotted around the peaceful gardens that envelop the chapel and museum. To reach here from the subway exit, take the second turn left and follow the covered railway line for 700m; it's less than a 10-minute walk.

KT&G SANGSANGMADANG ARCHITECTURE

Map p218 (KT&G 상상마당; ☎02-330 6200; www.sangsangmadang.com; 65 Eoulmadang-ro, Mapo-gu; ⊙shop noon-11pm, gallery 1-10pm; Ⓢ Line 2 to Hongik University, Exit 5) Funded by Korea's top tobacco company, this visually striking building is home to an art-house cinema, a concert space (hosting top indie bands) and galleries that focus on experimental, fringe exhibitions. There's also a great design shop for gifts on the ground floor. The architect Bae Dae-yong called his design the 'Why Butter Building' as the pattern of concrete across its glazed facade is said to resemble both butterfly wings and butter spread on toast.

MODERN DESIGN MUSEUM MUSEUM

Map p218 (근현대디자인박물관; www.designmuseum.or.kr; 36 Wausan-ro 30-gil, Mapo-gu; adult/child ₩5000/4000; ⊙10am-6pm Tue-Sun; Ⓢ Line 2 to Hongik University, Exit 9) The items displayed on the two floors of this small museum trace the history of modern design in Korea from the 1880s to contemporary times. Not much is labelled in English but it's still a fascinating collection that spans a wide range of products, from 19th-century books and newspapers to 1960s toys and electronics and posters for the 1988 Olympics.

EWHA WOMANS UNIVERSITY ARCHITECTURE, MUSEUM

(www.ewha.ac.kr; Ewhayeodae-gil, Seoudaemun-gu; Ⓢ Line 2 to Ewha Womans University, Exit 2) Come to this venerable university, founded in 1886 by American Methodist missionary Mary Scranton, to view Dominque Perrault's stunning main entrance, a building that dives six storeys underground and is split by a broad cascade of steps leading up to the Gothic-style 1935 Pfeiffer Hall. Walking through here feels like going through the parting of the Red Sea.

Inside, on the ground floor, you'll find cafes, shops and the **Arthouse Momo** (www.cineart.co.kr; Ewha Womans University main entrance bldg; tickets ₩9000) cinema.

EWHA WOMANS UNIVERSITY MUSEUM MUSEUM

(이화여자대학교박물관; ☎02-3277 3151; http://museum.ewha.ac.kr; 51 Ewhayeodae-gil, Seodaemun-gu; ⊙9.30am-5pm Mon-Sat; Ⓢ Line 2 to Ewha Womans University, Exit 2) FREE To the left of the university entrance, the exhibits spread over three floors here conjure up the extinct world of the *yangban* (aristocratic) elite with wonderful examples of their refined taste in ceramics, art, furniture and clothing.

WAR & WOMEN'S HUMAN RIGHTS MUSEUM MUSEUM

Map p218 (전쟁과여성인권박물관; ☎02-365 4016; www.womenandwar.net; 20 World Cup Buk-ro 11-gil, Mapo-gu; adult/child under 14yr/youth 14-19yr ₩3000/1000/2000; ⊙1-6pm Tue, Thu-Sat, 3-6pm Wed; Ⓢ Line 2 to Hongik University, Exit 1, then 🚌6, 15, 7711, 7011, 7016 or 7737) In Korea the survivors of sexual slavery by the Japanese military during WWII (known euphemistically as 'comfort women') are respectfully called *halmoni* (grandmother). When you enter this well-designed and powerfully moving museum you'll be given a card printed with the story of a *halmoni*, helping you to connect with the tragic history of these women.

The end of the exhibition brings the story up to date with images of the protests that occur every Wednesday at noon outside the Japanese embassy in Seoul, and broadens out the focus to the plight of women in wars and conflicts around the world.

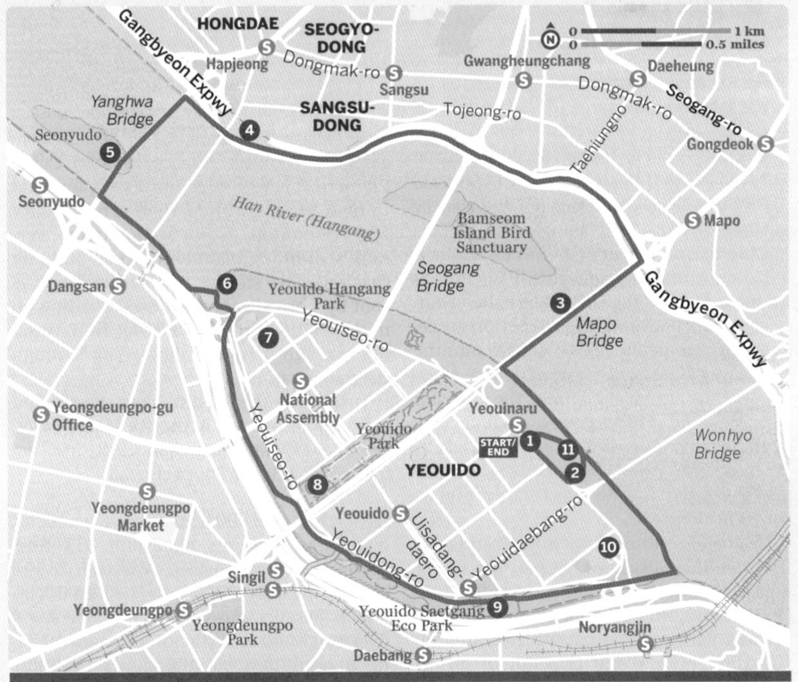

Neighbourhood Walk
Han River & Yeouido

START YEOUINARU STATION, EXIT 3
END YEOUIDO PARK
LENGTH 15KM; THREE HOURS

It's possible to walk this 15km route around Yeouido and across the river via the island park of Seonyudo, but it's quicker and more fun to use a bicycle, which you can rent at several outlets in Yeouido Hangang Park, near the starting point for the ride. Walk east from the 1 **subway exit** towards the Hangang Cruise Terminal in Yeouido Hangang Park, where you'll find a 2 **bicycle rental stall** (first hour ₩3000, every extra 15 minutes ₩500; ⏲9am to 5pm); bring some form of photo ID for staff to keep as a deposit.

Cycle west and out of the park across the 3 **Mapo Bridge**, taking the blue ramp down to the north bank of the river. Head west for about 4km until you reach a steep cliff, at the top of which is 4 **Jeoldusan Martyrs' Shrine**. Continue west to the Yanghwa bridge and carry your bike up the stairs to the pathway on the west side. On an island about halfway along the bridge is the beautifully landscaped 5 **Seonyudo Park** (p89). There are wonderful river views from the park (which used to be a water-filtration plant) as well as a cafe at which you can take a break.

Continue from the park back to the south bank of the Han River and pedal back towards Yeouido. At the western tip of the island you can pause to view the ritzy 6 **Seoul Marina** and the 7 **National Assembly** (p89). Also have a look around central 8 **Yeouido Park**, which includes a traditional Korean garden.

Continue along the bike paths on the southern side of the island; 9 **Yeouido Saetgang Eco Park** here is wilder and more natural. As you round the eastern tip of Yeouido look up to see clouds reflected in the gold-tinted glass of the skyscraper 10 **63 City** (p88). After returning your bike to the rental stall, look out for the quirky 11 **monster sculpture** based on the hit horror movie *The Host*.

WORTH A DETOUR

MULLAE ARTS VILLAGE

Artists and designers have started to move in beside the steel workers and welders in the light-industrial area of Mullae-dong, bringing to the area street art, small restaurants, cafes and a handful of quirky shops. Rebranded as **Mullae Arts Village** (문래예술촌; Mullae-dong, Yoengdeungpo-gu; S Line 2 to Mullae, Exit 7), it's a photogenic area with a backpackers hostel, **Urban Art Guest House** (p151), should you wish to stay. From the subway exit head straight and you'll soon hit the warren of factories and artist studios.

Chichipopo Library (☎02-2068 1667; www.facebook.com/chichipopolibrary; 428-1 Dorim-ro, Yeongdeungpo-gu; ⏰10am-11.30pm Mon-Fri, 11am-11pm Sat & Sun; 📶; S Line 2 to Mullae, Exit 7) A relaxing place to hang out, with mismatched furniture, cheap Western-style eats and drinks and a rooftop garden, this self-serve cafe, library and gallery space is something of a creative hub for Mullae.

Seoul Arts Space – Mullae (☎02-2676 4300; http://english.sfac.or.kr; 5-4 Gyeongin-ro 88-gil, Yeongdeungpo-gu; S Line 2 to Mullae, Exit 7) It's worth finding out what's happening at this arts and performance space which includes a studio theatre and gallery. Events that are part of the springtime Festival Bom (p20) are staged here.

WORLD CUP PARK PARK

(월드컵공원; http://worldcuppark.seoul.go.kr; 251 World Cup-ro, Mapo-gu; S Line 6 to World Cup Stadium, Exit 1) These five connected parks (Pyeonghwa, Nanjicheon, Nanji Hangang, Haneul Park and Noeul) were created for the 2002 FIFA World Cup out of former landfill and waste ground. Today it's one of Seoul's largest green spaces, threaded through with cycling and walking paths, sporting facilities and leafy relaxation spots. Climb hilly Haneul Park for great views across the area.

⊙ Yeouido & Around

63 SQUARE VIEWPOINT

Map p220 (☎02-789 5663; www.63.co.kr; 50 63-ro, Yeongdeungpo-gu; S Line 5 to Yeouinaru, Exit 4) From the basement of the gold-tinted glass skyscraper **63 City**, one of Seoul's tallest buildings, you can access five different attractions, the pick of which is **63 Sky Art Gallery** (adult/child under 14yr/youth 14-19yr ₩13,000/11,000/12,000; ⏰10am-10pm). This combines a 60th-floor observation deck, offering panoramic views, with top-class, regularly changing art exhibitions.

If you have more time to kill, there's also **63 Art Hall** (adult/child ₩12,000/11,000; ⏰10am-5.30pm), an IMAX theatre showing hourly movies with an English-language commentary; the lame mini Madame Tussaud's–like **63 Wax Museum** (adult/child ₩15,000/13,000; ⏰10am-10pm); a theatre; and an aquarium, **63 Seaworld** (adult/child under 14yr/youth 14-19yr ₩19,000/16,000/17,000; ⏰10am-10pm), which has penguins, seals and sea lions. This might do as a way of distracting kids on a rainy day, but the shows involving marine life have also received criticism by animal-welfare groups who claim such shows are debilitating and stressful for the animals, and that this is exacerbated by human interaction.

There are discount packages for three or more attractions, plus a further small foreigner discount (if you ask).

YEOUIDO FULL GOSPEL CHURCH CHURCH

Map p220 (☎02-783 4135; http://yfgc.fgtv.com; 15 Gukhoe-daero 76-gil, Yeongdeungpo-gu; ⏰services 7am-7pm Sun, 5am, 6am & 7am Mon-Sat, 10.30am Wed, 9pm Fri, 10.30am Sat; S Line 9 to National Assembly, Exit 1) FREE Founded in 1958, this giant Pentecostal church, with some 830,000 members, has been based on Yeouido since 1973. A visit during the Sunday services, when tens of thousands pack the circular, cathedral-sized building, is highly recommended. Huge TV screens flank the altar and there's a 150-member choir and orchestra. The foreigners' sections, where headphones provide a translation of the service, are on the 3rd and 4th floor in the balcony.

NATIONAL ASSEMBLY BUILDING

Map p220 (☎02-788 3656; www.assembly.go.kr; 1 Uisadang-daero Yeongdeungpo-gu; ⏰9am-5pm Mon-Fri, to 4pm Sat & 1st Sun of month; Ⓢ Line 9 to National Assembly, Exit 1) FREE Home to South Korea's parliament since 1975, the pleasant grounds here with a fountain and an elaborate **hanok** (traditional wooden house; used for official functions) are worth a wander. The interior of the green domed building can be viewed only as part of a tour; apply three days in advance via the website.

The central **Rotunda Hall** is impressive, as is the **Plenary Chamber** where the MPs sit, but on weekends, only the separate **Memorial Hall** section of the complex is open.

SEONYUDO PARK PARK

(http://hangang.seoul.go.kr; ⏰6am-midnight; Ⓢ Line 9 to Seonyudo, Exit 2) FREE A former water-filtration plant on an island in the Han River has been transformed into this award-winning park. The old industrial buildings have been cleverly adapted as part of the new landscaping and gardens which include lily-covered ponds, plant nurseries and exhibitions halls. Either walk here from the subway station or cycle from Yeouido (p87).

EATING

Hongdae & Around

★**MENYA SANDAIME** JAPANESE $

Map p218 (☎02-332 4129; www.menyasandaime.com; 24 Hongik-ro 3-gil, Mapo-gu; mains ₩7000-9000; ⏰noon-10pm; 📖; Ⓢ Line 2 to Hongik University, Exit 9) On a street with several other Japanese restaurants, this atmospheric ramen shop is the real deal and proof that being part of a chain need not compromise food quality. It's a great place for single diners who can sit at the counter by the open kitchen watching the hip, tattooed chefs carefully craft bowls of delicious noodles.

LOCAL KNOWLEDGE

SEOUL OFF THE BEATEN TRACK

Seoul-based teacher and writer Charles Usher began his blog **Seoul Sub→urban** (http://seoulsuburban.com) in 2009 with an ambitious target: to document in words and photos the areas around each of the city's 500-odd subway stops. As of April 2015 he'd got 154 covered, with the *Guardian* newspaper in the UK tipping him as their blogger of choice for Seoul. We asked him to nominate his favourite Seoul neighbourhoods that are off the tourism radar.

Mullae-dong

Seoulites tend to look down on the industrial Yeongdeungpo district a bit. Many factories are still around and you can come across grids of streets with all manner of manufacturing shops producing everything from small machine parts to surprisingly large-scale equipment. However, in recent years, the area's low rents have attracted many artists and the area is now home to the Mullae Arts Village (p88).

Yeonnam-dong

As Hongdae has become more corporate and expensive, some of the smaller indie businesses are moving to this neighbourhood to the north. Many Chinese live here, and it's long been known for its Chinese restaurants, but now you can find other cuisines, as well as many coffee shops and craft beer bars around the Dongjin Market (p94). My favourite Thai restaurant in Seoul, Tuk Tuk Noodle Thai (p90), is here.

Sindang

Southeast of Dongdaemun, this is a really old-school neighbourhood. Poke around and you'll find tons of furniture stores, a huge flea market and a kitchen-supply street selling everything from pots and pans to industrial-sized ovens and mixers. Best of all is Jungang Market (p122), Seoul's third biggest but completely untouristy – nobody goes here except old Koreans, although there is an interesting contemporary arts space (p121) beneath it.

★**TUK TUK NOODLE THAI** THAI $
(☎070-4407 5130; http://blog.naver.com/tuktuknoodle; 37 Yeonhui-ro, Mapo-gu; mains ₩7500-12,000; ⊙noon-3pm & 5-10.30pm; 📋; Ⓢ Line 2 to Hongik University, Exit 3) Credited with kicking off a trend for more authentic Thai restaurants in Seoul, Tuk Tuk is a jauntily decorated basement space close by Dongjin Market. Thai chefs whack out a broad menu of spicy dishes that don't compromise on flavour.

Their success has led them to opening **Soi Yeonnam** (☎02-323 5130; 267 Donggyo-ro, Mapo-gu; mains ₩7,500-12,000; ⊙noon-3pm & 5-9.30pm; 📋; Ⓢ Line 2 to Hongik University, Exit 3), also in Yeonnam-dong and serving Thai street food.

LOVING HUT VEGAN $
Map p218 (www.lovinghut.com; 35 Yonsei-ro, Seodaemun-gu; mains ₩5000-6000; ⊙11.30am-3.30pm & 4.30-9pm Mon-Fri, 11.30am-9pm Sat & Sun; 📶✏📋; Ⓢ Line 2 to Sinchon, Exit 2) A variety of slogans in English urge diners on to a more compassionate, meat-free life at this pastel-shaded, pleasantly modern cafe. It serves very tasty and good-value Korean meals with rice, noodles, vegies – and no animal products.

FELL & COLE ICE CREAM $
Map p218 (www.fellncole.com; 39-21 Wausan-ro, Mapo-gu; 1 scoop ₩4200; ⊙noon-10pm; 📋; Ⓢ Line 6 to Sangsu, Exit 1) A sweet diversion in Hongdae, Fell & Cole's fabulous flavours of ice cream and sorbet are changing all the time but might include perilla leaf, parsley lemonade, burnt banana and *kalimotxo* (aka Jesus Juice).

★**SLOBBIE** KOREAN $$
Map p218 (☎02-3143 5525; www.facebook.com/slobbie8; 5th fl, 10 Hongik-ro 6-gil, Mapo-gu; meals ₩8000; ⊙11.30am-11.30pm Mon-Sat; 📶📋; Ⓢ Line 2 to Hongik University, Exit 9) 🍃 Simple, tasty dishes such as bibimbap and *jjigae* (stews) are served in pleasant, modern surroundings at this admirable social enterprise training young chefs from challenged backgrounds and providing jobs for single mothers. The restaurant name is pronounced 'Slow-bee', indicating its aim to promote a slower, healthier and more organic lifestyle for Seoulites.

CIURI CIURI ITALIAN $$
Map p218 (☎02-749 9996; www.ciuriciuri.co.kr; 2nd fl, 314-3 Sangsu-dong, Mapo-gu; mains ₩7000-18,000; ⊙noon-3pm & 6-11pm Mon-Fri, noon-11pm Sat & Sun; Ⓢ Line 6 to Sangsu, Exit 1) Run by Italian couple Enrico and Fiore, the tasty and unusual – for Seoul – specialities here hail from Sicily, such as *arancine* (saffron-flavoured risotto balls), *anelletti* (small ring pasta) and a special type of sausage. The place is decorated as if you're on holiday in Sicily itself, with staw-hat lampshades and colourfully painted tiled tables and water bottles.

TAVERNA DE PORTUGAL PORTUGUESE $$
Map p218 (☎02-3144 4189; 9 Wausan-ro 13-gil Mapo-gu; mains from ₩14,000; ⊙noon-3.30pm & 5-10pm Wed & Thu, noon-10pm Fri-Sun; Ⓢ Line

NORYANGJIN FISH MARKET

Noryangjin Fish Market (노량진수산시장; Map p220; www.susansijang.co.kr; 688 Nodeul-ro, Dongjak-gu; ⊙24hr; Ⓢ Line 1 to Noryangjin, Exit 1) Providing terrific photo opportunities, Korea's largest fish market supplies every kind of aquatic life form to restaurants, fish shops and the general public. At the time of writing, a multistorey, state-of-the-art complex was nearing completion and should by now be housing the 700 stalls and numerous restaurants that make up the market.

If you want to view the market at its liveliest, get here for the auctions, which kick off around 1am. Otherwise, the best time to come is around mealtimes, when the apron-clad vendors will happily sell you produce directly – be it still-live crabs, prawns, the dark-orange-and-red *meongge* (Korean sea squirt, very much an acquired taste) or prepared platters of *hoe* (raw fish slices). You can then take your seafood to several restaurants within the market who will either serve it up to you with a variety of side dishes (usually around ₩3000 person), or prepare and cook it (starting from an extra ₩5000 depending on what you have). A good one is **Busan Ilbeonji** (부산일번지; ☎02-813 7799; 2nd fl; mains ₩15,000-30,000; ⊙10.30am-10.30pm).

6 to Sangsu, Exit 1) Porto-native Augusto and his Korean wife Heera have made their mark in Hongdae serving up authentically spicy and very moreish piri-piri grilled whole chicken or the Fracesinha, a chunky sandwich of pork and sausage smothered in melted cheese and dowsed with a tomato-and-beer sauce. Their set menus (₩26,000) are big enough for two to share.

SHIM'S TAPAS SPANISH $$

Map p218 (☎02-3141 2386; 48-14 Wausan-ro 29-gil Mapo-gu; tapas ₩5000-15,000; ⏰noon-midnight; 📶🍴; Ⓢ Line 2 to Hongik University, Exit 8) This adorable tapas bar whips up authentic and creative Spanish-style nibbles, including light-as-a-feather tortilla and homemade anchovies. Wash it all down with a sangria, glass of cava or one of the fine dry martinis.

Yeouido & Around

63 BUFFET PAVILION BUFFET $$$

Map p220 (☎02-789 5731; www.63buffet.co.kr; 63 City, 50 63-ro, Yeongdeungpo-gu; lunch Mon-Fri ₩65,000, dinner ₩78,000; ⏰noon-3pm & 6-10pm Mon-Fri, 11am-3.30pm & 5-10pm Sat & Sun; Ⓢ Line 5 to Yeouinaru, Exit 4) With too many temptations to count, this gourmet buffet is a good way to sample a range of Asian and other cuisines. Children up to 18 eat for about half-price.

DRINKING & NIGHTLIFE

Hongdae & Around

★ANTHRACITE CAFE

Map p218 (www.anthracitecoffee.com; 10 Tojeong-ro 5-gil; ⏰11am-midnight; 📶; Ⓢ Line 6 to Sangsu, Exit 4) An old shoe factory is the location for one of Seoul's top independent coffee-roaster and cafe operations. Drinks are made using the hand-drip method at a counter made out of an old conveyor belt. Upstairs is a spacious lounge and there's outdoor seating on the roof.

★WOLHYANG BAR

Map p218 (☎02-332 9202; www.tasteofthemoon.com; 27 Wausan-ro 29-gil, Mapo-gu; ⏰11.30pm-2am Mon-Sat, to 1am Sun; 📶; Ⓢ Line 2 to Hongik University, Exit 8) Specialising in *makgeolli* (milky rice wine) from around Korea and other local liquors, this brightly decorated, spacious 2nd-floor bar is a great place to sample traditional alcoholic drinks. It also has various fruity and nutty flavours of *makgeolli* as well as decent food such as savoury pancakes.

★CAFÉ SUKKARA CAFE, BAR

Map p218 (☎02-334 5919; www.sukkara.co.kr; Sanullim Bldg, 327-9 Seogyo-dong, Mapo-gu; ⏰11am-midnight Tue-Sun; 📶; Ⓢ Line 2 to Hongik University, Exit 9) You'll find a fantastic range of drinks and some very tasty things to eat (try the butter-chicken curry) at this shabby-chic, farmhouse-style cafe that has a contemporary Japanese flair. Juices and liquors are made in-house – be sure to try the black shandy gaff, which is a mix of homemade ginger ale and Magpie Brewery dark beer.

MAGPIE BREWING CO. PUB

Map p218 (www.magpiebrewing.com; 6-15 Wausan-ro 19-gil, Mapo-gu; ⏰5pm-2am Tue-Thu, 5pm-3am Fri, 2pm-3am Sat, 2pm-2am Sun; Ⓢ Line 2 to Hongik University, Exit 9) You don't need to be in Itaewon to sample local microbrewery Magpie's refreshing range of ales. This outlet close by Hongdae's playground keeps it low key with a just the company's cute birdy logo on the building facade.

KEG B PUB

Map p218 (☎02-334 1979; 19 Wausan-ro 13-gil, Mapo-gu; ⏰5pm-midnight; Ⓢ Line 6 to Sangsu, Exit 1) This cosy craft beer pub on the top floor of a small backstreet block is a good place to savour a pint or two. Choose between four local beers on tap and scores of bottled ales from around the world, served alongside snacks such as pizza, fried chicken and nachos.

AA CAFÉ CAFE, BAR

Map p218 (www.aadesignmuseum.com; 19-18 Wausan-ro 17-gil, Mapo-gu; ⏰cafe noon-midnight, shop to 8pm; 📶; Ⓢ Line 6 to Sangsu, Exit 1) Soaring ceilings and space, filled with designer and retro furniture, set apart this cafe. It's a pleasure to hang out here, while in the basement you can browse classic furniture pieces in the shop-museum.

HONGDAE'S ANIMAL CAFES

For the price of a drink, you can have quality time with a variety of cuddlesome creatures at theme cafes around Hongdae.

Thanks Nature Cafe (Map p218; ☎02-335 7470; www.facebook.com/TNcafe; 121 Prugio Bldg, 10 Hongik-ro, Mapo-gu; ⊙11am-10pm; **S** Line 2 to Hongik University, Exit 9) Every six months a different couple of cute sheep come to live in the enclosure outside this cafe which otherwise specialises in waffles and high-quality coffee. The interior has a sheep theme going on, too.

Bau House (☎070-7550 5153; www.baumall.co.kr; 64 Yanghwa-ro, Mapo-gu; ⊙1.30-11pm Mon-Sat, 12.30-11pm Sun; **S** Line 2 or 6 to Hapjeong, Exit 3) Korea may be known as a place where people eat dog meat, but at Bau House patrons are only interested in playing with the 30-odd pedigree pooches, whose names, breeds and ages you can learn from an English menu.

TableA (Map p218; www.table-a.co.kr; 146 Wausan-ro, Mapo-gu; ⊙8am-1am; **S** Line 2 to Hongik University, Exit 7) There are 11 cats and several kittens at this appealing cafe, one of several, in a chain around Hongdae. This one is peppered with great doodles and illustrations by art students from the nearby colleges.

YRI CAFE
CAFE

Map p218 (http://cafe.naver.com/yricafe; 27 Wausan-ro 3-gil, Mapo-gu; ⊙11am-1am Mon-Fri, to 2am Sat & Sun; **S** Line 6 to Sangsu, Exit 4) Browse local and imported books and magazines on art and design at this convivial boho hang-out that works just as well as a daytime cafe as it does a night-time drinks venue.

FOX WINE BISTRO
WINE BAR

Map p218 (포도먹는 여우; ☎02-3143 7191; www.foxwinebistro.com; 14 Dongmak-ro 9-gil, Mapo-gu; ⊙6pm-2am Mon-Sat; **S** Line 6 to Sangsu, Exit 1) A sign of Hongdae's growing sophistication as a nightlife destination is this classy wine bar on the building's 2nd floor. There are over 400 different bottles on the menu; unfortunately little is sold by the glass. The pasta and salads are also highly rated.

LABRIS
LESBIAN

Map p218 (라브리스; ☎02-333 5276; 81-Wausan-ro, Map-gu; ⊙7pm-2am Mon-Thu, to 5am Fri-Sun; **S** Line 6 to Sangsu, Exit 1) This is a comfortable women-only space that's lesbian-oriented but not exclusively so. DJ nights are Friday to Sunday, when the minimum charge for a drink and compulsory *anju* (bar snacks) is ₩15,000. You'll find it on the 8th floor of the same building as On the Spot boutique.

M2
CLUB

Map p218 (☎02-3143 7573; www.ohoo.net/m2; 20-5 Jandari-ro, Mapo-gu; Sun-Thu ₩10,000, Fri & Sat ₩20,000; ⊙9.30pm-4.30am Sun-Thu, 8.30pm-6.30am Fri & Sat; **S** Line 6 to Sangsu, Exit 1) Deep underground is M2, one of the largest and best Hongdae clubs. It has a high ceiling and plenty of lights and visuals. Top local and international DJs spin mainly progressive house music.

CLUB MWG
CLUB

Map p218 (www.facebook.com/clubmwg1; 6-5 Wausan-ro 19-gil, Mapo-gu; ⊙10pm-5am Fri & Sat; **S** Line 2 to Hongik University, Exit 2) Myoung Wol Gwan (MWG) translates as 'bright moon house' but lunar sightings are not on the agenda from this dark, basement venue, one of Hongdae's longest-running venues. Come here for the LGBT-friendly **Meet Market** (www.facebook.com/meetmarketseoul) queer party events as well as indie bands and DJ nights.

CHLORIS TEA GARDEN
TEAHOUSE

Map p218 (www.cafechloris.co.kr; 52 Yonsei-ro 4-gil, Seodaemun-gu; ⊙10am-midnight; **S** Line 2 to Sinchon, Exit 3) Drunken revels may be in full flight around it, but gentility reigns at this tea shop offering an impressive range of black and flavoured brews, dainty cakes served on real china and comfy chairs for quiet enjoyment. It also runs the similar Café de Chloris on the same street.

ENTERTAINMENT

Hongdae & Around

★MUDAERUK LIVE MUSIC

Map p218 (무대륙; ☎02-332 8333; www.mudaeruk.com; 12 Tojeong-ro 5-gil, Mapo-gu; admission from ₩10,000; 📶; Ⓢ Line 6 to Sangsu, Exit 4) The 'Lost Continent of Mu' has been hiding out in Sangsu-dong all these years? Join in-the-know hipsters for shows by bands and DJs specialising in electronic music in the basement on weekends. Upstairs is a stylish cafe-bar with craft beer, sharing boards of food and great fish and chips.

★CLUB EVANS JAZZ

Map p218 (☎02-337 8361; www.clubevans.com; 63-Wausan-ro, Mapo-gu; admission ₩10,000; ⏰7.30pm-midnight Sun-Thu, to 2am Fri & Sat; Ⓢ Line 6 to Sangsu, Exit 1) Appealing across the generations, Evans offers top-grade jazz and a great atmosphere. Get here early if you want a seat or book ahead. It releases its own label CDs, too. Monday is jam night.

★FF LIVE MUSIC

Map p218 (☎011 9025 3407; www.facebook.com/pages/Club-FF/213154478733706; Hongdae; admission ₩10,000; ⏰7pm-6am; Ⓢ Line 6 to Sangsu, Exit 1) A top live venue with up to eight local indie bands playing at the weekend until midnight. Afterwards it becomes a dance club with DJs.

★SU NORAEBANG KARAOKE

Map p218 (수노래방; ☎02-322 3111; www.skysu.com; 67 Eoulmadang-ro, Mapo-gu; r per hour ₩2000-20,000; ⏰24hr; Ⓢ Line 6 to Sangsu, Exit 1) Karaoke your heart out and be noticed: some rooms have floor-to-ceiling windows fronting onto the street so you can show off your K-Pop moves. Rates rise from noon to 6am with the most expensive period from 8pm to the early hours.

CAFÉ BBANG LIVE MUSIC

Map p218 (카페 빵; http://cafe.daum.net/cafebbang; 12 Wausan-ro 29-gil, Mapo-gu; ⏰7pm-6am; Ⓢ Line 2 to Hongik University, Exit 8) You're sure to catch something interesting here: apart from gigs by indie artists and bands, it also hosts film screenings, art exhibitions and parties.

DGBD LIVE MUSIC

Map p218 (디지비디; ☎02-322 3792; http://cafe.daum.net/dgbd; 23 Jandari-ro, Mapo-gu; admission ₩10,000; ⏰8-11pm; Ⓢ Line 2 or 6 or Hapjeong, Exit 3) First generation K-Indie bands such as Crying Nut came into the spotlight at this legendary live-music venue. It's standing room only and there's a balcony.

CLUB TA LIVE MUSIC

Map p218 (☎02-6085 5150; www.facebook.com/theliveclubta; 10 Wausan-ro 17-gil, Mapo-gu; admission from ₩15,000; ⏰7pm-3am Tue-Thu, to 5am Fri-Sun; Ⓢ Line 6 to Sangsu, Exit 1) The hub of Hongdae's ska and ska-punk scene, sets at Ta usually run from around 9.30pm until midnight Friday to Sunday. It's bit more comfortable than your average Hongdae live-gig house.

INDIE ART-HALL GONG PERFORMING ARTS

(☎02-2632 8848; www.gongcraft.net; 30 Seonyuseo-ro 30-gil, Yeongdeungpo-gu; 📶; Ⓢ Line 5 to Yangpyeong, Exit 2) Marked by a huge brick chimney, this still-operating steel-product factory has a large space on its 2nd floor devoted to a wide range of arts. Expect everything from visual- and performance-art shows to live gigs by K-Indie rockers. There's a shop selling some art and a cafe too. It's a couple of subway stations or a short taxi hop from Mullae.

CINEMATEQUE KOFA CINEMA

(한국영상자료원; ☎02-3153 2001; www.koreafilm.org; 400 World Cup buk-ro, Mapo-gu; Ⓢ Line 6 to Susaek, Exit 2) FREE Free classic and contemporary Korean films are on the bill at one of the three cinemas in this home of the Korean Film Archive. See the website for directions from the subway exit.

SHOPPING

Hongdae & Around

★KEY ARTS, CRAFTS

Map p218 (www.welcomekey.net; 48-5 Wausan-ro 29-gil; ⏰noon-10pm Tue-Sun; Ⓢ Line 2 to Hongik University, Exit 8) Representing scores of artists and craftspeople, several of whom also sell their goods at the Free Market on Saturday, this small gallery and showroom offers affordable, exclusive items, from jewellery to pottery to fabric art and paintings.

★**FREE MARKET** SOUVENIRS

Map p218 (www.freemarket.or.kr; Hongik University Playground, 19-3 Wausan-ro 21-gil, Mapo-gu; ⏲1-6pm Sat Mar-Nov; S Line 2 to Hongik University, Exit 9) Going strong since 2002, this lively weekly market helps to propel talented young creatives on to big-time retail. It's a great opportunity to meet the crafters and buy a unique souvenir, be it a hand-painted baseball cap, a colourful piece of jewellery or a leather bag. A good line-up of singers and bands play all afternoon, too.

★**GENTLE MONSTER** ACCESSORIES

Map p218 (www.gentlemonster.com; 48 Dongmak-ro 7-gil, Mapo-gu; S Line 2 or 6 to Hapjeong, Exit 3) Sunglasses at night is *the* Hongdae look and this hip place is where to pick up the edgiest of shades and frames as worn by K-Popsters and TV stars. Imaginative and fun art installations change roughly every 25 days on the ground floor.

OBJECT RECYCLE ACCESSORIES

Map p218 (www.insideobject.com; 110 Wausan-ro, Mapo-gu; ⏲11am-10pm; S Line 2 to Hongik University, Exit 9) Although there's a bigger branch of Object in Hongdae, this one is notable for specialising in products that involve some element of re- or up-cycling, such as jeans and shirts made into bags, clocks from LP records and side tables from cardboard boxes.

LITTLE FARMERS ACCESSORIES

Map p218 (www.littlefarmers.co.kr; 112 Wausan-ro, Mapo-gu; ⏲11.30am-8.30pm; S Line 2 to Hongik University, Exit 8) Ecofriendly shoes, bags and other goods, some made from recycled products, are sold at this attractive basement store. Look for the wallets and bags made from recycled newspapers and magazines. You'll also find a few K-Indie CDs here and other colourful accessories.

ÅLAND AFTER ÅLAND FASHION

Map p218 (www.a-land.co.kr; 19-12 Wausan-ro 17-gil, Mapo-gu; ⏲noon-10pm; S Line 6 to Sangsu, Exit 1) Bag bargains at Åland's discount and end-of-lines outlet store – some clothing here by local as well as international designers goes for up to 90% off original prices.

DONGJIN MARKET MARKET

(www.facebook.com/makedongjin; 198 Seongmisan-ro, Mapo-gu; ⏲1-6pm Sat; S Line 2 to Hongik University, Exit 3) An old market arcade has become a Saturday hot spot for browers in hip Yeonnam-dong. Secondhand clothing, homemade jams and cookies and various crafts can be picked up here, among other things.

The rest of the week a few bars and cafes stay open in and around around the market, such as the Mexican joint B'Mucho, gourmet coffee roasters Cafe Libre and Vietnamese *bánh mì* stall Lie Lie Lie.

MECENATPOLIS MALL MALL

(www.mecenatpolismall.co.kr; 45 Yanghwa-ro, Mapo-gu; ⏲10am-10pm; S Line 2 or 6 to Hapjeong, Exits 9 or 10) Local and international brands, including Uniqlo and Muji, are arranged on several levels around open plazas at one of Seoul's newest and best-designed malls. Stars from K-Pop groups such as Big Bang live in the ritzy apartments that tower above the complex.

SPORTS & ACTIVITIES

WORLD CUP STADIUM STADIUM

(서울월드컵경기장; www.seoulworldcupst.or.kr; 240, World Cup-ro, Mapo-gu; museum adult/child ₩1000/500; ⏲museum 9am-5.30pm; S Line 6 to World Cup Stadium, Exit 1) Built for the 2002 Football World Cup, this 66,000-seat venue is still used as a sports and events stadium. Die-hard soccer fans may want to visit the small museum here that focuses on the World Cup event.

Also in the stadium is multiplex cinema, shopping store Homeplus, a gym, swimming pool and 24-hour sauna **World Cup Spaland** (www.sponspa.co.kr; admission ₩8000-9000; ⏲24hr).

ELAND CRUISES CRUISE

Map p220 (www.elandcruise.com; Han River Park, Yeouido; cruises from ₩12,000; ⏲11am-8.40pm; S Line 5 to Yeouinaru, Exit 3) A variety of day and night short sightseeing cruises depart from this Yeouido pier, one of three that the company's boats pause at along the Han River.

Itaewon & Around

Neighbourhood Top Five

❶ Survey centuries of Korean culture and art at the mammoth **National Museum of Korea** (p97) and take time to explore the attached gardens.

❷ Get inspired by the art and architecture of the **Leeum Samsung Museum of Art** (p99).

❸ Pay homage to those who gave their lives for the nation at the **War Memorial of Korea** (p98).

❹ Indulge in some of Seoul's most varied cuisine with an impressive array of world food, often with a Korean twist such as at **Vatos** (p99).

❺ Join the party and head out for a hedonistic night on a pub crawl, starting off with craft beer at **Craftworks Taphouse** (p102).

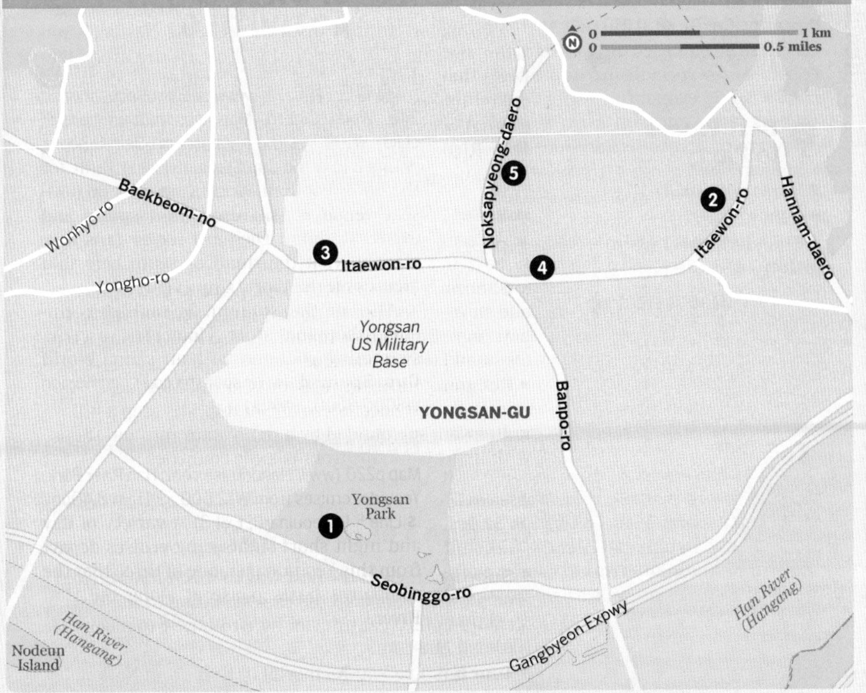

For more detail of this area see Maps p222 and p224

Lonely Planet's Top Tip

If a visit to the Korean War Museum is on your itinerary (which it should be), aim to visit at 2pm on a Friday from April to June and October to November for the entertaining military parade. It's an awesome display of precision and weapon twirling by the honour guards.

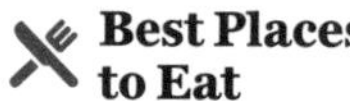

Best Places to Eat

- Linus' BBQ (p100)
- Vatos (p99)
- Atelier du Saint-Ex (p101)

For reviews, see p99 

Best Places to Drink

- Craft Beer Valley (p102)
- Damotori (p101)
- Southside Parlor (p101)

For reviews, see p101

Best Places to Party

- Cakeshop (p101)
- Venue/ (p101)
- Thunderhorse Tavern (p104)

For reviews, see p101

Explore Itaewon & Around

Immediately south of Namsan, Yongsan-gu has for many decades been defined by the presence of the US army base on a massive tract of land. Next door is Itaewon, a centre for army personnel and expats to shop and relax in an international mix of restaurants, bars and, umm, other places. For this reason it has had a dodgy rep, and was a place many Koreans feared to tread. While it maintains its gritty edge, and the hostess and transvestite bars of 'Hooker Hill' are still there (as is a cluster of Seoul's most foreigner-friendly gay hang-outs on 'Homo Hill'), it's now one of Seoul's trendiest dining and shopping districts, attracting people from across the city.

The vibe is spilling over into adjacent areas. Head down Itaewon-ro, the main drag, in one direction and you'll swiftly hit classy Hannam-dong, where you'll find the excellent Leeum Samsung Museum of Art, boutiques and cool cafes. In the other direction is happening Haebangchon (aka HBC) and Gyeongridan, home to laidback restaurants, cafes and craft beer bars. In all these areas you're as likely to hear English spoken as Korean – and not just by the expats.

Up on the hill near the mosque is 'Halal Hill', home to Seoul's Islamic community with a large Arabic-speaking population. Just down from there along Usadan-ro is also a new happening strip which came about with the arrival of artists relocating here to set up studio spaces.

Two major cultural institutions – the National Museum and the War Memorial of Korea – are area highlights and there are fine opportunities to de-stress, either in one of Seoul's most elaborate *jjimjil-bang* (sauna) complexes or by strolling or cycling along the Han River Park, which can be accessed in around a 15-minute downhill walk from Itaewon.

Local Life

- **Shopping** Itaewon is the best place to find clothes and shoes in foreigner-friendly large sizes as well as to have something tailor-made. It's also now getting a rep for small fashion boutiques.
- **Religion** The beautiful Seoul Central Mosque, Korea's largest such house of worship, sits atop a hill in Itaewon, surrounded by halal restaurants and shops with imported items from Islamic countries.

Getting There & Away

- **Subway** Line 6 is the best way to reach Itaewon and around, with Samgakji the closest station to the War Memorial of Korea; transfer here to Line 4 to reach the National Museum.
- **Tour bus** The War Memorial of Korea and National Museum are both stops on the City Tour Bus route.

TOP SIGHT
NATIONAL MUSEUM OF KOREA

Korea's National Museum occupies a grand, marble-lined complex, set in landscaped parklands. The massive Great Hall displays a fraction of the museum's 270,000 treasures from prehistoric times to the Joseon dynasty.

Exhibits & Gardens

Hour-long, English-language tours leave from the **Great Hall** at 10am, 11am and 2pm Tuesday to Friday, and 11am and 2pm weekends; alternatively you can rent an audioguide (₩1000).

The size of the museum is overwhelming, and would takes days to do properly, but among the must-see exhibits in the ground-floor galleries are the **Baekje Incense Burner**, an extraordinary example of the artistry of the 6th- to 7th-century Baekje Kingdom; and the **Golden Treasures for the Great Tomb of Hwangham**, a delicate 5th-century gold belt and crown dripping with jade gems.

In the 3rd-floor sculpture and craft galleries, search out the **Pensive Bodhisattva** from the 7th century. Also look down on the top of the Goryeo-dynasty **Ten Storey Pagoda** carved from marble. The surrounding park is best appreciated in good weather, when the Great Hall is perfectly reflected in the large **Reflecting Pond**. The original **Bosingak Bell** is in the grounds near the picturesque **Dragon Falls**.

Other Facilities

Outside is the **Special Exhibition Hall**, which hosts blockbuster shows with tickets costing around ₩10,000. Those interested in Korean language can visit the **National Hangeul Museum** (Map p224; www.hangeul.go.kr; 139 Seobinggo-ro; ⏲9am-6pm Tue, Thu & Fri, to 9pm Wed & Sat, to 7pm Sun) FREE, which provides an overview of its relatively recent history.

Kids don't miss out either, with the **Children's Museum** offering a snapshot of Korean culture with plenty of hands-on features and play spaces.

For picnic snacks in the park, there's a convenience store near the main entrance, as well as several cafes and restaurants in the complex.

DON'T MISS

- The Great Hall
- Reflecting Pond
- Dragon Falls

PRACTICALITIES

- 국립중앙박물관
- Map p224
- www.museum.go.kr
- 137 Seobinggo-ro
- admission free
- ⏲9am-6pm Tue, Thu & Fri, to 9pm Wed & Sat, to 7pm Sun
- S Line 1 or 4 to Ichon, Exit 2

TOP SIGHT
WAR MEMORIAL OF KOREA

This huge three-floor museum documents the history of warfare in Korea. Its main focus is the Korean War Room, with photos, maps and artefacts giving a fascinating insight into what the Korean War (1950–53) was like. It takes at least three hours to browse the whole place, so try to arrive before 3pm.

Indoor Exhibits

Exhibits cover the surprise 4am attack from the North (spearheaded by 240 Russian-made tanks), the build-up of UN (mainly US) forces in Busan, the daring amphibious landing at Incheon and the sweep north followed by the surprise Chinese attack.

Displays on the 3rd floor cover Korea's involvement in the Vietnam War (4700 Koreans died), North Korean attacks on the South since 1953, and Korea's UN peacekeeping roles.

On the 1st floor are paintings and panoramic displays illustrating many fierce battles fought against invading Mongol, Japanese and Chinese armies. There's also a scale replica of one of Admiral Sun-sin's famous iron-clad turtle warships (called *geobukseon*), which he used to defeat the Japanese navy in the 1590s.

DON'T MISS

- Korean War Room
- Statue of Brothers
- Outdoor exhibit areas

PRACTICALITIES

- 전쟁기념관
- Map p224
- www.warmemo.co.kr
- 29 Itaewon-ro
- admission free
- 9am-6pm Tue-Sun, Free one-hour tours at 10am and 2pm daily
- S Line 4 or 6 to Samgakji, Exit 12

Outdoor Exhibits

Outside there's plenty of large military hardware, including tanks, helicopters, missiles and a B-52 bomber. There are also stirring monuments and giant statues, most notably the 11m-high **Statue of Brothers** showing the reconciliation of two brothers from South and North Korea.

Time your visit to see the **Honour Guard Ceremony** (2pm Fri early Apr-end Jun, mid-Oct–end Nov) when a military band performs, and a marching parade culminates in an awesome display of military precision and weapon twirling.

SIGHTS

NATIONAL MUSEUM OF KOREA MUSEUM

See p97.

WAR MEMORIAL OF KOREA MUSEUM

See p98.

EATING

With an astounding selection of restaurants spanning the globe, eating in Itaewon is all about embracing its multiculturalism. Here you'll find authentic Mexican, Middle Eastern, American BBQ, Indian, African, Thai, Malaysian, Italian, Spanish, French and Russian restaurants among many others, all run by immigrants who know their stuff. Up the hill near the mosque are many halal restaurants and international supermarkets selling items you won't find elsewhere in Seoul.

★VATOS MEXICAN $

Map p222 (☎02-797 8226; www.vatoskorea.com; 2nd fl, 1 Itaewon-ro 15-gil; 2 tacos from ₩6900; ⏰11.30am-11pm Sun-Thu, from noon Fri & Sat; 📶📋; Ⓢ Line 6 to Itaewon, Exit 4) Tacos have long been popular as a snack of choice for GIs and expats in Itaewon but these guys make the shift from Tex-Mex to hipster LA-food-truck-style tacos with a Korean twist. Expect soft corn tortillas filled with *galbi* (beef ribs), a side of *kimchi carnitas* fries (fries with slow-cooked pork and *kimchi*) and cocktails like its 'makgeolita'.

PLANT VEGAN $

Map p222 (www.facebook.com/studioplant; 20 Itaewon-ro 16-gil; mains from ₩10,000; ⏰11am-8pm Tue-Sat; 🥕📋; Ⓢ Line 6 to Itaewon, Exit 4) Set up by the creator of the popular vegetarian blog **Aliens Day Out** (www.aliensdayout.com), this cosy vegan cafe specialises in dairy- and meat-free baked goods. The menu changes daily, but you can expect the likes of tempeh meatball subs, mock-chorizo pasta and awesome cakes such as salted-caramel pumpkin pie.

PASSION 5 BAKERY, DESSERTS $

Map p222 (272 Itaewon-ro; sandwiches from ₩5000; ⏰7.30am-10pm; 📋; Ⓢ Line 6 to Hangangjin, Exit 2) Offering a Fortnum & Mason–like experience, this homage to fine food is a good place to check out a gourmet choice

TOP SIGHT

LEEUM SAMSUNG MUSEUM OF ART

A masterful combination of contemporary architecture and exquisite art, Leeum is made up of three contrasting buildings designed by leading international architects. It's fronted by a **sculpture garden**, containing Anish Kapoors' tower of steel mirrored-orbs *Tall Tree and Eye* and his satellite-like dish *Sky Mirror.*

The three main buildings cover a mix of modern and traditional art. Contemporary-art lovers will want to focus on **Museum 2**, featuring early- and midcentury paintings, sculptures and installations by esteemed Korean and international artists. Here you'll find three floors of works by the likes of Lee Joong-seop, Nam Jun Paik, Damien Hirst, Andy Warhol, Francis Bacon, Jean-Michel Basquiat and Jeff Koons. Getting an audioguide is highly recommended, or you can visit at 3pm weekends for the free 1½-hour tours in English.

For traditional Korean art, **Museum 1** is a must. Though there's a lot to cover, with four floors separated into fine art and calligraphy, ceramics and celadon, metalwork and Buddhist art.

The museum's third element, the **Samsung Child Education & Culture Center**, is used for special exhibitions of Korean and international shows.

DON'T MISS

- Museums 1 and 2
- Samsung Child Education & Culture Center
- Jeff Koons outdoor art installations

PRACTICALITIES

- Map p222
- www.leeum.org
- 60-16 Itaewon-ro 55-gil
- adult/child ₩10,000/4000, temporary exhibition ₩7000/4000, day pass ₩13,000/6000
- ⏰10.30am-6pm Tue-Sun
- Ⓢ Line 6 to Hangangjin, Exit 1

LOCAL KNOWLEDGE

ARTY ITAEWON

If the top of the hill near Seoul Central Mosque wasn't intriguing enough – with its extraordinary diversity that mixes Seoul's Islamic community among its LGBTIQ community and red-light district – the enclave of artists who've relocated to Usadan-ro adds another layer of interest. Since rent prices in Hongdae have skyrocketed, this art community has moved in and set up studios, galleries, pop-up shops and cool hole-in-the-wall bars and eateries. Aim to visit on the last Saturday of each month for its **Stairway Flea Market** (Usadan-ro) with a street-party like atmosphere as local artists sell their works on the stairs and stalls set up along the strip.

Also check out the adjoining suburb of Haebangchon (HBC), a historically impoverished neighbourhood that's undergone a dramatic gentrification. The **HBC Art Village** (Map p224; http://arthill100.com; S Line 6 to Noksapyeong, Exit 2) has recently been developed with murals and art installments throughout its backstreets.

of goods, from house-baked breads, sandwiches and soups (including a sourdough clam chowder), to handmade chocolates and lavish cakes. There's also a Champagne bar and European-style deli items.

COREANOS KITCHEN — MEXICAN $

Map p222 (www.coreanoskitchen.com; 46 Noksapyeong-daero 40-gil; tacos from ₩3300; noon-11pm; ; S Line 6 to Itaewon, Exit 2) Trading off the success of its Gangnam branch, Coreanos brings its fusion of Mexican/Korean street food to Itaewon in a prime location overlooking the main strip.

★LINUS' BBQ — AMERICAN, BARBECUE $$

Map p222 (www.facebook.com/linusbbq; 136-13 Itaewon-ro; mains from ₩15,000; 11.30am-3.30pm & 5.30-10pm; ; S Line 6 to Itaewon, Exit 4) Specialising in authentic southern-style American BBQ, Linus' does a range of Alabaman and Texan-style dishes that involve heaped plates of pulled pork or beef brisket, and excellent sandwiches. There's a *M*A*S*H* theme going (less tacky than it sounds) with its khaki canvas-covered terrace, combined with a 1950s Americana soundtrack. It's hard to find; take the entrance next door to McDonald's on the main strip and head down the stairs.

BUA — THAI $$

Map p222 (2nd fl, 9 Bogwang-ro 59-gil; mains from ₩13,000; 11.30am-3pm & 6-10pm Tue-Sat, 12.30-9.30pm Sun; S Line 6 to Itaewon, Exit 4) An ambience that succeeds in mixing classy with homely, Bua does authentic fragrant dishes from northern Thailand, as well as traditional and royal Thai cooked up by chefs from Chang Mai. Everything is made from scratch, including rotis and curry pastes using fresh ingredients.

BLOC PARTY — BURGERS $$

Map p222 (www.facebook.com/blocpartyseoul; Usadan-ro 10-gil 51; mains from ₩12,000; noon-1am; ; S Line 6 to Itaewon, Exit 3) On the hill among the artist community who've set up along Usadan-ro, this hole-in-the-wall bar and grill is run by a friendly New Yorker who knows how to do a mean cheeseburger. It has incredible views overlooking Hannam from its large gallery window.

SUJI'S — AMERICAN $$

Map p222 (www.sujis.net; 134 Itaewon-ro; breakfast from ₩3900, sandwiches from ₩15,000; 8am-8.30pm; ; S Line 6 to Noksapyeong, Exit 2) In a city where a decent Western breakfast is hard to find, this upstairs New York–style deli delivers. Grab a stool, a paper and go the well-priced egg-salad-muffin-coffee combo, or a full-scale greasy cook up. It also bakes delicious cakes, and has burgers and steaks on the menu.

BAKER'S TABLE — BAKERY, CAFE $$

Map p222 (http://blog.naver.com/mirabakery; 244-1 Noksapyeong-daero, Gyeongridan; mains from ₩10,000; 8am-9pm; ; S Line 6 to Noksapyeong, Exit 2) Opened by a German baker, this very popular terrace cafe serves gourmet-style sandwiches made using home-baked breads, as well as other freshly baked pastries. You'll find hearty German mains such as schnitzels and wurst, plus reasonably priced house wine by the glass. Its proper breakfasts are another reason to stop by.

HBC GOGITJIP
KOREAN, BARBECUE $$

Map p222 (HBC고깃집; 46-5 Yongsandong 2-ga, Haebangchon; meals ₩15,000-25,000; ⏲5pm-1am Mon-Fri, from 3pm Sat & Sun; 📶; Ⓢ Line 6 to Noksapyeong, Exit 2) Popular among expats, this lively Korean-barbecue restaurant is famous for its all-you-can-eat rib eye on Monday nights (₩15,000). Other nights it's still worth checking out.

TARTINE
CAFE $$

Map p222 (☎02-3785 3400; www.tartine.co.kr; 4 Itaewon-ro 23-gil; mains ₩9000-38,500; ⏲10am-10.30pm; 📋; Ⓢ Line 6 to Itaewon, Exit 1) Looking for dessert? You won't go wrong with the sweet pies at this charming bakery-cafe run by an American baker. It also has a diner opposite with plenty of brunch options.

ZELEN
BULGARIAN $$

Map p222 (☎02-749 0600; Itaewon 2-gil; mains from ₩13,000; ⏲11.30am-2.30pm & 6-10pm; 📋; Ⓢ Line 6 to Itaewon, Exit 1) Run by a couple of Bulgarian guys, this is a warm and welcoming restaurant. Meat lovers have plenty of options, like *kiufte* meatballs, served on a big white platter, while the *giuvedje* stew is smaller but packed with meat.

ATELIER DU SAINT-EX
FRENCH $$$

Map p222 (☎02-795 2465; Itaewon 2-gil; mains ₩21,000-49,000; ⏲noon-11pm, to 2am Fri & Sat; 📶📋; Ⓢ Line 6 to Itaewon, Exit 1) A revamped version of this acclaimed French bistro has seen it converted to a more casual affair while maintaining the quality service and delicious dishes such as grilled herb chicken and caramelised pork belly.

LOBSTER BAR
AMERICAN, SEAFOOD $$$

Map p222 (www.lobsterbar.co.kr; 3rd fl, 140-1 Itaewon-ro; mains from ₩21,000; ⏲noon-10pm Mon-Sat, to 9pm Sun; Ⓢ Line 6 to Itaewon, Exit 4) The hip and roomy upstairs Lobster Bar is packed with diners sinking their teeth into rolls filled with soft, juicy lobster mixed with mayo and melted butter, served with fries. Good craft beer selection, too.

DRINKING & NIGHTLIFE

★SOUTHSIDE PARLOR
COCKTAIL BAR

Map p222 (www.facebook.com/SouthsideParlor; 218 Noksapyeong-daero, Gyeongridan; ⏲6pm-midnight; Ⓢ Line 6 to Noksapyeong, Exit 2) Having outgrown their roots in a hipster food truck in Texas, these artisan cocktail makers have set up shop in Itaewon. The mixologists know their stuff, concocting labour-intensive original and classic cocktails, served at an old-school copper bar. If the weather's nice check out the AstroTurf rooftop. There's also a quality menu of pulled-pork sandwiches, burgers etc.

★CAKESHOP
CLUB

Map p222 (www.cakeshopseoul.com; 134 Itaewon-ro; entry incl 1 drink ₩20,000; ⏲Tue-Sat 10pm-5am; Ⓢ Line 6 to Noksapyeong, Exit 2) Head underground to Itaewon's hippest club for electronic beats spun by international and top local DJs. Its attracts a lively, mixed crowd and is very popular so expect long queues.

★DAMOTORI
BAR

Map p222 (다모토리; 31 Sinheung-ro, Haebangchon; ⏲6pm-1am Sun-Thu, to 2am Fri & Sat; 📶; Ⓢ Line 6 to Noksapyeong, Exit 2) A locals' favourite along HBC's main strip, the dimly lit Damotori specialises in quality *makgeolli* (milky rice wine), hand-picked from provinces around the country. The food is also excellent, especially the seafood pancakes.

★VENUE/
CLUB

Map p222 (www.facebook.com/venuerok; 165-6 Itaewon-ro; ⏲10pm-6am; Ⓢ Line 6 to Itaewon, Exit 1) This dive-y basement club attracts a fun-loving, unpretentious crowd for quality DJs spinning hip hop and electronica. There's no cover charge, but there's a queue after midnight.

FOUR SEASONS
BAR

Map p222 (사계; www.facebook.com/craftpub4seasons; Basement, 7 Bogwang-ro 59-gil; ⏲6pm-1am Mon-Thu, to 2am Fri, 2pm-2am Sat, to midnight Sun; Ⓢ Line 6 to Itaewon, Exit 4) Set up by a bunch of local beer geeks who brew their own ales, this basement bar has 10 craft beers on tap and a good stock of bottled varieties in the fridge.

PET SOUNDS
BAR

Map p222 (www.facebook.com/petsoundsbar; 21 Hoenamu-ro; ⏲6pm-3am; Ⓢ Line 6 to Noksapyeong, Exit 2) Named after the young owner's love affair with the Beach Boys' *Pet Sounds* album, this popular upstairs rock bar provides a paper and pen to put in your requests to knowledgable DJs. Has a good selection of drinks, too.

CRAFT BEER VALLEY

At the epicentre of the craft beer revolution in Seoul, Noksapyeong (in Gyeongridan up from Itaewon) is home to a string of brewers who have set up shop in what's now known locally as Craft Beer Valley. In a short time over a few years, this localised scene has paved the way for a greater diversity and quality of beer, resulting in a shift in tastes that's seen locals gain a thirst for India pale ales (IPAs), amber ales, German-style wheat beers and smoky stouts.

Until recently government restrictions have meant the industry has been dominated by a handful of major brewers that's resulted in a lack of variation in taste. While mainstream lagers such as Hite, Cass and OB are perfectly drinkable, they're best described as unremarkable, diluted lagers.

It was this lack of choice that led to an article in the *Economist* criticising the industry and stating that North Korean beer tasted infinitely better. Such a remark sparked outrage among the industry, and led to a loosening of restrictions for small-scale breweries to produce commercially. The rest is history, and now every second bar in Itaewon advertises craft beer, most of which is produced domestically.

Craftworks Taphouse (Map p222; craftworkstaphouse.com; 651 Itaewon 2-dong, Gyeongridan; ⏲11am-midnight Mon-Fri, to 2am Sat & Sun; 🅢Line 6 to Noksapyeong, Exit 2) The original brewer to kick off Noksapyeong's craft beer scene has secured a treasured place in the hearts of Seoul's ale lovers. Order the paddle to sample its seven beers (₩10,500) and then decide which one to savour in a pint. It also features guest breweries, house wine and a quality menu of pub grub. Happy hour is 4pm to 6pm. It also has branches in Itaewon (Map p222; 214-1 Itaewon-ro; 🅢Line 6 to Itaewon, Exit 3) – which has a greater beer selection – and downtown at Euljiro (p81).

Magpie Brewing Co. (Map p222; www.magpiebrewing.com; Noksapyoungro 54gil 7, Gyeongridan; ⏲3pm-1am; 🅢Line 6 to Noksapyeong, Exit 2) A big player in Seoul's craft beer movement, Magpie is split into two parts. Downstairs is Magpie Basement, a beer bunker with low-lying lamps, serving its eight beers on tap and pizza (from ₩9000). Otherwise there's the more intimate Brew Shop, which does occasional home-brew classes and tastings for ₩60,000. It's also opened bars in Hongdae (p91) and Jeju Island.

Booth (Map p222; www.theboothpub.com; Itaewon-dong 705, Gyeongridan; ⏲noon-1am; 🅢Line 6 to Noksapyeong, Exit 2) The original brew pub has pop-art murals on its walls, and is known for its flagship Bill's pale ale and pepperoni pizza by the slice. There's also a divey industrial **Booth Mansion** (Map p222; 36 Itaewon-ro 27ga-gil; beer ₩5000; ⏲5pm-1am Sun-Thu, 2pm-3am Fri & Sat; 🅢Line 6 to Itaewon, Exit 1) branch near Itaewon station, and in Gangnam.

Made in Pong Dang (Map p222; www.pongdangsplash.com; 222-1 Noksapyeong, Gyeongridan; ⏲4pm-midnight Sun-Thu, 2pm-2am Fri & Sat; 🅢Line 6 to Noksapyeong, Exit 2) In a scene dominated by North Americans, this is an all-Korean affair, producing six of its own beers on taps pulled from the wood-panelled bar, including pale ale, Belgian Blonde ale and seasonals such as oatmeal stout.

White Rabbit (Map p222; 242 Noksapyeong-daero, Gyeongridan; ⏲6pm-1am; 🅢Line 6 to Noksapyeong, Exit 2) Run by a local surfer, White Rabbit has an extensive selection of Korean and international craft beers on tap and bottled; also brews a few of its own ales.

FLOWER GIN — BAR

Map p222 (250 Noksapyeong-daero, Gyeongridan; ⏲2pm-midnight Mon, Wed & Thu, from noon Fri-Sun; 🅢Line 6 to Noksapyeong, Exit 2) An inspired mix of florist-meets-gin-bar, the perfumed scents here match the drinks superbly. Run by a young female owner, this tiny bar only does gin-based drinks using Hendricks, infused with a slice of cucumber and freshly plucked flower.

LOVIBOND — BAR

Map p222 (136-1 Itaewon-ro; ⏲5pm-midnight Sun-Thu, to 2am Fri, 2pm-2am Sat; 🅢Line 6 to Itaewon, Exit 4) Head down the stairs to this cool little basement bar specialising in craft beer, including three of its own India Pale Ales (IPAs) to go with a rotating selection of guest breweries and bottled beers.

BLUE 55
BAR

Map p222 (이태원 블루55; 3 Bogwang-ro 55-gil; ⌚4pm-2am; 📶; Ⓢ Line 6 to Itaewon, Exit 4) A double-storey house converted to a shabby-chic bar, Blue 55 is a good spot for craft beer, including its cheap (and very drinkable) house beer. Visit Wednesdays for all-day happy hour.

TAKEOUT DRAWING
CAFE

Map p222 (www.takeoutdrawing.com; Noksa pyeong-daero, Gyeongridan; ⌚2pm-10am; Ⓢ Line 6 to Noksapyeong, Exit 2) This arty cafe is a cool place to hang out and enjoy graphic art, books and magazines with coffee, organic teas and other beverages. There's another branch in **Hannam** (Map p222; Itaewon-ro; 📶; Ⓢ Line 6 to Hanganjjin, Exit 3).

WOLHYANG
BAR

Map p222 (월향, Taste of the Moon; http://tasteofthemoon.com; 13 Itaewon-ro 54-gil; ⌚noon-2am; Ⓢ Line 6 to Hangangjin, Exit 3) This upmarket *makgeolli* bar and restaurant has an interesting range of sweetened and unsweetened hand-crafted rice wines (₩9000 per litre) from around Korea. Go for the house organic brown-rice *makgeolli*. Happy hour is from noon to 4pm.

MOWMOW
BAR

Map p222 (모우모우; 54-3 Itaewon-ro 27ga-gil; ⌚3pm-3am; Ⓢ Line 6 to Itaewon, Exit 1) There are usually more brands of *makgeolli* (starting from ₩6500) to choose from than are listed on the menu at this airy bar and eatery up the hill from the main Itaewon dining alley. Try one of the *makgeolli* cocktails (₩9000).

WAYS OF SEEING
CAFE, BAR

Map p222 (683-134 Hannam-dong; ⌚11am-midnight Mon-Sat, to 10pm Sun; 📶; Ⓢ Line 6 to Hangangjin, Exit 3) This is as good a place as any to suss out the area's pulse and hang with hipsters while sipping your latte or beer. It does food and hosts events including art shows and the **Fifty Seoul** (www.facebook.com/fiftyseoul) flea market.

AGAINST THE MACHINE
BAR

Map p222 (ATM; 48 Itaewon-ro 54-gil, Hannam-dong; ⌚6pm-3am; Ⓢ Line 6 to Itaewon, Exit 3) Hidden in the backstreets of Hannam-dong, this small open-air bar attracts a friendly, cool local crowd for beers and cocktails.

ROSE & CROWN
PUB

Map p222 (6 Itaewon-ro 19-gil; ⌚3pm-3am; Ⓢ Line 6 to Itaewon, Exit 1) Foreigner-friendly Itaewon wouldn't be complete without a British pub, and this three-storey boozer delivers with its pints of ale, fish and chips and live Premier League on the telly.

GRAND OLE OPRY
BAR

Map p222 (16 Usadan-ro 14-gil; ⌚6pm-3am; Ⓢ Line 6 to Itaewon, Exit 3) Bang in the middle of Itaewon's red-light district, this honky-tonk dive bar is an old-school GI hang-out and something straight out of a movie. The original owner Mama Kim still works behind the bar and is good for a chat about Itaewon's colourful history. The 'Star-Spangled Banner' is played at the stroke of midnight, as it has been here for over 40 years.

BURN
BAR

Map p222 (www.burninhal.com; 305-7 Itaewon-dong; ⌚6pm-late; Ⓢ Line 6 to Noksapyeong, Exit 2) All kinds of cigars, including top-class Cuban ones, single malt whiskies and quality rums are the poisons of choice at this classy upstairs bar which also features live jazz.

PROST
BAR

Map p222 (www.districtprost.com; 1st fl, 116-1 Hamilton Hotel Annex, Itaewon-dong; ⌚11.30am-2.30am; Ⓢ Line 6 to Itaewon, Exit 1) On the ground floor of District – a warehouse-style complex of bars behind the Hamilton Hotel – this European-chic gastro-pub has a huge selection of draught beers, including its own brews, and hearty pub-style meals.

G'DAY
CAFE

Map p222 (10 Noksapyeong-daero 46-gil, Gyeongridan; coffee ₩4000; ⌚10am-11pm; Ⓢ Line 6 to Noksapyeong, Exit 2) Say g'day to one of the few places in Seoul to offer a flat white coffee. The Sydney-style cafe also does Aussie beers, Tim Tam shakes and cheese-and-avocado jaffles.

B1
CLUB

Map p222 (entrance Sat ₩10,000; ⌚8pm-4am Sun-Thu, 9am-5.30am Fri & Sat; Ⓢ Line 6 to Itaewon, Exit 1) On the main drag, B1 is a good place to kick on to after the pub, and it's one of Itaewon's most known clubs, as evidenced by the long line to get in.

ON THE HILL

Squished between 'Hooker Hilll', 'Tranny Hill' and 'Halal Hill' (aka Little Arabia, the strip by the Seoul Mosque), 'Homo Hill' is a 50m alley so-called because of its cluster of gay-friendly bars and clubs. Most hardly have room to swing a handbag, so on warm weekends the crowds often spill into the street. All genders and sexual persuasions will feel welcome here. To reach here from Exit 3 of Itaewon station head uphill and take the first major road right; Homo Hill is the second street on the left.

Always Homme (올웨이즈옴므; Map p222; www.facebook.com/AlwaysHommeBar; Usadan-ro 12-gil; ⏲8pm-4am Sun-Thu, to 6am Fri & Sat; Ⓢ Line 6 to Itaewon, Exit 3) A homely gay bar with flirty-friendly staff, low-playing music and a cosy open-air lounge set-up.

Why Not (Map p222; Usadan-ro; ⏲7.30pm-3am Sun-Thu, to 5am Fri & Sat; Ⓢ Line 6 to Itaewon, Exit 3) This small gay dance club is fitted out with lights and lasers and plenty of K-Pop.

Miracle (Map p222; Usadan-ro; ⏲8pm-5am; Ⓢ Line 6 to Itaewon, Exit 3) One of Korea's few exclusively lesbian bars, this tiny little bar sits atop Homo Hill and gets going around midnight.

Trance (Map p222; http://.cafe.daum.net/trance; Usadan-ro; admission incl 1 drink ₩10,000; ⏲10.30pm-5am; 🚻; Ⓢ Line 6 to Itaewon, Exit 3) Pouting drag princesses entertain in their own utterly unique style at this small gay club with a DJ and a stage. The shows don't begin until 2.30am, otherwise this red-and-black dance club serves up mixed dance music.

Queen (Map p222; www.facebook.com/queenbar; 7, Usadan-ro 12-gil; ⏲8pm-5am Tue-Sun; Ⓢ Line 6 to Itaewon, Exit 3) The eternally popular Queen offers sit-and-chat zones though it usually gets very crowded with mostly everyone dancing.

Soho (Map p222; Usadan-ro; ⏲10pm-5am; Ⓢ Line 6 to Itaewon, Exit 3) A smart and friendly gay bar (lesbians welcome) with a relaxed vibe and dance-club section for later in the evening.

ENTERTAINMENT

THUNDERHORSE TAVERN — LIVE MUSIC

Map p222 (www.thunderhorsetavern.com; Noksapyeong 220, Gyeongridan; ⏲8.30pm-midnight; Ⓢ Line 6 to Noksapyeong, Exit 2) Take the stairs down to this dingy basement venue for a regular roster of local and expat bands playing anything from indie and punk to metal.

ALL THAT JAZZ — JAZZ

Map p222 (☎02-795 5701; www.allthatjazz.kr; 3rd fl, 12 Itaewon-ro 27ga-gil; admission ₩5000; ⏲6pm-1am Sun-Thu, to 2.30am Fri & Sat; Ⓢ Line 6 to Itaewon, Exit 2) A fixture on the Seoul jazz scene since 1976, top local musicians regularly perform here; table reservations are recommended for the weekend. During the week live music starts at 8.30pm, with additional earlier 6.30pm shows on Fridays and weekends. There's also a late 11.30pm show on Friday and Saturday.

ROCKY MOUNTAIN TAVERN — LIVE MUSIC

Map p222 (www.rockymountaintavern.com; 210 Itaewon-ro; ⏲4pm-midnight, to 2am Fri & Sat; Ⓢ Line 6 to Itaewon, Exit 3) Adding to Itaewon's multicultural make-up, this Canadian-themed pub does draught beers and *poutine* (fries with cheese curds and sauce) burgers, and hosts live bands on weekends and stand-up comedy the first Thursday of each month.

SHOPPING

MILLIMETRE MILLIGRAM — GIFTS

Map p222 (www.mmmg.net; Itaewon-ro; ⏲11am-9pm; Ⓢ Line 6 to Itaewon, Exit 3) Usually shortened to MMG, this is the spot to pick up quirky stationery and bags, including the Swiss brand Freitag. There's a cafe as well as a basement gallery/furniture store and, on the 3rd floor, the boutique art-book and magazine shop **Post Poetics** (Map p222; www.postpoetics.org; 3rd fl, Itaewon-ro; ⏲1-8pm Mon-Sat; Ⓢ Line 6 to Itaewon, Exit 3).

YONGSAN ELECTRONICS MARKET — ELECTRONICS

Map p224 (용산전자랜드; 125 Cheongpa-ro; ⏲10am-7.30pm; Ⓢ Line 1 Yongsan, Exit 3) If it plugs in, you can find it at this geeky universe of high-tech marvels. Computer prices are usually marked but prices on other goods are lacking, so do what the locals do – check out the prices online before arriving. It's also a good spot for well-priced (and barely used) secondhand phones. The area is being redeveloped, and is now spread across several buildings.

Leave the train station plaza via Exit 3, turn right, then left and walk through the pedestrian overpass to enter the first building of Yongsan Electronics Land on the 3rd floor. It's partly closed the first and third Sundays of the month. If all this is too much, try discount electronics chain E-Mart in the nearby I'Park Mall.

WHAT THE BOOK — BOOKS

Map p222 (02-797 2342; www.whatthebook.com; 151 Itaewon-ro; 10am-9pm; Line 6 to Itaewon, Exit 3) Itaewon's best bookshop sells new releases and secondhand English-language fiction and nonfiction, plus an interesting range on Korean culture and international magazines.

STEVE J & YONI P — FASHION

Map p222 (02-796 4766; www.steveandyonip.com; Hannam-dong; 11.30am-7.30pm; Line 6 to Hanganjin, Exit 3) Collaborating on the superfashionable streetwear in this boutique are local designers Steve J and Yoni P. Their T-shirts, sweatshirts and colourful printed clobber is stocked by high-class boutiques around the world, but their flagship store is down this happening little street in Hannam-dong.

I'PARK MALL — MALL

Map p224 (www.iparkmall.co.kr; Yongsan; Line 1 to Yongsan, Line 4 to Sinyongsan, Exit 3 or 4) There's pretty much everything you need from brand-name fashion to digital goods at this mall that sprawls around the major overground Yongsan station.

EELSKIN SHOP — ACCESSORIES

Map p222 (Itaewon-ro; 9.30am-8pm; Line 6 to Itaewon, Exit 4) A good place to purchase ultrasoft eel-skin handbags, belts, wallets and purses. Eel-skin goods are an Itaewon speciality that make popular gifts. Wallets start at ₩15,000 and purses at ₩25,000.

COMME DES GARCONS — FASHION

Map p222 (261 Itaewon-ro; 11am-8pm; Line 6 to Hangangjin, Exit 1) This hip boutique of the Japanese label has a maze-like, five-floor layout with superfashionable men's and women's clothing.

HAMILTON SHIRTS — FASHION

Map p222 (www.hs76.com; 153 Itaewon-ro; 10am-7.30pm; Line 6 to Itaewon, Exit 1) One of the larger and most reliable of the dedicated men's shirt makers that are clustered along Itaewon-ro where you pick the material before being fitted. A 100% cotton shirts start from ₩41,000. It also has a branch in Myeong-dong, and a store in Gangnam for women.

DYNASTY TAILOR — FASHION

Map p222 (02-3785 3035; www.dynastytailor.com; 14 Itaewonro 14-gil; 10am-8pm; Line 6 to Itaewon, Exit 4) The suits here are all handmade in the traditional way by expert tailors just a few doors down from the shop. Ask to see the workshop. Pure-wool suits cost ₩380,000 to ₩450,000 and take about three days to make.

ANDO — ANTIQUES

Map p222 (www.ando.or.kr; 99 Bogwang-ro; 10am-7pm Mon-Sat; Line 6 to Itaewon, Exit 4) In a street famous in Seoul for its antique and vintage furniture stores (which originated when departing US soldiers sold their belongings), Ando is one of the most well known, selling stylish early-20th-century European and British pieces. It ain't cheap, though.

SPORTS & ACTIVITIES

DRAGON HILL SPA & RESORT — JJIMJIL-BANG

Map p224 (드래곤힐스파; 010 4223 0001; www.dragonhillspa.co.kr; 40-713, Hangangno 3(sam)-ga; Mon-Fri day/night ₩10,000/12,000, Sat & Sun all day ₩12,000; 24hr; Line 1 to Yongsan, Exit 1) This foreigner-friendly *jjimjil-bang* – a noisy mix of gaudy Las Vegas bling and Asian chic – is one of Seoul's largest. In addition to the outdoor unisex pool, all manner of indoor saunas and ginseng and cedar baths, there is a cinema, arcade games, beauty treatment rooms and multiple dining options.

ITAEWONLAND — JJIMJIL-BANG

Map p222 (02-749 4122; www.itaewonland.com; 34 Usadan-ro 14-gil; sauna ₩6000; 24hr; Line 6 to Itaewon, Exit 2) This *jjimjil-bang* with a traditional gate facade is up a flight of steep steps from Itaewon-ro. A scrub down is an extra ₩20,000/28,000 (male/female); an hour-long massage is ₩60,000.

Gangnam & South of the Han River

Neighbourhood Top Five

1. Stroll around **Olympic Park** (p108), where there are 1700-year-old fortifications, museums and 200 quirky sculptures.
2. Join in the amusement-park fun of **Lotte World** (p109), with its thrill rides and fairy-tale carousel and castle.
3. Make a lotus lantern and sip tea with monks at the venerable temple **Bongeun-sa** (p110).
4. Pay your respects at **Seonjeongneung** (p110), the tombs of past Korean kings in Seolleung Park.
5. Head to Seoul Grand Park to enjoy the **National Museum of Modern and Contemporary Art** (p112) and science museum.

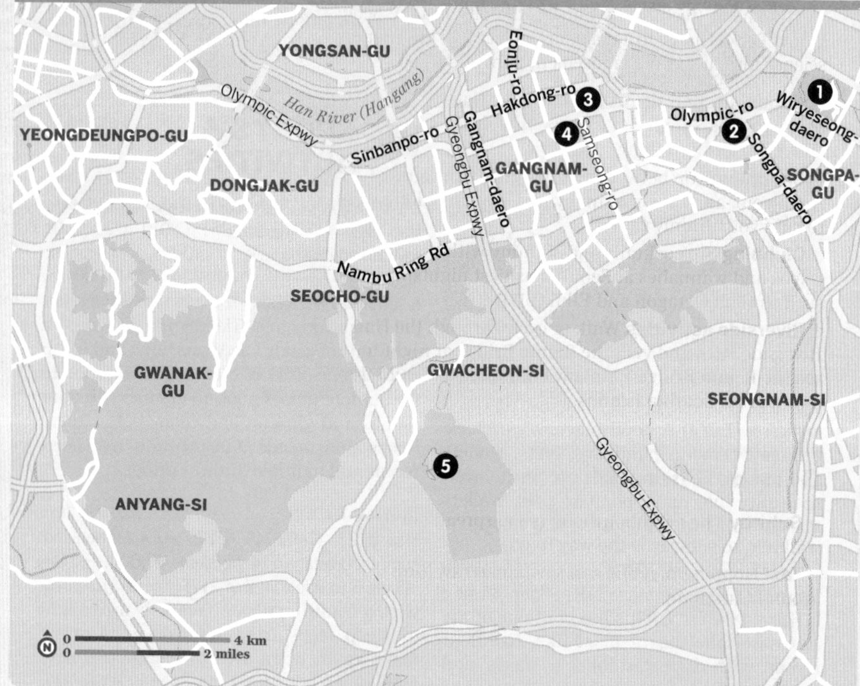

For more detail of this area see Maps p228 and p230

Explore Gangnam & South of the Han River

Meaning 'South of the River', Gangnam refers to an administrative area, Gangnam-gu, and the parts of Seoul that lie south of the Han. Looking at the ranks of tower blocks bisected by broad highways, it's hard to imagine that there wasn't much of the city here a few decades ago.

The area saw much development for the 1988 Olympics, the legacy of which is Olympic Park, one of the area's main sights with its green space, museums and galleries. Gangnam's wide open spaces allowed Lotte to create its giant theme park, plus Seoul's tallest building nearby. But mainly this newer part of Seoul is a ritzy residential address, entertainment district and business hub with major company headquarters, such as Samsung D'Light, and the COEX complex with its convention centre and shopping mall.

Retail is as flash as it gets in upscale Apgujeong and Cheongdam. Checking out the eye-boggling design boutiques, with even more eye-boggling price tags on the merchandise, can be fun even if you lack the funds for purchases. More affordable is the shopping on nearby tree-lined Garosu-gil.

Further south the Seoul Arts Center promotes traditional and modern culture, Korean and Western, while in Gwacheon (technically outside the city limits), Seoul Grand Park is home to a major art gallery and kid-friendly science museum, a big amusement park and a zoo.

Local Life

- **Shopping** Hop between the designer boutiques of Apgujeong and Cheongdam by taxi – you wouldn't want to ruin your Jimmy Choos!
- **Clubbing** Sip cocktails and shimmy with the rich, celebs and wannabes at Seoul's flashiest nightspots, such as Club Octagon and Ellui (p114).
- **Riverside activities** Walk or cycle through the Han Riverside Park and visit the Banpo Bridge at night to see the Banpo Bridge Rainbow Fountain (p111) and the illuminated floating Islands.

Getting There & Away

- **Subway** The neighbourhood is too spread out for walking, so subway is the way to go.
- **Taxi** Hopping in a taxi can save time travelling around Gangnam.

Lonely Planet's Top Tip

Drop by Banpo Bridge in the evening for both the spectacle of its Rainbow Fountain performance and the floating islands illuminated at Some Sevit.

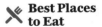

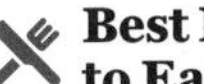

Best Places to Eat

- Jungsik (p113)
- Samwon Garden (p113)
- Coreanos Kitchen (p113)

For reviews, see p113

Best Places to Drink

- Neurin Maeul (p114)
- Booth (p114)
- Greenmile Coffee (p114)

For reviews, see p114

Best Places to Shop

- 10 Corso Como Seoul (p116)
- COEX Mall (p116)
- Galleria (p116)

For reviews, see p116

SEBASTIAN CZAPNIK / DREAMSTIME ©

TOP SIGHT
OLYMPIC PARK

This large and pleasant park, a focus of the 1988 Olympics, has an interesting variety of sights that makes it worthy of a visit. As well as a place to stroll among greenery and lakes past the Olympic sights, there's plenty of art to admire, from open-air sculptures to the modern-art museum. It contains many stadiums used during the Games as well as the remains of the Mongchon-toseong (Mongchon Fortress).

Museums & Galleries

Olympic Park's bunker-like **SOMA** (소마미술관, Seoul Olympic Museum of Art; Map p230; 02-425 1077; www.somamuseum.org; adult/child ₩3000/1000; 10am-8pm Tue-Sun; S Line 5 to Olympic Park, Exit 3) features modern and contemporary art in six galleries. Most are special paid exhibitions, covering local and big-name international artists. Also check out the quirky sculptures scattered like buckshot around the park.

Seoul Baekje Museum (Map p230; http://baekjemuseum.seoul.go.kr; Wiryeseong-daero, Songpa-gu; 9am-9pm Mon-Fri, to 6pm Sat & Sun; S Line 5 to Olympic Park, Exit 3) FREE illuminates the history and culture of Hanseong (18 BC–AD 475), when this part of Seoul was the capital of the Baekje kingdom.

Less interesting is the smaller **Mongchon Museum** (Map p230; 02-424 5138; 9am-6pm Tue-Sun; S Line 8 to Mongchontoseong, Exit 5) FREE, which exhibits some precious golden relics of the Baekje kings and the usual ceramic pots.

Olympic Memorials

Standing at the main entrance is the colossal **World Peace Gate** (Map p230; S Line 8 to Mongchontoseong, Exit 1), with its striking winged arches designed for the 1988 Olympics.

The **Seoul Olympic Museum** (Map p230; www.88olympic.or.kr; 10am-6pm Tue-Sun; S Line 8 to Mongchontoseong, Exit 1) FREE relives the highlights of the 1988 Olympics with screens showing footage, together with a brief history of the games.

DON'T MISS

- World Peace Gate
- Seoul Baekje Museum
- SOMA
- Mongchon-toseong (Mongchon Fortress)

PRACTICALITIES

- 올림픽공원
- Map p230
- www.olympicpark.co.kr
- 424 Olympic-ro Songpa-gu
- admission free
- S Line 8 to Mongchontoseong, Exit 1 or Line 5 to Olympic Park, Exit 3

JTB PHOTO / AGE FOTOSTOCK ©

TOP SIGHT
LOTTE WORLD

Kids *and* adults love the massive entertainment hub of Lotte World. It's a Korean version of Disneyland with the chipmunk-like Lotty and Lorry standing in as the park's iconic duo.

Lotte World Adventure

One of the world's largest indoor theme parks, Lotte World Adventure is an enchanting place for kids. Along with its spinning rides and bumper cars, it has an old-world charm with its **ice-skating rink** (롯데월드 아이스링크; ☎for English 02-1330; www.lotteworld.com/icerink; B3 fl, Lotte World Adventure; per session incl rental adult/child ₩15,000/14,000; ⊙hours vary), a monorail, 'flying' hot-air balloons, regular parades and a beautifully decorated carousel with 64 horses. The outdoor **Magic Island**, in the middle of Seokchon Lake, is the place for the more thrilling rides. Centred on a Magic Castle, here you'll hear the screams of excitement from people on roller-coaster rides, gyro swings and free-fall drops, as well as more child-friendly rides such as a Ferris wheel. Note, it's closed in bad weather.

Folk Museum

The 3rd-floor **Folk Museum** (⊙9.30am-8pm) uses imaginative techniques such as dioramas, scale models and moving waxworks to bring scenes from Korean history to life. Entrance is included in the day-passport ticket. Other attractions include a theatre, multiplex cinema, department store, shopping mall, hotel and restaurants. Note that tickets are discounted for entry after 4pm (adult/child/youth ₩26,000/20,000/23,000) and 7pm (₩17,000/13,000/15,000).

DON'T MISS

- Lotte World Adventure
- Magic Island
- Folk Museum
- Ice-skating rink

PRACTICALITIES

- 롯데월드
- Map p230
- ☎02-1661 2000
- www.lotteworld.com
- 240 Olympic-ro, Songpa-Gu
- adult/child/youth ₩31,000/25,000/28,000, passport incl most rides adult/child/youth ₩46,000/36,000/40,000
- ⊙9.30am-10pm
- Ⓢ Line 2 or 8 to Jamsil, Exit 3

SIGHTS

OLYMPIC PARK PARK

See p108.

LOTTE WORLD AMUSEMENT PARK

See p109.

COEX AQUARIUM AQUARIUM

Map p230 (☎02-6002 6200; www.coexaqua.com; COEX Mall, 513, Yeongdong-daero, Gangnam-gu; adult/child under 13yr/child 13-18yr₩22,000/16,000/19,000; ⏰10am-8pm; Ⓢ Line 2 to Samseong, Exit 6) Seoul's largest aquarium exhibits thousands of fish and other sea creatures from around the world. You can see live coral, sharks, turtles, rays, electric eels, octopus, evil-looking piranhas and pulsating jellyfish. Its only downside is the smallish enclosures for the seals and manatees.

SEONJEONGNEUNG TOMB

Map p230 (선정릉; http://jikimi.cha.go.kr/english; Seonjeongneung Park, 1 Seolleung-ro 100-gil, Gangnam-gu; adult/child under 13yr/youth 13-18yr ₩1000/free/500; ⏰6am-8pm Tue-Sun; Ⓢ Line 2 or Bundang Line to Seolleung, Exit 8) Seonjeongneung Park contains two main burial areas for kings and queens from the Joseon dynasty. The first tomb is for **King Seongjong** (Map p230), who reigned 1469 to 149; he was a prolific author and father – he had 28 children by 12 wives and concubines. Go around the side and you can walk up to the tomb for a closer look. Nearby is the tomb of King Seongjong's second wife, **Queen Jeonghyeon Wanghu** (Map p230).

A 10-minute walk further on through the thickly wooded park is the tomb of King Seongjong and Queen Jeonghyeon's second son, **King Jeongjong** (Map p230), who reigned from 1506 to 1544. Although he ruled for 38 years he was a weak king and court factions held the real power, as they often did during the Joseon period. At this tomb you can see the full layout – the gateway and the double pathway to the pavilion where memorial rites were carried out – but you can't go near the tomb.

There is another Joseon-dynasty tomb complex at Donggureung (p122), about 20km northeast of Seoul.

SONGEUN ARTSPACE GALLERY

Map p230 (☎02-3448 0100; www.songeunartspace.org; 6 Apgujeong-ro 75-gil; ⏰11am-7pm

TOP SIGHT
BONGEUN-SA

The shrines and halls of the Buddhist temple Bongeun-sa, with its tree-filled hillside location, stand in direct juxtaposition to its corporate high-rise surrounds. Founded in AD 794, the buildings have been rebuilt many times over the centuries. Entry to the temple is through **Jinyeomun** (Gate of Truth), protected by its guardians, the four celestial kings. On the left is a small office where an English-speaking volunteer guide is usually available.

The main shrine, **Daewungjeon**, is decorated with symbols and art that express Buddhist philosophy and ideals. A small 14th-century bell is hidden in one corner. On the right is the **funeral hall**, while behind are smaller **shrine halls** and a 23m-high statue of the Maitreya (Future) Buddha. Nearby is the oldest hall, **Panjeon**, constructed in 1856, which houses more than 3000 150-year-old woodblocks with Buddhist scripture and art carved into them.

It's highly recommended to visit on Thursday to take part in the **Templelife program** (tour ₩20,000; ⏰2-4pm Thu), which includes lotus-lantern making, *dado* (tea ceremony), a temple tour and Seon (Zen) meditation. There's also an opportunity to stay overnight in the two-day templestay program (₩70,000), which includes activities and monastic meals; book three weeks in advance.

DON'T MISS

- Jinyeomun
- Daewungjeon
- Panjeon
- Templelife program

PRACTICALITIES

- 봉은사
- Map p230
- ☎02-3218 4895
- www.bongeunsa.org
- 531 Bongeunsa-ro, Gangnam-gu
- Ⓢ Line 2 to Samseong, Exit 6

K-WAVE IN GANGNAM

As the Korean Wave surged into a worldwide tsunami following Psy's 2012 smash hit 'Gangnam Style', the interest sparked in Korean pop culture has reached unprecedented levels. And there's nowhere better to ride the wave than in Gangnam itself – the hang-out for K-Pop stars and actors, and where the talent agencies and record labels are based.

The rise of *hallyu* (the term referring to the global rise of Korean pop culture since the 1990s, aka the Korean Wave) is a trend not lost on the tourism department. They named Psy as official tourism ambassador in 2013, before opening a shiny new Gangnam Tourist Information Center (p192) to offer a range of *hallyu*-themed tours and sights to capitalise on the phenomenon.

K-Wave Experience (Map p228; 2nd fl, Gangnam Tourist Information Center, 161 Apgujeong-ro, Gangnam-gu; ⌚10am-7pm; S Line 3 to Apgujeong, Exit 6) Upstairs from the Gangnam Tourist Center, this is the place to live out all your K-Pop fantasies, with a full makeover to transform you into a K-Pop star. Choose from a wardrobe of clothing, wigs and bling, as well as make- up, for that cheesy photo op. Also here is a bunch of CDs, DVDs and kitschy K-Wave souvenirs.

K-Star Road (Hallyu Star Avenue; Map p228; Apgujeong Rodeo St; S Bundang Line to Apgujeong Rodeo, Exit 7) Gangnam's 'Hallyuwood Walk of Fame' pays homage to K-Pop stars in the form of cutesy bear sculptures dedicated to K-Wave singers and actors.

Gangnam Style 'Horse Dance' Stage (Map p228; Gangnam-daero; S Line 2 to Gangnam, Exit 11) Outside Gangnam subway is the multimedia Gangnam Style stage, a shrine to Psy – somewhat ironic given the song was a parody of the neighbourhood. While you're here head down Gangnam-daero (redubbed U-Street) to see 12m-high, 1.4m-wide media poles displaying video art. Visit early evening to soak up the electric atmosphere.

Mon-Sat; S Bundang Line to Apgujeong Rodeo, Exit 2) FREE In the heart of Gangnam's fashionable Cheongdam district, this contemporary-art gallery promotes works by emerging and established Korean artists with regular exhibitions over several floors.

HORIM MUSEUM — MUSEUM

Map p228 (www.horimmuseum.org; 6 Dosan-daero 45-gil, Gangnam-gu; adult/child ₩8000/5000; ⌚10.30am-6pm Mon-Sat; S Line 3 to Apgujeong, Exit 3) Within the lustrous walls of the stylish Horim Art Center, this museum has three floors devoted to Korean ceramic masterpieces and temporary exhibits on traditional Korean art.

313 ART PROJECT — GALLERY

Map p228 (www.313artproject.com; 313 Dosan-daero, Gangnam-gu; S Line 3 to Apgujeong, Exit 3) In the middle of Apgujeong's chic art hub, this slick gallery shows contemporary works by emerging and established artists, both local and from abroad.

OPERA GALLERY — GALLERY

Map p228 (☎02-3446 0070; www.operagallery.com/ang/eastern-asia/seoul.html; 1F, SB Tower, 318 Dosan-daero, Gangnam-gu; ⌚10am-7pm; S Line 3 to Apgujeong, Exit 3) FREE This high-end commercial gallery is worth popping into for a gawk at works (and price tags) by artists such as Damien Hirst, Joan Miró, Salvador Dalí as well as local contemporary painters.

FIFTY FIFTY — GALLERY

Map p228 (www.fiftyfifty.kr; 53 Nonhyeon-ro 153-gil, Gangnam-gu; ⌚noon-9pm; S Line 3 to Sinsa, Exit 8) FREE A decent art gallery with a fantastic space for its regularly rotating art shows by emerging local artists.

SOME SEVIT — ARCHITECTURE

Map p228 (세빛섬; Sebitseom; www.somesevit.com; Hanggan Riverside Park; S Line 3, 7 or 9 to Express Bus Terminal, Exit 8-1) FREE At the south end of Banpo Bridge are these three artificial floating islands interconnected by walkways. Each features futuristic buildings in a complex that comprises restaurants, an exhibition hall and an outdoor stage. Definitely aim to visit at night when its buildings are lit up spectacularly by LED lights, as is the **Banpo Bridge Rainbow Fountain** (반포대교 달빛무지개분수).

Covered with 10,000 lights, the fountain's rainbow-coloured water rains down in graceful arcs from the double-decker bridge. Spanning 1140m, it's the world's longest fountain and is best viewed from the island's observation deck or **Banpo Hangang Park**.

The 20-minute show happens from late April to the end of August at noon, 8pm and 9pm Monday to Friday and noon, 6pm, 8pm, 8.30pm and 9pm on Saturday and Sunday. Shows are cancelled if it's raining.

SAMSUNG D'LIGHT — BUILDING

Map p228 (www.samsung.com/us/experience/dlight; Samsung Electronics Bldg, 11 Seocho-daero 74-gil, Seocho-gu; ⏲10am-7pm Mon-Sat; ⓈLine 2 to Gangnam, Exit 8) FREE Spread over three floors, one of which is devoted to selling the latest lines of gadgets, this showroom showcases the technology of the Korean electronics giant Samsung, whose headquarters are in the same building. Whether you're a techno geek or not, it's fun to play around with the interactive displays and digital gizmos.

SEOUL ARTS CENTER — ARTS CENTRE

Map p228 (예술의전당, SAC; www.sac.or.kr; 2406 Nambusunhwan-ro, Seocho-gu; ⏲11am-8pm; ⓈLine 3 to Nambu Bus Terminal, Exit 5) FREE As well as being home to Seoul's premier concert halls (p115), this art centre also has three art galleries. **Seoul Calligraphy Museum** is devoted to hand-drawn *hangeul* (Korean phonetic alphabet) and Chinese characters, showcasing both traditional and contemporary examples of this art form. The **Hangaram Art Museum** is spread over four levels featuring rotating art shows, while **Hangaram Design Museum** has exhibits which focus on contemporary art and design.

To reach the complex, walk straight on from the subway exit and turn left at the end of the bus terminal, around a 15-minute walk – or jump in a taxi.

MUSEUM OF GUGAK — MUSEUM

Map p228 (☎02-580 3300; www.gugak.go.kr; 2364 Nambusunhwan-ro, Seocho-gu, National Gugak Center; ⏲9am-6pm Tue-Sun; ⓈLine 3 to Nambu Bus Terminal, Exit 5) FREE A part of the National Gugak Center (p115), this engaging museum covers *gugak* (traditional Korean music) with displays of Korean stringed instruments and unique drums among others that are rarely heard today. Some you're able to play, such as the Jeongak *gayaguem* (12-stringed zither dating from Joseon dynasty). It's a five-minute walk from Seoul Arts Center.

SEMA NAM SEOUL LIVING ARTS MUSEUM — GALLERY

(남서울생활미술관; www.sema.seoul.go.kr; 2076 Nambusunhwan-ro, Gwanak-gu; ⏲10am-8pm Tue-Fri, to 6pm Sat & Sun; ⓈLine 2 or 4 to Sadang, Exit 6) FREE Housed within a beautiful colonial building (c 1901) that was the former Belgian consulate, this branch of SEMA labels itself as a 'living arts museum' with changing exhibits that range from furniture to design and art installations.

NATIONAL MUSEUM OF MODERN AND CONTEMPORARY ART — MUSEUM

(MMCA; ☎02-2188 6000; www.moca.go.kr; Seoul Grand Park, Gwacheon; ⏲10am-6pm Tue-Fri & Sun, to 9pm Sat & Wed; ⓈLine 4 to Seoul Grand Park, Exit 4, then shuttle bus) FREE The best reason for making the trip out to Seoul Grand Park is to visit this large and striking museum spread out over three floors and surrounded by a sculpture garden. The dazzling highlight is Nam June Paik's *The More the Better*, an 18m-tall, pagoda-shaped video installation that uses 1000 flickering screens to make a comment on our increasingly electronic universe. Special exhibition entry costs vary.

GWACHEON NATIONAL SCIENCE MUSEUM — MUSEUM

(www.sciencecenter.go.kr; Seoul Grand Park, Gwacheon; adult/under 7yr/child ₩4000/free/2000, planetarium adult/child ₩2000/1000; ⏲9.30am-5.30pm Tue-Sun; ⓈLine 4 to Seoul Grand Park, Exit 6) While aimed at kids, this interactive science museum can be enjoyed by all. Set within a gigantic futuristic building, there are plenty of entertaining, hands-on exhibits that cover all aspects of science and technology; don't miss the hourly robot dance performing 'Gangnam Style'! Note that a lot of exhibits have limited capacity, so check upon arrival if you need a ticket, which are free inside. The traditional Korean **Science Hall** is also worth checking out for cultural insights.

There's an extra charge for the **planetarium shows** (in English at 11.30am). Outdoor exhibits include a **dinosaur park**.

SEOUL LAND — AMUSEMENT PARK

(☎02-509 6000; www.seoulland.co.kr; Seoul Grand Park, Gwacheon; day pass adult/child/youth

₩36,000/29,000/32,000; ⏲9.30am-10pm summer, to 6pm winter; Ⓢ Line 4 to Seoul Grand Park, Exit 2) Keep the children happy all day at this family amusement park with five themed areas, special shows and the main attraction: thrill rides and roller coasters that spin you like a top or drop you like a stone. Everland (p138) and Lotte World (p109) are better overall, but small kids will still be very happy here. It's near to Seoul Zoo, accessed via the **Elephant Tram Car** (adult/child ₩1000/7000) which links it with the subway.

EATING

COREANOS KITCHEN — MEXICAN $

Map p228 (www.coreanoskitchen.com; Basement, 25 Seolleung-ro 157-gil, Gangnam-gu; tacos from ₩3300, burritos from ₩9000; ⏲noon-11pm; 🗒; Ⓢ Bundang Line to Apgujeong Rodeo, Exit 5) What was originally a hipster food truck in Austin, USA, Coreanos (which is Spanish for 'Korean') brings its winning formula of *kimchi* tacos to Seoul. Tastes here are a fusion of authentic Mexican street food with Korean flavours, with its hand-pressed soft-corn tortilla tacos filled with anything from *galbi* (beef ribs) to *kimchi* pork belly. It also does *tortas* (sandwiches), burritos and craft beer. There's another branch in Itaewon (p100).

NONHYEON SAMGYETANG — KOREAN $

Map p228 (720 Eonju-ro, Gangnam-gu; mains ₩8000-18,000; ⏲24hr; Ⓢ Line 7 to Hak-dong, Exit 10) The original branch of this popular restaurant is a good place to sample Korean specialities such as *samgyetang* (ginseng chicken soup) or steaming bowls of hearty *juk* (rice porridge) done with seafood or vegetarian servings.

HA JUN MIN — KOREAN $

Map p228 (332 Apgujeong-ro, Gangnam-gu; buffet ₩8000; ⏲24hr; 🖉; Ⓢ Bundang Line to Apgujeong Rodeo, Exit 6) Keeping it real in the heart of ritzy Apgujeong Rodeo St, this long-established no-frills Korean restaurant offers amazing-value, all-you-can-eat dishes, including great vegetarian options. For BBQ it's ₩18,000, but you'll need two people. There's no English sign but it's 200m west across the road from Galleria.

LAY BRICKS — CAFE $

Map p228 (46 Nonhyeon-ro 153-gil, Gangnam-gu; ⏲11am-midnight Mon-Sat, from noon Sun; Ⓢ Line 3 to Sinsa, Exit 8) A popular hang-out with a passing array of characters – artists, models and hipsters – this industrial brick coffeehouse does a delicious *patbingsu* (red bean and fruit on milky shaved ice), particularly popular in summer, as well as sandwiches. It roasts its own coffee and has a decent selection of craft beer, too.

SEASONS TABLE — KOREAN, BUFFET $$

Map p230 (www.seasonstable.co.kr; Olympic Park; lunch weekday/weekend ₩13,900/22,900, dinner ₩22,900; ⏲10am-10.30pm; 🖉; Ⓢ Line 5 to Olympic Park, Exit 3) Located within the main Olympic Park gate, this earthy open-plan restaurant buzzes with diners here for excellent-value, all-you-can-eat Korean and fusion dishes. There's an excellent spread of traditional and seasonal-based dishes of grilled meats, stews, savoury pancakes and good vegetarian options.

GILBERT'S BURGERS & FRIES — BURGERS $$

Map p228 (47 Dosan-daero 15-gil, Gangnam-gu; burgers from ₩10,000; ⏲11am-10pm Mon-Thu, 11.30am-11pm Fri-Sun; Ⓢ Line 3 to Sinsa, Exit 8) From the moment those salivating aromas of sizzling burgers hit you, there's no return from this underground diner which is a homage to American food. Its signature burger is the well-stacked Mr President, which comes with a 7oz beef patty. Wash it down with a good choice of American craft beers and sodas.

★JUNGSIK — NEO-KOREAN $$$

Map p228 (정식당; ☎02-517 4654; http://jungsik.kr; 11 Seolleung-ro, 158-gil Gangnam-gu; 4-course lunch/dinner from ₩50,000/90,000; ⏲noon-3pm & 5.30-10.30pm; Ⓢ Bundang Line to Apgujeong Rodeo, Exit 4) Voted number 10 in Asia's 50 Best Restaurants in 2015; neo-Korean cuisine hardly gets better than this. At the Apgujeong outpost of the New York restaurant named after chef-owner Yim Jungsik, you can expect inspired and superbly presented contemporary mixes of traditional and seasonal ingredients over multiple courses. Book at least one month in advance.

★SAMWON GARDEN — KOREAN $$$

Map p228 (삼원가든; ☎02-548 3030; www.samwongarden.com; 835 Eonju-ro, Gangnam-gu; mains from ₩43,000; ⏲11.30am-10pm; Ⓢ Line 3 to Apgujeong, Exit 2) Serving top-class *galbi* for over 30 years, Samwon is a Korean idyll, surrounded by beautiful traditional gardens including several waterfalls. It's one of the best places in the city for this kind of barbecued-beef meal. There are also more inexpensive dishes such as *galbitang* (beef short rib soup) for ₩13,000.

HANMIRI NEO-KOREAN **$$$**

Map p228 (한미리; ☎02-569 7165; www.hanmiri.co.kr; Basement, Star Tower, 152 Teheran-ro, Gangnam-gu; set lunch/dinner from ₩33,000/45,000; ⊙noon-3pm & 6-8.30pm; Ⓢ Line 2 to Yeoksam, Exit 2) You'll be treated like royalty by *hanbok*-clad staff in this oasis of old-fashioned service and decor. The dozen well-presented dishes are modernised versions of royal cuisine. It's located downstairs in the basement of the Gangnam Finance Center within Star Tower, as part of a labryinthe upmarket food court.

QUEENS PARK INTERNATIONAL **$$$**

Map p228 (☎02-542 4073; www.queens-park.co.kr; 22 Apgujeong-ro 60-gil, Gangnam-gu; mains ₩19,000-50,000; ⊙10am-midnight Mon-Fri, from 8am Sat & Sun; Ⓢ Bundang Line to Apgujeong Rodeo, Exit 4) This is *the* place for fashionistas to see and be seen. Run by the bakery behemoth Paris Croissant, it has a classy bakery section and dining area with a soaring ceiling and great design. For late risers it's perfect as the brunch dishes, including an English breakfast, are available until 5.30pm.

DRINKING & NIGHTLIFE

★CLUB OCTAGON CLUB

Map p228 (www.cluboctagon.co.kr; 645 Nonhyeon-ro, Gangnam-gu; admission before 11pm & after 4am ₩10,000, after 11pm ₩30,000; ⊙Thu-Sat 10pm-6am; Ⓢ Line 7 to Hak-dong, Exit 4) Voted number six in the world's top clubs by *DJ Mag* in 2015, Octagon is one of Gangnam's best for serious clubbers. High-profile resident and guest DJs spin house and techno over its powerful Funktion 1 sound system to an appreciative crowd here to party till dawn.

NEURIN MAEUL BAR

Map p228 (느린마을; ☎02-587 7720; 7 Seocho-daero 73-gil, Seocho-gu; ⊙11am-11pm; Ⓢ Line 2 to Gangnam, Exit 9) FREE The Gangnam branch of this Baesangmyeon Brewery bar is a bit snazzier than others, but remains a good place to sample quality traditional Korean alcohol. Its signature Neurin Maeul *makgeolli* (milky rice wine) is the standout – it's divided into the four 'seasons', which refers to the differing production stages; you can sample each before ordering. You're likely to have to order food here.

Jugs cost ₩8000 per litre (or ₩3000 takeway). Sign up for its free membership to get two hours unlimited *makgeolli* for ₩10,000. There's another **branch** (느린마을; Map p216; ☎02-587 7720; Center 1, 26 Eulji-ro 5-gil, Jung-gu; ⊙11am-11pm; Ⓢ Line 2 to Euljiro 1-ga, Exit 3 or 4) in Myeong-dong.

BOOTH BAR

Map p228 (www.theboothpub.com; 2nd fl, 11 Gangnam-daero 53-gil, Seocho-gu; beer from ₩5000; ⊙11.30am-1am; Ⓢ Line 2 to Gangnam, Exit 5) A popular brew pub with its roots in Noksapyeong's Craft Beer Valley (p102), this Gangnam branch has several of its beers on tap, including its signature Bill's Pale Ale. It has a casual set-up of camping chairs, oil-drum tables and murals on the walls, and does pizza by the slice (₩4000).

GREENMILE COFFEE CAFE

Map p228 (www.facebook.com/greenmilecoffee; 11 Seolleung-ro 127-gil, Gangnam-gu; coffee from ₩3500; ⊙8am-9pm Mon-Fri; 📶; Ⓢ Line 7 to Gangnam-gu Office, Exit 2) Fitted out in designer furniture and caffeine-related paraphernalia, this cool little cafe is one of Seoul's best spots for coffee. It roasts all its single-origin beans on-site, sourced from Africa to Latin America. As well as the usual espresso, pour-overs and cold drip, it's also the proud owner of laboratory-like, halogen-powered equipment which does sensational siphon brews.

ELLUI CLUB

Map p230 (www.facebook.com/ellui.club; 551 Dosan-daero, Gangnam-gu; admission ₩30,000; ⊙10pm-8am Fri & Sat; Ⓢ Line 7 to Cheongdam, Exit 13) If you're going to visit just one mega-club in Gangnam, Ellui is the one. It's a massive space with a dazzling light-and-sound system and multiple dance floors.

PONGDANG MICROBREWERY

Map p228 (www.pongdangsplash.com; 49 Apgujeong-ro 2-gil, Gangnam-gu; ⊙5pm-1am Sun-Thu, 4pm-2am Fri & Sat; Ⓢ Line 3 to Sinsa, Exit 6) The original bar for this Korean microbrewery does a good selection of pale ales, Belgian and wheat beers, enjoyed at Pongdang's bar or tables surrounded by arcade machines.

MOON JAR
BAR

Map p228 (달빛술담; ☎02-541 6118; 38 Apgujeong-ro 46-gil, Gangnam-gu; 750ml makgeolli from ₩7000; ⏰5.30pm-2am; 📶; Ⓢ Line 3 to Apgujeong, Exit 3) Rustic charm meets Apgujeong chic at this convivial *makgeolli* bar and cafe spread over two floors. The menu has several different types of quality *makgeolli* served in kettles with the usual menu items such as *pajeon* (seafood pancakes).

SJ KUNSTHALLE
CLUB, BAR

Map p228 (☎010 2014 9722; http://sjkunsthalle.com; 5 Eonju-ro 148-gil; ⏰11am-1am Mon-Sat; 📶; Ⓜ Line 3 to Apgujeong, Exit 3) What's not to love about this bar/gallery/events space created like a giant's Lego set from old shipping containers. There's live music and a wide variety of other events. Opening hours vary, so check the website for upcoming events.

STEAMERS COFFEE FACTORY
CAFE

Map p228 (80 Dosan-daero 1-gil, Gangnam-gu; coffee ₩5000; ⏰8.30am-10pm Mon-Fri, from noon Sat; 📶; Ⓢ Line 3 to Sinsa, Exit 6) Bringing third-wave coffee to Seoul, Steamers does Ethiopian and Colombian single-origin brews in its shabby-chic industrial brick cafe.

MEAKJUGO
BAR

Map p228 (맥주고; 13 Gangnam-daero 96-gil, Gangnam-gu; ⏰5pm-2am; Ⓢ Line 2 to Gangnam, Exit 11) Translating to 'Beer High School', this basement craft beer bar is done up in the theme of a 1980s Korean classroom. Grab a desk, and order from its top range of draught and bottled craft beers. Visit midweek for all-you-can-drink craft beer (₩12,900, two hours).

CLUB MASS
CLUB

Map p228 (415 Gangnam-daero, Seocho-gu; weekday/weekends ₩10,000/20,000; ⏰9pm-6am Tue-Sun; Ⓢ Line 2 to Gangnam, Exit 5) One of Gangnam's original clubs, this huge basement space attracts a young, beautiful crowd here for techno and house, and a dazzling light show. It doesn't getting kicking till after 3am.

OKTOBERFEST
BEER HALL

Map p228 (옥토버페스트; ☎02-3481 8881; www.oktoberfest.co.kr; 12 Seocho-daero 73-gil, Seocho-gu; beers ₩4000; ⏰4pm-1am; Ⓢ Line 2 to Gangnam, Exit 9) It's much quieter than Oktoberfest at this long-running microbrewery, but the quality is good, serving up four freshly produced brews. It's in a large, bare-brick and natural-wood cellar bar with brewing equipment on display. German-style meats are served by frock-clad lasses.

TAKE URBAN
CAFE

Map p228 (테이크어반; ☎02-519 0001; www.takeurban.co.kr; 476 Gangnam-daero, Gangnam-gu; ⏰8am-midnight; Ⓢ Line 9 to Sinnonhyeon, Exit 3) On the ground floor of a building that looks like a giant concrete beehive is this sophisticated and spacious cafe, with indoor and outdoor options, heaps of designer-style, fresh bakery items and organic coffee.

☆ ENTERTAINMENT

★NATIONAL GUGAK CENTER
TRADITIONAL MUSIC

Map p228 (☎02-580 3300; www.gugak.go.kr; 2364, Nambusunhwan-ro, Seocho-gu; tickets from ₩10,000; Ⓢ Line 3 to Nambu Bus Terminal, Exit 5) Traditional Korean classical and folk music and dance are performed, preserved and taught at this centre, which is home to the Court Music Orchestra, the Folk Music Group, Dance Theater and Contemporary Gugak Orchestra. The main theatre, Yeakdang, puts on an ever-changing program by leading performers every Saturday, usually at 3pm.

SEOUL ARTS CENTER
PERFORMING ARTS

Map p228 (예술의전당, SAC; ☎02-580 1300; www.sac.or.kr; 2406 Nambusunhwan-ro, Seocho-gu; tickets from ₩10,000; Ⓢ Line 3 to Nambu Bus Terminal, Exit 5) The national ballet and opera companies are based at this sprawling arts complex, which includes a circular opera house with a roof shaped like a Korean nobleman's hat. It also houses a concert hall and a smaller recital hall in which the national choir, the Korea and Seoul symphony orchestras and drama companies stage shows.

There are regular free shows, which are held at weekends on the outdoor stage. Check the website for the extensive program.

LG ARTS CENTER
PERFORMING ARTS

Map p228 (☎02-2005 0114; www.lgart.com; 508 Nonhyeon-ro, Gangnam-gu; Ⓢ Line 2 to Yeoksam, Exit 7) Major local and international artists and companies perform at this multihall, state-of-the-art venue.

COSMETIC SURGERY

In a city that has one of the highest rates per capita in the world for cosmetic surgery, nowhere is this industry more visible than downtown Gangnam. As you stroll along Apgujeong-ro and Dosan-daero in Sinsa-dong, you'll find the streets lined with hundreds of boutique clinics, surgeries and high-rise medical centres that all specialise in plastic surgery. The sight of postoperative patients walking around in sunglasses with bruised, busted up faces is not uncommon.

While estimates from the BBC have reported around 50% of Korean women in their 20s having received work, it's an industry that also caters to an international clientele. Around one-third of patients are from abroad, mainly Chinese, Japanese and Russian. It's an industry not lost on the tourism department, which has set up the Gangnam Medical Tour Center. Sharing space with the main tourist office in Gangnam, not only does it produce shelfloads of leaflets listing medical centres, but also interactive features where you can get a range of 'before' and 'after' photos, as well as have your skin analysed, which will give you a rundown on your flaws and the work you need to have done.

The Korean Wave pop phenomenon seems to have had a negative influence in shaping the public consciousness about what defines beauty. Sadly this has seen not only the standard nip, tucks and implants, but more disturbing trends such as the double eye lift widening to create a more Westernised appearance.

ONCE IN A BLUE MOON — JAZZ

Map p228 (원스인어블루문; ☎02-549 5490; www.onceinabluemoon.co.kr; 824 Seolleung-ro, Gangnam-gu; ⏰6pm-1am; Ⓢ Bundang Line to Apgujeong Rodeo, Exit 4) FREE An intimate and classy club with live jazz from two groups of performers every night, each playing two sets between 7.30pm and 12.30am.

SHOPPING

★10 CORSO COMO SEOUL — FASHION

Map p228 (www.10corsocomo.co.kr; 416 Apgujeong-ro, Gangnam-gu; ⏰11am-8pm; Ⓢ Bundang Line to Apgujeong Rodeo, Exit 3) Inspired by its shopping complex in Milan, this outpost of the fashion and lifestyle boutique is about as interesting as Gangnam retail can get. The blend of fashion, art and design includes several local designers. There's also a brilliant selection of international books and CDs to browse, and a chic cafe for an espresso or glass of wine.

COEX MALL — MALL

Map p230 (☎02-6002 5300; www.coexmall.com; 513 Yeongdongdae-ro, Gangnam-gu; ⏰10am-10pm; Ⓢ Line 2 to Samseong, COEX Exit) One of Seoul's premier malls, the shiny COEX is a vast maze of department stores loaded with shops selling fashion, lifestyle, accessories and electronics, as well as a multiplex cinema and aquarium (p110). It's also a launching point to the airport (p185), and has several hotels.

GALLERIA — DEPARTMENT STORE

Map p228 (☎02-344 9414; http://dept.galleria.co.kr; Apgujeong-ro, Gangnam-gu; ⏰10.30am-8pm; Ⓢ Bundang Line to Apgujeong Rodeo, Exit 7) Department stores in Seoul don't get more luxurious than this. If you want to play Audrey Hepburn staring wistfully into Tiffany's, don a Helen Kaminski hat, try on a Stella McCartney dress or slip into a pair of Jimmy Choos, the east wing of fashion icon Galleria is the place to be.

Dozens of top fashion-designer stores are packed into the two Galleria buildings, the west wing of which is covered in glass discs that turn psychedelic at night.

GAROSU-GIL — STREET

Map p228 (Ⓢ Line 3 to Apgujeong, Exit 5) One of Gangnam's most famous strips, this tree-lined street is worth a stroll for brand-name stores and cute fashion boutiques, plus art galleries, restaurants and cafes.

HYUNDAI DEPARTMENT STORE — DEPARTMENT STORE

Map p228 (www.ehyundai.com/lang/en/index.do; 65 Apgujeong-ro, Gangnam-gu; ⏰10.30am-8pm; Ⓢ Line 3 to Apgujeong, Exit 6) Hyundai is a classy department store in Apgujeong where you're greeted by uniformed doormen that exude old-fashioned elegance circa 1920s New York. It's mostly about high-end fashion and accessories, including Korean designers on the 3rd floor.

BOON THE SHOP — CLOTHING

Map p228 (☎02-2056 1228; www.boontheshop.com; 17 Apgujeong-ro 60-gil, Gangnam-gu; SBundang Line to Apgujeong Rodeo, Exit 4) There are two close-by branches of this multibrand boutique that's a byword for chic, high-end fashion. The original, worth a look if only for its gorgeous sculpture of a giant string of pearls hanging in the midst of an atrium, is the women's store. It stocks mainly exclusive niche designer brands from overseas; if you need to ask the price you can't afford to shop here.

The men's **store** (Map p228; www.boontheshop.com; 21 Apgujeong-ro 60-gil; SBundang Line to Apgujeong Rodeo, Exit 3) is a two-minute walk around the corner.

LOTTE WORLD MALL — MALL

Map p230 (www.lwt.co.kr/en/main.do; 300 Olympic-ro, Songpa-gu; ⏲10.30am-10pm; SLine 2 or 8 to Jamsil, Exit 1) At the base of Korea's tallest building lies its largest shopping mall, comprising six floors of luxury and duty-free department stores, a mega cinema complex, concert hall and aquarium. There's also a department store at the nearby amusement park (p109).

BOY+ BY SUPERMARKET — FASHION

Map p228 (16 Seolleung-ro 157-gil, Gangnam-gu; ⏲11am-10pm; SBundang Line to Apgujeong Rodeo, Exit 5) A clothing shop in Apgujeong that's not haute couture, this unisex store does affordable and wearable street fashion by mostly K-designers.

PUNGWOLDANG — MUSIC

Map p228 (www.pungwoldang.kr; 4th fl, 39 Dosan-daero 53-gil, Gangnam-gu; ⏲noon-9pm Mon-Sat; SBundang Line to Apgujeong Rodeo, Exit 5) One for lovers of classical music, this art nouveau–styled CD and DVD shop has an attached cafe where you can sip a free coffee.

SPORTS & ACTIVITIES

The designated bike paths along the Han River are wonderful spots to cycle. There are several spots south of the river where you can hire bikes, including from the free stall at Jamsil subway (p42).

SEOUL SPORTS COMPLEX — STADIUM

Map p230 (서울종합운동장, Jamsil Sports Complex; ☎02-2240 8800; http://stadium.seoul.go.kr; 10 Jamsil-dong, Songpa-gu; tickets from ₩7000; SLine 2 or 8 to Sports Complex, Exit 6) Even if you're not a baseball fan it's worth coming along to **Jamsil Baseball Stadium** (admission ₩15,000-25,000), part of the Seoul Sports Complex, for a game for its raucous atmosphere and off-field entertainment such as K-Pop cheerleaders. Also here is **Olympic Stadium**, which is used for major concerts.

SPA LEI — SPA

Map p228 (스파레이; ☎02-545 4121; www.spalei.co.kr; Cresyn Bldg, 5 Gangnam-daero 107-gil, Seocho-gu; admission ₩14,000, massage from ₩30,000; ⏲24hr; SLine 3 to Sinsa, Exit 5) Luxurious women-only spa providing excellent services in an immaculate, stylish environment. Staff are helpful and used to dealing with foreigners.

KUKKIWON — TAEKWONDO

Map p228 (국기원(세계태권도본부); ☎02-567 1058; www.kukkiwon.or.kr; 32 Teheran-ro 7-gil, Gangnam-gu; ⏲office 9am-5pm Mon-Fri; SLine 2 to Gangnam, Exit 12) There's no better place to watch Korea's very own home-grown martial arts than here at the world headquarters for taekwondo. It hosts a regular schedule of taekwondo displays, training courses and tournaments. Call ahead to see when you might be able to see a training session. Also check out its museum while you're here.

GANGNAM CITY TOUR — BUS TOUR

(☎02-3448 5519; www.gangnamtour.go.kr; adult/child/youth ₩7000/5000/6000; ⏲10am-8pm) A hop-on, hop-off trolley-bus tour divided into two routes that covers Gangnam district's main sights.

Dongdaemun & Eastern Seoul

Neighbourhood Top Five

❶ Uncover layers of Seoul's history, from its foundation as the capital of the Joseon dynasty to its 21st-century incarnation, at the **Dongdaemun Design Plaza & Park** (p120).

❷ Cruise the malls and buzzing streets of **Dongdaemun Market** (p123) into the early hours of the morning.

❸ Cycle around **Seoul Forest** (p121), past the wetlands, the riverside and Sika deer.

❹ Explore the **Seoul Art Space Sindang** (p121) in the underground arcade beneath Jungang Market.

❺ Learn about your yin and yang and the traditional Korean approach to medicine at the **Seoul Yangnyeongsi Herb Medicine Museum** (p121).

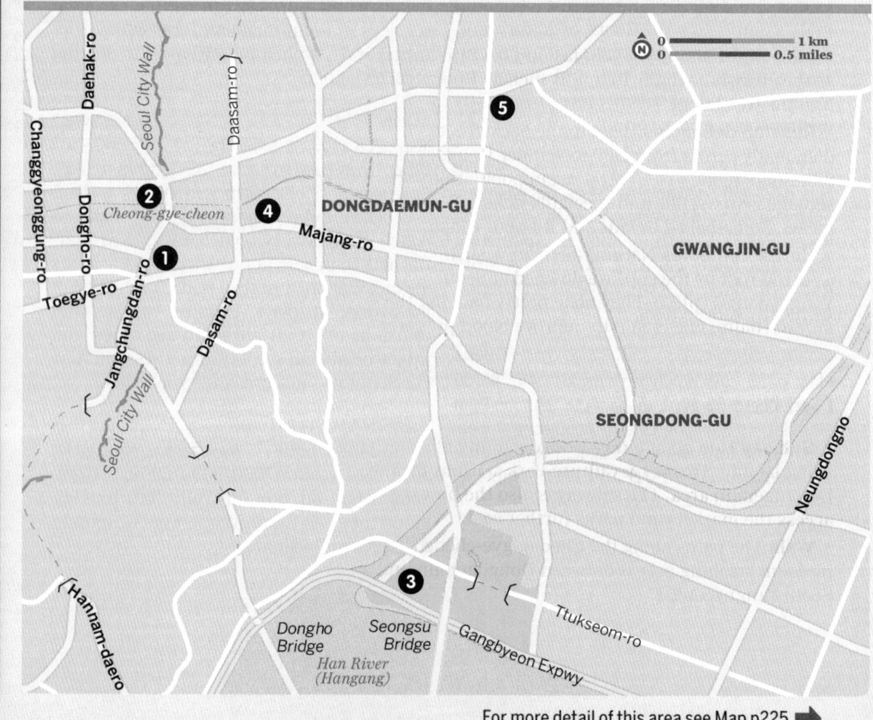

For more detail of this area see Map p225 ➡

Explore Dongdaemun & Eastern Seoul

Taking its name from the Great East Gate (Heunginjimun) to the city, Dongdaemun – an area synonymous with shopping for centuries in Seoul – is now famous for the Zaha Hadid–designed Dongdaemun Design Plaza & Park (DDP), an architectural showpiece so complex that it wasn't ready in time for Seoul's stint as World Design Capital in 2010.

With the DDP now fully formed, it's fascinating to explore the ribbon of indoor markets that stretch around it and along either side of Cheong-gye-cheon, spilling out into side streets where you can find anything and everything from succulents and sewing-machine parts to every hue of zipper and variety of *kimchi*. Much of the action is wholesale, with traders haggling over deals until the break of dawn, but there's also plenty of retail, particularly in fashion goods.

Further east there are more interesting markets to discover, including ones devoted to herbal medicines, antiques and secondhand goods. A couple of big green spaces – Seoul Forest Park and the Children's Grand Park – provide natural relief from the commercial activity.

Local Life

- **Late-night shopping** Join fashion bargain-hunters as they trawl the high-rise malls such as Doota (p123) into the wee hours.
- **Russian delicacies** Head to the backstreets diagonally across from DPP to wander Dongdaemun's Silk Road, home to a Central Asian population, where signage is in Cyrillic and speciality delis sell smoked meats, home-baked breads and Russian vodka.
- **Herbal remedies** Natural medicines, such as arrowroot by the cup, are downed at Seoul Yangnyeongsi (p123). They taste pretty bad, but the *maesil* (plum) one is said to improve blood pressure.

Getting There & Away

- **Subway** Hop off at either Dongdaemun or Dongdaemun History & Culture Park stations for the Dongdaemun area. The subway is also the best way to access the markets and parks further east.
- **Walk** The paths along the Cheong-gye-cheon provide pleasant strolling access between Dongdaemun and Seoul Yangnyeongsi.

Lonely Planet's Top Tip

Gwangjang Market isn't just a great place for food, its upstairs arcade in the northwestern corner is packed with stalls selling secondhand and vintage clothing.

Best Parks

- Seoul Forest (p121)
- Children's Grand Park (p121)

For reviews, see p121

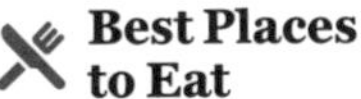

Best Places to Eat

- Gwangjang Market (p122)
- Samarkand (p122)
- Woo Rae Oak (p122)

For reviews, see p122

Best Places to Shop

- Seoul Folk Flea Market (p123)
- Dongdaemun Market (p123)
- Doota (p123)

For reviews, see p123

TOP SIGHT
DONGDAEMUN DESIGN PLAZA & PARK

Seoul's striking contemporary masterpiece, the DDP is a showcase for Korean and international design. As well as its silver futuristic-looking building with its streamlined free-flowing curves, it's a creative hub and cultural space home to galleries, event halls and design studios. Attached is Dongdaemun History & Culture Park with several museums that highlight past uses of this area, including a a 16th-century military camp and baseball stadium. Tours of the complex can be arranged by calling ahead.

Architecture & Exhibitions

Dongdaemun Design Plaza is architect Zaha Hadid's sleek concept, a curvaceous concrete structure with a silvery sci-fi facade. Covered in 45,000 aluminium panels, it's fitted with LED lights that pulsate meditatively at night. Its undulating layout leads to public spaces, convention centres and an underground plaza as well as lawns that rise up on to its roof.

The interior of this cultural complex is equally impressive. Its amorphous structure is filled with floors of galleries, exhibition spaces, design shops and studios interconnected by long flowing pathways and sculpted staircases. Ticket prices for exhibitions range from free to ₩10,000.

Dongdaemun History & Culture Park

During the site's excavation, major archaeological remains from the Joseon dynasty were uncovered, including original sections of Seoul's City Wall. The remains have been incorporated into the park and include the arched floodgate **Yigansumun**. The **Dongdaemun History Museum** (⌚10am-7pm) FREE imaginatively displays the pick of the 2575 artefacts from the site and provides the historical background to the ancient foundations preserved outside. Look for the patterned section of pavement made from clay tiles.

The **Dongdaemun Stadium Memorial** (⌚10am-9pm) FREE relives key moments from the stadium's history. Built by the Japanese in 1925, it was used primarily for soccer and baseball matches until it was demolished in 2007. Several of the stadium floodlights remain standing.

DON'T MISS

- Dongdaemun Design Plaza
- Dongdaemun History Museum
- Dongdaemun Stadium Memorial
- Dongdaemun History & Culture Park

PRACTICALITIES

- DDP, 동대문디자인플라자
- Map p225
- ☎02-2153 0408
- www.ddp.or.kr
- 28 Eulji-ro, Jung-gu
- ⌚10am-7pm Tue, Thu, Sat & Sun, to 9pm Wed & Fri
- S Line 2, 4 or 5 to Dongdaemun History & Culture Park, Exit 1

SIGHTS

DONGDAEMUN DESIGN PLAZA & PARK — CULTURAL CENTRE

See p120.

HEUNGINJIMUN — GATE

Map p225 (Dongdaemun; S Line 1 or 4 to Dongdaemun, Exit 6) The Great East Gate to Seoul's City Wall has been rebuilt several times in its 700-year history and, after recent renovations, today it's looking majestic. Stranded in a traffic island, it's not possible to enter inside the gate; but there are plenty of good photo ops from Naksan Park.

SEOUL CITY WALL MUSEUM — MUSEUM

Map p225 (한양도성박물관; ☎02-724 0243; http://seoulcitywall.seoul.go.kr; 283 Yulgok-ro, Jongno-gu; ⏲9am-7pm Tue-Sun; S Line 1 or 4 to Dongdaemun, Exit 1) FREE On the Naksan Park hill overlooking Heunginjimun (Dongdaemun), near a stretch of the City Wall, this modern museum offers an engaging history of the 18.6km-long wall that surrounds the city. There are plenty of high-tech interactive displays, combined with artefacts from the original wall and a model of Sungnyemun gate built from Lego.

Originally built in the 14th century, with many sections rebuilt several times since, the city wall continues to be restored by the city, which is aiming to have it inscribed on Unesco's World Heritage list.

SEOUL ART SPACE SINDANG — GALLERY

Map p225 (http://http://english.sfac.or.kr/html/artspace/sindang_intro.asp; Sindang Underground Shopping Center, 87 Majang-ro, Jung-gu; ⏲10am-6pm; S Line 2 to Sindang, Exit 1 or 2) FREE In the underground arcade that runs beneath the Jungang Market (p122), this collection of design and art studios has popped up in unoccupied shops. A part of a citywide project to foster up-and-coming artists, sections of the arcade itself have been turned into a gallery of the artists' work, which shares space with raw-seafood restaurants.

CHEONGGYECHEON MUSEUM — MUSEUM

(청계천박물관; ☎02-2286 3434; www.cgcm.go.kr; 530, Cheonggyecheon-ro, Seongdong-gu; ⏲9am-7pm Tue-Sun; S Line 2 to Yongdu, Exit 5) FREE To fully comprehend what a mammoth and expensive effort it was to resurrect Seoul's long-covered-over Cheong-gye-cheon, pay a visit to this well-designed museum about the stream. It's a good starting point for a walk along the riverside park. Across from here is the **Cardboard House museum** (Cheonggyecheon-ro, Seongdong-gu; ⏲10am-8pm Tue-Sun; S Line 2 to Yongdu, Exit 5) FREE, a wooden shack that was typical of the slum houses that used to line the river back in the 1950s. It displays paraphernalia of Seoul dating from this period of time.

SEOUL YANGNYEONGSI HERB MEDICINE MUSEUM — MUSEUM

(서울약령시 한의약박물관; ☎02-3293 4900; http://museum.ddm.go.kr; B2 Donguibogam Tower, 128 Wangsan-ro, Dongdaemun-gu; ⏲10am-6pm Tue-Sun; S Line 1 to Jeji-dong, Exit 3) FREE Learn about the history and practice of traditional Korean medicine at this imaginative museum. The displays have plenty of English, and the kind ladies here will give you herbal tea and allow you to work out which of the four Sasang constitutions you have. To get here take a left at the subway and look for the building with a big Korean flag on it; it's located a bit back of this. Across the road is the Seoul Yangnyeongsi Herb Medicine Market (p123).

SEOUL FOREST — PARK

(서울숲; http://parks.seoul.go.kr; 685 Seongsu 1-ga 1-dong, Seongdong-gu; ⏲24hr, rental stall 9am-10pm; S Bundang Line 2 to Seoul Forest, Exit 2) FREE A hunting ground in Joseon times, this park makes for a very pleasant area to enjoy some time in natural surroundings. It's big, so to see it all it's best to hire a bicycle (₩3000 per 1½ hours) or a pair of rollerblades (₩4000 per hour) from the rental stall by Gate 2 across from Seoul Forest subway. Among the trees and lakes are deer enclosures, eco areas, an insect exhibition, a plant nursery and fountains. It's a lovely spot for a picnic.

CHILDREN'S GRAND PARK — PARK

(서울 어린이대공원; ☎02-450 9311; www.childrenpark.or.kr; 216 Neungdong-ro, Gwangjin-gu; amusement park rides ₩4000; ⏲5am-10pm, amusement park 9am-5pm, zoo 10am-6pm; 👪; S Line 5 or 7 to Children's Grand Park, Exit 1) FREE Let your little ones run wild in this enormous playground, which includes amusement rides, a zoo, botanical garden, wetland eco area and a giant musical fountain.

WORTH A DETOUR

ROYAL TOMBS OF THE JOSEON DYNASTY

The 40-odd royal tombs of the Joseon dynasty are World Heritage listed and scattered across Seoul and Gyeonggi-do with a couple also in the North Korean city of Kaesong. In these tombs are buried every Joseon ruler right up to the last, Emperor Sunjong (r 1907–10). The most central tomb in Seoul is Seonjeongneun (p110).

Further afield is **Donggureung** (동구릉; http://jikimi.cha.go.kr/english; adult/child ₩1000/500; ⌚6am-5pm Tue-Sun) in Guri, around 20km northeast of central Seoul. It's the largest and most attractive of the tomb complexes. Here lie seven kings and 10 queens, including the dynasty's founder King Taejo: in contrast to the other neatly clipped plots in this leafy park, his mound sprouts rushes from his home town of Hamhung (now in North Korea) that – in accordance with the king's predeath instructions – have never been cut. To reach the complex take subway Line 2 to Gangbyeon to connect with bus 1, 1-1 or 1115-6, around a two-hour trip from central Seoul.

EATING

★**GWANGJANG MARKET** KOREAN $

(광장시장; Kwangjang; www.kwangjangmarket.co.kr; 88 Changgyeonggung-ro, Jongno-gu; dishes ₩4000-10,000; ⌚8.30am-10pm; Ⓢ Line 1 to Jongno-5ga, Exit 8, or Line 2 or 5 to Euljiro 4-ga, Exit 4) Best known as Seoul's largest *meokjagolmok* (food alley), the Gwangjang Market is home to some 200 stalls set up among *kimchi* and fresh-seafood vendors. Its speciality is the golden fried *nokdu bindaetteok* (mung-bean pancake; ₩5000) – paired beautifully with *makgeolli* (milky rice wine).

JUNGANG MARKET MARKET $

Map p225 (서울중앙시장; 87 Majang-ro, Jung-gu; dishes from ₩6000; ⌚noon-4pm Mon-Sat; Ⓢ Line 2 to Sindang, Exit 1 or 2) One of Seoul's traditional arcade markets, Jungang Market is very much a local affair with vendors selling street food, *kimchi* and fresh produce. Seafood is a speciality here, from *samchi* (grilled Spanish mackerel) and *haemul pajeon* (seafood pancake) to raw fish dishes in the underground arcade section – where you can also check out Seoul Art Space Sindang (p121).

DONGDAEMUN MARKET MARKET $

Map p225 (동대문시장; dishes from ₩6000; ⌚10am-10pm; Ⓢ Line 1 or 4 to Dongdaemun, Exit 8) Within the Dongdaemun Shopping Complex of the main market, here there's an excellent choice of street food from vendors to small restaurants, including several that specialise in charcoal BBQ *samchi*.

WOO RAE OAK NOODLES, BARBECUE $$

(우래옥; ☎02-2265 0151; 62-29 Changgyeonggung-ro, Jung-gu; mains ₩11,000-43,000; ⌚11.30am-10pm; 📋; Ⓢ Line 2 or 4 to Euljiro 4ga, Exit 4) Tucked away in the sewing-machine-parts section of Dongdaemun's sprawling market streets is this elegant old-timer specialising in *bulgogi* and *galbi* (barbecued beef; from ₩29,000, could feed two). But its delicious *naengmyeon* (buckwheat cold noodles) make the best lunch paired with delicious *kimchi*.

SAMARKAND CENTRAL ASIAN $$

Map p225 (사마르칸트; 159-10 Mareunnae-ro, Jung-gu; mains from ₩8000; ⌚10am-11pm; Ⓢ Line 2, 4 or 5 to Dongdaemun, Exit 12) This family-run Uzbekistan restaurant is a part of Dongdaemun's 'Little Silk Road', an intriguing district that's home to a community of Russian-speaking traders from the 'Stans, Mongolia and Russia. It has delicious halal home cooking, including lamb shashlik that goes beautifully with fresh *lepeshka* bread and Russian beer. The area is worth a look around; signage is in Cyrillic.

DRINKING & NIGHTLIFE

HIDDEN TRACK MICROBREWERY

(숨겨진음악; www.facebook.com/hiddentrack; 6 Yangnyeongsi-ro, Dongdaemun-gu; beers from ₩5000; ⌚6pm-1am Mon-Sat; Ⓢ Line 6 to Anam, Exit 3) Set up by the BBB Brewing Company, this basement pub serves five of its own beers on tap including the signature India Pale Ale (IPA) and a few German-style beers. The brewing vats sit behind the bar. It's a 10-minute walk south from Anam subway, located just off the roundabout.

ENTERTAINMENT

KLIVE LIVE PERFORMANCE

Map p225 (☎02-2265 0810; www.klive.co.kr; 9th fl, Lotte Fitin Bldg, 264 Eulji-ro, Jung-gu; adult/child ₩33,000/16,000; ⊙shows 2pm, 4pm, 6pm & 8pm Tue-Sun; S Line 2, 4 or 5 to Dongdaemun History & Culture Park, Exit 11) One for the K-Pop fans, with nightly concerts using state-hologram technology with scarily real effects. It's all in Korean, but there are English subtitles.

SHOPPING

DONGDAEMUN MARKET MARKET

Map p225 (동대문시장; Dongdaemun; ⊙7-10pm Mon-Sat; S Line 1 or 4 to Dongdaemun, Exit 8) Take Seoul's commercial pulse at this colossal retail and wholesale market. It sprawls across a wide area on both sides of the Cheong-gye-cheon. On one side is the multilevel **Pyoung Hwa Clothing Market** (평화시장), crammed with stalls selling wholesale clothing and accessories. The other side of the stream is **Dongdaemun Shopping Complex** (⊙9am-6pm Mon-Sat), with a more eclectic range of goods, plus atmospheric food alleys.

The bargaining never stops. The wholesale clothing sections operate mainly through the night, but even during the day it's a buzz to wander the network of buildings and streets. You can buy practically anything, although it's mainly clothing that drags in the punters, though don't expect any high standard of fashion. And while there are plenty of bargains, you often need to buy in bulk.

DOOTA DEPARTMENT STORE

Map p225 (☎02-3398 3114; www.doota.com; 275 Jangchungdan-ro, Jung-gu; ⊙10.30am-midnight Sun-Thu, to 5am Fri & Sat; S Line 2, 4 or 5 to Dongdaemun History & Culture Park) Cut through Dongdaemun's commercial frenzy by heading to its leading fashion mall full to the brim with domestic brands. Ten floors above and below ground are dedicated to clothing, accessories, beauty items and souvenirs. When you start flagging, there are plenty of cafes and a good food court on the 7th floor.

SEOUL FOLK FLEA MARKET MARKET

(서울풍물시장; 19-3 Cheonho-daero 4-gil, Dongdaemun-gu; ⊙10am-7pm, closed 2nd & 4th Tue of month; S Line 1 or 2 to Sinseol-dong, Exit 6 or 10) Spilling out of a two-storey building into the surrounding area, here you'll find a fascinating collection of artworks, collectables and general bric-a-brac from wooden masks and ink drawings to Beatles LPs and valve radios.

GWANGJANG MARKET CLOTHING

(광장시장; 2nd & 3rd fl, West Gate 2, 88, Changgyeonggung-ro, Jongno-gu; ⊙10am-7pm Mon-Sat, from 11am Sun; S Line 1 to Jongno 5-ga, Exit 8, or Line 2 or 5 to Euljiro 4-ga, Exit 4) As well as the food and fabrics sold here, head upstairs for vintage clothing stalls. There's the usual flannel shirts, vintage dresses, army jackets, sunglasses and Doc Martens, mixed in with some local fashion. Access is by the stairs to the upper floor outside exit 2.

SEOUL YANGNYEONGSI HERB MEDICINE MARKET TRADITIONAL MEDICINE

(www.seoulya.com; Jegi-dong; ⊙9am-7pm; S Line 1 to Jegi-dong, Exit 2) Also known as Gyeongdong Market, Korea's biggest Asian medicine market runs several blocks back from the traditional gate on the main road and includes thousands of clinics, retailers, wholesalers and medicine makers. If you're looking for a leaf, herb, bark, root, flower or mushroom to ease your ailment, it's bound to be here.

DAPSIMNI ANTIQUES MARKET ANTIQUES

(⊙10am-6pm Mon-Sat; S Line 5 to Dapsimni, Exit 2) One for serious collectors, this sprawling collection of antique shops is spread over three separate precincts. Here you can browse through old dusty treasures – from *yangban* (aristocrat) pipes and horsehair hats to wooden shoes, fish-shaped locks and embroidered status insignia – dating anywhere from 100 to 600 years old.

At the subway exit walk over to the orange-tiled Samhee 6 building behind the car park. A similar arcade on the left is Samhee 5. After visiting them, walk back to Exit 2 and go left along the main road for 10 minutes to reach a brown-tiled arcade, Janganpyeong, with another section behind it.

SPORTS & ACTIVITIES

JANGCHUNG GYMNASIUM STADIUM

Map p225 (장충체육관; ☎02-2236 4197; http://new.sisul.or.kr/global/main/en/sub/gymnasium.jsp; 241 Dongho-ro, Jung-gu; S Line 3 to Dongguk University, Exit 5) Major *ssireum* (Korean wrestling) competitions are held at this 7000-seat indoor arena, which looks like a huge cooking pot.

Northern Seoul

Neighbourhood Top Five

1. Hike up **Bukaksan** (p132), the tallest of Seoul's four guardian mountains, following an intact and heavily guarded section of the city's original fortress walls.

2. Admire the traditional buildings and elegant furnishings at the **Korea Furniture Museum** (p126).

3. Learn about the horrors of the Japanese colonial period at the **Seodaemun Prison History Hall** (p129).

4. Meditate at a templestay at serene **Gilsang-sa** (p129) in leafy Seongbuk-dong.

5. Witness ancient shamanistic ceremonies at **Inwangsan Guksadang** (p130).

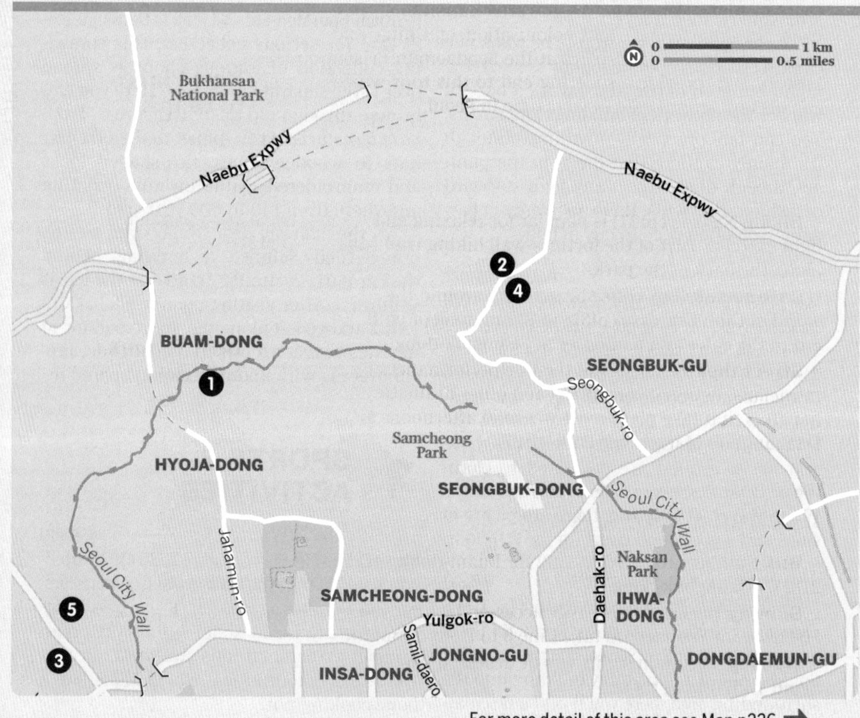

For more detail of this area see Map p226

Explore: Northern Seoul

The city's northern districts seldom figure prominently on international tourist itineraries, which is a pity as they are home to some of Seoul's most charming neighbourhoods and some fascinating sights, including the best sections of the old fortress walls. Start exploring in the university district of Daehangno, a performing-arts hub with some 150 theatres ranging from intimate fringe-style venues to major auditoriums such as the Arko Art Theater.

Hike to Naksan Park and follow the wall northwest over to Seongbuk-dong, a leafy mountainside community known as the Beverly Hills of Seoul because of its grand mansions, many of them home to ambassadors and CEOs. Here you'll find the outstanding Korea Furniture Museum and serene Buddhist temple Gilsang-sa.

It's a stiff climb, but views of the city from the summit of Bukaksan repay the effort of getting there. Come down to Buam-dong, where the high-security trappings of the mountain overlooking the presidential compound are replaced by relaxed teahouses, cafes and galleries.

Continue following the walls to the summit of Inwangsan with its weirdly eroded rocks, temples and Guksadang shrine. The area has a special atmosphere because of the outdoor shamanist ceremonies that invoke the spirits of the departed. At the foot of the mountain is the large Seodaemun Independence Park, with monuments that celebrate Korea's march towards nationhood, free from the interference and colonisation of China and Japan. The haunting displays at the Seodaemun Prison History Hall provide a sobering end to this tour which can occupy several days of your time in Seoul.

Local Life

- **Hiking** Naksan (p127) is popular for relaxing and light exercise. Part of the fortress-wall hiking trail runs along the back of the park.
- **Cafe society** Buy coffee beans from around the world at Club Espresso (p132) in Buam-dong or chill out in the cafes and teahouses of Seongbuk-dong.
- **Street theatre** Check out the free performances by musicians, dancers, comedians and other dramatic hopefuls that take place most weekend afternoons at Daehangno's Marronnier Park (p127).

Getting There & Away

- **Bus** Numbers 1020, 7022, 7212 for Buam-dong, 1111 or 2112 for Seongbuk-dong.
- **Subway** Daehangno is easily accessed by Line 4 to Hyehwa; for Seodaemun take Line 3 to Dongnimmun.
- **Walking** The main sights can be accessed from the Seoul Wall hiking route.

Lonely Planet's Top Tip

For info on what's showing at the scores of venues in Daehangno, and discounts on tickets of up to 50%, go to the **Theatre Ticket Office** (Map p226; Marronnier Park, 104 Daehak-ro, Jongno-gu; ⌚11am-8pm Tue-Sat, to 7pm Sun; **S** Line 4 to Hyehwa, Exit 2) or the **Seoul Theater Center** (Map p226; www.e-stc.or.kr; 3 Daemyeong-gil, Jongno-gu; ⌚1-8pm Tue-Fri, 11am-8pm Sat, 11am-7pm Sun; **S** Line 4 to Hyehwa, Exit 4).

Best Places to Eat

- Jaha Sonmandoo (p130)
- Deongjang Yesool (p130)
- Serious Deli (p130)

For reviews, see p130 ➡

Best Places to Drink

- Mix & Malt (p131)
- Dallyeora Gaemi 1 (p131)
- Suyeon Sanbang (p131)

For reviews, see p131 ➡

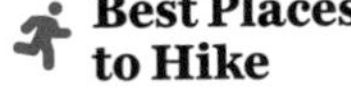

Best Places to Hike

- Bukaksan (p132)
- Inwangsan (p132)
- Ansan (p132)

For reviews, see p132 ➡

TOP SIGHT
KOREA FURNITURE MUSEUM

Almost as exclusive as its hillside location in leafy Seongbuk-dong, this architecture and traditional furniture museum is a gem in which 10 beautiful buildings serve as the appetiser to the main course: a collection of furniture, including chests, bookcases, chairs and dining tables made from varieties of wood, such as persimmon, maple and paulownia, some decorated with lacquer, mother-of-pearl or tortoise shell.

Buildings & Gardens

The museum is the personal project of a former Yonsei University professor who has amassed some 2500 pieces, of which around 500 are on show at any one time. Equally impressive is the compound's collection of wooden buildings, such as the **kitchen house** with its seemingly contemporary design of windows, as well as a **villa** that was once part of Changdeokgung. The **panoramic views** from the gardens and inside the buildings are also lovely.

There are plans to add a boutique-style hotel to the compound and create a cluster of nearby museums, each dedicated to different Korean traditional crafts.

Visiting the Museum

Advance reservations are required for the hour-long guided tours of the compound.

The easiest way to get here is to take a taxi from the subway exit.

DON'T MISS

- Furniture collection
- Kitchen house
- Villa from Changdeokgung

PRACTICALITIES

- 한국가구박물관
- ☎02-745 0181
- www.kofum.com
- 121 Daesagwan-ro, Seongbuk-gu
- tour without/with tea ₩20,000/40,000
- ⌚11am-5pm Mon-Sat
- Ⓢ Line 4 to Hangsung University, Exit 6

SIGHTS

CHANGGYEONGGUNG PALACE

Map p226 (창경궁, Palace of Flourishing Gladness; ☎02-762 4868; http://english.cha.go.kr; 185 Changgyeonggung-ro, Jongno-gu; adult/child ₩1000/500; ⏲9am-6.30pm Tue-Sun; Ⓢ Line 4 to Hyehwa, Exit 4) Originally built in the early 15th century by King Sejong for his parents, the oldest surviving structure of this palace is the **Okcheongyo** stone bridge (1483) over the stream by the main gate. The main hall, 1616 **Myeongjeongjeon** (Map p226), has lovely latticework and an ornately carved and decorated ceiling.

Look out for dates (usually in early May) when the palace is open for night viewing and illuminated, making it a romantic spot – if you can ignore the crowds.

The stone markers in the front courtyard show where the different ranks of government officials had to stand during major state ceremonies.

The smaller buildings behind the main hall were where the kings and queens lived in their separate households. Beyond here paths passing through a spacious wooded garden with an ornamental pond, **Chundangji**, lead to the **Great Greenhouse** (Map p226), Korea's first modern conservatory built in 1909 by the Japanese.

Like the other palaces, Changgyeonggung was destroyed twice by the Japanese – first in the 1590s and then again during the colonial period from 1910 until 1945, when the palace suffered the indignity of being turned into a zoo. Only a fifth of the palace buildings survived or have been rebuilt.

MARRONNIER PARK PARK

Map p226 (마로니에공원; 104 Daehak-ro, Jongno-gu; Ⓢ Line 4 to Hyehwa, Exit 2) This free performance area and sculpture park in Daehangno usually has something happening on afternoons and evenings on the outdoor stage. It's named after the chestnut trees planted here and was once part of Seoul National University, before that institution was moved to Gwanak Campus in the mid-1970s.

ARKO ART CENTER GALLERY

Map p226 (아르코미술관; ☎02-760 4850; www.arkoartcenter.or.kr/nr3; 3 Dongsung-gil, Jongno-gu; ⏲11am-7pm; Ⓢ Line 4 to Hyehwa, Exit 2) FREE Interesting, often avant-garde, art is assembled in three large galleries, run by the Arts Council Korea. The big red-brick complex (designed by Kim Swoo Geun, one of Korea's most famous postwar architects) overlooks Marronnier Park.

IHWA MAEUL AREA

Map p226 (이화 벽화 마을; Ihwa-dong, Jongno-gu; Ⓢ Line 4 to Hyehwa, Exit 2) High on the slopes of Naksan is an old *daldongnae* (literally 'moon village') where refugees lived in shacks after the Korean War. Sixty years later it has morphed into a tourism hot spot thanks to a growing collection of quirky sculptures and imaginative murals on walls along the village's steep stairways and alleys. It's a great area for casual wandering, but if you drop by the Lock Museum you can pick up an English map to the village.

The euphemistic name *daldongnae* alludes to the fact that residents had a great view of the moon from their hovels high on the hillside. There are still wonderful views of the city but try to come early in the day – and certainly avoid weekends – unless you like being surrounded by mobs of selfie-stick-toting tourists.

NAKSAN PARK PARK

Map p226 (낙산공원; http://parks.seoul.go.kr; 54 Naksan-gil, Jongno-gu; Ⓢ Line 4 to Hyehwa, Exit 2) In Korean *nakta* means 'camel' and it's thought that the shape of this mountain resembles a camel's hump. The park on the slopes above Daehangno provides fantastic views of the city and contains an impressive section of the Seoul City Wall that you can follow in either direction (and often on both sides) between Dongdaemun and Seongbuk-dong.

LOCK MUSEUM MUSEUM

Map p226 (쇳대박물관; ☎02-766 6494; 100 Ihwajang-gil, Jongno-gu; adult/child ₩4000/3000; ⏲10am-6pm Tue-Sun; Ⓢ Line 4 to Hyehwa, Exit 2) One of Seoul's quirkier private collections makes for a surprisingly absorbing exhibition. It focuses on the artistry of locks, latches and keys of all kinds, mainly from Korea but also with international examples, including a gruesome-looking chastity belt. The Corten steel-clad building contrasts nicely with a colourful wall mural nearby.

Come here also to pick up an English-language map to the mural art and small house museums of Ihwa Maeul.

HYEHWAMUN HISTORIC BUILDING

Map p226 (혜화문; 1-1 Seongbukdong 1-ga, Seongbuk-gu; Ⓢ Line 4 to Hyehwa, Exit 4) One

Neighbourhood Walk
Inwangsan Shamanist Walk

START DONGNIMMUN STATION, EXIT 2
END SEODAEMUN PRISON HISTORY HALL
LENGTH 4KM; THREE HOURS

On this hillside walk you can see Seoul's most famous shamanist shrine, small Buddhist/shamanist temples and part of Seoul's medieval city walls, as well as enjoy a bird's-eye view from Inwangsan's summit. Treat the area and people with respect, and remember that taking a photograph could interfere with an important ceremony.

To get here, take subway Line 3 to Dongnimmun station. From ❶ **exit 2** of the subway turn down the first small alley on your left. At the five-alley crossroads, fork right up the steps and you'll soon reach the colourful ❷ **entrance gate** to the shamanist village.

Turn left where the houses and small temples are terraced up the rocky hillside. Most are decorated with colourful murals of birds and blossom on their outside walls, and wind chimes clink in the breeze.

On the main path is a temple, ❸ **Seonamjeong** and, up the steps, the shamanistic shrine ❹ **Inwangsan Guksadang** (p130). Walk left and up some steps to the extraordinary ❺ **Seonbawi** (Zen Rocks), so called because they are thought to look like a pair of giant monks in prayer. A path continues up around the Dalí-esque rocks and you can climb to higher ❻ **giant boulders** for expansive views across the city.

To reach Inwangsan's peak, head back to Guksadang and follow the paths up the gully to where they meet the path along the mountain ridge and the lower side of the Seoul City Wall. At a set of ❼ **wooden steps** you can climb over to the other side of the wall. From here it's around a 15-minute hike to the summit of ❽ **Inwangsan** (p132).

Retrace your steps down the wall to where it ends, and turn right along the road for 10 minutes until you reach ❾ **Dongnimmun** (p130), and Seodaemun Independence Park across the road. Finish your walk by having a look around the ❿ **Seodaemun Prison History Hall** (p129).

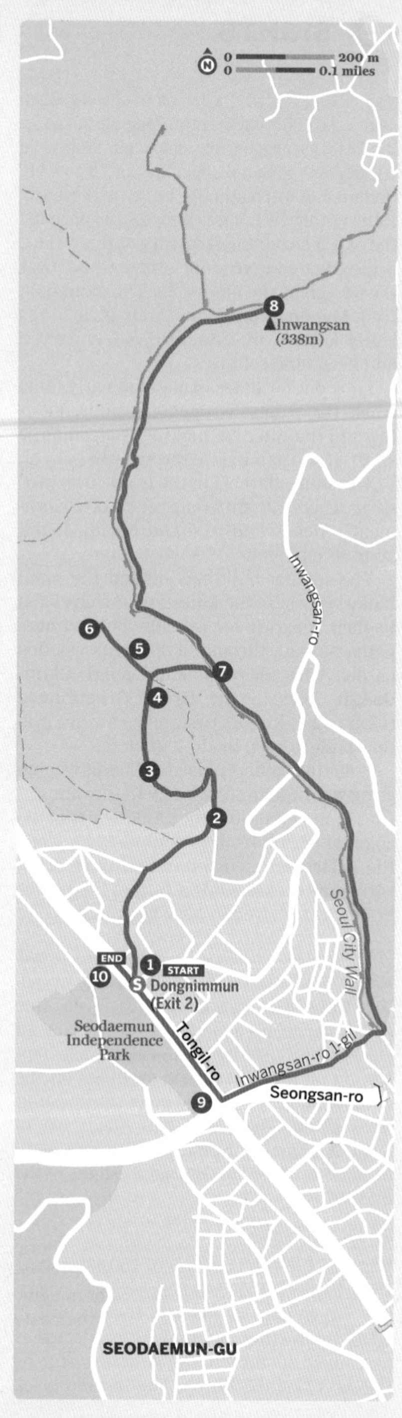

of the four subgates of Seoul City Wall, Hyehwamun is also known as Dongsomun, meaning 'small east gate'. Originally built in 1396, it was reconstructed in 1992 in this spot above the main road where it used to stand.

CHOI SUNU HOUSE HOUSE

Map p226 (최순우 옛집; 9 Seongbuk-ro 15-gil, Seongbuk-gu; ⏲10am-4pm Tue-Sat Apr-Nov; Ⓢ Line 4 to Hangsung University, Exit 6 then 🚌1111 or 2112) FREE The charming *hanok* (traditional wooden home) of a former director of the National Museum of Korea and academic on Korean arts is now looked after by the National Trust of Korea. Built in the 1930s, it follows a traditional pattern with a box of outer walls containing the L-shaped inner and outer wings of the home and gardens. Find it off the main road near the bus stop and behind a hat shop.

GILSANG-SA TEMPLE

(길상사; ☎02-3672 5945; www.gilsang sa.or.kr; 68 Seonjam-ro 50-gil, Seongbuk-gu; ⏲10am-6pm Mon-Sat; Ⓢ Line 4 to Hangsung University, Exit 6) This delightful hillside temple is beautiful to visit at any time of year, but particularly so in May when the grounds are festooned with lanterns for Buddha's birthday. There's a small teahouse and the temple offers an overnight templestay program on the third weekend of the month.

A shuttle bus runs roughly once an hour between 8.30am and 4.30pm to the temple from near the subway exit – see the website for details.

The buildings here once housed the elite restaurant Daewongak, where *gisaeng* (female entertainers accomplished in traditional arts) performed. In 1997 the property was donated by its owner, a former *gisaeng*, to a Buddhist monk to be turned into a temple.

WHANKI MUSEUM MUSEUM

(환기미술관; ☎02-391 7701; www.whankimu seum.org; 63 Jahamun-ro 14-gil, Jongno-gu; adult/student ₩7000/5000; ⏲10am-6pm Tue-Sun; Ⓢ Line 3 to Gyeongbokgung, Exit 3, then 🚌1020, 7022, 7212) Surrounded by sculptures, this attractive museum showcases works by Kim Whan-ki (1913–74), a local pioneer of modern abstract art who is known as the 'Picasso of Korea'. Apart from some of Kim's works, the gallery also hosts

TOP SIGHT
SEODAEMUN PRISON HISTORY HALL

Now a museum, Seodaemun Prison History Hall was built by the colonial Japanese in 1908 to house 500 prisoners. Up to 3500 were packed inside during the height of the 1919 anti-Japanese protests. The factories where prisoners were forced to make bricks and military uniforms have gone, but some of the prison-made bricks with Chinese characters on them have been used to make pavements, and the whole complex has been expertly restored.

In the **main exhibition hall** chilling tableaux display the various torture techniques employed on Korean patriots. Photographs of the prison are on view along with video footage, and you can go into cells in the **central prison building**. The most famous victim was Ryu Gwan-sun, an 18-year-old Ewha high-school student, who was tortured to death in 1920. You can see the **underground cell** where this happened, as well as a separate **execution building** where other prisoners were killed and the tunnel where their bodies were secretly removed. The prison continued to be used by Korea's various dictatorships in the postwar years right up until its closure in 1987.

DON'T MISS

- Exhibition hall
- Central prison building
- Ryu Gwan-sun's cell

PRACTICALITIES

- 서대문형무소역사관
- www.sscmc.or.kr/culture2/foreign/eng/eng01.html
- 251 Tongil-ro, Seodaemun-gu
- adult/child/youth ₩3000/100/1500
- ⏲9.30am-6pm Tue-Sun Mar-Oct, to 5pm Tue-Sun Nov-Feb
- Ⓢ Line 3 to Dongnimmun, Exit 5

various exhibitions, some of which have cutting-edge themes and include interesting installations.

SEOUL MUSEUM MUSEUM

(서울미술관; ☎02-395 0100; www.seoulmuseum.org; 4-1 Changuimun-ro 11-gil, Jongno-gu; adult/child/youth ₩9000/3000/5000; ⏲11am-6pm Tue-Sun Mar-Nov, 10.30am-5.30pm Tue-Sun Dec-Feb; SLine 3 to Gyeongbokgung, Exit 3 then 🚌1020, 1711, 7016, 7018, 7022, 7212) The spacious modern galleries here have a variety of shows through the year. The highlight, though, is **Seokpajeong**, the elegant remains of a 19th-century wooden mansion, and parts of its landscaped grounds on the hillside behind the gallery.

The roof garden also provides pleasant views of the surrounding suburb. The closest bus stop to the museum is Jahamun Tunnel Entrance.

SEODAEMUN INDEPENDENCE PARK PARK

(서대문독립공원; 247 Jiha Tongil-ro, Seodaemun-gu; SLine 3 to Dongnimmun, Exit 4) Apart from the former prison, this park, dedicated to those who fought for Korean independence, also features **Dongnimmun**, an impressive granite archway modelled after the Arc de Triomphe in Paris. Built by the Independence Club in 1898, it stands where envoys from Chinese emperors used to be officially welcomed to Seoul.

A tribute of gold, tiger skins, green tea, ginseng, horses, swords, ramie cloth, straw mats and eunuchs would be handed over by the Koreans. This ritual symbolised Chinese suzerainty over Korea, which only ended when King Gojong declared himself an emperor in 1897.

INWANGSAN GUKSADANG SHRINE

(인왕산 국사당; Inwangsan, Seodaemun-gu; SLine 3 to Dongnimmun, Exit 2) Originally located on Namsan, this is Seoul's most famous shamanist shrine and a place where you may witness *gut*, sacrifices to the spirits made by *mudang* (shamans) who are usually female. The Japanese demolished the original shrine on Namsan in 1925, so Korean shamanists rebuilt it here. The simple shrine with turquoise-painted doors is above the temple **Seonamjeong** (선암정사), marked by a bell pavilion and gates painted with a pair of traditional door guardians.

EATING

★JAHA SONMANDOO KOREAN $

(자하손만두; ☎02-379 2648; www.sonmandoo.com; 12 Baekseondong-gil, Jongno-gu; mains ₩7000-10,000; ⏲11am-9.30pm; 📋; SLine 3 to Gyeongbokgung, Exit 3 then 🚌1020, 7022, 7212) Around lunchtime and on weekends Seoulites flock to this mountainside dumpling house for the steamed and boiled vegetable, beef and pork parcels. A couple of plates is enough of these whoppers; the sweet cinnamon tea to finish is free.

SCOFF BAKERY $

(☎070-8801 1739; www.scoff.co.kr; 149 Changuimun-ro, Jongno-gu; baked goods ₩2000-5000; ⏲10am-7.30pm Tue-Sun; SLine 3 to Gyeongbokgung, Exit 3 then 🚌1020, 1711, 7016, 7018, 7022, 7212) Young Brit baker Jonathan exhibits admirable bake-off skills in his selection of sweet treats ranging from scones and chelsea buns to delicious cakes – try the lemon sponge. Ideal for a takeaway nibble while wandering Buam-dong.

★DEONGJANG YESOOL KOREAN $$

Map p226 (된장예술; ☎02-745 4516; 9-2 Daehak-ro 11-gil, Jongno-gu; set meal ₩9500; ⏲9am-11pm; 🌿📋; SLine 4 to Hyehwa, Exit 3) Serves a tasty fermented-bean-paste-and-tofu stew with a variety of nearly all vegetarian side dishes at a bargain price – no wonder it's well patronised by the area's student population. Look for the stone carved lions flanking the door.

★SERIOUS DELI PIZZA $$

Map p226 (☎070-7723 9686; 119 Seongbuk-ro, Seongbuk-gu; mains ₩15,000-19,000; ⏲10.30am-10.30pm; 📶📋; SLine 4 to Hangsung University, Exit 6 then 🚌bus 1111 or 2112) They are serious about pizza at this busy, rustic space, its walls lined with shelves of tinned goods. The supercrispy, thin-crust pies come with a variety of toppings; they also serve pasta dishes and chunky homemade burgers.

WOOD AND BRICK BAKERY $$

Map p226 (www.woodnbrick.com; 120 Seongbuk-ro, Seongbuk-gu; items ₩7000-16,000; ⏲bakery-cafe 8am-10pm, restaurant noon-8pm; 📶📋; SLine 4 to Hangsung University, Exit 6 then 🚌1111 or 2112) Sandwiches, bakery and deli items to go or to eat in this pleasant bakery-cafe, part of a small chain known for its baked good and macarons. Should you want something fancier there's the posh European restaurant upstairs.

DRINKING & NIGHTLIFE

★**MIX & MALT** BAR

Map p226 (☎02-765 5945; www.facebook.com/MixMalt; 3 Changgyeonggung-ro 29-gil, Jongno-gu; ⏲7.30am-2am Sun-Thu, to 3am Fri & Sat; 📶; Ⓢ Line 4 to Hyehwa, Exit 4) Even without the advantage of the owner's delightful golden retriever Louis padding around, this would be a superb cocktail and malt-whisky bar (some 50 plus single malts) to hunker down in. It also serves tasty US comfort food and has plenty of room on two levels with sofas and a fireplace for winter and an outdoor deck for warmer days.

★**SUYEON SANBANG** TEAHOUSE

Map p226 (수연산방; 8 Seongbuk-ru 26-gil, Seongbuk-gu; ⏲11.30am-10pm; Ⓜ Line 4 to Hangsung University, Exit 6 then 🚌1111, 2112) Seoul's most charming teahouse is based in a 1930s *hanok* that was once the home of novelist Lee Tae-jun and is surrounded by a peaceful garden. Apart from a range of medicinal teas and premium-quality, wild green tea, it also serves traditional sweets; the salty-sweet pumpkin soup with red-bean paste is a taste sensation.

Find it around the corner from the Seongbuk Museum of Art and avoid weekend afternoons when it gets busy.

DALLYEORA GAEMI 1 BAR

Map p226 (달려라 개미 1; ☎02-3676 5955; 22-14 Naksan-gil, Jongno-gu; ⏲4-11pm; Ⓢ Line 4 to Hyehwa, Exit 2) Purists may snub the fruit-flavoured slushies made from *makgeolli* (a mild milky rice alcohol) but the fact is that they are not a bad choice at this fun update on a *pocha* (tent bar). There's a second branch higher up the hill in the heart of Ihwa Maeul also serving breads and other baked items made with *makgeolli*. The name means 'Ants Run'.

SANMOTOONGE CAFE

(산모퉁이; ☎02-391 4737; www.sanmotoonge.co.kr; 153 Baekseokdong-gil, Jongno-gu; ⏲11am-10pm; Ⓢ Line 3 to Gyeongbokgung, Exit 3, then 🚌1020, 7022, 7212) Being featured in a Korean TV drama can do wonders for your business, but customers would still come to Sanmotoonge regardless for the wonderful views from its outdoor terraces and quirky interior design. Order drinks and snacks at the counter.

HAKRIM CAFE

Map p226 (www.hakrim.pe.kr; 119 Daehak-ro, Jongno-gu; ⏲10am-midnight; 📶; Ⓢ Line 4 to Hyehwa, Exit 3) Little has changed in this retro Seoul classic since the place opened in 1956, save for the price of drinks. Apart from coffee it also serves tea and alcohol. The cosy wooden booths and dark corners make it popular with couples.

ON THE HILL CAFE CAFE

Map p226 (☎02-743 7044; 68-7 Yulgok-ro 19-gil, Jongno-gu, 10.30am-10.30pm; 📶; Ⓢ Line 4 to Hyehwa, Exit 2) Beside the flowers-on-the-steps mural in Ihwa Maeul, this is a good spot for a breather and has a broad outdoor terrace providing fine views over the rooftops that's particularly pleasant around sunset.

SLOW GARDEN CAFE

Map p226 (www.slowgarden.co.kr; 111 Seongbuk-ro, Jongno-gu; ⏲9am-11.30pm; 📶; Ⓢ Line 4 to Hangsung University, Exit 6, then 🚌1111, 2112) Chandeliers and recycled wood make up the shack-chic decor of this pleasant self-serve cafe where you can have brunch, grab a sandwich or waffle or just sip wine or coffee.

☆ ENTERTAINMENT

JAZZ STORY JAZZ

Map p226 (☎02-725 6537; www.jazzstory.co.kr; 86 Daehak-ro 12-gil, Jongno-gu; cover ₩5000; ⏲5pm-3am; Ⓢ Line 4 to Hyehwa, Exit 2) Lined with shelves of old LPs and some rather extraordinary metalwork decor, this shack-like building is certainly one of Seoul's more striking bars; you can catch live sets by the house jazz band at 8.30pm (8pm on Sunday).

ARKOPAC THEATRE

Map p226 (☎02-3668 0007; www.koreapac.kr; 17 Daehak-ro 10-gil, Jongno-gu; Ⓢ Line 4 to Hyehwa, Exit 2) In this large, red-brick complex, designed by Kim Swoo-geun, are the main and small halls of both the Arko Art Theater and Daehangno Arts Theater. Come here for a varied dance-oriented program of events and shows.

DONGSOONG ARTS CENTER THEATRE

Map p226 (☎02-766 3390; www.dsartcenter.co.kr; 122 Dongsung-gil, Jongno-gu; Ⓢ Line 4 to Hyehwa, Exit 1) Major theatre complex where you can see Korean and international performance arts in a variety of genres. The centre includes a puppet theatre, smaller performances spaces and a museum devoted to *kokdu* (wooden dolls and effigies with spiritual properties).

SHOPPING

★BAEK BAEK — CERAMICS

Map p226 (백백; 100 Seongbuk-ro, Seongbuk-gu; ⏲10am-7pm Mon-Sat; Ⓢ Line 4 to Hangsung University, Exit 6 then 🚌1111, 2112) There's a mix of attractive products for sale at this shop organised around the traditional pottery of Seyong Lee. You can also buy nicely packaged Korean foods such as seaweed, cooking oils and fermented bean pastes – ideal for making favourite local dishes at home.

HYOJAE — TRADITIONAL FABRICS

(효재; 69 Seonjam-ro 5-gil, Seongbuk-gu; ⏲10am-6pm Mon-Sat; Ⓢ Line 4 to Hangsung University, Exit 6) Opposite Gilsang-sa, this gift shop with a sign in Chinese characters sells pretty, good-quality *bojagi* (Korean wrapping cloths), embroidered pillowcases, placemats, clothes and other trinkets.

CLUB ESPRESSO — COFFEE

(www.clubespresso.co.kr; 132 Changuimun-ro, Jongno-gu; ⏲9am-10pm; Ⓢ Line 3 to Gyeongbokgung, Exit 3; then 🚌1020, 7022, 7212) The choice of coffee lovers for the fine range of roasted beans from around the world. You can sample some of the brews before buying.

10X10 — FASHION

Map p226 (www.10x10.co.kr; 31 Daehak-ro 12-gil, Jongno-gu; ⏲11am-10pm; Ⓢ Line 4 to Hyehwa, Exit 1) Korean-designed youthful clothing and accessories are just a few of the types of colourful goods sold at this multistore alongside stationery, kitchenware, candles and the like. It's typical of the kind of cheap, student-orienated retail that's abundant in this area.

FILIPINO SUNDAY MARKET — MARKET

Map p226 (288 Changgyeonggung-ro, Jongno-gu; ⏲9am-6pm Sun; Ⓢ Line 4 to Hyehwa, Exit 1) Seoul's Filipino community gathers every Sunday to shop, meet, chat and eat Filipino food. Street stalls sell tropical treats such as coconut drinks, cassava cakes and fried bananas on a stick, as well as various tinned and dried goods and international telephone calling cards.

SPORTS & ACTIVITIES

★BUKAKSAN — HIKING

(북악산; www.bukak.or.kr; ⏲9am-3pm Apr-Oct, from 10am Nov-Mar; 🚌1020, 7022, 7212 to Changuimun) FREE At 342m, the tallest of Seoul's four guardian peaks, Bukaksan (also transliterated Bugaksan and Baegaksan) was off limits to the public for 38 years following an assassination attempt by North Korean agents on then-President Park Chung-hee in 1968. Security remains tight along this spectacular 2.5km section of the Seoul City Wall that undulates between **Changuimun**, the old subgate in Buam-dong, and the Malbawi Information Center near **Sukjeongmun**, the main north gate, which can be accessed from Samcheong Park.

This section of the wall is open only during daylight hours and photography is allowed at designated spots only, such as **Baekakmaru**, the summit viewpoint. The wall is in excellent condition and with plenty of soldiers and CCTV cameras, there's a vivid sense of its original purpose as the city's last line of defence.

INWANGSAN — HIKING

(인왕산; Ⓢ Line 3 to Dongnimmun, Exit 5) After Bukaksan, the next most spectacular section of Seoul City Wall is that snaking up and down the flanks of Inwangsan (339.9m). Near the summit are the enigmatic **Seonbawi** (Zen Rocks), while lower down is the shamanistic shrine Inwangsan Guksadang (p130). Access can be either from near Changuimun, the subgate in the wall in Buam-dong, or from just east of Dongnimmun (p128).

ANSAN — HIKING

(안산; Ⓢ Line 3 to Dongnimmun, Exit 5) At 295.9m Ansan is a relatively easy mountain to climb and is topped with **bongsudae**, a set of the smoke-signal beacons used during the Joseon dynasty. You can also have a very pleasant walk around Ansan at a lower level through woodlands following the **Ansan Jarak-gil**, a broad, generally level path partly made up of wooden decking. Access this by walking uphill from Seodaemun Prison History Hall (p129) and looking for direction signs behind the military compound there.

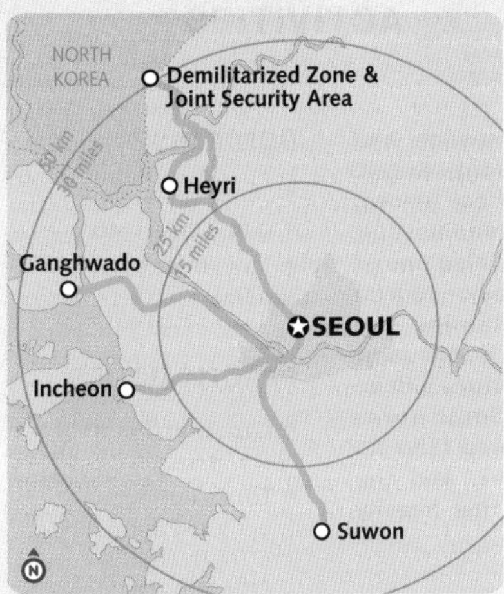

Day Trips from Seoul

Demilitarized Zone & Joint Security Area p134

For history buffs and collectors of weird and unsettling experiences, a visit to the Demilitarized Zone (DMZ) buffer between North and South Korea is not to be missed; in the Joint Security Area (JSA) you can straddle the line between the two countries.

Heyri p136

The art and culture village of Heyri is a charming place to browse galleries and while away time in cafes; nearby Paju Book City is all about its contemporary architecture.

Suwon p137

Stride around the World Heritage–listed, 18th-century fortress walls, drop by the restored Joseon-dynasty temporary palace and enjoy the charms of the Korean Folk Village.

Incheon p140

Korea opened up to the world at the end of the 19th century in this port city where you'll find a colourful Chinatown, creative Art Platform and pleasant beaches on nearby islands.

Ganghwado p143

Connected to the mainland by bridge, this island has a rich history that briefly saw it as the capital of Korea in the 13th century. Today it's all about peaceful surrounds, temples and delicious seafood.

TOP SIGHT
DEMILITARIZED ZONE & JOINT SECURITY AREA

The Demilitarized Zone (DMZ) is a 4km-wide and 240km-long buffer splitting North from South Korea. Lined on both sides by tank traps, electrical fences, landmines and two armies in full battle readiness, it is one of the scariest places on earth. It is also one of the most surreal since it has become a major tourist attraction with several observatories allowing you to peek into North Korea. The key sight is the Joint Security Area (JSA), inside of which is the truce village of Panmunjeom – there's nowhere else in South Korea where you can get so close to North Korea (and its soldiers) without being arrested or shot, and the tension is palpable. The only way into this heavily restricted area is on an organised tour.

DON'T MISS

- JSA (Panmunjeon)
- Dora Observatory
- Third Infiltration Tunnel

PRACTICALITIES

- **Location** 55km north of Seoul
- **Tours** Koridoor Tours and Panmunjom Travel Center are the two main tour operators.

JSA (Panmunjeom)

Unquestionably the highlight of any trip to the DMZ is a visit to the JSA at Panmunjeom. An improbable tourist destination, it's here where the infamous **Military Demarcation Line** separates South and North Korea. Soldiers from both sides often stand metres apart eyeballing one another from their respective sides of the blue-painted UN buildings. You'll be taken inside the **meeting room** – where the truce between North and South Korea was signed – the only place where you can safely walk into North Korea.

Tours kick off with a briefing by US or Republic of Korea (ROK) soldier guides at **Camp Bonifas**, the joint US–ROK army camp just outside the DMZ, before being transferred to another bus to the JSA.

Within the blue **conference room** at the JSA, where official meetings are still sometimes held, microphones on the tables constantly record everything said, while ROK soldiers stand guard inside and out in a modified taekwondo stance – an essential photo op. Their North Korean counterparts keep a steady watch, usually, but not always, from a distance.

Though your tour will be a quiet one, the soldier guide will remind you that this frontier is no stranger to violent incidents. One of the most notorious being in 1976 when two US soldiers were hacked to death with axes by North Korean soldiers after the former had tried to chop down a tree obstructing the view from a watchtower. Camp Bonifas is named after one of the slain soldiers.

Back on the bus you'll be taken to one of Panmunjeom's lookout posts from where you can see the two villages within the DMZ: **Daeseong-dong** in the South and **Gijeong-dong** in the North. You'll also see the site of the axe-murder incident and the **Bridge of No Return** where POW exchange took place following the signing of the Armistice Agreement in 1953.

The forested surrounds are Korea's most ecologically pristine and allegedly home to the Siberian tiger.

Observatory Decks

At **Dora Observatory** (binoculars ₩500; ⏲10am-5pm Tue-Sun) you can peer through binoculars for a closer look at **Kaesong city** and **Kaesong Industrial Complex** in the Democratic People's Republic of Korea (DPRK; North Korea), where cheap North Korean labourers are employed by South Korean conglomerates.

In between Heyri and Paju, **Odusan Unification Observatory** (오두산통일전망대; www.jmd.co.kr; adult/child/teen ₩3000/1000/1600; ⌚9am-5.30pm Apr-Sep, to 5pm Oct-Mar, to 4.30pm Nov-Feb) provides another chance to gaze across the DMZ into North Korea. There's also an **exhibition hall** with interesting displays on the conflict.

Third Infiltration Tunnel

The **Third Infiltration Tunnel** (제3땅굴; ⌚9am-5pm Tue-Sun) is one of four tunnels running under the DMZ found since 1974, dug by the North Koreans so that their army could launch a surprise attack. Walking along 265m of the 73m-deep tunnel is not for the claustrophobic or the tall: creeping hunched over, you'll realise why they issue hard hats. The guide will point out how the North Koreans painted the rocks black so they might claim it was a coal mine!

Dorasan Station & Imjingak

Awaiting the next departure to Pyongyang (and onward trans-Eurasian intercontinental travel), **Dorasan train station** (admission ₩500) stands as a symbol of the hope for the eventual reunification of the two Koreas. The shiny new international customs built in 2002 remains unused. Trains to Seoul still run here four times daily.

Imjingak park is dedicated to the 10 million South Koreans separated from their families postwar when the peninsula was divided. Also here is **Freedom Bridge**, connecting North and South, where 13,000 POWs were exchanged in 1953, plus a **steam train** derailed during the war.

Getting There & Away

The only way to visit the DMZ is on an organised tour. The following are recommended:

Run by the United Service Organizations (USO), the US army's social and entertainment organisation, **Koridoor Tours** (☎02-795 3028; www.koridoor.co.kr; tours ₩96,000; ⌚office 8am-5pm Mon-Sat; Ⓢline 1 to Namyeong, Exit 2) has long been regarded as one of the best. Lunch isn't included; bring a packed lunch, or budget around ₩10,000 for lunch at the restaurant stop.

A reputable company with knowledgable guides, **Panmunjom Travel Center** (☎02-771 5593; http://panmunjomtour.com; 6th fl, Lotte Hotel main bldg, Sogong-dong, Jung-gu; tours ₩77,000-120,000) is notable for having a North Korean defector who comes along (but not always) to answer your questions. Prices are inclusive of lunch.

TOP TIPS

- Book at least two weeks in advance for the popular Koridoor Tours tour, which includes the JSA. If booking other tours, check that they include the JSA.
- Don't forget your passport, you'll need it to gain clearance at the JSA.

Citizens of certain countries are not allowed on tours that include the JSA. There are also strict dress and behavioural codes; usually collared shirts for men, and no ripped jeans, revealing clothing or open-toed shoes. Alcohol consumption is also prohibited. Only children over 10 years are permitted.

Heyri

Explore

Less than 10km south of the DMZ, Heyri (헤이리) is a charming village of small-scale contemporary buildings that couldn't be more of a contrast to the heavily fortified, doom-laden border. Conceived as a 'book village' connected to the nearby publishing centre of Paju Book City, it has blossomed into a community of artists, writers, architects and other creative souls. There are scores of small art galleries, cafes, boutique shops and quirky private collections turned into mini museums.

Just wandering around the village is a pleasure. Be sure to check out the residential area with its interesting examples of modern architecture. Most are created with materials that reflect and fit in with the natural environment. Roads twist naturally and the village is beautifully landscaped and sculptures abound.

The Best...

- **Sight** Blume Museum of Contemporary Art
- **Place to Eat** Foresta Book Cafe
- **Place to Stay** Motif #1

Top Tip

At Heyri's tourist office you can pick up a good English map that details the many places to see in the village.

Note that on Mondays most places shut down in Heyri.

Getting There & Away

- **Bus** Express Bus 2200 (₩2000; 45 minutes) and local bus 200 (₩1800, one hour 20 minutes) both leave from stop 16 near Hapjeong station on subway Lines 2 and 6 in Seoul. Both pass through Paju on the way to Heyri; the local bus also stops near Odusan. The last bus back is around 10.30pm.

Need to Know

- **Area Code** ☎031
- **Location** 48km north of Seoul
- **Tourist Office** (☎031-946 8551; www.heyri.net; Gate 1; ⏰10am-6pm Tue-Sun)

SIGHTS

BLUME MUSEUM OF CONTEMPORARY ART GALLERY

(BMOCA; www.bmoca.or.kr; Gate 3; admission ₩3000; ⏰11am-6pm Mon-Sat, 1-6pm Sun) Within a postmodern building that incorporates a giant tree into its facade, this contemporary gallery exhibits a mix of emerging and established artists across all mediums.

WHITE BLOCK ART CENTER GALLERY

(www.whiteblock.org; Gate 1; ⏰11am-6.30pm) In the centre of the village, this is one of Heyri's larger-scale galleries with three floors showcasing contemporary art. Outside stands the blue *Greeting Man* sculpture.

GALLERY SOSO GALLERY

(☎031-949 8154; www.gallerysoso.com; Gate 7; ⏰11am-6pm Tue-Sun) There's nothing so so about this classy gallery backing on to the forest. It offers artist residency programs and has a guesthouse too.

EATING & DRINKING

In Heyri practically every gallery (and there are many) has an attached cafe or gallery.

FORESTA BOOK CAFE CAFE $$

(www.heyribookhouse.co.kr; Gate 3; drinks from ₩5000, pizza ₩15,000; ⏰10.30am-9pm; 📶📖) Foresta's backdrop comprises a colossal floor-to-ceiling wall of books, with plenty of tables to enjoy house-roasted Ethiopian coffee, sandwiches and pizzas. The attached bookshop sells art books on Heyri.

KOKOPELLI BAR

(http://blog.daum.net/lookipc; Gate 4; beer ₩5500; ⏰noon-midnight) A good spot for a drink, Kokopelli stays true to its motto of 'Not war, make beer' by brewing its own ales.

SLEEPING

★MOTIF #1 GUESTHOUSE $$

(☎031-949 0901; www.motif1.co.kr; Gate 1; d weekday/weekend ₩120,000/140,000; ❄📶) The bohemian-chic home of Ansoo Lee – traveller, writer and president of the art council – is typical of Heyri. It's packed with art and has beautifully designed rooms worthy of a boutique hotel, plus a library of 10,000 books to browse. All four doubles and one family room have bathrooms, and guests can use the kitchen.

WORTH A DETOUR

PAJU BOOK CITY

If you enjoyed Heyri's arty vibe and contemporary architecture, you should definitely add a stop to nearby Paju. The hub of Korea's book industry, there are some 300 publishing houses and bookshopss set within a complex of futuristic, award-winning buildings – a must for architectural buffs.

Your first port of call should be the **Asia Publication Culture & Information Center** (아시아출판문화정보센터; www.pajubookcity.org/english; ⌚10am-5pm) to pick up a walking-tour map and guide to the area. Here you can check out the 'Forest of Wisdom', a corridor lined with towering 8m-high shelves containing 200,000 books; titles on its top shelf are accessed by crane!

If you want to stay the night, there's the boutique **Guesthouse Jijihang** (☎031-955 0090; http://pajubookcity.org/jijihyang; Asian Publication Culture Centre; d/tr ₩132,000/154,000; ❄📶) attached to the Asian Publication Culture Center, which also has an Italian restaurant and book cafe. Across the street, **Café Hesse** (sandwiches ₩4500; ⌚9am-8pm Sun-Thu, 10am-9pm Fri & Sat) is just the place to soak up Paju's literary vibes.

Paju Book City is 10km south of Heyri. Buses 2200 and 200 both stop en route to Seoul; disembark at Eunseokgyo bus station.

★**FOREST GARDEN** GUESTHOUSE $$$
(☎010 4363 2660, 031-8071 0127; www.forestgarden.kr; Gate 1; d weekday/weekend incl breakfast ₩170,000/200,000; ❄📶) English-speaking Mr Kim, retired from the Korea Tourism Organisation, and his artist wife Son Yeong-won own this award-winning home that was built climbing up the hillside. Large rooms are comfortable and stylish, and there is a lovely lounge and rooftop sitting area.

Suwon

Explore

It was King Jeongjo, the 22nd Joseon dynasty ruler, who had the idea of moving the national capital from Seoul to Suwon, 48km south, in 1794. The fortress walls that surrounded the original city were constructed but the king died and power stayed in Seoul. Named Hwaseong, Suwon's impressive World Heritage–listed fortifications remain the best reason for visiting the city, where you'll also find the faithfully restored palace Hwaseong Haenggung. Suwon is also close to the Korean Folk Village and Everland Resort and can be used as a base to visit both.

The Best...

- **Sight** Hwaseong
- **Place to Eat** Yeonpo Galbi (p140)
- **Place to Drink** Bom Cafe (p140)

Top Tip

At the Yeonmudae **archery centre** (10 arrows ₩2000; ⌚9.30am-5.30pm, every 30min) you can practice a traditional sport in which Koreans often win Olympic medals.

Getting There & Away

- **Subway** Line 1 connects Seoul to Suwon (₩1850, one hour) but make sure you're on a train that heads to the city before the line splits at Guro.
- **Train** KTX trains from Seoul are speedier (from ₩4600, 30 minutes) but less frequent.

Need to Know

- **Area Code** ☎031
- **Location** 48km south of Seoul
- **Tourist Office** (☎031-228 4673; http://english.swcf.or.kr; ⌚9am-6pm; Ⓢ Suwon, exit 4)
- **Information Booth** (☎031 228 4672; Suwon Cultural Foundation; ⌚9am-6pm). Next to Hwaseong Haenggung.

SIGHTS

HWASEONG FORTRESS
(화성; http://ehs.suwon.ne.kr; adult/child ₩1000/500; ⌚24hr) The World Heritage–listed fortress wall that encloses the original town of Suwon is what brings most travellers to the city. Snaking up and down Mt Paldal (143m), the fortification wall stretches a scenic 5.7km past four majestic gates, command posts, pavilions, observation towers and fire-beacon

WORTH A DETOUR

EVERLAND RESORT

Set in lush hillsides 40km south of Seoul, this mammoth amusement park is regarded as one of Korea's best.

The main theme park, **Everland** (☎031-320 5000; www.everland.com; adult/child/teen ₩48,000/31,000/34,000; ⏲9.30am-10pm Sep-Jun, to 11pm Jul & Aug), is filled with fantasy buildings, fairground attractions, impressive seasonal gardens, live music and parades. Lit up at night, the park takes on a magical atmosphere and there are always fireworks. The highlight for many is the wooden roller-coaster, supposedly the steepest in the world. Expect long queues for all rides. Next door is **Caribbean Bay** (adult/child from ₩35,000/27,000; ⏲10am-5pm Sep-Jun, 9.30am-11pm Jul & Aug), a superb indoor and outdoor water park with plenty of thrill rides.

A free shuttle bus runs from Everland's main entrance to the **Hoam Art Museum** (http://hoam.samsungfoundation.org; adult/child ₩4000/3000, with Everland ticket free; ⏲10am-6pm Tue-Sun) and you are well advised to take it. The serenely beautiful Hee Won Korean gardens induce a calm frame of mind so that visitors can fully appreciate the gorgeous art treasures inside the museum, including paintings, screens and celadon.

To get here from Seoul take bus 5002 (₩2000, 50 minutes, every 15 minutes) from Gangnam. From outside Suwon's train station, hop on bus 66 or 66-4 (₩1700, one hour, every 30 minutes).

platforms. Built by King Jeongjo and completed in 1796, it was constructed of earth and faced with large stone blocks and grey bricks, nearly all of which have been restored.

It takes around two hours to complete the circuit. Try to go outside the wall for at least part of the way, as the fortress looks more impressive the way an enemy would see it.

Start at **Paldalmun**, also known as Nammun (South Gate), and follow the steep steps off to the left up to the **Seonam Gangu**, an observation point near the peak of Paldalsan. Near the command post, **Seojang-dae**, is the large **Hyowon Bell** you can toll (₩1000) and **Seono-dae**, a tower on the summit that was used by crossbow archers and has spectacular panoramic views of the city.

On the wall's north side is **Hwahongmun**, a watergate over a stream. Nearby **Dongbukgongsimdon**, another watchtower, has a unique design – a high, tapering structure with rounded corners, stone base and brick tower. Further on, the **Bongdon Beacon Towers** were used to send messages around the country.

If you don't fancy the walk, head up the hill at the rear of the palace to the find the 54-seat **Hwaseong Trolley** (adult/child/teen ₩1500/700/1100; ⏲10am-5.20pm) that winds in and out of the fortress wall to the archery field at Yeonmu-dae.

HWASEONG HAENGGUNG PALACE

(화성행궁; adult/child ₩1500/700; ⏲9am-6pm, changing of the guard 2pm Sun Mar-Nov, martial-arts display 11am & 3pm Tue-Sun Mar-Nov) Sitting at the base of Mt Paldal, King Jeongjo's palace was built in the late 18th century as a place for him to stay on his visits. It's been meticulously reconstructed after being destroyed during the Japanese occupation. From March to November, various traditional performances are held at the plaza in front of the palace, including a changing of the guard ceremony and martial-arts display.

Find out how detailed court records aided the reconstruction process and see how the area used to look at the **Suwon Cultural Foundation** (⏲9.30am-6pm Mar-Oct, to 5pm Nov-Feb) FREE on the south side of the plaza in front of the palace.

Every October a grand royal procession is reenacted as part of Suwon's annual festival.

KOREAN FOLK VILLAGE CULTURAL CENTRE

(한국민속촌; ☎031-288 0000; www.koreanfolk.co.kr; 90 Minsokchon-ro, Yongin-si; adult/chil/teen ₩15,000/10,000/12,000; ⏲9.30am-6.30pm May-Sep, to 6pm Oct-Apr) Showcasing traditional Korean culture, this 245-acre folk village comprises thatched and tiled traditional houses and buildings from around Korea. It takes at least half a day to wander the picturesque grounds, where you'll encounter artisans wearing *hanbok* (traditional clothing) making pots and handmade paper, while others tend to vegetable plots and livestock. The **Folk Museum** offers a fascinating snapshot of 19th-century Korean life.

Throughout the day there are entertaining performances by traditional musicians, dancers, acrobats and tightrope walkers, and you can watch a staged wedding ceremony. There are also kid-specific attractions including an amusement park, which costs extra, plus several traditional restaurants.

A free shuttle bus leaves Suwon's main tourist information centre (30 minutes, at 10.30am, 12.30 and 2.30pm). The last shuttle bus leaves the folk village at 4.30pm (5pm on weekends). After that time, walk to the far end of the car park and catch city bus 37 (₩1300, one hour, every 20 minutes) back to Suwon station.

HAENGGUNG-DONG MURAL VILLAGE — AREA

This is a neighbourhood of street art featuring work by a mix of international muralists, as well as excellent art galleries **Alternative Art Space Noon** (www.spacenoon.co.kr; noon-7pm) and **Space Bom** (noon-10pm), which both exhibit local artists.

JI-DONG MURAL VILLAGE — AREA

Just outside Suwon's city walls, Ji-dong's labyrinth of alleyways burst with vibrant murals that decorate its walls. To get here, head through Jidgan Market arcade and take the first left at Changnyongmon-ro, from where it's a 500m walk.

MR TOILET HOUSE — MUSEUM

(Haewoojae; 031-271 9777; www.haewoojae.com; 458-9 Jangan-ro, Jangan-gu; 10am-6pm Tue-Sun, to 5pm winter) FREE A contender as Korea's wackiest museum, Mr Toilet House (the former residence of Suwon's mayor, the late Sim Jae-duck) is designed like a toilet. As well as hilarious poo-related exhibits and a sculpture garden, it also covers more serious sanitation issues. Kids especially will love it, and there's a children's museum across the road with an observatory deck for viewing the toilet house.

Jae-duck was famous for his efforts in beautifying Suwon's public toilets during the lead-up to the 2002 Soccer World Cup, decorating them in art, flowers and classical music – most of which remain around the city today.

It's important to note it's not just a quirky museum, but an NGO that was established to improve public health worldwide. Visit its website for more details.

To get here take bus 64, 65 or 98 from Hwasseong Haenggung (25 minutes) and get off at Dongwon High School, from where it's a 10-minute walk.

NAM JUNE PAIK ART CENTER — GALLERY

(031-201 8500; http://njpac-en.ggcf.kr; 10 Paiknamjune-ro, Giheung-gu, Yongin-si; admission

WORTH A DETOUR

BUKHANSAN NATIONAL PARK

Granite peak-studded **Bukhansan National Park** (북한산 국립공원; 031-873 2791; http://bukhan.knps.or.kr; S Line 1 to Dobongsan) is so close to Seoul that it's possible to visit by subway – which partly accounts for why it sees over 10 million hikers a year. It offers sweeping mountain-top vistas, maple leaves, rushing streams and remote temples. Even though it covers nearly 80 sq km, the park's proximity to the city (45 minutes by subway) means it gets crowded, especially on weekends.

Popular for hiking and rock climbing, the park is divided into two sections, the Baegundae and Dobongsan areas. Both are separate destinations that feature multiple scenic trails leading to mountain peaks. Neither are a stroll in the park, and quite strenuous. Bring plenty of water.

In the northern area a popular hike is the climb up **Dobongsan** (740m), which climaxes with the spectacular ridge-top peak climb. Along the way be sure to take signed detours to visit atmospheric forested temples **Cheonchuk-sa** (천축사) on the way up and **Mangwol-sa** (망월사) upon descent – all up around a four-hour trek.

The southern part has South Korea's highest peak in **Baegundae** (836m), a 3½-hour return trip via the Bukhansanseong trail. For rock climbers, nearby **Insubong** (810m) has some of the best multipitch climbing in Asia and routes of all grades.

For Dobongsan, take subway Line 1 to Dobongsan station, a 15-minute walk from Dobong Park Information Center, which has a basic hiking map in English. If you take the route down via Wondolbong (recommended) you'll finish at Mangwolsa station.

Baegundae is accessed from Bukhansanseong or Jeongneung, both of which have information centres with maps. For Bukhansanseong take subway Line 3 to Gupabal station and take bus 70. For Jeongneung take Line 4 to Gireum station and bus 110B or 143.

₩4000; ⏲10am-6pm) Not far from the Korean Folk Village, this gallery features the work of internationally acclaimed avante-garde artist Nam June Paik (1932–2006). It shows a changing collection of his pioneering new-media work, namely his signature TV sets.

From Suwon station take bus 10, 66, 66-4, 10-5 or 37; from Seoul take the Budang Line subway to Sanggal station, from where it's a 10-minute walk. En route you'll pass **Gyeonggi Provincial Museum** (http://old.musenet.or.kr/english; 6 Sanggal-ro, Giheung-gu, Yongin-si; ⏲10am-8pm Mon-Fri, to 10pm Sat & Sun) FREE, worth a stop for its fine collection of cultural artefacts.

EATING & DRINKING

Suwon is renowned for its *galbi* (beef) dishes, including *galbitang* (meaty bones in a broth).

YEONPO GALBI KOREAN $$

(연포갈비; 56-1 Jeongjo-ro 906beon-gil; meals ₩10,000-40,000; ⏲11.30am-10pm) Down the steps from Hwahongmun, this famous restaurant serves up its special Suwon version of *galbitang* (big ribs in a seasoned broth with noodles and leeks; ₩10,000), only served at lunch.

BOM CAFE CAFE

(Haenggung-dong Mural Village; ⏲noon-10pm) A cool, arty cafe attached to its eponymous gallery (p139), Bom specialises in traditional teas and also sells quality homemade crafts.

Incheon

Explore

This major port is where Korea opened up to the world in the 1880s, ending centuries of self-imposed isolation. The layers of history here are fascinating and include memorials to the daring landing behind enemy lines of UN forces led by US General Douglas MacArthur in 1950. Its colourful Chinatown, Korea's largest such community, is next to the Open Port area with Japanese colonial-era buildings and the brick warehouses transformed into a contemporary arts centre. Incheon can also be used as a stepping stone to the West Sea islands and their beaches.

The Best...

- **Sight** Incheon Art Platform
- **Place to Eat** Tochon (p142)
- **Place to Stay** Harbor Park Hotel (p143)

Top Tip

Visit midweek to avoid massive queues for restaurants on weekends in Chinatown.

Getting There & Away

- **Subway** Line 1 connects Seoul to Incheon (₩1850, 1¼ hours) but make sure you're on a train that heads to the city before the line splits at Guro.

Need to Know

- **Area Code** ☎032
- **Location** 36km west of Seoul
- **Tourist Information Centre** (Map p141; ☎032-777 1330; http://eng.icjg.go.kr/index.asp; Incheon station; ⏲9am-6pm)

SIGHTS

INCHEON ART PLATFORM ARTS CENTRE

Map p141 (www.inartplatform.kr; Open Port; ⏲9am-6pm Tue-Sun) FREE This complex of 1930s and '40s brick warehouses was turned over to the Incheon Foundation for Arts and Culture, and it has created gallery spaces and artist residency studios. Performances and events are also held here, and there is a light-filled cafe with plenty of art books.

It offers three-month residency programs for artists; visit the website for info.

JAYU PARK PARK

Map p141 (Open Port) This beautiful hillside park, designed by a Russian civil engineer in 1888, makes a good spot for a stroll. It contains the monument for the centenary of Korea–USA relations and a statue of General MacArthur.

INCHEON GRAND FISHERY MARKET MARKET

Map p141 (www.asijang.co.kr; Yeonan; ⏲5am-9pm; 🚌12 and 24 from Ⓢ Dongincheon) Even if you've already visited Noryangjin (p90) in Seoul, this fish and seafood market is still worth seeing. It's a more intimate, brightly lit place displaying hundreds of types of marine products, all of which you can eat on the spot at several small restaurants and cafes.

Incheon

INCHEON OPEN PORT MUSEUM MUSEUM

Map p141 (인천개항박물관; www.icjgss.or.kr/open_port; Open Port; adult/child/teen ₩500/200/300; ⌚9am-6pm) One of three former Japanese bank buildings on the same street, this is an interesting museum of the history of Incheon since the port's opening in 1883.

MODERN ARCHITECTURE MUSEUM MUSEUM

Map p141 (Open Port; adult/child/youth ₩500/200/300; ⌚9am-6pm) Housed within a former colonial Japanese bank, this museum sheds insight into Incheon's multiculturalism through its architecture. It includes displays of Incheon's buildings, ranging from modernism, gothic, French Renaissance, Japanese imperial and Chinese styles.

SONGWOL-DONG FAIRY TALE VILLAGE PUBLIC ART

Map p141 (인천동화마을) Like a princess has waved a magic wand over its streets, this once-gritty neighbourhood has been transformed into a children's wonderland of brightly coloured fairy-tale-themed murals.

Incheon

Sights (p140)

1 Incheon Art Platform D2
2 Incheon Grand Fishery Market B4
3 Incheon Open Port Museum D2
4 Jayu Park D1
5 Korean Emigration History Museum A2
6 Modern Architecture Museum D2
7 Songwol-dong Fairy Tale Village C1
8 Wolmi Observatory B2
9 Wolmi Park A2
10 Wolmido B2

Eating (p142)

11 Dada Bok C1
12 Pungmi C1
13 Shinpo-sijang D2
14 Tochon D1

Sleeping (p143)

15 Harbor Park Hotel C2

WORTH A DETOUR

YEONGJONGDO & MUUIDO

Also part of Incheon's municipality are the 100-plus islands scattered off the coast including Yeongjongdo, home to Incheon International Airport and connected to the mainland by bridges, train lines or a brief ferry ride from Wolmido (adult/child ₩3000/1000, 7am to 9pm). Buses run from the airport, or the town of Incheon (outside the subway station) to **Eulwangri Beach** on the island's western tip.

Nicer than Yeongjongdo is Muuido, which can be reached via a five-minute ferry trip (₩3000 return, half-hourly until 7pm, until 6pm in winter) from Jamjindo, a tiny islet connected by a causeway to the southwest tip of Yeongjongdo.

On Muuido, **Hanagae Beach** (하나개 해수욕장; 032-751 8833; www.hanagae.co.kr; adult/child ₩2000/1000) and **Silmi Beach** (실미 해수욕장; 032-752 4466; adult/child ₩2000/1000) are top relaxation spots where you can either camp or stay in cabins.

Muuido has plenty of *minbak* (homestays) and pensions. The best budget option is the basic **Hanagae Beach Huts** (Hanagae Beach; huts without bathroom ₩30,000), plonked right on the beach. Otherwise **Island Garden** (010 3056 2709; www.islandgardenkr.com; camping ₩50,000 r weekday/weekend ₩100,000/150,000;) has its own private beach and all rooms look out to the water. The friendly owners speak good English.

To get here, head to Incheon Airport from where you catch bus 222 and 2-1 (₩1000, 20 minutes, hourly) to the islet of Jamjindo for the connecting ferry to Muuido.

While it's aimed at kids, it's quirky enough to warrant a visit for all.

WOLMIDO — AREA

Map p141 (월미도; http://wolmi.incheon.go.kr) Once an island, Wolmido was later a military base and site of the Incheon Landing Operation during the Korean War. Today it's a leisure area with atmospheric Coney Island–style waterfront boardwalk and amusement park. It also has the forested **Wolmi Park** (월미공원; Map p141; http://wolmi.incheon.go.kr/index.do; Wolmi-do; 6am-10pm, garden 9am-8pm) FREE with tranquil walking trails leading to traditional gardens and the hilltop **Wolmi Observatory** (Map p141; Wolmi Park; 6am-10pm) FREE with wonderful 360-degree views of Incheon and beyond.

At the base of the park, the **Korean Emigration History Museum** (Map p141; http://mkeh.incheon.go.kr; 9am-6pm Tue-Sun) FREE offers an interesting insight to the journey of Korean migrants, with a focus on settlers' experiences in the US and the Americas.

INCHEON LANDING OPERATION MEMORIAL HALL — MUSEUM

(인천상륙작전기념관; www.landing915.com; Song-do; 9am-6pm Tue-Sun; 6-1, 8 and 16 from Dongincheon) FREE Some 70,000 UN and South Korean troops took part in the surprise landing in Incheon in 1950, supported by 260 warships. Find out about the attack at this sombre museum. The displays include newsreel films of the Korean War, plus guided missiles and LVT landing crafts.

INCHEON METROPOLITAN CITY MUSEUM — MUSEUM

(인천광역시립박물관; Song-do; 9am-6pm Tue-Sun) FREE Next to the Memorial Hall is the city's main museum, offering an excellent collection of celadon pottery and some interesting historical displays dating from the Three Kingdoms (57 BC to AD 668).

EATING

In Chinatown you can sample local variations of Chinese cuisine, including *jjajangmyeon* (noodles in a savoury-sweet black-bean sauce), *jjampong* (noodles in a spicy seafood soup) and *onggibyeong* (crispy dumplings baked inside large clay jars).

TOCHON — KOREAN $

Map p141 (토촌; mains ₩8000-15,000; 10am-10pm) At the bottom of Jayu Park, Tochon is one of Incheon's most atmospheric Korean restaurants, with traditional ceramics, lush greenery, a small waterfall and aquarium-lined walls. It's a sit-down affair serving bulgogi (grilled marinated beef) and bibimbap (rice, egg, meat and vegies with chilli sauce) with an impressive array of sides.

DADA BOK — CHINESE $

Map p141 (dumplings ₩4500; 11am-8pm) Just back from the bedlam of Chinatown, this unassuming restaurant is the local pick for Incheon's tastiest dumplings. There's a choice of pork or shrimp, steamed or pan-fried.

SAMCHI ST SEAFOOD
(동인천 삼치거리; Dongincheon; samchi from ₩6000; S Exit 8, Dongincheon) This strip of lively restaurants specialises in cheap, delicious grilled *samchi* (Spanish mackerel), which when accompanied by a few bottles of *makgeolli* (milky rice wine) makes for a fun boozy evening. It's a short walk from the station.

SHINPO-SIJANG KOREAN $
Map p141 (신포시장; Shinpo-dong; street eats ₩1000-10,000; ⏲10am-8pm) Locals line up here for takeaway boxes of *dakgangjeong* (spicy sweet-and-sour deep-fried chicken). It's well worth sampling, as are other street eats along the twin covered arcades, including giant candy-coloured *madu* (dumplings).

PUNGMI CHINESE $
Map p141 (풍미; ☎032-772 2680; Chinatown; meals ₩5000-10,000; ⏲9am-9.30pm; ▣) In business since 1957, this is a good place to sample *jjajangmyeon,* a local speciality.

SLEEPING

HARBOR PARK HOTEL HOTEL $$
Map p141 (하버파크 호텔; ☎032-770 9500; www.harborparkhotel.com; 217 Jemullyang-ro; r from ₩110,000; ❄@☜) Sporting sleek design inside and out, the rooms at the Harbor Park provide great views of the working harbour and hillsides. There's a good gym and tempting top-floor buffet restaurant (adult/child ₩35,000/23,000), also with stellar views.

Ganghwado

Explore

For a brief period in the mid-13th century, when the Mongols were rampaging through the mainland, the island of Ganghwado (now linked by bridge to the mainland) became the location of Korea's capital. Situated at the mouth of the Han River, South Korea's fifth-largest island continued to have strategic importance and was the scene of bloody skirmishes with French and US forces in the 19th century as colonial powers tried to muscle in on the 'hermit kingdom'.

It's not just Ganghwado's history that makes it worth visiting. Given over to small-scale agriculture, the island provides a welcome respite from sometimes-crazy Seoul.

Ganghwado's main town, **Ganghwa-eup** (강화읍), is not particularly scenic, but is just 2km beyond the northern bridge and acts as a base for visiting all attractions.

The Best...

- **Sight** Jeondeung-sa
- **Place to Eat** Wang Jajeong (p144)
- **Place to Stay** Namchidang (p144)

Top Tip

A 15km cycle path runs alongside the seaside highway passing fortifications that line the east coast including Gwangseongbo (광성보) and Chojijin (초지진). Bikes (₩9000 per day) can be rented from 9am to 4pm at the souvenir stall beside the fortification Gapgot Dondae (갑곶돈대), close to the northern bridge.

Getting There & Away

- **Bus** There are frequent buses running to Ganghwa-eup (₩2100, 1½ hours, every 10 minutes from 4am to 10pm) near Seoul's Sinchon station. From Incheon, you can jump on bus 90 from Bupyeong subway. While buses from Ganghwa-eup connect all points of the island, they run infrequently, usually on the hour, so it pays to get info for bus schedules.
- **Tour** The island is big, and buses infrequent, so consider taking a tour: several leave from Seoul; check with the KTO Tourist Information Center (p192).

Need to Know

- **Area Code** ☎032
- **Location** 56km from Seoul
- **Tourist Office** (☎032 930 3515; www.ganghwa.incheon.kr; Ganghwa-eup Bus Terminal; ⏲9am-6pm)

SIGHTS

JEONDEUNG-SA BUDDHIST TEMPLE
(전등사; ☎032-937 0125; www.jeondeungsa.org; adult/child/youth ₩3000/1000/2000; ⏲7am-sunset) In Ganghwado's southeast, Jeondeung-sa has a tranquil forested hilltop setting within the walls of Samrangseong Fortress. Founded in 1259, it's one of Korea's oldest Buddhist temples. Here the *Tripitaka Koreana*, 80,000 wooden blocks of Buddhist scriptures, were carved between 1235 and 1251. You can also stay overnight and sip traditional teas at the charming teahouse.

BOMUN-SA TEMPLE

(보문사; Seongmodo; adult/child/youth ₩2500/1000/1700, ferries adult/child ₩2000/1000, cars ₩16,000; ⏲9am-6pm, ferries 7am-9pm Mar-Nov, to 5.30pm Dec-Feb) Situated high in the pine-forested hills of the west-coast island of Seongmodo (steep walk and many stairs – catch your breath at the top), this temple has some superbly ornate painting on the eaves of its buildings. The grotto and 10m-tall Buddha rock carving are standouts.

To get here, take bus 31 from Ganghwa-eup terminal to Oepo-ri (₩1200, 20 minutes), 13km away on the west coast, and take a ferry across to Seongmodo (10 minutes, every 35 minutes). From here there's a bus (₩1200; hourly on weekdays, every 30 minutes on weekends) to the temple.

MT MANISAN MOUNTAIN

(마니산; adult/child ₩2000/700; ⏲9am-6pm) It's a steep one-hour climb, with more than 900 steps, to reach the top of Mt Manisan (469m). At its summit is **Chamseongdan** (참성단; ⏲10am to 4pm), a large stone altar said to have been originally built and used by Dangun, the mythical first Korean. There's also a helipad and rocky outcrops, which both offer splendid views. It's 14km from Ganghwa-eup; bus 41 leaves here hourly (30 minutes).

GANGHWA PEACE OBSERVATION DECK OBSERVATORY

(adult/child ₩2500/1700, binoculars per 2min ₩500; ⏲9am-6pm) Only 2km from North Korea, this multiplex observatory offers views into the hermit kingdom. Through binoculars you can spy villages, workers in rice fields, military towers and distant mountain ranges. There's a short, introductory video in English but you'll need to request it to be played. Bus 1 will get you here, with bus 2 returning to Ganghwa-eup terminal.

GANGHWA HISTORY MUSEUM MUSEUM

(http://museum.ganghwa.go.kr; adult/youth/child ₩1500/1000/1000; ⏲9am-6pm Tue-Sun) Covering 5000 years of the island's history, this museum's range of exhibits is engaging and modern. There's good info on Ganghwa's Unesco Heritage–listed dolmen sites, while the replica of the US Navy attack on Ganghwado in 1871 takes you into the thick of the battle. It's a 30-minute ride (bus 1 or 2) from Ganghwa-eup bus terminal.

GORYEOGUNGJI PALACE PALACE

(고려궁지; Ganghwa-eup; adult/child ₩900/600; ⏲9am-6pm) In Ganghwa-eup are the remains of the small palace built in 1231, once surrounded by an 18km fortress wall. The fortress was destroyed in 1866 by French troops, who invaded Korea in response to the execution of nine French Catholic missionaries. Some 2km of walls and three major gates have since been renovated. It's a 10-minute walk from the bus terminal.

Directly down the hill from the palace is **Ganghwa Anglican Church** (c 1900), built in traditional Korean style with arched-tiled roof. Follow the alleyway down to the **Yongheunggung Royal Residence**, where King Cheoljong used to live.

EATING & DRINKING

Gourmands flock to Ganghwado to sample seafood at the different fishing villages on the island. At Bomun-sa there's heaping plates of inexpensive *twigim* (tempura) seafood and mugwort, accompanied by local ginseng *makgeolli*. On the east coast head to Deurih-mi for seaside restaurants specialising in local eel dishes.

At Jeondeung-sa Temple there are many traditional restaurants, or you can drop by for a free vegetarian lunch within the temple (wash your own dishes afterwards).

WANGJAJEONG KOREAN $$

(왕자정; Ganghwa-eup; meals ₩7000-25,000; ⏲10am-9.30pm; 🖉) Dine on the terrace, enjoying healthy, delicious vegetarian dishes such as *mukbap* (acorn jelly rice) and *kongpiji* (bean soup), while overlooking the walls of Goryeogungji Palace.

JUNGNIM DAWON TEAHOUSE

(죽림다원; Jeongeungsa Temple; tea ₩5000; ⏲8.30am-7.30pm May-Oct, 9.30am-4.30pm Nov-Apr) Within Jeondeung-sa, this atmospheric tea garden is frequented by resident monks and pilgrims sipping on traditional teas.

SLEEPING

★**NAMCHIDANG** HANOK GUESTHOUSE $$$

(남취당; ☎010 9591 0226; http://kyl3850.com/pension/index.php?uid=3; Tosuk Tofu Maeul; r from ₩100,000; ❄📶) In the south of the island, a couple of kilometres from Jeondeung-sa, this beautiful purpose-built *hanok* has traditional wood-fired *ondol* (underfloor-heating) rooms. There are free bikes to get around, and lessons in traditional painting on cotton. Buses 2, 3 and 41 run from Ganghwa-eup.

Sleeping

Seoul has an excellent range of budget backpacker guesthouses and top-end hotels. In the midrange, however, blandness predominates, with the standout options being charming traditional hanok *guesthouses and a handful of design-conscious hotels scattered around the city.*

Backpacker Guesthouses

Backpacker guesthouses are concentrated around Myeong-dong, Itaewon and Hongdae but you'll find them in other districts, too. Rooms – dorms and doubles – tend to be tiny, but nearly always have a bathroom. Helpful staff speak English and there are good communal facilities, including lounges, kitchens, free washing-machine use and internet access.

Hanok Guesthouses & Homestays

Traditional *hanok* (one-storey wooden houses built around a courtyard) are increasingly being turned into guesthouses – you'll find most in Bukchon and Ikseon-dong. Staying in one is a unique and memorable experience; some offer cultural programs such as dressing in *hanbok* (traditional Korean clothing) or cooking classes.

Rooms are small and you'll usually sleep on *yo* (padded quilts and mattresses) on the floor, but underfloor heating systems *(ondol)* keep them snug in winter. At cheaper *hanok* you'll share the bathroom, but some have en suite rooms; note bathrooms are tiny. Rates often include breakfast.

Some *hanok* are also family homes. Families may offer pick-ups and dinner. Jongno-gu runs a *hanok* homestay program (http://homestay.jongno.go.kr/homestayEngMain.do).

Motels, Love Motels & Hotels

Budget hotels are scattered throughout Seoul. The rooms are always on the small size but have bathrooms and come with plenty of facilities. However, staff rarely speak English.

Love motels cater for couples seeking some by-the-hour privacy, but they also accept conventional overnight guests. They tend to be clustered in nightlife areas and can be spotted by the plastic curtains shielding the parked cars from prying eyes. Don't be put off, as they can be an excellent option; some of the extravagantly decorated rooms are a bargain compared with what you'd pay for similar facilities at a top-end hotel.

Seoul has relatively few hotels that could truly be described as 'boutique' although the top international brands are all here.

Serviced Apartments & Longer-Term Rentals

Even for short stays, serviced apartments can be a great option, offering conveniences such as proper kitchen and laundry facilities. Renting an apartment long-term can be tricky because of the traditional payment system that involves paying a huge deposit to the landlord and/or having to pay all your rent up front.

Browse websites www.nicerent.com, www.nearsubway.com or www.airbnb.com for what's on offer.

Accommodation Websites

Lonely Planet (lonelyplanet.com/south-korea/seoul/hotels) Bookings for all kinds of accommodation in Seoul.

Korean Hotel Reservation Center (www.khrc.com) Check for low rates on top-end hotels.

Koreastay (www.koreastay.or.kr) Booking site run by the Korea Tourism Organization.

Homestay Korea (www.homestaykorea.com) If you wish to stay with a Korean family.

Best Guesthouse in Seoul (www.guesthouseinseoul.org) Reviews of Seoul guesthouses.

NEED TO KNOW

Price Ranges

$ less than ₩60,000

$$ ₩60,000–250,000

$$$ more than ₩250,000

Weekend Rates

Rates at many places are a few thousand won higher on Friday and Saturday nights

Taxes & Service Charges

Budget and midrange places usually include a value-added tax (VAT) of 10% in their rates; rates listed here include all taxes. Most top-end hotels will slap a service charge of 10% on the bill as well as VAT (so a total of 20% over the quoted rate).

Tipping

Not expected.

Transport

Only a handful of top-end hotels are not near a subway station; those that aren't provide shuttle buses. Alternatively, use a taxi.

Wi-Fi

Often free, but sometimes only in the hotel lobby. Top-end hotels may charge by the day for internet access.

Lonely Planet's Top Choices

Hide & Seek Guesthouse (p148) Worth tracking down this gem near Gyeongbokgung.

Minari House (p154) Creative, arty base at the foot of Ihwa-dong.

Park Hyatt Seoul (p153) Sophisticated, contemporary design hotel overlooking COEX.

Small House Big Door (p149) Art hotel in downtown Seoul full of designer touches.

Itaewon G Guest House (p152) Grungy apartment block converted to cool backpackers with a sensational rooftop hang-out

K Hostel (p154) Vibrant backpackers full of murals and a cool rooftop with couches.

Best By Budget

$

Urbanwood Guesthouse (p150) Cool, colourful apartment living in the heart of Hongdae.

Kimchee Gangnam Guesthouse (p152) Friendly backpackers inside a posh Gangnam apartment building.

Zaza Backpackers (p149) Pick of the hostels in Myeong-dong's backpacker enclave.

Doo Guesthouse (p148) Best of the budget *hanok* guesthouses.

$$

Hotel Sunbee (p148) Huge double beds in tastefully decorated rooms.

Lee Kang Ga (p151) Attractive Korean design features in the rooms here.

Metro Hotel (p149) Splashes of style abound at this Myeong-dong base.

$$$

Grand Hyatt Seoul (p152) Oozing class on the hillside of Namsan overlooking Itaewon.

Plaza (p150) Large rooms look down upon grassy Seoul Plaza and the historic-meets-contemporary facade of City Hall.

Best Hanok Guesthouses

Rak-Ko-Jae (p149) Beautifully restored *hanok*, with an enchanting garden and traditional sauna.

Eugene's House (p154) Family run and a bit more spacious than you'll find elsewhere.

Chi-Woon-Jung (p149) *Hanok* guesthouses don't come any more luxurious than this beauty.

Best Love Motels

Hotel the Designers (p148) Take your pick from 18 different designer suites.

H Avenue Hotel (p153) Classy motel notable for rooms with private roof-deck pools.

Hotel D'Oro (p152) Best value in the Itaewon area.

Best Serviced Apartments

Fraser Suites (p149) Top-class serviced apartments in Insa-dong.

Oriens Hotel & Residences (p150) Great location and professional service for a reasonable price.

Where to Stay

Neighbourhood	For	Against
Gwanghwamun & Jongno-gu	Ideal for exploring the city on foot with the palaces, Insa-dong and Bukchon on your doorstep. Plenty of characterful *hanok* guesthouses and homestays.	Light on top-end hotels. Parts of Insa-dong and Bukchon are very heavily trafficked with tourists.
Myeong-dong & Jung-gu	Central location and direct access to Namsan and shopping in Myeong-dong and Namdaemun. Good selection of accommodation at all levels.	Streets in the heart of Myeong-dong are perpetually busy – not a place for those seeking peace and tranquillity.
Western Seoul	Best for budget travellers who want to party with students and hipsters in Hongdae and surrounds. Yeouido is recommended only if you have business on the island.	You will spend a fair amount of time on the subway to get to the major sights.
Itaewon & Around	Reasonably central location close to some major sights. Perfect if you want to take full advantage of Itaewon's plentiful dining and nightlife options.	The most 'Western' area of Seoul. You'll be catching taxis or taking the subway to major sights north of Namsan.
Gangnam & South of the Han River	For those who will settle for nothing less than major top-end brands. There's buzzing nightlife in Apgujeong and Gangnam. Handy for COEX if you're visiting for a convention there.	Very light on budget options. The grid-like layout, barrelling highways and dearth of historical sights make it way less appealing than north of the Han.
Dongdaemun & Eastern Seoul	Shopping nirvana, particularly for those who love markets. Night owls will be thrilled by the 24-hour activity.	Hotels on Walker Hill are a long drive from the city and not close to the subway either.
Northern Seoul	Several backpacker guesthouses near the theatre district of Daehangno.	Not all areas here are accessible by subway.

Gwanghwamun & Jongno-gu

At the time of writing the new Four Seasons Hotel Seoul was nearing completion. The 25-story building's opening will bring five-star luxury next to Gwanghwamun Sq.

★HOSTEL KOREA 11TH HOSTEL $

Map p212 (☎070-4705 1900; www.cdg.hostelkorea.com; 85 Donhwamun-ro, Jongno-gu; dm/tr/q from ₩20,000/129,000/149,000, d & tw ₩99,000; ❄@📶; Ⓢ Line 3 to Anguk, Exit 4) The best of the larger hostels popping up in this area. This one has a colourful, fun design, great location, roomy capsule-style dorm beds and a fabulous rooftop chill-out area with views.

★DOO GUESTHOUSE HANOK GUESTHOUSE $

Map p208 (☎02-3672 1977; www.dooguesthouse.com; 103-7 Gyedong-gil; s/d/tr/q incl breakfast ₩50,000/60,000/100,000/120,000; ❄@📶; Ⓢ Line 3 to Anguk, Exit 3) Mixing old and new is this enchanting *hanok* in a garden setting with a traditional-style room where breakfast is served. The shared bathrooms are high quality, with bidets and walk-in showers. The rooms have TVs and DVD players.

BEEWON GUESTHOUSE GUESTHOUSE $

Map p212 (비원게스트하우스; ☎02-765 0677; www.beewonguesthouse.com; 77-4 Donhwamun-ro 11ga-gil; dm/d/tr ₩17,000/43,000/47,000; ❄@📶; Ⓢ Line 3 to Anguk, Exit 4) Combining facility-filled motel-style rooms (some with *ondol* options) with free, guesthouse-style communal facilities, the clean-and-tidy Beewon is generally quiet and friendly, plastered with photos of happy past guests.

INN DAEWON HANOK GUESTHOUSE $

Map p210 (대원여관; ☎02-735 7891; www.geocities.jp/newdaewon2006; 133-10 Sajik-ro, Jongno-gu; dm/s/d without bathroom ₩19,000/27,000/35,000; ❄📶; Ⓢ Line 3 to Gyeongbokgung, Exit 4) The Daewon's greatest asset is its kindly owners, who live next door. Simple rooms with shared bathrooms surround a covered courtyard. Guests sleep on floor mattresses, except in the dorm, reached up a steep flight of stairs.

★HOTEL THE DESIGNERS BOUTIQUE HOTEL $$

Map p212 (☎02-2267 7474; www.hotelthedesigners.com; 89-8 Supyo-ro, Jongno-gu; r/ste from ₩90,000/150,000; ❄📶; Ⓢ Lines 1 or 3 Jongno 3-ga, Exit 15) Eighteen designers were given free reign to decorate the suites at this sophisticated love motel. Check the website for the themes: our favourite is Camp Ruka-baik with a tent, deck chairs, tree-bark-covered poles and guitar for a city camping experience. If you just want a taste of these fantasy rooms, then short stays (fours hours Sunday to Thursday, three hours Friday and Saturday) are also available for ₩40,000.

★HIDE & SEEK GUESTHOUSE GUESTHOUSE $$

Map p210 (☎02-6925 5916; www.hidenseek.co.kr; 14 Jahamun-ro 6-gil, Jongno-gu; s/tw/tr incl breakfast from ₩56,000/77,000/105,000; ❄📶; Ⓢ Line 3 to Gyeongbokgung, Exit 5) Stylish design marks out this appealing five-room guesthouse, tucked away in Tongui-dong, beside the remains of an ancient pine tree, and occupying a modern, two-storey house with a broad outdoor terrace. Breakfast is served in the cute Stella's Kitchen cafe.

★HOTEL SUNBEE HOTEL $$

Map p212 (호텔썬비; ☎02-730 3451; www.hotelsunbee.com; 26 Insa-dong 7-gil, Jongno-gu; d/tw/ondol incl breakfast ₩100,000/120,000/140,000; ❄@📶; Ⓢ Line 3 to Anguk, Exit 6) The friendly Sunbee offers huge double beds in tastefully decorated rooms with wide-screen TVs and computers, for a lower price than similar business hotels nearby. A simple breakfast is served in the ground-floor cafe.

MOON GUEST HOUSE HANOK GUESTHOUSE $$

Map p212 (☎02-745 8008; www.moonguesthouse.com; 31-16 Samil-daero 32-gil, Jongno-gu; s/d incl breakfast from ₩50,000/80,000; ❄📶; Ⓢ Line 3 to Anguk, Exit 4) The seven rooms at this 50-year-old *hanok* have been renovated to a high standard. Rooms are tiny and the cheapest have shared bathrooms. Various traditional cultural experiences are offered to guests.

WWOOF KOREA GUESTHOUSE HANOK GUESTHOUSE $$

Map p208 (☎070-8288 1289; www.wwoofkoreaguesthouse.com; 52-11 Gyedong-gil, Jongno-gu; s/d incl breakfast from ₩70,000/100,000, without bathroom from ₩60,000/90,000; ❄📶; Ⓢ Line 3 to Anguk, Exit 1) This rustic courtyard *hanok* is run by Helen, the director of the Korea branch of World Wide Opportunities on Organic Farms (WWOOF). Breakfast is all organic and you can buy the organic plum juice as a souvenir.

SOPHIA GUEST HOUSE HANOK GUESTHOUSE $$

Map p208 (☎02-720 5467; www.sophiagh.com; 74-11 Yulgok-ro 1-gil, Jongno-gu; s/d incl breakfast without bathroom from ₩50,000/90,000; ❄📶; S Line 3 to Anguk, Exit 1) Rooms surround a pretty courtyard shaded by a pine tree, at this place run by hospitable Sophia. It's one of the larger properties of its type with nine rooms, all of which share bathrooms. It has an antique feel, but rooms have TVs.

★**RAK-KO-JAE** HANOK GUESTHOUSE **$$$**

Map p208 (락고재; ☎02-742 3410; www.rkj.co.kr; 98 Gyeo-dong; s/d incl breakfast & dinner ₩198,000/275,000; ❄@; S Line 3 to Anguk, Exit 2) This beautifully restored *hanok*, with an enchanting garden is modelled after Japan's ryokan. The guesthouse's mud-walled sauna is included in the prices. The en suite bathrooms are tiny, though.

CHI-WOON-JUNG HANOK GUESTHOUSE **$$$**

Map p208 (취운정; ☎02-765 7400; www.chiwoonjung.co.kr; 31-53 Gahoe-dong; s/d from ₩500,000/1,000,000; ❄📶; S Line 3 to Anguk, Exit 2) The *hanok* as an exclusive luxury experience doesn't get much finer than this stunning property that has just four elegant guest rooms, all with beautifully tiled bathrooms and pine-wood tubs. Completely remodelled since Korean president Lee Myung Bak once lived there, it is decorated with beautiful crafts and has a Zen-calm garden.

FRASER SUITES APARTMENT **$$$**

Map p212 (☎02-6262 8888; www.frasershospitality.com; 18 Insadong 4-gil, Jongno-gu; 1-/2-/3-bedroom apt incl breakfast ₩330,000/440,000/550,000; ❄@📶🏊; S Line 1, 3 or 5 to Jongno 3-ga, Exit 5) These fully equipped serviced apartments are modern, light and spacious, great for a long-term stay (discounts available). The staff tries hard to make this a home away from home and its location, steps away from Insadong-gil, is ideal for sightseeing.

Myeong-dong & Jung-gu

ZAZA BACKPACKERS HOSTEL **$**

Map p216 (자자 백팩커스; ☎02-3672 1976; www.zazabackpackers.com; 32-3 Nansandong-2ga, Jung-gu; s/d ₩50,000/60,000; ❄@📶; S Line 4 to Myeondong, Exit 3) In the backpacker enclave along the hill to Namsan, Zaza is one of the best with its contemporary building full of design touches and a friendly young staff. It runs the nearby **Global Hostel** (서울 글로벌 호스텔; Map p216; ☎02-587 5776; www.seoulglobalhostel.com; 38 Sogong-ro 6-gil; s/d/tr/q ₩50,000/60,000/80,000/100,000; ❄📶; S Line 4 to Myeongdong, Exit 3), which also resembles something out of an architectural magazine. It has modern, comfortable rooms and a spacious kitchen and dining area.

NAMSAN GUESTHOUSE BACKPACKERS **$**

Map p216 (남산게스트하우스; ☎02-752 6363; www.namsanguesthouse.com; 79-3 Toegye-ro 18-gil, Jung-gu; dm/d/tr/q incl breakfast ₩30,000/55,000/85,000/95,000; ❄@📶; S Line 4 to Myeongdong, Exit 2) Taking over the neighborhood on the slopes of Namsan, this long-running backpackers now has five locations in the immediate area. Some have pod-style dorms fitted with TVs, others rooftop terraces, but all make for good budget choices. See the website for specifics of each branch.

MYEONGDONG TOMATO GUESTHOUSE HOSTEL **$**

Map p216 (명동 토마토 게스트하우스; ☎02-318 9800; www.tomato.testors.net; 8-1 Toegye-ro 20ga-gil, Jung-gu; s/d/tr incl breakfast ₩50,000/60,000/85,000; S Line 4 to Myeongdong, Exit 4) Tucked down an alleyway, this friendly guesthouse has stylish design elements, plus bright, clean rooms, a large homely kitchen and a rooftop with views of Namsan.

★**SMALL HOUSE BIG DOOR** HOTEL **$$**

Map p216 (스몰 하우스 빅 도어; ☎02-2038 8191; www.smallhousebigdoor.com; 6 Namdaemun-ro 9-gil, Jung-gu; r incl breakfast from ₩115,000-250,000; ❄📶; S Line 2 to Euljiro 1-ga, Exit 1, 2) Down a narrow street in downtown Seoul, this suave little art hotel is quite the find. Its white-toned rooms all feature locally designed, handmade furniture and beds, and maximise the use of space with ingenious slide-out desks and TVs. Pricier rooms have outdoor sitting areas and sky windows. Head upstairs to its rooftop lounge to hang out, or downstairs to the lively cafe with gallery and performance space.

★**METRO HOTEL** HOTEL **$$**

Map p216 (메트로호텔; ☎02-2176 3199; www.metrohotel.co.kr; 14 Myeong-dong 9ga-gil, Jung-gu; s/d incl breakfast from ₩110,000/143,000; ❄@📶; S Line 2 to Euljiro 1-ga, Exit 6) An excellent mid-range choice, this small, professionally run hotel has boutique aspirations. Splashes of style abound, from the flashy, metallic lobby to its laptops. Room size and design vary; ask for one of the larger ones with big windows (room numbers which end in 07).

CRIB49 GUESTHOUSE **$$**

Map p216 (크립 49 게스트하우스; ☎070-8128 5981; www.crib49.com; 49 Toegye-ro 20na-gil, Jung-gu; d/tr incl breakfast from ₩80,000/100,000;

❄@📶; ⓈLine 4 to Myeongdong, Exit 3) Up the hill near Namsan's cable car, the *ondol* rooms at Crib49 have floor mattresses, and minimalist decor with Scandanavian-style shelving and plasma TVs. Its rooftop deck has Namsan views and there's a small kitchen.

NINE TREE HOTEL MYEONG-DONG HOTEL $$

Map p216 (나인트리호텔 명동; ☎02-7500 999; www.ninetreehotel.com; 51 Myeongdong 10-gil, Jung-gu; s/d incl breakfast ₩170,000/190,000; ❄📶; ⓈLine 4 to Myeongdong, Exit 8) There's plenty to like about this snazzy hotel in the heart of Myeong-dong's shopping district. The smart boutique-y rooms have city views, a pillow menu, Japanese-style electronic toilets, clothes press, foot-massage machines, minibar and a coffee maker. Plus there are substantial discounts if you book online.

HOTEL PRINCE HOTEL $$

Map p216 (프린스호텔; ☎02-752 7111; www.princeseoul.com; 130 Toegye-ro, Jung-gu; d/tw/ondol incl breakfast ₩143,000/170,500/220,000; ❄@📶; ⓈLine 4 to Myeongdong, Exit 2) Rooms at this centrally located business hotel are smallish but sparkling, with some bright primary colours to alleviate the otherwise all-white regime. Book online for discounts.

ORIENS HOTEL & RESIDENCES APARTMENT $$

Map p216 (오리엔스 호텔 & 레지던스; ☎02-2280 8000; www.hansuites.com; 50 Samil-daero 2-gil; studio/1-bedroom apt from ₩90,000/231,000; ❄@📶; ⓈLine 3 or 4 to Chungmuro, Exit 4) A great location, friendly and professional service and reasonable rates make this one of the best serviced apartments for short or long stays. Rooms are plainly furnished but have everything you need. Note that many of the cheaper studios have windows onto an internal light well, so can be rather gloomy.

PACIFIC HOTEL HOTEL $$

Map p216 (퍼시픽호텔; ☎02-777 7811; www.thepacifichotel.co.kr; 2 Toegye-ro, 20-gil, Jung-gu; d/tw from ₩145,000/170,000; ❄@📶; ⓈLine 4 to Myeongdong, Exit 3) Bell boys in caps greet you at this old-fashioned hotel, where light neutral colours, greenery and a natural-wood effect are the style. Bathrooms are a tad cramped, but there's a big sauna and spa bath in the building, as well as a small rooftop garden.

★**PLAZA** HOTEL $$$

Map p216 (더 플라자; ☎02-771 2200; www.hoteltheplaza.com; 23 Taepyeong-ro 2-ga; r from ₩300,000; ❄@📶🏊; ⓈLine 1 or 2 to City Hall, Exit 6) Opposite the striking glass edifice of City Hall, you couldn't get more central than the Plaza. Rooms sport a smart design with giant anglepoise lamps, circular mirrors and crisp white linens contrasting against dark carpets. It also has some chic restaurants and a good fitness club with a swimming pool.

WESTIN CHOSUN SEOUL HOTEL $$$

Map p216 (웨스틴 조선호텔 서울; ☎02-771 0500; www.westin.com/seoul; 106 Sogong-ro, Jung-gu; r from ₩410,000; ❄@📶🏊; ⓈLine 2 to Euljiro 1-ga, Exit 4) Dating from the late 1970s, this is not Seoul's most spectacular hotel, but the relaxing atmosphere and the conscientious staff keep it a cut above the rest. Each stylish room decorated in soft caramel tones comes with a coffee maker, shaving mirrors, bathroom scales and a choice of 10 types of pillows. Keep an eye out for the Henry Moore sculpture in the lobby.

LOTTE HOTEL SEOUL HOTEL $$$

Map p216 (롯데호텔서울; ☎02-771 1000; www.lottehotelseoul.com; 30 Eulji-ro; r from ₩380,000; ❄@📶🏊; ⓈLine 2 to Euljiro 1-ga, Exit 8) This twin-towered hotel with over 1000 rooms has a marble-lined lobby long enough for Usain Bolt training runs. The new wing's standard rooms are bigger than those in the old but don't have as modern a design; some come with City Hall views. There's also a ladies-only floor with a book-lined lounge.

Renowned French chef Pierre Gagnaire's new restaurant (p81) is on the 35th floor.

Western Seoul

★**URBANWOOD GUESTHOUSE** HOSTEL $

Map p218 (☎070-8613 0062; www.urbanwood.co.kr; 3rd fl, 48-20 Wausan-ro 29-gil, Mapo-gu; s/d incl breakfast from ₩60,000/80,000; ❄📶; ⓈLine 2 to Hongik University, Exit 8) Creatively decorated in bright colours and modern furnishings, this cosy guesthouse feels like a cool arty apartment. Martin, the convivial English-speaking host, knows the area well and will whisk you up a mean coffee on the professional barista machine in the well-appointed kitchen Also rents apartments in the area.

ROI HOUSE GUESTHOUSE $

(☎070-811 2626; http://roihouse.wix.com/english; 14 Donggyo-ro 41-gil, Mapo-gu; dm/tw/q incl breakfast from ₩22,000/70,000/130,000; ❄@📶; ⓈLien 2 to Hongik University, Exit 3) Modern, with larger rooms than most guesthouses and on a quiet, tree-lined street in Yeonnam-dong, this is a very pleasant place to stay that's within walking distance of Hongdae. Owner Park Simon speaks good English.

V MANSION BACKPACKERS $

Map p218 (☎070-8877 0608; vmansion.com; 133 Tojeong-ro, Mapo-gu; d ₩80,000, dm/s/tw without bathroom incl breakfast ₩28,000/50,000/70,000; ❄@📶; Ⓢ Line 6 to Sangsu, Exit 3) Offers something quite unexpected from a Seoul backpackers – space and a big garden! Exhibitions by local artists and various arty events are held here to help visitors connect with Seoul's more creative spirits.

BLU: HOME GUEST HOUSE BACKPACKERS $

Map p218 (☎02-4065 7218; www.bluguesthouse.com; 142-16 Donggyo-ro, Mapo-gu; dm/s/d incl breakfast from ₩15,000/50,000/60,000; ❄@📶; Ⓢ Line 2 to Hongik University, Exit 1) Decked out in plenty of blue paint, and in two locations close to Hongdae, this is an appealing backpackers lodge with all the usual facilities, friendly staff and a free basic breakfast thrown into the bargain. Long-term residency is a possibility here too.

TRAVELERS PLANET HOSTEL HOSTEL $

Map p218 (☎02-335 0063; http://tphostel.com; 54-8 Donggyo-ro 25-gil, Mapo-gu; s/d incl breakfast from ₩90,000/100,000, without bathroom from ₩55,000/60,000; ❄@📶; Ⓢ Line 2 to Hongik University, Exit 1) Good-value rooms here in an old apartment block turned into a hostel; there are no dorms but the rooms are pretty inexpensive especially if you buddy up. It's all nicely decorated and kept very clean. Pluses include a big kitchen, roof-top area and staff preparing Korean breakfasts at the weekend.

The same management run the similar **Studio 41st hostel** (Map p218; ☎070 4402 0041; www.studio41st.com; 30 Seongmisan-ro 22-gil; d or tw from ₩90,000, tr ₩110,000; ❄@📶; Ⓢ Line 2 to Hongik University, Exit 2) which is a bit of a further walk from Hongdae.

COME INN BACKPACKERS $

Map p218 (☎070-8958 7279; www.comeinnkorea.com; 20-10 Wausan-ro 21-gil, Mapo-gu; dm/s/d without bathroom incl breakfast from ₩15,000/43,000/58,000; ❄@📶; Ⓢ Line 2 to Hongik University, Exit 9) Bang in the centre of Hongdae is this compact 3rd-floor guesthouse offering the usual mix of dorms and private rooms, all of which share common bathrooms. There's a comfy lounge and a broad outdoor terrace with views across the area.

URBAN ART GUEST HOUSE HOSTEL $

(☎070-4137 3565; www.facebook.com/urbanart; 98 Mullae-ro, Yeongdeungpo-gu; dm/d from ₩15,000/35,000; ❄@📶; Ⓢ Line 2 to Mullae, Exit 7) Pine bunk beds, Tibetan prayer flags, shabby sofas and street art: this crash pad fits right in with Mullae's boho vibe. It's not the pick of Seoul's backpackers but it does run weekly BBQ parties and tours of the local street art as well as Korean language classes.

★LEE KANG GA GUESTHOUSE $$

Map p218 (☎02-323 5484; www.leekanghouse.com; 4th fl, 12 World Cup-buk-ro 11-gil, Mapo-gu; d incl breakfast from ₩80,000; ❄@📶; Ⓢ Line 2 to Hongik University, Exit 1, then 🚌15, 7711, 7737 or 7016) Near the War and Women's Human Rights Museum, this appealing guesthouse is worth the schlep from Hongdae. Rooms are attractively decorated with *hanji* (traditional paper) wallpaper, silky pillows and pine-wood furniture and a few have balconies and washing machines. There are great views from the rooftop kitchen and garden.

HAEMIL GUESTHOUSE $$

(☎070-4530 7131; thehaemil.com; 30 Donggyo-ro 46gil, Mapo-go; d/tw incl breakfast ₩77,000/88,000; ❄@📶; Ⓢ Line 2 to Hongik University, Exit 3) Among the guesthouses in Yeonnam-dong, Haemil stands out for its rustic Korean design touches such as the use of natural wooden furniture and colours. Rooms are compact but have private bathrooms and there's a lounge and rooftop garden.

MARIGOLD HOTEL HOTEL $$

Map p218 (☎02-332 5656; www.hotelmarigold.co.kr; 112 Yanghwa-ro, Mapo-gu; tw from ₩130,000; ❄@📶; Ⓢ Line 2 to Hongik University, Exit 9) Part of the reliable business-hotel chain Benikea, the Marigold's rooms are spacious and aim for contemporary chic with amber onyx tiles and fake animal-skin headboards on the beds. The deluxe rooms even stretch to copies of Eames recliner chairs.

A buffet breakfast is ₩15,400 extra and guests get a discount at the Happy Day Spa in the basement.

CONRAD SEOUL HOTEL $$$

Map p220 (☎02-6137 7000; conradseoul.co.kr; 23-1 Yeouido-dong, Yeongdeungpo-gu; s/d from ₩330,000/374,000; ❄@📶🏊; Ⓢ Line 5 or 9 to Yeouido, Exit 3) Superior service, luxe rooms in natural tones, and sweeping views of the Han River and city are what you'd expect here – and it absolutely delivers. The natural choice for business travel on the island.

Itaewon & Around

★ITAEWON G GUEST HOUSE HOSTEL $

Map p222 (이태원 G 게스트하우스; ☎010 8774 7767; www.gguest.com; 14-38 Bogwang-ro 60-gil; dm/s/d incl breakfast ₩15,000/40,000/70,000; ❄📶; Ⓢ Line 6 to Itaewon, Exit 3) Owned by ultra-friendly Shrek and Fiona, this hostel stands above for its attention to thought and detail. Set in a renovated industrial-chic apartment building, its private rooms and dorms are clean, spacious and have quality thick mattresses. There's also **G Guest Home** that'll suit those looking for a more a low-key stay.

It's a good place to meet others, whether hanging out in its basement or on the awesome rooftop with weekly BBQs. Other perks include free laundry, filter coffee and bikes for the nearby Han River cycling path. Room rates go up around ₩5000 on weekends.

SP@ITAEWON GUESTHOUSE HOSTEL $

Map p222 (SP@이태원게스트하우스; ☎02-796 6990; www.spguest.com; Itaewon-dong 112-11; dm/s/f from ₩15,000/32,000/70,000; ❄📶; Ⓢ Line 6 to Itaewon, Exit 1) Run by a friendly team of international staff, this Serbian-owned hostel is just up the hill from Itaewon's main drag. It attracts an eclectic crowd of backpackers, long-term residents and local students who congregate in the old-school party-house garage downstairs. The same owners also run the **Itaewon Hostel & Inn** (이태원 호스텔 과 여관; Map p222; ☎02-6221 0880; www.itaewoninn.com; 103-2 Bogwang-ro; dm ₩16,000, s/d ₩50,000/70,000, s without bathroom ₩35,000; Ⓢ Line 6 to Itaewon, Exit 4) with a cool rooftop.

GUESTHOUSE YACHT GUESTHOUSE $

Map p222 (요트게스트하우스; ☎010 6556 1125; www.guesthouseyacht.com; 23 Itaewon-ro 23-gil; dm/s/d with breakfast ₩20,000/40,000/60,000; ❄@📶; Ⓢ Line 6 to Itaewon, Exit 1) Steered by 'the Captain' (the owner was the first Korean to sail by yacht across the Pacific) and his trusty crew, this friendly guesthouse has a good selection of rooms with shared bathrooms, including a 'penthouse' with its own piano. The highlight is the small rooftop decked out in astroturf. Once a month guests are invited on sailing trips to the West Sea.

POP@ITAEWON GUESTHOUSE GUESTHOUSE $

Map p222 (팝 앳 이태원 게스트하우스; ☎070-7797 9244; www.guesthouseseoul.net; 9 Noksapyeong-daero 32-gil; dm/d ₩14,000/48,000; ❄📶; Ⓢ Line 6 to Noksapyeong, Exit 2) Down a laneway in the heart of Itaewon, this vibrant little guesthouse has basic rooms with desks, plasma TV, and replica murals by Warhol and Keith Haring. Its rooftop is a good place to relax and there's a kitchen and small lounge.

IP BOUTIQUE HOTEL HOTEL $$

Map p222 (IP 부티크 호텔; ☎02-3702 8000; www.ipboutiquehotel.com; 737-32 Hannam-dong; r from ₩170,000; ❄@📶🏊; Ⓢ Line 6 to Itaewon, Exit 2) Trying a bit too hard to be hip with bold artworks and quirky design, this boutique wannabe is in a great location and stands out in a city of fairly generic-style hotels.

HOTEL D'ORO LOVE MOTEL $$

Map p222 (디오로호텔; ☎02-749 6525; 34-34 Itaewon-ro 27-gil, Yongsan-gu; d from ₩88,000; ❄@📶; Ⓢ Line 6 to Itaewon, Exit 2) This above-average love motel offers some style, modern equipment and furnishings, plus free soft drinks rather than an expensive minibar.

★GRAND HYATT SEOUL HOTEL $$$

Map p222 (그랜드 하얏트 서울; ☎02-797 1234; www.seoul.grand.hyatt.com; 322 Sowol-ro; r from ₩360,000; ❄@📶🏊; Ⓢ Line 6 to Hangangjin, Exit 1) Making the most of its hilltop views, the Grand Hyatt oozes class. Rooms are a bit smaller than at rivals but all have been freshly renovated and sport a contemporary look. Pamper yourself in the spa, dance the night away at popular club JJ Mahoney's or swim in the excellent outdoor pool which, come winter, is turned into an ice rink.

Gangnam & South of the Han River

KIMCHEE GANGNAM GUESTHOUSE HOSTEL $

Map p228 (김치 강남 게스트하우스; ☎02-518 6696; www.kimcheeguesthouse.com; 23 Seolleung-ro 133-gil, Gangnam-gu; dm/s/d incl breakfast ₩25,000/35,000/60,000; ❄@📶; Ⓢ Line 7 to Gangnam-gu Office, Exit 3) A rare budget choice for ritzy Gangnam, this friendly guesthouse is set in a posh-looking old apartment building in a residential street. The mixed dorms are modern and spacious, while private rooms are more on the boxy side. Unwind in the basement with stylish cafe, vintage furniture and full kitchen.

24 GUESTHOUSE GANGNAM CENTER GUESTHOUSE $

Map p228 (24게스트하우스 강남 센터점; ☎02-538 1177; http://gangnamcenter.24guesthouse.co.kr; 52 Bongeunsa-ro 20-gil, Gangnam-gu; dm/s/d/tr incl breakfast ₩30,000/50,000/60,000/80,000;

; Line 2 to Yeoksam, Exit 4) In a residential backstreet of Gangnam, this guesthouse has a location that's close enough to the action, yet far enough away to enjoy a peaceful stay. Rooms share bathrooms and lack character, but make up for it with a laid-back homely atmosphere and full kitchen. There's also a branch along **Garosu-gil** (Map p228; 02-540 7742; http://garosu-gil.24guesthouse.co.kr; 31-5 Dosan-daero 13-gil, Gangnam-gu; r with bathroom ₩80,000, s/d without bathroom incl breakfast ₩60,000/70,000; ; Line 3 to Sinsa, Exit 6).

SEOUL OLYMPIC PARKTEL HOTEL $

Map p230 (서울올림픽파크텔; 02-421 2114; www.parktel.co.kr; Olympic Park, 88-8 Bang-dong, Songpa-gu; dm ₩22,000; ; Line 8 to Mongchontoseong, Exit 1) If you're a youth-hostel member you can stay in this business hotel at a youth-hostel rate. It's a long way from most sights, but the dorms – actually hotel rooms with two double bunks and two pull-out beds – have big windows with park views.

LA CASA HOTEL $$

Map p228 (라까사 호텔 서울; 02-546 0088; www.hotellacasa.kr; 83 Dosan-daero 1-gil, Gangnam-gu; s/d incl breakfast from ₩178,000/215,000; ; Line 3 to Sinsa, Exit 6) The first venture into the hospitality business by classy Korean furniture and interior-design store Casamia packs plenty of chic style. The rooms are attractive and spacious with details such as travel-themed pillowcases, while the lobby also has plenty of design features and art books. It's handy for Garosu-gil.

MERCURE SEOUL AMBASSADOR GANGNAM SODOWE HOTEL $$

Map p228 (머큐어 서울 앰배서더 강남 쏘도베; 02-2050 6000; www.mercureseoul.com; 642 Teheran-ro 25-gil, Gangnam-gu; r from ₩147,400; ; Line 2 to Yeoksam, Exit 4) Well located, this business-smart hotel is decorated in candy colours and arty flourishes. Rooms with city views cost extra, as does the sauna (₩5000), but laundry is included and good discounts are available by booking online. There's also the upstairs Rooftop Kloud bar with great views and single-malt selection.

H AVENUE HOTEL LOVE MOTEL $$

Map p228 (에이치 에비뉴 호텔; 02-508 6247; 12 Teheran-ro 29-gil, Gangnam-gu; r from ₩60,000; ; Line 2 to Yeoksam, Exit 8) Fantastic value, this hotel is most notable for its roof-terrace rooms which come with their own roof-deck swimming pools and views over Namsan and the cathedral; stay midweek for the best deals. While a love motel, it comes without all the usual weird trappings.

M CHEREVILLE APARTMENT $$

Map p228 (엠쉐르빌; 02-532 9774; www.mchereville.net; 1316-31 Seocho 4-dong, Seocho-gu; studio/1-/2-bedroom apt from ₩110,000/132,000/165,000; ; Line 2 to Gangnam, Exit 9) These spacious apartments come fully furnished and suit a longer stay, with cooking facilities, fridge, water dispenser, DVD player, washer/dryer and dishwasher. You'll find its friendly staff at reception on the 6th floor.

PRINCESS HOTEL MOTEL $$

Map p228 (프린세스호텔; 02-544 0366; 17 Apgujeong-ro 46-gil, Gangnam-gu; r from ₩80,000; ; Bundang Line to Apgujeong Rodeo, Exit 6) If you need to be close to Apgujeong's shopping action, this easy-to-locate motel with English-speaking staff is just the ticket. Rooms are dark, but spacious and good value.

TRIA HOTEL HOTEL $$

Map p228 (호텔 트리아; 02-553 2471; www.triahotel.co.kr; 16 Teheran-ro 33-gil, Gangnam-gu; r/ste from ₩95,000/150,000; ; Line 2 to Yeoksam, Exit 8) An excellent-value option that's very affordable for this end of town, 50-room boutiquey Tria has lots going for it. Opt for any room above standard and you'll get a whirlpool bath. The hotel is tucked away in the streets behind the Renaissance Hotel, a five-minute walk from the subway exit.

★**PARK HYATT SEOUL** HOTEL $$$

Map p230 (파크 하얏트 서울; 02-2016 1234; www.seoul.park.hyatt.com; 606 Teheran-ro, Gangnam-gu; r from ₩450,000; ; Line 2 to Samseong, Exit 1) A discrete entrance – look for the rock sticking out of the wall – sets the Zen-minimalist tone for this gorgeous property. Each floor only has 10 rooms with spotlit antiquities lining the hallways. Spacious open-plan rooms are glassed in with floor-to-ceiling windows that boast city views and come with luxurious bathrooms classed among the best in Asia.

RITZ-CARLTON SEOUL HOTEL $$$

Map p228 (리츠칼튼 서울; 02-3451 8000; www.ritzcarltonseoul.com; 120 Bongeunsa-ro, Gangnam-gu; r from ₩423,500; ; Line 9 to Shinnonhyeon, Exit 4) Traditional but not old-fashioned, the Ritz Carlton wraps guests in soothing luxury with high levels of service, plenty of facilities and a European atmosphere stretching from the furniture to the food. Some rooms have huge balconies, and views of the city or Namsan. Book online for discounts.

LOTTE HOTEL WORLD HOTEL $$$
Map p230 (롯데호텔월드; ☎02-419 7000; www.lottehotelworld.com; 240 Olympic-ro, Songpa-gu; r from ₩360,000; ❄@📶🏊; Ⓢ Line 2 or 8 to Jamsil, Exit 4) Purely for those with kids in tow, this luxury hotel has rooms that open directly to the theme park that will fulfill every child's wildest imagination. The 7th-floor rooms are the ones you're after, all decorated with cartoon characters as well as PlayStations.

Dongdaemun & Eastern Seoul

★K HOSTEL HOSTEL $
Map p225 (케이 호스텔; ☎02-2233 9155; www.khostel.net; 384 Jong-ro, Jongno-gu; d with bathroom ₩55,000, dm/s/tw without bathroom incl breakfast ₩20,000/30,000/50,000; ❄📶; Ⓢ Line 2 to Dongmyo, Exit 2) Your quintessential Western-style backpackers, this lively hostel (one of many branches in Seoul) has a homely kitchen, comfy lounge and sensational rooftop with BBQ, couches and views. Rooms are clean and more spacious than most. It's a 15-minute walk to Dongdaemun market.

DONGDAEMUN HOSTEL & INN BACKPACKERS $
Map p225 (동대문 호스텔; ☎070-7785 8055; www.dongdaemunhostel.com; 43-1 Gwanghui-dong 2-ga, Jung-gu; s/d/tr from ₩20,000/40,000/50,000; 📶; Ⓢ Lines 2, 4 & 5 to Dongdaemun History & Culture Park, Exit 4) A lot is crammed into the tiny single rooms at this backpackers guesthouse, including computer, desk and a shower/toilet cubicle. In the laneway behind is Dongdaemun Inn with doubles and triples.

TOYOKO INN SEOUL DONGDAEMUN HOTEL $$
Map p225 (토요코인 서울 동대문; ☎02-2267 1045; www.toyoko-inn.com; 337 Toegye-ro, Jung-gu; s/d incl breakfast from ₩60,500/77,000; ❄@📶; Ⓢ Lines 2, 4 & 5 to Dongdaemun History & Culture Park, Exit 4) The small, clean rooms at this Japanese business hotel are great value, and well located for Dongdaemun's main sights.

W SEOUL WALKERHILL HOTEL $$$
(W 서울 워커힐 호텔; ☎02-465 2222; www.whotels.com/seoul; 177 Walkerhill-ro, Gwangjin-gu; r from ₩357,000; ❄@📶🏊; Ⓢ Line 5 to Gwangnaru, Exit 2) One of the city's best-designed hotels, with hip public areas and generally fablicious rooms with striking colour schemes and river or mountain views. The spa, pool, gym, restaurants and Woobar are so nice you probably won't want to stray far, which is just as well as it's distant from most sights. There's a free shuttle to Gwangnaru station every 10 minutes from 6am to 11pm.

JW MARRIOTT DONGDAEMUN SQUARE HOTEL $$$
Map p225 (JW 메리어트 동대문 스퀘어 서울; ☎02-2276 3000; www.jwmarriottdongdaemun.com; 279 Cheonggyecheon-ro, Jongno-gu; r from ₩300,000; Ⓢ Line 1, 4 to Dongdaemun, Exit 9) In a prime location next door to Dongdaemun Market and opposite Heunginjium Gate, the five-star Marriot is a more intimate branch than usual. All rooms have desks, bath-tubs equipped with TVs, top-notch sound systems and coffee capsules. It's worth upgrading to a room with views of Heunginjium and retractable blinds that open to the stars.

Northern Seoul

INSIDE BACKPACKERS BACKPACKERS $
Map p226 (☎02-3672 1120; http://insideseoulhostel.com; 5 Sungkyunkwan-ro 4-gil, Jongno-gu; tw ₩49,000, dm/s/tw without bathroom ₩16,000/25,000/40,000; @📶; Ⓢ Line 4 to Hyehwa, Exit 4) A friendly if slightly scruffy place with plenty of character and room options – although note most are very tiny with thin walls. Rates are a few thousand won higher for stays on Friday and Saturday nights.

★MINARI HOUSE GUESTHOUSE $$
Map p226 (미나리 하우스; ☎070-8656 3303; www.minarihouse.com; 3 Ihwajang 1na-gil, Jongno-gu; dm/s/d/tw incl breakfast ₩35,000/70,000/100,000/130,000; ❄📶; Ⓢ Line 4 to Hyehwa, Exit 2) Designed as a base for artists and creatives, the four rooms here sport minimalist design and arty touches. Breakfast is served in a lovely gallery cafe on the which opens out onto a spacious tiered garden. Located near Ihwa-dong, and overlooking the grand *hanok* of Korea's first president Syngman Rhee, it also runs an artist residency.

EUGENE'S HOUSE HANOK GUESTHOUSE $$
Map p226 (☎02-741 3338; www.eugenehouse.co.kr; 36 Hyehwa-ro 12-gil, Jongno-gu; s/d incl breakfast from ₩70,000/110,000, s/tw without bathroom ₩50,000/100,000; ❄📶; Ⓢ Line 4 to Hyehwa, Exit 1) The friendly family running this *hanok* homestay speak English and have another *hanok* around the corner where they conduct various cultural experiences. These homes have larger courtyards than in Bukchon, and a pleasing, lived-in quality.

Understand Seoul

Seoul Today

Former human-rights lawyer Park Won-soon has won two elections to become Seoul's mayor on a platform of simple improvements to the daily lives of citizens, such as plans to ease road traffic and build more parks. The national right-wing government, in the wake of the *Sewol* ferry tragedy, faces criticism over corruption and policing of public safety, so does he now have the chops to take on the presidency in 2017?

Best on Film

The Host (2006) Seoul-based classic monster movie that juggles humour, poignancy and heart-stopping action.

The King and the Clown (2005) Courtly politics and relationships in the Joseon dynasty, with a homosexual subtext.

Modern Family (2012) Four short movies including the prize-winning *Circle Line* about an unemployed man killing time on a Seoul subway train.

Best in Print

I'll Be Right There (Shin Kyung-sook; 2014) A city wracked by prodemocracy protests in the 1980s is elegantly evoked by this award-winning contemporary Korean author.

The Red Queen (Margaret Drabble; 2005) Seoul's past and relative present overlap when a female British academic becomes obsessed with an 18th-century Korean princess.

Meeting Mr Kim (Jennifer Barclay; 2008) Based on the author's experiences in Seoul in 2000, this is an amusing, easy read with fresh insights.

The Popular Park

It was his independent status that marked out Park Won-soon at his first election victory as Seoul's mayor in 2011. Although he has since aligned with the left-of-centre Democratic Party, Park's policies, such as building more pavements and pedestrian-only zones and expansion of the subway, continue to stoke his popularity. His administration is also building the new Skyline park on the old Seoul station overpass.

However it hasn't all been roses. Park had to withdraw plans for a human-rights charter for Seoul following protests from church and conservative groups about it covering discrimination based on sexual orientation and gender identity. Park, who is on record as in favour of same-sex marriage, subsequently made a public apology to LGBT activists occupying City Hall.

However, Park was praised for his rapid response to the outbreak of the Middle Eastern Respiratory Syndrome (MERS) virus in Seoul in mid-2015, in contrast to slower action from national government. Although he has said he's not interested in the top job, there's a growing number of people pushing him forward as a candidate for the 2017 presidential race.

Plastic Surgery Rules

Just as the city seems to be constantly refashioning itself, so do its citizens. Seoul takes the medal for plastic-surgery capital of the world. Gangnam (of the famous 'Gangnam Style') is the city's self-improvement quarter, with up to 500 clinics and hospitals offering procedures within a square mile for both men and women seemingly desperate to go under the knife. Walk the streets here and you'll not fail to miss ads for plastic surgery ('Everyone but you has done it', is the tagline for one) and postop clients with swollen, bruised and bandaged heads.

It's hardly surprising that looks should matter so much in a place where it's par for the course to present a photograph with your job application and normal for parents to give their teenage kids a nose job or double-eyelid surgery as a present. Despite this there are horror stories aplenty about procedures gone wrong plus other dodgy practices: in 2014 a clinic was fined around ₩3 million for exhibiting on its premises an installation made up of thousands of jaw fragments, each with the previous owner's name written on it.

Fighting for Justice

Tensions ran high in central Seoul around 15 April 2015, the first anniversary of the tragic sinking of the ferry *Sewol*, with the loss of 304 passengers and crew, most of them school children. Thousands of police and national-service conscripts blocked streets around Gwanghwamun Sq, where a sea of yellow ribbons, flickering memorial candles and placards demanding truth and justice marked the encampment of the families and friends of the bereaved. Their stand-off with the government over further investigation of the sinking and punishment of those involved resulted in violent clashes and shows little sign of abating, despite President Park Geun-hye's accession to one of their key demands: the raising of the 6825-tonne vessel, which could take up to 18 months and cost over US$140 million.

Anyone who doubts how tenacious Koreans can be in these matters need only look at the protest that has been going on every Wednesday at noon since 1992 in front of Seoul's Japanese Embassy over full acknowledgement of the Japanese military's use of sexual slavery during WWII.

Surrounded by Enemies?

Less than 50km from the border, Seoul is literally on the front line with North Korea. South Korea expressed concerns in May 2015 over North Korea's test firing of a submarine-launched ballistic missile. However, most of the time the only indication you'll have of heightened tensions with the North is if there's increased security mounted around the Blue House, official home of the president.

Likewise, despite the sometimes uneasy diplomacy between South Korea and its neighbours China and Japan over a variety of territorial and economic issues, the welcome extended to visitors from both countries in Seoul is effusive. Around the royal palaces, in department stores and Gangnam's plastic-surgery clinics, a seemingly never-ending stream of Chinese, in particular, are greeted with open arms for their spending power which is said to be keeping Seoul's economy afloat.

population per sq km

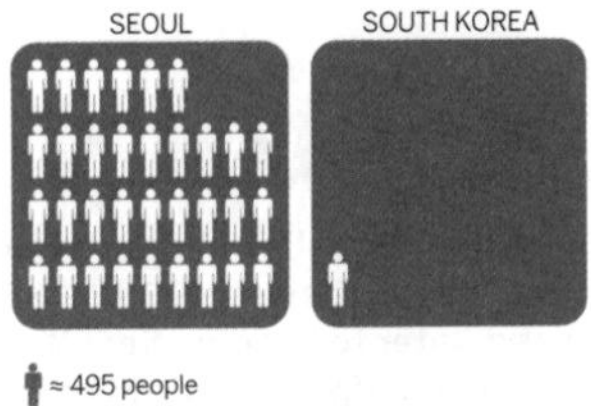

ethnic groups

(% of population)

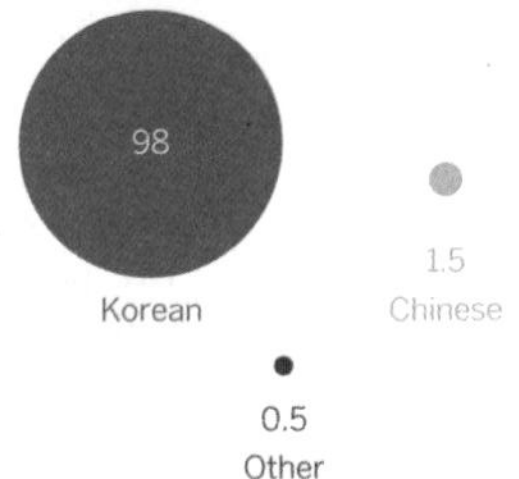

if Seoul were 100 people

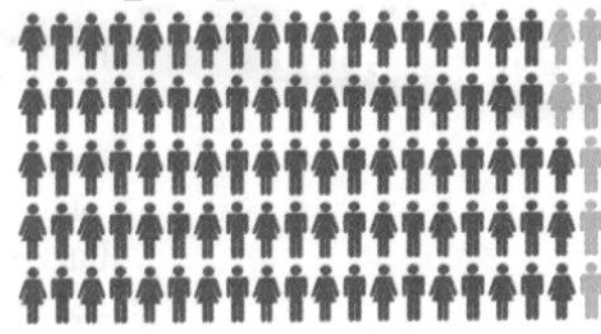

History

The mighty walls of Korea's modern capital rose in 1394, when King Taejo, founder of the Joseon dynasty (1392–1897), settled the government seat in the valley of Hanyang (later to become Seoul) and ordered the building of Gyeongbokgung, the Palace of Shining Happiness, at the foot of Bukaksan. But the city's roots stretch back many centuries before that, while its development in recent times into an economic powerhouse and second-largest metropolitan area in the world has been breathtaking.

Seoul, meaning 'capital' in Korean, has only been the official name of the city since 1945. Before the Joseon dynasty it was known as Hanyang, afterwards Hanseong. During Japanese rule it was called Keijo in Japanese, Gyeongseong in Korean.

Japanese Colonisation

Since recorded time, external forces have cast designs upon Korea – Japan to the east, China and Mongolia to the west. Brutal invasions – many lasting and painful – comprise the fabric of Korean history. Japanese armies rampaged through the peninsula in 1592, burning temples and palaces to the ground, but were forced out five years later by Koreans aided by the Chinese.

However, three centuries later, Japan returned with vengeance. When a large-scale peasant rebellion raged uncontrollably in Korea in 1894, Japan stepped in to 'help'. One year later, Japanese assassins fatally stabbed Queen Min, King Gojong abdicated in 1907, and in 1910 the cession was complete.

This period marked the subjugation, and attempted eradication, of Korean identity. Locals were made to take Japanese names and were forbidden to speak their national tongue. As Japan exploited Korea's resources, only 20% of Koreans were able to even start elementary school. Though some Koreans collaborated with their colonial rulers and reaped great profit, most were unable to rise above second-class citizenship in their own land.

Korean Versus Korean

Down the ages there has been no shortage of internal conflict, either, on the Korean peninsula. The Three Kingdoms period, preceding the Goryeo dynasty (from which comes the name 'Korea'), was marked by

TIMELINE

c 18 BC

Hanseong, capital of the kingdom of Baekje (Paekche), is established in the Seoul area. For four centuries Baekje rules the peninsula until falling to the Goguryeo kingdom.

10th century

After conquering the Shilla dynasty, the Goryeo dynasty change the name of Hanseong to Namgyeong, meaning 'southern capital', and make it one of their three capital cities.

1392

Having overthrown the Goryeo dynasty, General Yi Seong-gye ascends the throne, naming himself King Taejo and establishing the Joseon dynasty that rules Korea for 500 years.

continual feuds. Korea was unified in AD 918, but peasant rebellions remained commonplace throughout the Joseon era.

The Korean War (1950–53) represents another such conflict along internally riven lines – the more agrarian south had always resented the wealthier north, and vice versa. When the nation was at last returned to Korea with the Allied victory in 1945, the decision to divide the country into protectorates – the north overseen by the USSR and the south by the US – soon led to rival republics. On 25 June 1950, under the cover of night, the North Korean army marched over the mountains that rim Seoul, marking the start of the brutal civil war.

Seoul's sudden fall to the North caught the populace by surprise; the government of President Syngman Rhee fled southward, destroying the only Han River highway bridge and abandoning the remaining population to face the communists. During its 90-day occupation of the city, North Korea's army arrested and shot many who had supported the Rhee government.

History Books

The Dawn of Modern Korea (Andrei Lankov)

Korea's Place in the Sun (Bruce Cumings)

The Korean War (Max Hastings)

End & Aftermath of the Korean War

In September 1950, UN forces led by US and South Korean troops mounted a counterattack. After an amphibious landing at Incheon, they fought their way back into Seoul. During a series of bloody battles, whole districts of the capital were bombed and burned in the effort to dislodge Kim Il Sung's Korean People's Army. When at last UN forces succeeded in reclaiming the city, much of it lay in smouldering ruins.

Later that year, as UN forces pushed northward, the Chinese Army entered the war on the North Korean side and pushed back down into Seoul. This time the invaders found a nearly empty city. Even after the UN regained control in March 1951, only a fraction of Seoul's population returned during the two years of war that raged along the battle-front until the armistice in July 1953. Instead, they holed up in rural villages and miserable camps, slowly trickling back into the shattered capital that was once their home.

Widespread hunger, disease, crime and misery comprised daily life for hundreds of thousands. On the slopes of Namsan a wretched village called Haebang-chon (Liberation Town) housed tens of thousands of war refugees, widows and beggars. Sex workers lined up at the gates of the US military bases in Yongsan in a desperate effort to earn a few dollars. Even a decade after the war, average male life expectancy hovered barely above 50.

1394

King Taejo decrees Hanyang (Seoul) as the capital of the Joseon kingdom, mobilising some 200,000 labourers to surround the city with a great wall, remnants of which still remain.

1446

Sejong the Great oversees the invention of *hangeul*, Korea's unique script, which is announced to the public in the document known as the Hunminjeongeum.

1796

King Jeongjo moves the royal court to Suwon to be closer to his father's grave, and builds the Hwaseong fortress (now a World Heritage site) to protect the new palace.

1897

As an independence movement grows in Korea, King Gojong declares the founding of the Korean Empire, formalising the end of the country's ties to China.

Military Rule

Historically, Seoul was never an egalitarian society. A registry from the mid-1600s suggests that perhaps three-quarters of the city's population were slaves. Social inequality continued through the Japanese colonial period, and after the Korean War dictatorships sprang up in the South.

In 1968 North Korean agents launched an assassination attempt on then-president Park Chung-hee by climbing over Bukaksan in an attempt to infiltrate the presidential compound Cheongwadae.

The Syngman Rhee regime (1948–60) rigged its own re-election (by mass arrests of opposition leaders and changes to the constitution) several times until 19 April 1960, when a popular rebellion led by unarmed students sought to overthrow the president. Police opened fire on the group, which had gathered in downtown Seoul; by dusk, nearly 200 people lay dead. Rhee's right-hand man, Gibung Lee, committed suicide, as did his family. Rhee resigned a few days later and was spirited away to exile in Hawaii by the US Air Force.

What came to be known as the April Revolution resulted in eight months of democracy under a cabinet system of government led by Prime Minister Chang Myon. However, on 16 May 1961, the civilian government was replaced by a military junta led by Major General Park Chung-hee. In 1963 Park was narrowly elected South Korea's president. He would retain an iron grip on power for 16 years, during which scores of political dissidents were executed or disappeared.

Miracle on the Han

After forcibly taking the reins of the government, Park quickly went to work defining national economic goals. He often followed patterns set by Imperial Japan, such as fostering big businesses (*zaibatsu* in Japanese, *jaebeol* in Korean) as engines of growth. Conglomerates such as Hyundai and Samsung achieved – and still retain – incredible economic influence.

In 1969 the completion of the Hannam Bridge kicked off Seoul's major expansion south of the Han River, and Namsan Tower (now N Seoul Tower) was erected.

Under Park, fear and brutal efficiency combined to deliver results. Wages were kept artificially low to drive exports, and by the mid-1970s Seoul was well on its way to becoming a major world city. Slums were bulldozed, and the city spread in all directions. Expressways, ring roads and a subway network connected these new districts.

Seoul was undoubtedly at the heart of a Korean economic miracle, but the city was also the scene of increasingly strident protests and demonstrations for an end to effective military rule. Park was assassinated in 1979 by his own chief of central intelligence. He was succeeded by another general – Chun Doo-hwan – who crushed prodemocracy uprisings all over the country (most notoriously in the southwestern city of Gwangju). However, by 1987, as over a million citizens participated in

1900

Modernistaion continues as a railroad between the port of Incheon and Seoul opens and an electricity company provides public lighting and a streetcar system.

1910

After gradually increasing its power and forcing King Gojong to abdicate to Seoul's Russian legation three years earlier, Japan annexes Korea, beginning 35 years of colonial rule.

1948

The Republic of Korea is founded in the southern part of the peninsula, while Kim Il Sung sets up the Democratic People's Republic of Korea in the north.

1950–53

North Korean forces occupy Seoul for 90 days before UN forces led by US and South Korean troops mount a counterattack. An armistice ends the Korean War three years later.

KING SEJONG'S GIFT

As the seat of government, Seoul has born the brunt of bad policies during periods of lacklustre rule, but has reaped the fruits of the thinking of its wisest leaders. The greatest of these leaders was King Sejong (r 1418–50), who sponsored many cultural projects, consolidated border defences and served as a model of Confucian probity. At his direction, court scholars devised the phonetic *hangeul* alphabet, a simple system of writing the Korean language that made it possible for anyone to learn to read. King Sejong's alphabet is one reason why Korea enjoys universal literacy today.

the nationwide antigovernment protests, Chun had little choice but to step down to allow democratic elections.

Democracy – At Long Last

The result of the first direct presidential election for 16 years in 1988 was that Roh Tae-woo, a former military man and supporter of Chun, won out over a divided opposition. The country's first civilian president in 30 years, Kim Young-sam, was elected in 1992, and replaced in 1998 by former dissident Kim Dae-jung, a 'radical' who had survived several assassination attempts during the Park Chung-hee reign.

Once in power, Kim worked to achieve détente with North Korea under what was known as a 'Sunshine Policy'. His presidency was followed by that of equally liberal Roh Moo-hyun (who committed suicide in May 2009 following his involvement in a bribery scandal).

Geomancy (feng shui, or *pungsu-jiri* in Korean) decreed Seoul's location: the Han River supplied yin force and access to the sea, and the Bukhan mountain range supplied yang energy and protection from the north.

Economic Powerhouse

South Korea's 17th president (and former Seoul mayor), Lee Myung-bak, was a fascinating change from the previous two administrations. Formerly the hard-nosed CEO of the Hyundai construction *jaebeol* (huge, often family-run, corporation), Lee was nicknamed 'the bulldozer' – derisively by those who loathe him, glowingly by his supporters – for his penchant for ramming through his policies. It was under Lee's tenure as mayor that the Cheong-gye-cheon stream project was begun.

Under Lee's administration, Seoul consolidated its grip on the nation's economy and was ranked as one of the most competitive cities in the world. In 2010 it was appointed a Unesco City of Design in recognition of its cultural heritage and promotion of strong design policies, and hosted the G20 Economic Summit.

1960–61

Popular protests oust President Syngman Rhee. Attempts at democratic rule fail, a military coup topples the unstable elected government and installs General Park Chung-hee into power.

1979

After surviving a couple of assassination attempts (one of which kills his wife), Park is finally shot dead by the trusted head of his own Central Intelligence Agency.

1987

Following sustained national protests, with the strongest concentration in Seoul, Korea's last military dictatorship, under Chun Doo-hwan, steps down to allow democratic elections.

1988

Seoul hosts the Summer Olympics, building a huge Olympic Park and major expressway. The international showcase leads to increased trade and diplomatic relations.

A New Vision

In 2012 many government ministries were shifted to a 'mini capital' at Sejong City, 120km south of Seoul. The aim is decentralisation and moving part of the nation's administration away from the northern border.

South Korea's national politics is dominated by the currently governing Saenuri Party (a centre-right party) and the liberal opposition Democratic Party – a successor to the former Democratic United Party (DUP). After the South Korean president, the mayor of Seoul is the second-most powerful job in the country – so it was something of a wake-up call for both of Korea's major political parties when the previously unelected and politically unaffiliated Park Won-Soon won the election. Known for promoting a chain of thrift shops for the poor, Park portrayed himself as the nation's first 'welfare mayor' (South Korea has a minimal social safety net and the gap between rich and poor is widening).

In February 2012, Park affiliated himself with the DUP. However, in the National Assembly elections in April 2012, the beleaguered Saenuri Party, dogged by a series of scandals and corruption cases involving President Lee Myung-bak's aides and relatives, held on to its majority status in the country's parliament. Much of that victory was put down to the relentless campaigning of Park Geun-hye, daughter of South Korea's former dictator, Park Chung-hee. Later the same year, Park Geun-hye emerged as the victor in the presidential elections to become the country's first female head of state in February 2013.

Since winning a second term as Seoul's mayor in June 2014, Park Won-Soon is being talked up as a candidate for the presidential elections in 2017.

2002

Seoul serves as one of the host cities for the World Cup, with the opening game of the soccer tournament held at the new World Cup Stadium.

2010

Seoul hosts the G-20 Economic Summit and becomes World Design Capital, but its centrepiece – Dongdaemun Design Plaza & Park, by architect Zaha Hadid – remains uncompleted.

2011

Independent candidate and former human-rights lawyer Park Won-soon is elected Seoul's mayor. He puts the brakes on major construction projects and focuses on welfare spending.

2014

Protestors are arrested as a candlelight vigil in Seoul turns into angry demands for the Park Geun-hye government to resign over the *Sewol* ferry disaster.

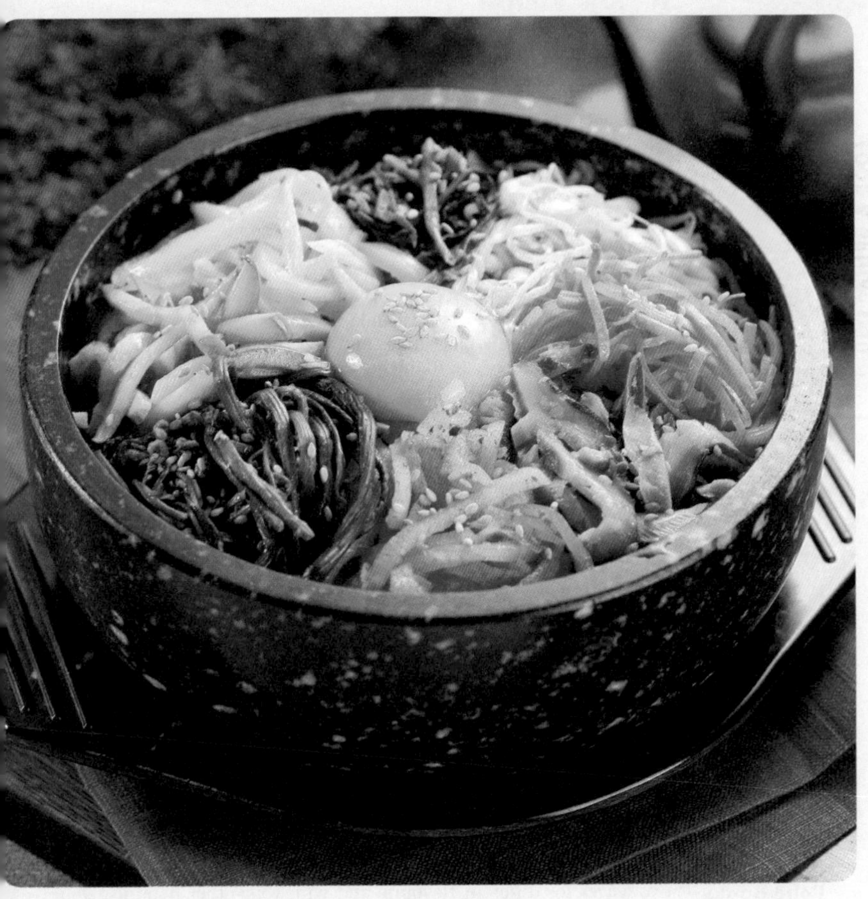

Food & Drink

So you thought Korean cuisine was mainly about *kimchi* and barbecued beef? A few days in Seoul will swiftly bring you up to speed. Prepare to be blown away by the amazing diversity and spicy deliciousness of the nation's cuisine, ranging from rustic stews and tasty street snacks to glorious royal banquets involving elaborate preparation and presentation. The leisurely sampling of soothing traditional teas and herbal infusions is also one of Seoul's great pleasures, as is the chance to sample a variety of local alcoholic beverages.

Food

A traditional Korean meal (either breakfast, lunch or dinner) typically consists of meat, seafood or fish served at the same time as soup, rice and a collection of dipping sauces and *banchan*, the ubiquitous cold side dishes. The fermented *kimchi* cabbage or radish is the most popular side dish, but there are many others, such as bean sprouts, black beans,

Above: *Dolsot bibimbap* (bibimbap in stone hotpot)

RULES OF KOREAN DINING

- Take off your shoes in traditional restaurants where everyone sits on floor cushions.
- Pour drinks for others if you notice that their glasses are empty. It's polite to use both hands when pouring or receiving a drink. Don't pour drinks for yourself (unless you're alone).
- Ask for *gawi* (scissors) if you're trying to cut something and your spoon won't do it.
- Don't touch food with your fingers, except when handling *ssam* (salad leaves used as edible wrapping for other foods).
- Use a spoon rather than chopsticks to eat rice.
- Don't leave your chopsticks or spoon sticking up from your rice bowl. This is taboo, only done with food that is offered to deceased ancestors.
- Don't blow your nose at the table.

dried anchovy, spinach, quail eggs, shellfish, lettuce, acorn jelly and tofu. It's a healthy and balanced approach to eating – no wonder Korean cooks refer to food as 'medicine'.

The pinnacle of Korean dining is *jeongsik* or *hanjeongsik*. These banquets that cover the table with food include fish, meat, soup, *dubu jjigae* (spicy tofu stew), *doenjang jjigae* (soybean-paste stew), rice, noodles, steamed egg, shellfish and lots of cold vegetable side dishes, followed by a cup of tea. It's invariably too much to eat and it's meant to be – don't feel obliged to eat everything put in front of you. When going for such a set meal, it's a good idea to choose the one with the least number of courses.

Joseon kings and queens used to scoff specially prepared *juk* (rice porridge) with abalone, pine nuts and sesame seeds as a pre-breakfast meal.

Specialities

Barbecue

The many barbecue restaurants have a grill set into the tables on which to cook slices of beef *(bulgogi)*, beef ribs *(galbi)*, pork *(samgyeopsal)*, chicken *(dak)*, seafood or vegetables. The server often helps out with the cooking. The inexpensive *samgyeopsal* is fatty slices of pork belly. These meals are usually only available in servings for two or more.

Bulgogi, *galbi* and *samgyeopsal* are served with a bunch of *ssam*, typically lettuce and sesame leaves. Take a leaf in one hand (or combine two leaves for different flavours) and with your other hand use your chopsticks to load it with meat, side-dish flavourings, garlic and sauces. Then roll it up into a little package and eat it in one go.

Food Books

- *Eumsik dimibang (Lady Jang; 1670)*
- *Traditional Food: A Taste of Korean Life (Korean Foundation; 2011)*
- *A Korean Mother's Cooking Notes (Chang Sun-young; 1997)*
- *Korean Cuisine: A Cultural Journey (Chung Haekyung; 2009)*
- *Growing Up in a Korean Kitchen (Hi Soo Shin Hepinstall; 2001)*

Rice Dishes

Bibimbap is a tasty mixture of rice, vegetables and minced beef, often with a fried egg on top. Add *gochujang* (red-chilli paste) to taste and thoroughly mix it all together with a spoon before digging in. *Sanchae bibimbap* is made with mountain-grown greens; *dolsot bibimbap* is served in a stone hotpot, which makes some of the rice nicely crispy. *Boribap* is rice with barley mixed in.

Similar to sushi rolls, but not exactly the same, are *gimbap* (rice rolled in dried seaweed with strips of carrot, radish, egg and ham in the centre). 'Nude' *gimbap* has no dried seaweed wrap. There are also *samgak gimbap*, triangular-shaped rice parcels filled with beef, chicken, tuna or *kimchi*, wrapped in *gim* (dried seaweed). Sold mainly in convenience stores, it's a tasty snack once you've mastered the art of taking it out of the plastic.

Traditional, slow-cooked rice porridge *(juk)* is mixed with a wide choice of ingredients and is popular as a healthy, wellbeing food that is not spicy.

Chicken

Samgyetang is a small whole chicken stuffed with glutinous rice, red dates, garlic and ginseng root, and boiled in broth. *Dakgalbi* is pieces of spicy chicken, cabbage, other vegetables and pressed rice cakes, all grilled at your table. *Jjimdak* is a spiced-up mixture of chicken pieces, transparent noodles, potatoes and other vegetables. Many informal *hof* (pubs) serve inexpensive barbecued or fried chicken to accompany the beer.

Fish & Seafood

Fish *(saengseon)* and other seafood *(haemul)* is generally served broiled, grilled or in a soup, while *hoe* is raw fish like sashimi. Fish is usually served whole with both the head and guts. Visit Noryangjin Fish Market (p90) to indulge in raw fish, steamed crab, grilled prawns or barbecued shellfish feasts. *Nakji* (octopus) is usually served in a spicy sauce; if you're brave, try the raw version of *sannakji* (baby octopus) – the chopped-up tentacles still wriggle on the plate when brought to the table. *Haemultang* is a seafood soup containing so much chilli that even locals have to mop their brows.

Royal palace cuisine, a style of cooking now replicated in fancy restaurants for the general public, requires elaborate preparation and presentation. It includes dishes such as *gujeolpan* (snacks wrapped in small pancakes) and *sinseollo* (hotpot).

Vegetarian & Vegan

Although rice and vegetables make up a considerable part of their diet, few Koreans are fully vegetarian. It can be a struggle for vegetarians in ordinary restaurants. Many otherwise seemingly vegetarian dishes have small amounts of meat, seafood or fish sauce added for flavour. The same is true of *kimchi*. Generally less risky things to order include bibimbap (you'll need to request without meat, or egg), *beoseotjeongol* (mushroom hotpot), *doenjang jjigae*, *dubu jjigae*, *jajangmyeon* (noodles and sauce), vegetable *pajeon* (pancakes), and pumpkin *juk*.

Soups & Stews

Soups (*tang* or *guk*) are a highlight of Korean cuisine. 'A meal without soup is like a face without eyes', goes a traditional saying. They vary from spicy seafood and tofu soups to bland broths such as *galbitang* and *seolleongtang*, made from beef bones; the latter is a Seoul speciality.

STREET FOOD

Some of the best food you'll taste in Seoul is off the street; from food stalls set up in market alleyways, street carts on main roads or late-night *pojenchmacha* (plastic tent bars) outside subway stations. Food is always freshly cooked and can range from inexpensive mains such as *bindaetteok* (mungbean pancakes) and *sundae* (blood sausage), to bimbimbap or ready-made snacks to chow down on the run.

Tteokbokki (hot rice cakes slathered in a bright-red spicy sauce) is a quintessential Korean favourite, along with skewered snacks ranging from spicy grilled meats and *odeng* (boiled fish cakes) to an assortment of sausages on a stick. Also ubiquitous is *Twigim*, deep-fried battered prawns, squid or vegetables that's similar to Japanese tempura.

Freshly baked sweet snacks are abundant. Steaming *gyeran ppang* (egg cooked within an oval-shaped bread) are popular in winter, while *bungeoppang* (fish-shaped pastry filled with sweet red-bean paste) and *hotteok* (deep-fried dough pancakes made with brown sugar, nuts, honey and cinnamon) are all delicious comfort foods.

Pressed fish and dried squid are both old-school snacks, and a popular accompaniment to beer. Those feeling more adventurous can snack on *beondegi* (silkworm larvae), which are sold by the cup from street vendors.

For something more Westernised, 'toast' is a trusty favourite – fried toasted sandwiches filled with egg, ham, cheese and usually sweetened with kiwi jam. Good for breakfast or a late-night drunken snack.

Gamjatang is a spicy peasant soup with meaty bones and a potato. Tip: if a soup is too spicy, mix in some rice.

Stews *(jjigae)* are usually served sizzling in a stone hotpot with plenty of spices. Popular versions are made with tofu *(dubu jjigae)*, soybean paste *(doenjang jjigae)* and *kimchi*. *Beoseotjeongol* is a less spicy but highly recommended mushroom hotpot.

Dating from 1670, the Joseon-era cookbook *Eumsik dimibang* was written by Lady Jang (1598–1680), a member of the *yangban* ruling class. It's regarded as Korea's first cookbook written in *hangeul* (the Korean phonetic alphabet), and today its 340-year-old recipes are making a comeback with the book's relaunch in 2015.

Kimchi

Traditionally, *kimchi* was made to preserve vegetables and ensure proper nutrition during the harsh winters, but it's now eaten year-round and adds zest, zip and a long list of health benefits to any meal. A cold side dish of the spicy national food is served at nearly every Korean meal, whether it's breakfast, lunch or dinner.

Generally made with pickled and fermented cabbage seasoned with garlic and red chilli, it can be made from cucumbers, white radish or other vegetables. Note, *kimchi* is not always vegetarian as it can have anchovies added. *Mul kimchi* is a cold, gazpacho-type minimalist soup, and is not spicy.

Dumplings, Noodles & Pancakes

Mandu are small dumplings and *wangmandu* are large ones; both can be filled with minced meat, seafood, vegetables and herbs. They are often freshly made to a special recipe by restaurant staff during quiet times. Fried, boiled or steamed, they make a tasty snack or addition to a meal. *Manduguk* is *mandu* in soup with seaweed and makes a perfect light lunch.

There's a whole range of *guksu* (noodles) to sample. A much-loved Pyongyang speciality is *naengmyeon*, chewy buckwheat noodles in an icy, sweetish broth, garnished with shredded vegetables and topped with half a hard-boiled egg – add red-chilli paste or *gyeoja* (mustard) to taste. Popular in summer, it is often eaten after a meat dish like *galbi*. Use the scissors provided to cut up the noodles so they're easier to eat.

Kalguksu are thick, hand-cut noodles usually served in a bland clam-and-vegetable broth. *Ramyeon* are instant noodles often served in a hot chilli soup. Seoulites believe in fighting fire with fire and claim it's a good cure for hangovers.

Pajeon are thick, savoury pancakes the size of pizzas, often filled with spring onions and seafood. *Bindaetteok* are just as big and even more filling, made from ground mung beans with various fillings and fried until a crispy, golden brown – they're best eaten at Gwangjang Market (p122).

MAKGEOLLI APPRECIATION

In line with the current-day revival of traditional Korean culture among the younger generation, traditional alcohols such as *makgeolli* (milky rice wine) have become revered. It's a trend worth exploring, akin to the craft beer movement, where local brewers strive for chemical-free, top-quality, handcrafted products. However it's very much a local scene, and one that's hard to crack. So thankfully several expat groups have come about, all on a mission to spread the word about the wonder that is *makgeolli*.

Makgeolli Makers (www.facebook.com/makgeollimakers; Susubori Academy, 47 Kyonggidae-ro, Seodaemun-gu; course ₩45,000; S Line 2 or 5 to Chungjeongno, Exit 7) Run by an extremely knowledgable American couple, Makgeolli Makers offers lessons on how to brew your own *makgeolli* based on recipes from the 340-year-old cookbook *Eumsik dimibang*.

Makgeolli Mamas & Papas (MMPKorea; mmpkorea.wordpress.com) Established by the passionate Mama Julia, this outfit runs regular meet ups for tastings and traditional liquor brewery tours, among other events. It's also incredibly well-informed.

Dining Etiquette

If you're invited out by Korean colleagues or friends, it's difficult or impossible to pay the bill or even contribute towards it. Arguing about who should have the honour of paying the restaurant bill is a common scene at the cashier's desk.

Meals are usually eaten communally, so dishes are placed in the centre of the table and diners put a little from each common dish in their own dish or bowl.

At some traditional restaurants, customers sit on cushions on the floor (the *ondol*, an underfloor heating system, is beneath). Before stepping up, always remove your shoes.

Nearly every restaurant in Seoul serves bottled or filtered water free of charge when you first arrive.

Budae jjigae (or *johnsontang*) is a unique Seoul dish that originated in the hungry years after the Korean War. At this time tins of ham, sausages and baked beans from American army bases (such as Yongsan) were bought on the black market and mixed with noodles and vegetable scraps to make a meal.

Drinks

Bottled and canned soft drinks are everywhere. Some uniquely Korean choices are grape juice with whole grapes inside and *sikhye*, rice punch with rice grains inside. Health tonics, made with fibre, vitamins, ginseng and other medicinal herbs, are available in shops and pharmacies; many claim to boost your virility.

Tea

Tea *(cha)* is a staple, with the term is also used to describe drinks brewed without tea leaves. The most common leaf tea is *nokcha* (green tea). *Hongcha* (black tea) is harder to find. Nonleaf teas include the ubiquitous *boricha* (barley tea), *daechucha* (red-date tea), *omijacha* (five-flavour berry tea), *yujacha* (citron tea) and *insamcha* (ginseng tea). They may be served hot or cold.

Alcoholic Beverages

Koreans drink enough *soju* – a highly potent mix of ethanol mixed with water and flavouring – that the Jinro-brand *soju* (you'll see the green bottles everywhere) is the top-selling brand of spirits *worldwide*. The size of the *soju* bottle is calculated to fill only seven shot glasses. The stuff might go down easily, but it can induce a killer hangover the next day. Go for the higher-quality stuff distilled from grain (try Andong Soju or Jeonju Leegangju); it offers a far more delicate flavour, but can have an alcohol content of up to 45%.

Makgeolli is a traditional farmer's brew made from unrefined, fermented rice wine. Generally around 5% alcohol, it has a cloudy appearance and a sweetish yoghurty flavour. It is traditionally served in a brass kettle and poured into shallow brass bowls, although Seoul has several bars now where higher-quality styles of *makgeolli* (as opposed to hangover-inducing convenience-store varieties), akin to the range of Japanese sake, are served and savoured.

A host of sweetish traditional spirits are brewed or distilled from grains, fruits and roots. Many are regional or seasonal. *Bokbunjaju* is made from wild raspberries, *meoruju* from wild fruit, *maesilju* from green plums and *insamju* from ginseng.

Beer is also a popular choice of beverage. The main local brands include Cass, Hite and OB, all of which are lagers and widely available from convenience stores and pubs. The past few years have seen the emergence of several microbreweries, which have set up around Itaewon, including Craftworks, Magpie Brewing Co. and the Booth. Since then the craft beer revolution has exploded, with brewpubs opening all over the city, many of which produce their own ales.

Food & Drink Glossary

FISH & SEAFOOD DISHES		
chobap	초밥	raw fish on rice
garibi	가리비	scallops
gwang-eohoe	광어회	raw halibut
hongeo	홍어	ray, usually served raw
jangeogui	장어구이	grilled eel
kijogae	키조개	razor clam
kkotgejjim	꽃게찜	steamed blue crab
modeumhoe	모듬회	mixed raw-fish platter
nakji	낙지	octopus
odeng	오뎅	processed seafood cakes in broth
ojingeo	오징어	squid
saengseongui	생선구이	grilled fish
saeugui	새우구이	grilled prawns
ureok	우럭	rockfish

GIMBAP	김밥	
chamchi gimbap	참치김밥	tuna *gimbap*
modeum gimbap	모듬김밥	assorted *gimbap*
yachae gimbap	야채 김밥	vegetable *gimbap*

KIMCHI	김치	
baechu kimchi	배추김치	cabbage *kimchi*; the classic spicy version
kkakdugi	깍두기	cubed radish *kimchi*
mul kimchi	물김치	cold *kimchi* soup

MEAT DISHES		
bossam	보쌈	steamed pork with *kimchi*, cabbage and lettuce wrap
bulgogi	불고기	barbecued beef slices and lettuce wrap
dakgalbi	닭갈비	spicy chicken pieces grilled with vegetables and rice cakes
donkkaseu	돈까스	pork cutlet with rice and salad
dwaeji galbi	돼지갈비	pork ribs
galbi	갈비	beef ribs
heukdwaeji	흑돼지	black pig
jjimdak	찜닭	spicy chicken pieces with noodles
jokbal	족발	steamed pigs' feet
kkwong	꿩	pheasant
metdwaejigogi	멧돼지고기	wild pig
neobiani/tteokgalbi	너비아니/떡갈비	large minced-meat patty
samgyeopsal	삼겹살	barbecued baconlike streaky pork belly
tangsuyuk	탕수육	Chinese-style sweet-and-sour pork
tongdakgui	통닭구이	roasted chicken
yukhoe	육회	seasoned raw beef

NOODLES

bibim naengmyeon	비빔냉면	cold buckwheat noodles with vegetables, meat and sauce
bibimguksu	비빔국수	noodles with vegetables, meat and sauce
jajangmyeon	자장면	noodles in Chinese-style black-bean sauce
japchae	잡채	stir-fried 'glass' noodles and vegetables
kalguksu	칼국수	wheat noodles in clam-and-vegetable broth
kongguksu	콩국수	wheat noodles in cold soybean soup
makguksu	막국수	buckwheat noodles with vegetables
naengmyeon	물냉면	buckwheat noodles in cold broth
ramyeon	라면	instant noodles in soup

RICE DISHES

bap	밥	boiled rice
bibimbap	비빔밥	rice topped with egg, meat, vegetables and sauce
bokkeumbap	볶음밥	Chinese-style fried rice
boribap	보리밥	boiled rice with steamed barley
daetongbap	대통밥	rice cooked in bamboo stem
dolsot bibimbap	돌솥비빔밥	bibimbap in stone hotpot
dolsotbap	돌솥밥	hotpot rice
dolssambap	돌쌈밥	hotpot rice and lettuce wraps
gulbap	굴밥	oyster rice
hoedeopbap	회덮밥	bibimbap with raw fish
honghapbap	홍합밥	mussel rice
jeonbokjuk	전복죽	rice porridge with abalone
juk	죽	rice porridge
pyogo deopbap	표고덮밥	mushroom rice
sanchae bibimbap	산채비빔밥	bibimbap with mountain vegetables
sinseollo	신선로	meat, fish and vegetables cooked in broth
ssambap	쌈밥	assorted ingredients with rice and wraps

SNACKS

anju	안주	bar snacks
beondegi	번데기	boiled silkworm larvae
bungeoppang	붕어빵	fish-shaped waffle with red-bean paste
dakkochi	닭꼬치	spicy grilled chicken on skewers
gukhwappang	국화빵	flower-shaped waffle with red-bean paste
hotteok	호떡	wheat pancake with sweet or savoury filling
jjinppang	찐빵	giant steamed bun with sweet-bean paste
goguma twigim	고구마튀김	fried sweet potato
nurungji	누룽지	crunchy burnt-rice cracker
patbingsu	팥빙수	shaved-iced dessert with *tteok* and red-bean topping
tteok	떡	rice cake
tteokbokki	떡볶이	rice cakes in a sweet and spicy sauce

SOUPS

bosintang	보신탕	dog-meat soup
chueotang	추어탕	minced loach-fish soup
dakbaeksuk	닭백숙	chicken in medicinal herb soup
dakdoritang	닭도리탕	spicy chicken and potato soup
galbitang	갈비탕	beef-rib soup
gamjatang	감자탕	meaty bones and potato soup
haejangguk	해장국	bean-sprout soup ('hangover soup')
haemultang	해물탕	spicy assorted seafood soup
hanbang oribaeksuk	한방 오리백숙	duck in medicinal soup
kkorigomtang	꼬리곰탕	ox-tail soup
maeuntang	매운탕	spicy fish soup
manduguk	만두국	soup with meat-filled dumplings
oritang	오리탕	duck soup
samgyetang	삼계탕	ginseng chicken soup
seolnongtang	설렁탕	beef and rice soup
yukgaejang	육개장	spicy beef soup

STEWS

budae jjigae	부대찌개	'army stew' with hot dogs, Spam and vegetables
dakjjim	닭찜	braised chicken
doenjang jjigae	된장찌개	soybean-paste stew
dubu jjigae	두부찌개	spicy tofu stew
galbijjim	갈비찜	braised beef ribs
gopchang jeongol	곱창전골	tripe hotpot
kimchi jjigae	김치찌개	*kimchi* stew
nakji jeongol	낙지전골	octopus hotpot

OTHER

banchan	반찬	side dishes
bindaetteok	빈대떡	mung-bean pancake
dotorimuk	도토리묵	acorn jelly
gujeolpan	구절판	eight snacks and wraps
hanjeongsik	한정식	Korean-style banquet
jeongsik	정식	set menu or table d'hôte, with lots of side dishes
mandu	만두	filled dumplings
omeuraiseu	오므라이스	omelette with rice
pajeon	파전	green-onion pancake
sangcharim	상차림	banquet of meat, seafood and vegetables
sigol bapsang	시골밥상	countryside-style meal
sujebi	수제비	dough flakes in shellfish broth
sundae	순대	noodle and vegetable sausage
sundubu	순두부	uncurdled tofu
twigim	튀김	seafood or vegetables fried in batter
wangmandu	왕만두	large steamed dumplings

Barbecue with side dishes and *naengmyeon* (buckwheat noodles in cold broth)

NONALCOHOLIC DRINKS

boricha	보리차	barley tea
cha	차	tea
daechucha	대추차	red-date tea
hongcha	홍차	black tea
juseu	주스	juice
keopi	커피	coffee
dikapein keopi	디카페인 커피	decaffeinated coffee
mul	물	water
nokcha	녹차	green tea
saengsu	생수	mineral spring water
seoltang neo-eoseo/ppaego	설탕 넣어서/빼고	with/without sugar
sikhye	식혜	rice punch
sujeonggwa	수정과	cinnamon and ginger punch
uyu	우유	milk
uyu neo-eoseo/ppaego	우유 넣어서/빼고	with/without milk

ALCOHOLIC DRINKS

bokbunjaju	복분자주	wild berry liquor
dongdongju	동동주	fermented rice wine
insamju	인삼주	ginseng liquor
maekju	맥주	beer
makgeolli	막걸리	traditional farmer's fermented rice wine
soju	소주	vodkalike drink

Religion & Culture

Seoul was once divided strictly along nearly inescapable class lines and hierarchical distinctions, but its sensibility is now much like any modern city. People often hold loyalties to school, company and church, but egalitarianism has given way to greater individualism. Still, strong traces of Korea's particular identity linger. Remnants of its Confucian past coexist alongside 'imported' spiritual beliefs, denting the myth that modernisation necessitates secularisation.

Main Belief Systems

Of the four streams of spiritual influence in Korea, Confucianism and Buddhism are the most important. Christianity, which first made inroads into Korea in the 18th century, also plays a major role in the lives of many, while the ancient superstitions of shamanism persist as well.

Above: Royal ancestral shrine musicians, Jongmyo (p54)

Confucianism

The state religion of the Joseon dynasty, Confucianism still lives on as a kind of ethical bedrock (at least subconsciously) in the minds of most Koreans, especially the elderly.

Visit the spirit shrines of Joseon royalty at the splendid Jongmyo. A grand Confucian ceremony honouring the deceased is held there every May.

The Chinese philosopher Confucius (552–479 BC) devised a system of ethics that emphasised devotion to parents and family, loyalty to friends, justice, peace, education, reform and humanitarianism. He also urged that respect and deference should be given to those in positions of authority – a philosophy exploited by Korea's Joseon-dynasty ruling elite. Confucius firmly believed that men were superior to women and that a woman's place was in the home.

These ideas led to the system of civil-service examinations *(gwageo)*, where one could gain position through ability and merit, rather than from noble birth and connections (though it was, in fact, still an uphill battle for the commonly born). Confucius preached against corruption, war, torture and excessive taxation. He was the first teacher to open his school to all students solely on the basis of their willingness to learn.

As Confucianism trickled into Korea, it evolved into neo-Confucianism, which combined the sage's original ethical and political ideas with the quasi-religious practice of ancestor worship and the idea of the eldest male as spiritual head of the family.

Buddhism

When first introduced during the Koguryo dynasty in AD 370, Buddhism coexisted with shamanism. Many Buddhist temples have a *samseionggak* (three-spirit hall) on their grounds, which houses shamanist deities such as the Mountain God.

The religion was persecuted during the Joseon period, when its temples were tolerated only in the remote mountains. It suffered another

THE CONFUCIAN MINDSET

Confucianism is a social philosophy, a prescription for achieving a harmonious society. Not everyone follows the rules, but Confucianism does continue to shape the Korean paradigm. Some of the key principles and practices:

- Obedience and respect towards seniors – parents, teachers, the boss, older brothers and sisters – is crucial. Heavy penalties (including physical punishment) are incurred for stepping out of line.
- Seniors get obedience, but they also have obligations. Older siblings help out younger siblings with tuition fees, and the boss always pays for lunch.
- Education defines a civilised person. Despite having built a successful business, a high-school graduate would still feel shame at their lack of scholastic credentials.
- Men and women have separate roles. A woman's role is service, obedience and management of household affairs. Men don't do housework or look after children.
- Status and dignity are critical. Every action reflects on the family, company and country.
- Everything on and beyond the earth is in a hierarchy. People never forget who is senior and who is junior to them.
- Families are more important than individuals. Everyone's purpose in life is to improve the family's reputation and wealth. No one should choose a career or marry someone against their parents' wishes – a bad choice could bring ruin to a family. Everyone must marry and have a son to continue the family line. For these reasons homosexuality is considered a grossly unnatural act.
- Loyalty is important. A loyal liar is a virtuous person.
- Be modest and don't be extravagant. Only immoral women wear revealing clothes. Be frugal with praise.

sharp decline after WWII as Koreans pursued more worldly goals. But South Korea's success in achieving developed-nation status, coupled with a growing interest in spiritual values, is encouraging a Buddhist revival. Temple visits have increased and large sums of money are flowing into temple reconstruction.

Korean Buddhism is also operating a templestay program for travellers at facilities across the country. Many Koreans take part in these templestays, regardless of whether they are Buddhist or not, as a chance to escape societal pressures and clear their minds.

About 90% of Korean Buddhist temples belong to the Jogye order (www.koreanbuddhism.net). Buddha's birthday in May is a national holiday, which includes an extravagant lantern parade in Seoul.

Christianity

Korea's first exposure to Christianity was in the late 18th century. It came via the Jesuits from the Chinese imperial court when a Korean aristocrat was baptised in Beijing in 1784. The Catholic faith took hold and spread so quickly that it was perceived as a threat by the Korean government and was vigorously suppressed, creating the country's first Christian martyrs.

Christianity got a second chance in the 1880s, with the arrival of American Protestant missionaries who founded schools and hospitals, and gained many followers – so many, in fact, that today Christianity is the nation's second-most-popular religion after Buddhism.

Shamanism

Historically, shamanism influenced Korean spirituality. It's not a religion but it does involve communication with spirits through intermediaries known as *mudang* (female shamans). Although not widely practised today, shamanist ceremonies are held to cure illness, ward off financial problems or guide a deceased family member safely into the spirit world.

Ceremonies involve contacting spirits who are attracted by lavish offerings of food and drink. Drums beat and the *mudang* dances herself into a frenzied state that allows her to communicate with the spirits and be possessed by them. Resentments felt by the dead can plague the living and cause all sorts of misfortune, so their spirits need placating. For shamanists, death does not end relationships. It simply takes another form.

On Inwangsan in northwestern Seoul, ceremonies take place in or near the historic Inwangsan Guksadang shrine.

Koreans give their family name first, followed by their birth name, which is typically two syllables, ie Lee Myung-bak. There are less than 300 Korean family names, with Kim, Lee (or Yi) and Park accounting for 45% of the total.

Competitive Lives

The country's recovery from the ashes of the Korean War, construction workers on the job seven days a week, or computer-game addicts: they're all strands cut from the same cloth, the country's tenacious, pit-bull spirit. Once Seoulites lock onto something, it's difficult to break away. Life is competitive and everything is taken seriously, be it tenpin bowling, hiking or overseas corporate expansion.

'A person without education is like a beast wearing clothes' is a proverb that nails Korea's obsession with education. To get into one of the top Seoul universities, high-school students go through a gruelling examination process, studying 14 hours a day, often in private cram schools at night, for their one annual shot at the college entrance test.

FORTUNE-TELLING

These days most people visit one of the city's street-tent fortune-tellers for a bit of fun, but no doubt some take it seriously. For a *saju* (reading of your future), inform the fortune-teller of the date, including the hour, of your birth; another option is *gunhap* (a love-life reading), when a couple gives their birth details and the fortune-teller pronounces how compatible they are. Expect to pay ₩10,000 for *saju* and double that for *gunhap*. If you don't speak the language, you'll also need someone to translate.

MINDING YOUR KOREAN MANNERS

Most locals understand that visitors do not mean disrespect when they commit a minor social faux pas. But you'll be even more warmly received when it is obvious that you've gone out of your way to burnish your graces, Korean style.

Shoes off In any residence, temple, guesthouse or Korean-style restaurant, leave your shoes at the door. And socks are better than bare feet.

Artful bow Though you may see members of the royal court drop to the ground to greet the king on Korean TV dramas, don't get inspired. A quick, short bow – essentially a nod of the head – is most respectful for meetings and departures.

All hands on deck Give and receive any object using both hands – especially name cards (essential for any formal and many informal meetings), money and gifts.

Giving gifts When you visit someone at their home, bring along a little token of your appreciation. The gift can be almost anything – flowers, fruit, a bottle of liquor, tea or something from your home country. Your host may at first strongly refuse your gift. This is a gesture of graciousness. Keep insisting, and they will accept it 'reluctantly'. For the same reason, your host will not open the package immediately.

Paying the bill Fighting to pay the bill is a common phenomenon, though the quid pro quo is that one person pays this time and the other fights a little harder to pick up the cheque next time. If a Korean takes you under their wing, it's difficult to pay for anything.

Get over here Don't beckon someone using your forefinger. Place your hand out, palm down and flutter all your fingers at once.

Loss of face In interpersonal relations, the least desirable outcome is to somehow *gibun* ('lower the harmony'). A mishandled remark or potentially awkward scene should be smoothed over as soon as possible, and if you sense someone actively trying to change the subject, go with the flow. An argument or any situation that could lead to embarrassment should be avoided at all costs.

Smile, you're embarrassed Often, potential loss of face – say, when someone realises they are clearly in the wrong – will result in an unlikely reaction: a wide smile. No, you're not being mocked; you've just been told 'I'm sorry'. So if a taxi driver almost mows you down, only to roll down his window and flash you a big grin, he's not off his rocker – he's showing his embarrassment, which is both a form of apology and a gesture of sympathy.

Seoulites are also fanatical about health. The millions of hikers who stream into the mountains on weekends are not only enjoying nature but also keeping fit. Thousands of health foods and drinks are sold in markets and pharmacies, which stock traditional as well as Western medicines. Nearly every food claims to be a 'wellbeing' product or an aphrodisiac – 'good for stamina' is the local phrase.

Contemporary & Traditional Culture

Driven by the latest technology and fast-evolving trends, Seoul can sometimes seem like one of the most cutting-edge cities on the planet. On subway trains and the streets, passengers tune into their favourite TV shows via their smartphones and tablet computers. In PC *bang* (computer-game rooms), millions of diehard fans battle at online games, while in *noraebang* (karaoke rooms), wannabe K-Popsters belt out the latest hit tunes.

General fashions tend to be international and up to the moment too. However, it's not uncommon to see some people wearing *hanbok*, the striking traditional clothing that follows the Confucian principle of unadorned modesty. Women wear a loose-fitting short blouse with long sleeves and a voluminous long skirt, while men wear a jacket and baggy trousers. Today *hanbok* is worn mostly at weddings or special events, and even then it may be a more comfortable 'updated' version.

Culture Books

- *Notes on Things Korean (Suzanne Crowder Han)*
- *Understanding Koreans and their Culture (Choi Joon-sik)*
- *Korea Bug (J Scott Burgeson)*
- *The 48 Keywords that Describe Korea (Kim Jin-woo & Lee Nam-hoon)*

Architecture

Seoul's skyline – dominated by skyscrapers and endless high-rise apartments – at first suggests no building has survived the war and economic modernisation. But examples of architecture from all periods of Seoul's history do remain, resulting in a juxtaposed hotchpotch that at times finds a quirky harmony. Explore the city and you'll discover not only fortress walls, grand palaces and decorative temples, but also charming early-20th-century *hanok* (traditional wooden homes) and dramatic contemporary structures, such as the new City Hall and Dongdaemun Design Plaza.

Traditional Architecture

There are three main types of traditional architecture found in Seoul: palaces, temples and homes. They are all primarily made of wood, with no nails used – a system of braces and brackets holds the elements together. They were (and often still are) heated using an ingenious system of circulating underfloor smoke tunnels called *ondol*.

Constructed around the 1st century AD, the Mongchon-to-seong (Mongchon Clay Fortress) was built on the southern banks of the Han River during the kingdom of Baekje (18 BC–AD 475). It's still there in Olympic Park.

Palaces

During the Joseon era (1392–1897), five main palaces were constructed in the royal capital. These were cities unto themselves, massive complexes with administrative offices, residences, pleasure pavilions and royal gardens, all hemmed in by imposing walls. A prominent feature of these structures is the roof, which is made from heavy clay tiles with dragons or other mythical beasts embossed on the end tile. The strikingly bold, predominantly green-and-orange paintwork under the eaves is called *dancheong*. Ceilings are often intricately carved and coloured.

Because of centuries of invasion and war, Seoul's palaces have all been painstakingly rebuilt countless times, sometimes changing their shape altogether.

Architecture Books

- *Hanoak – Traditional Korean Houses (various authors)*
- *Joseon Royal Court Culture (Shin Myung-ho)*
- *Seoul's Historic Walks (Cho In-Souk & Robert Koehler)*
- *City as Art: 100 Notable Works of Architecture in Seoul (Yim Seock-jae)*

Temples, Shrines & Royal Tombs

Korean temples, like palaces, are painted in natural colours. Outside murals depict the life of Buddha or parables of self-liberation; inside the shrines are paintings of Buddhist heavens – and occasionally hells. Look for intricately carved lattice in the Buddhist shrines, and for a *samseionggak*, or Mountain God Hall, which contains an image of the deity in question and represents the accommodation of Korean Buddhism to Korea's preexisting shamanist beliefs.

Also visually striking in their command of space and use of natural materials are the royal shrines and burial tombs of the Joseon dynasty, 40-odd of which are on the Unesco World Heritage list. In these tombs, each similarly arranged on hillsides according to the rules of Confucianism and feng shui, are buried every Joseon ruler right up to the last, Emperor Sunjong (r 1907–10).

Hanok

Hanok are complex in design yet masterfully understated. These one-storey homes are crafted entirely from wood, save for the clay tiled roofs, insulated with mud and straw. The windows are made of a thin

SAVING THE HANOK

'Thirty-five years ago there were around 800,000 *hanok* in South Korea; now there are less than 10,000', says Peter Bartholomew, an American expat in Korea. For over 40 years Bartholomew has been battling the predominant view among Koreans that such traditional houses are an anachronism in their modern country, unworthy of preserving.

Bartholomew has lived in *hanok* since he first came to Korea in 1968 as a Peace Corps volunteer and has owned one in the Dongsomun-dong area of northern Seoul since 1974. He bought an adjacent property in 1991. In 2009 Bartholomew and his neighbours won a two-year legal battle against the city over plans to redevelop the area. 'I deplore the assumption that these old houses are irreparable, dirty and unsanitary', he says, pointing out that traditional *hanok* are very easy to modernise in just the same way that centuries-old homes across the West have been adapted to contemporary life.

The proof of this lies in the Bukchon area, where some 900 *hanok* remain, the bulk concentrated in a few streets in Gahoe-dong (also transliterated as Kahoi-dong). 'The preservation program has only been achieved by the government providing financial incentives to owners for repairs and maintenance', says Bartholomew. However, according to some local residents, even in Bukchon the *hanok* as a private home is under threat. Gahoe-dong 'is being relentlessly destroyed', says David Kilburn, author of **Preservation of Kahoi-dong** (www.kahoidong.com), a website that documents the abuses of the preservation system over the past decade.

Contemporary Seoulites may shun *hanok* as places to live, but tourists clearly love them if the increasing number of *hanok* guesthouses is anything to go by. Ahn Young-hwan, owner of Rak-Ko-Jae, a *hanok* guesthouse in Bukchon, was one of the first people to suggest that *hanok* be used in this way. 'People thought I was crazy', he says, 'but now many more people are doing it'.

For Ahn, *hanok* are the 'vessels that contain Korean culture' and a way of experiencing the joys of an analogue life in an increasingly digital society. It's a view that Bartholomew underlines when he says that living in his *hanok* has 'filled my life with peace and beauty'.

translucent paper that allows daylight to stream in. They're heated by the underfloor system called *ondol*.

Unlike the ostentatious manor homes of Europe, even an aristocrat's lavish *hanok* was designed to blend with nature; they are typically left unpainted, their brown-and-tan earth tones giving off a warm, intimate feel. All of the rooms look onto a courtyard *(madang)*, which usually includes a simple garden. Life was lived on the floor, so all the furniture was low slung, and people sat and slept on mats rather than chairs and beds.

Social rank dictated the decorations, beam size, roof pitch and number of rooms – these rules were not relaxed until the 1930s. The traditional home was also divided into two sections: the *sarangchae* for men and the *anchae* for women. In larger homes, these comprised different buildings, surrounded by walls and gates. In the *anchae*, the women of the family raised children, did the cooking and ran the household. The *sarangchae* housed the library, an ancestral shrine and rooms in which to receive guests, who seated themselves on comfortable low cushions and enjoyed a tea service.

With South Korea's modernisation, desire to live in *hanok* waned. Their thin walls prevented privacy. There was no easy space to install indoor toilets. Rooms were small, and living on the floor had its inconveniences. In comparison, Seoul's modern high-rises offered amenities galore. Recently, however, Seoul has seen a revival of interest in traditional homes, with increased efforts to preserve their unique character.

Bukchon has Seoul's largest concentration of *hanok*, mostly dating from the 1930s. To see larger-scale *hanok* in a more traditional setting, visit Namsangol Hanok Village (p77) at the foot of Namsan.

Top Traditional Buildings

Gyeongbokgung, Gwanghwamun & Jongno-gu (p50)

Bosingak, Gwanghwamun & Jongno-gu (p62)

Jongmyo, Gwanghwamun & Jongno-gu (p54)

Sajikdan, Gwanghwamun & Jongno-gu (p59)

Sungnyemun (Namdaemun), Myeong-dong & Jung-gu (p74)

Deoksugung, Myeong-dong & Jung-gu (p75)

GANGNAM ARCHITECTURE

Given the wide-open spaces of Gangnam, architects have been able to push the envelope a bit more with their designs south of the river. Here are a few to look out for.

Some Sevit (p111) On three islands on the Han River are these futuristic buildings with glass, undulating facades covered in LEDs that glow colourfully each evening.

Tangent (Yeongdong-daero, Gangnam-gu; S Line 2 to Samseong, Exit 6) An enormous sculpture in glass, concrete and steel, reminiscent of a painting by Kandinsky.

Prugio Valley (337 Yeongdong-daero, Gangnam-gu; S Line 2 to Samseong, Exit 1) Looking like a giant music speaker crossed with a slab of Swiss cheese, this incredible steel-clad building was designed by Unsangdong Architects.

GT Tower East (411 Seocho-daero, Seocho-gu; S Line 2 to Gangnam, Exit 9) The slinkylike curvaceous stylings rises like a giant sculpture.

Early Modern & Colonial Architecture

In the late 19th century, Western and Japanese missionaries, traders and diplomats flooded into the Hermit Kingdom. The architecture of this period is often regarded as 'colonial', although some of it purely represents Korean attempts to modernise along Western lines.

Churches were usually designed by French, American or British missionaries, including wonderful examples of Gothic and Romanesque styles, but much of Seoul's early modern architectural heritage was built by the Japanese, who destroyed significant chunks of the capital's traditional buildings (particularly palaces) in the process.

Japanese colonial architects often emulated Western Renaissance and neo-baroque architectural styles, although you'll also find the occasional art nouveau or other modernist style thrown in.

Modern Architecture 1950s–1980s

Though the needs of post–Korean War reconstruction required a focus on more utilitarian concerns, much of Korea's modern architecture is distinct, usually following one of two trajectories: either an attempt to reinterpret traditional Korean architecture in concrete and steel, or to communicate Seoul's cutting-edge technological prowess.

First and perhaps foremost of Korea's postindependence architects was Japanese-trained Kim Swoo-geun, whose early work reflected the influence of Le Corbusier and Kenzo Tange. He is responsible for the curving lines of the Olympic Stadium and the ivy-clad Kyungdong Presbyterian Church (1981). Among other local architectural greats are Kim Chung-up, whose work includes the soaring Peace Gate at Olympic Park, and Kim Joong-up, responsible for the 31-storey smoked-glass Samil Building (1969), Seoul's first International-style skyscraper.

Heyri & Paju

Visiting the artist community of Heyri and publishing centre of Paju (less than one hour by bus from Seoul) are both highly recommended for their award-winning contemporary architecture.

Contemporary Architecture

Spurred on by its winning bid to be the World Design Capital in 2010, the city government and major construction firms went on a building spree, hiring such luminaries as Zaha Hadid for the Dongdaemun Design Plaza and Park, and US architecture firm Kohn Pedersen Fox for the sleek Lotte World Tower – Korea's highest building.

The work of these celebrated international architects shouldn't overshadow that of local talents, who have imposed their creative visions on a series of both small- and large-scale projects adding to Seoul's built beauty. The shopping complex Ssamziegil in Insa-dong (designed by Choi Moon-gyu and Gabriel Kroiz) and Bae Dae-young's Why Butter building in Hongdae (housing KT&G SangsangMadang) are both fine examples of contemporary buildings with a strong point of view.

Arts

Seoul has long been the nexus of Korea's spectacular range of arts. Rich, colourful costumes set the scene for passionate traditional *pansori* operas. Folk dances such as *samullori*, with its whirling dervish of dancers, seamlessly meld the cacophonous and melodic. Artisans preserve the ancient art of calligraphy with their silken strokes. Seoul takes national pride of place in the modern arts too. Korea's film directors are regularly feted at international festivals. The city's art museums and galleries burst with contemporary works. And as well as Asia going gaga for K-Pop, Seoul has also got a rockin' live-music scene too.

Visual Art

Traditional

Stone Buddhist statues and pagodas such as the one in Tapgol Park (p60) are among the oldest artworks in Seoul. Some marvellous examples of cast-bronze Buddhas can be seen in the National Museum of Korea (p97).

Above: Traditional dance performance at Korea House (p80)

SEOUL IN LITERATURE

Seoul has always been a city of writers. Part of the Joseon-era government-service exam *(gwageo)* involved composing verse. During the Joseon dynasty, literature meant *sijo*, short nature poems that were handwritten (using a brush and ink) in Chinese characters, even after the invention of *hangeul* (the Korean phonetic alphabet) in the 15th century.

In the 20th century, however, there was a sharp turn away from Chinese (and Japanese) influence of any kind. Western ideas and ideals took hold, and existentialism and other international literary trends found footing, but through a unique and pervasive Korean lens. A fascinating example is *Three Generations* (1931), a novel by Yom Sang-seop which follows the soap opera-ish and ultimately tragic lives of the wealthy Jo family under the Japanese occupation of the time.

More recent is Kim Young-ha's *I Have the Right to Destroy Myself* (2007), which delves into alienation in contemporary Seoul and *The Vegetarian* (2015) by Han Kang, a dark and disturbing Kafkaesque account of a lady's fantasy to turn into a tree.

Zen-style Buddhist art can be seen inside and outside Seoul's temples, Jogye-sa (p55) and Bongeun-sa (p110), and you'll find stone and wooden effigies of shamanist spirit guardians outside the National Folk Museum (p51) in the grounds of the main palace, Gyeongbokgung.

A fascinating traditional Korean art form is *hanji* (handmade paper). Often dyed soft colours, *hanji* can be pressed and lacquered so that it can serve as a waterproof cup or plate.

Chinese influence is paramount in traditional Korean painting. The basic tools (brush and water-based ink) are those of calligraphy, which influenced painting in both technique and theory. The brush line, which varies in thickness and tone, is the most important feature. Traditional landscape painting is meant to surround the viewer, and there is no fixed viewpoint as in traditional Western painting. A talented artist who painted everyday scenes was Kim Hong-do (1745–1816). Court ceremonies, portraits, flowers, birds and traditional symbols of longevity – the sun, water, rocks, mountains, clouds, pine trees, turtles and cranes – were popular subjects.

Modern & Contemporary

Seoul has a thriving contemporary-art scene with the best of local artists incorporating Korean motifs and themes, and sometimes traditional techniques, with a modern vision. Insa-dong, Bukchon, Samcheong-dong and Tongui-dong are all packed with small galleries, often with free shows; you'll also find major galleries south of the river in Cheongdam.

Major modern Korean artists include Nam June Paik (1932–2006), whose new-media installations can be seen at Nam June Paik Art Center and the National Museum of Contemporary Art, and Kim Tschang Yeul (1929–), whose work can be seen at the Leeum Samsung Museum of Art.

The city is fostering up-and-coming artists through its **Seoul Art Space Project** (http://eng.seoulartspace.or.kr) with 15 diverse arts spaces around Seoul. Projects vary from galleries and studios set up in factories in Mullae to underground arcades at Jungang Market in Sindang, as well as performance art and theatre.

There's a healthy street-art scene in Seoul too. Particularly in Hongdae near Hongik University subway (exit 4) with its backstreets and alleys full of cool stencils, murals, graffiti and paste-ups. Mullae Arts Village (p88) and HBC Art Village (p100) also have plenty of urban art to check out. You'll also find several mural villages where artists are commissioned to beautify downtrodden gritty neighbourhoods. Most well-known is Ihwa Maeul (p127), now a hugely popular tourist sight. Consider heading to Suwon (p137), which has similar projects, but without large numbers of tourists.

Seoul has a lively multiperformance art scene. **Crazy Multiply** (www.crazymultiply.com) puts on monthly shows that combine music, art and performance art; check its website for upcoming events. The annual **Festival Bo:m** (www.festivalbom.org; ⌚late Mar–Apr), which showcases dance, theatre, art, music and film, is also worth checking out.

Ceramics & Pottery

Archaeologists have unearthed Korean pottery that dates back some 10,000 years, although it wasn't until the early 12th century that the art form reached a peak, with skilled potters turning out wonderful celadon pottery with a warm green tinge. Visit the National Museum of Korea for one of the best displays. Original celadon fetches huge sums at auctions, but modern copies are widely available.

Music

Traditional

Korean traditional music *(gugak)* is played on stringed instruments, most notably the *gayageum* (12-stringed zither) and *haegum* (two-stringed fiddle) as well as on chimes, gongs, cymbals, drums, horns and flutes. Court music *(jeongak)* is slow and stately, while folk music such as *samullori* is fast and lively. In recent years there's been a revival of traditional Korean music among the younger generation, with audience numbers tripling to watch *gugak* performances. Young talents such as Song So-hee, and Luna Lee (who plays covers of Western hits on the *gayageum*) have both played roles in popularising *gugak*.

Similar to Western opera is *changgeuk*, which can involve a large cast of characters. An unusual type of opera is *pansori*. It features a solo storyteller (usually female) singing to the beat of a drum, while emphasising dramatic moments with a flick of her fan. The singing is strong and sorrowful: some say if *pansori* is done correctly, the performer will have blood in her mouth upon finishing. Only a few *pansori* dramas have survived; *Chunhyang*, the story of a woman's faith and endurance, is the most popular.

At the park in front of Jongmyo you may see pensioners dancing to 'trot' music. Short for 'foxtrot', this musical form combines Korean scales with Western harmonies and sounds similar to Japanese enka music.

K-Indie

Seoul is home to Korea's independent music scene. Known locally as K-Indie, it's an all-encompassing genre that includes bands playing original music ranging from indie, punk, garage and metal to shoegaze, electronica and hip-hop.

Hongdae is the home of Seoul's K-Indie scene, with dive-y venues catering to bands. The scene has flourished over the past few years, with many bands receiving international recognition. Some to watch out for include Jambinai, a postrock band who combine traditional instruments with heavy guitar riffs; alt-indie bands the Dead Buttons, the Koxx; the Patients and Yellow Monsters for punk rock; and electronica act Idiotape. All are regulars on the international festival circuit.

K-Pop

Dating back to the 1990s boy bands in Seoul, Korean pop (K-Pop) had been at the forefront of the Korean Wave (aka *hallyu*) well before Psy started busting out his crazy moves. The popularity of K-Pop has

GIG GUIDES & CULTURAL LISTINGS

Korea Gig Guide (www.koreagigguide.com)

Korean Indie (www.koreanindie.com)

Groove (www.groovekorea.com)

Seoul Magazine (http://magazine.seoulselection.com)

10 Magazine (www.10mag.com)

Beyond Hallyu (www.beyondhallyu.com)

reached fanatical levels among devotees in Korea, China and Japan, and this has extended into a worldwide phenomenon with fans from the Middle East to Latin America.

But of course it was in 2012, with Psy's smash hit 'Gangnam Style', when things really exploded. Topping the charts in nearly 30 countries, the song single-handedly thrust K-Pop into the spotlight of Western countries and still remains the world's most viewed YouTube clip, as of the time of writing.

Fans of K-Pop will have ample opportunity to enjoy tunes – both recorded and live – by their favourite singers and bands in Seoul. Other than Psy, among solo singers, few have attained the level of commercial success of BoA and her male counterpart Rain. Among the current-day K-Pop acts, popular ones include boy bands EXO, Bigbang, SHINee, the 13-member group Super Junior, and girl bands Wonder Girls and Girls' Generation.

Koreanfilm.org is a top resource covering all aspects of the industry and features numerous reviews.

Cinema

Seoul's Chungmuro neighbourhood has long been the heart of the nation's vibrant and critically acclaimed film industry, which has been a major component of *hallyu* or the Korean Wave of popular culture sweeping across Asia and the world.

Directors haven't shied away from major issues, such as the Korean War with *Taegukgi* (2004) and its turbulent political aftermath in *The President's Last Bang* (2005). Pervasive social issues in modern Seoul – such as the blistering pace of city life and the shifting notion of family – are tackled in films like *The Way Home* (2002) and *Family Ties* (2006), both quietly touching. The horror films *Memento Mori* (1999) and *A Tale of Two Sisters* (2003) provide gruesome shocks for the genre aficionado, and for an action-revenge flick – something Korea excels at – nothing tops the jaw-dropping *Old Boy* (2003), a regular contender for Korea's best film of all time. *Pieta* (2012) by art-house director Ki-duk Kim became the first Korean movie to win a best international film award, taking the Golden Lion at the Venice Film Festival.

Film-making used to be a boys' club. No longer: superb films by female directors are receiving greater recognition. These include Jeong Jae-eun's *Take Care of My Cat* (2001), the story of five girls in the suburbs outside of Seoul, and Yim Soon-rye's *Waikiki Brothers* (2001), a sobering exploration of those left behind by Korea's economic rise. Yim's *Forever the Moment* (2008) follows the Korean women's handball team into the 2004 Olympics.

Elegant court dances, accompanied by an orchestra and dating back 600 years, are performed in front of Jongmyo on the first Sunday of every May.

Theatre & Dance

Seoul's thriving theatre scene is based mainly around Daehangno, where more than 50 small theatres put on everything from rock musicals and satirical plays to opera and translations of Western classics. Nearly all shows are in Korean. More accessible are the many nonverbal shows such as Nanta and Jump (see p82 for details of both).

Korean folk dances include dynamic *seungmu* (drum dances), the satirical and energetic *talchum* (mask dances) and solo improvisational *salpuri* (shamanist dances). Most popular are *samullori* dance troupes, who perform in brightly coloured traditional clothing, twirling a long tassel from a cap on their heads at the same time as they dance and beat a drum or gong.

Survival Guide

Transport

ARRIVING IN SEOUL

Most likely you'll arrive at Incheon International Airport. If flying from within Korea, it's possible that your arrival point will be Gimpo International Airport, or Seoul or Yongsan train stations, or one of the long-distance bus stations. Ferries to Incheon, west of Seoul, connect the country with China. Flights, cars and tours can be booked online at www.lonelyplanet.com.

Incheon International Airport

The main international gateway is **Incheon International Airport** (☎02-1577 2600; www.airport.kr;), 52km west of central Seoul on the island of Yeongjong-do. This top-class operation also has a few domestic connections.

Bus

Two types of buses run from the airport to downtown Seoul. The **city limousine buses** (₩9000, 5.30am to 10pm, every 10 to 30 minutes) take around an hour to reach central Seoul depending on traffic. The deluxe **KAL limousine buses** (www.kallimousine.com; ₩14,000) run along four routes, dropping passengers at over 20 top hotels around Seoul.

Taxi

Regular taxis charge around ₩60,000 to ₩100,000 for the 70-minute journey to downtown Seoul. From midnight to 4am regular taxis charge 20% extra.

Train

There are two **A'REX** (Airport Railroad Express; www.arex.or.kr) trains from the airport to Seoul station. The **express train** costs ₩14,300 (43 minutes) departing every 30 minutes (note promo rates are ₩8000). The more frequent **commuter trains** cost ₩4250 (53 minutes; ₩4150 with T-card, p187). Trains run from 5.20am to 11.45pm.

Gimpo International Airport

The bulk of domestic flights (and a handful of international ones) arrive at **Gimpo International Airport** (☎02-1661 2626; http://gimpo.airport.co.kr; West Seoul), 18km west of the city centre.

Bus

City/KAL limousine buses run every 10 minutes to central Seoul (from ₩5000/7000, around 40 minutes, depending on traffic).

CLIMATE CHANGE & TRAVEL

Every form of transport that relies on carbon-based fuel generates CO_2, the main cause of human-induced climate change. Modern travel is dependent on aeroplanes, which might use less fuel per kilometre per person than most cars but travel much greater distances. The altitude at which aircraft emit gases (including CO_2) and particles also contributes to their climate change impact. Many websites offer 'carbon calculators' that allow people to estimate the carbon emissions generated by their journey and, for those who wish to do so, to offset the impact of the greenhouse gases emitted with contributions to portfolios of climate-friendly initiatives throughout the world. Lonely Planet offsets the carbon footprint of all staff and author travel.

Subway

Lines 5 and 9 connect the airport with the city (₩1450, 35 minutes).

Train

A'REX Trains run to Seoul station (₩1300, 15 minutes).

Taxi

A taxi costs around ₩35,000 to the city centre and takes from 40 minutes to an hour.

Seoul Station

Seoul station is the hub of the domestic rail network operated by **Korean National Railroad** (www.letskorail.com). Tickets can be bought up to one month in advance at many travel agents, as well as at train stations or online. Booking ahead is advised. If you plan to travel by train a lot over a short period, consider buying a 'KR pass' (see the website for details).

The fastest train is the KTX (Korea Train Express), which operates at speeds of 300km/h. A grade down are *saemaeul* services, which also only stop in major towns. *Mugunghwa* (limited-stop express trains) and other commuter trains are also comfortable and fast, but stop more often.

CITY AIR TERMINALS

If you're flying Korean Air, Asiana or Jeju Air, you can check in your luggage and go through immigration at the **City Airport Terminal** (english.arex.or.kr/jsp/eng/terminal/introduction.jsp; Seoul Station; ⏲5.20am-7pm; Ⓢ Line 1 or 4 to Seoul Station) inside Seoul Station, then hop on the A'REX train to Gimpo or Incheon. If you're south of the river, a similar service operates from **CALT** (☎02-551 0077; www.calt.co.kr; COEX Mall, 22 Teheran-ro 87-gil, Gangnam-gu; ⏲5.30am-6.30pm; Ⓢ Line 2 to Samseong, Exit 5) which allows check-ins for most major airlines, before transferring by limousine bus to Incheon (₩16,000, 65 minutes) or Gimpo (₩7500, 45 minutes) airports.

Bus & Taxi

City buses and taxis depart from the east side of the station.

Subway

Lines 1 and 4 connect Seoul station with the city.

Yongsan Station

Some long-distance trains from the south of Korea terminate at Yongsan station; many others pass through on their way to Seoul station.

Bus & Taxi

City buses and taxis depart from the east side of the station.

Subway

Line 1 and the Jungang line connect Yongsan station with the city.

Cheongnyangni Station

Some trains servicing Eastern Korea terminate at **Cheongnyangni station** (청량리역), including Chuncheon, Andong, Gangneung and Wonju.

Subway

Subway Line 1 connects Cheongnyangni station with the city.

BUS JOURNEYS FROM SEOUL

DESTINATION	EXPRESS/DELUXE (₩)	DURATION (HR)
Busan	23,000/34,200	4¼
Buyeo	11,600	2½
Chuncheon	6800	1¼
Gongju	8000/9000	1¾
Gwangju	17,000/26,100	3¼
Gyeongju	20,400/30,300	3¾
Jeonju	12,800/18,700	2½
Mokpo	20,000/30,000	3¾
Sokcho	18,100	2½

Seoul Express Bus Terminal

Long-distance buses arrive at the major station **Seoul Express Bus Terminal** (☎02-536 6460-2), split across two separate buildings: **Gyeongbu Line Terminal** (www.kobus.co.kr) serves mainly the eastern region, and **Central City Terminal** (www.hticket.co.kr) serves the southwestern region.

It's only necessary to buy tickets in advance for holidays and weekends. Deluxe-class buses have more leg room and cost more than ordinary buses. Buses that travel after 10pm have a 10%

surcharge and are generally deluxe. Children aged six to 14 go half price.

Subway

Lines 3, 7 and 9 connect the bus terminal with the city; use exit 1 for Gyeongbu Line Terminal, exit 7 for Honam Terminal.

Dong-Seoul Bus Terminal

This **terminal** (☎02-1688 5979; www.ti21.co.kr; 50 Gangbyeonnyeok-ro) in Jamsil serves the eastern part of Korea (1st floor) and major cities (2nd floor).

Subway

Line 2 to Gangbyeon, Exit 4.

Nambu Bus Terminal

Located in Gangnam, this **terminal** (☎02-521 8550; www.kobus.co.kr/web/eng/index.jsp; 292 Hyoryeong-ro) serves destinations south of Seoul.

Subway

Line 3 to Nambu Bus Terminal, Exit 5.

FREE SHUTTLE TO JEONJU

Those heading between Seoul and Jeonju can take the free tourist **shuttle bus** (http://shuttle.dongbotravel.com/en) departing Friday, Saturday and Sunday at 8am (three hours) from the parking lot at Dongwha Duty Free store. The bus returns from Jeonju at 5pm. Note it runs only March to December, and you need to bring your foreign passport.

Incheon Port

Ferries connect Incheon, west of Seoul, with a dozen port cities in China. Journey times vary from 12 to 24 hours. One-way fares start at ₩115,000 to most destinations but prices double for the more private and comfortable cabins. To reach Incheon's port (ferries leave from Yeonan Pier or International Terminal 2), take subway line 1 to Incheon station and then take a taxi (around ₩6000).

Ferries to a number of Japanese cities leave from the southern city of Busan. See www.korail.com for details of a Seoul–Japan rail-and-ferry through ticket.

GETTING AROUND SEOUL

Bicycle

Cycling the busy main streets of the city is not recommended but a pedal along the cycling lanes beside the Han River and through several parks can be a pleasure. Bicycles can be rented at several parks along the Han River including on Yeouido, Ttukseom Resort, Seoul Forest Park and Olympic Park. Rental is ₩3000 per hour and you'll need to leave some form of ID as a deposit. There's also free bicycle rental from designated subway stations (p42).

Bus

Seoul has a comprehensive and reasonably priced **bus system** (www.bus.go.kr; ⏲5.30am-midnight). Some bus stops have bus route maps in English, and most buses have their major destinations written in English on the outside and a taped

TRANSPORT APPS

Subway Korea Very handy free app for interactive Seoul subway map and real-time journey planner.

Seoul Topis (http://topis.seoul.go.kr/english.jsp) Provides route planning and real-time information in English for bus, subway and road journeys in the city. Use it to work out the most convenient public-transport routes and journey times between destinations.

announcement of the names of each stop in English, but few bus drivers understand English.

Using a T-Money card saves ₩100 on each bus fare and transfers between bus and subway are either free or discounted. Put your T-Money card to the screen as you exit as well as when you get on a bus, just as you do on the subway.

Red buses Long-distance express run to the outer suburbs.

Green buses Link subways within a district.

Blue buses Run to outer suburbs.

Yellow buses Short-haul buses that circle small districts.

Car & Motorcycle

Driving is on the right, but due to the traffic jams, the impatience and recklessness of other drivers and the lack of street names, directional signs and parking, we recommend first-time visitors to Seoul give driving a miss. Public transport and taxis are cheap and convenient.

Hire

To rent a car you must be over 21 and have both a driving licence from your own country and an International Driving Permit. The latter must be obtained abroad as they're not available in Korea. Incheon International Airport has a couple of car-rental agencies. Try **KT Kumho** (☎02-797 8000; www.ktkumhorent.com) or **Avis** (☎032 743 3300; www.avis.com; Incheon International Airport). Daily rates start at ₩80,000.

Subway

Seoul has an excellent, user-friendly **subway system** (www.smrt.co.kr; ⏰5.30am-midnight) which connects up with destinations well beyond the city borders, including Suwon and Incheon. The minimum fare of ₩1350 (₩1250 with a T-Money card) takes you up to 12km. In central Seoul the average time between stations is just over two minutes, so it takes around 25 minutes to go 10 stops. Some top-end hotels and a few sights are a 15-minute walk from a subway station but you can hail taxis from the closest station.

T-MONEY CARD

Bus, subway, taxi and train fares can all be paid using the rechargeable touch-and-go **T-Money card** (http://eng.t-money.co.kr), which gives you a ₩100 discount per trip. The basic card can be bought for a nonrefundable ₩2500 at any subway-station booth, bus kiosks and convenience stores displaying the T-Money logo; reload it with credit at any of the aforementioned places, and get money refunded that hasn't been used (up to ₩20,000 minus a processing fee of ₩500) at subway machines and participating convenience store before you leave Seoul.

Most subway stations have lifts or stair lifts for wheelchairs. Escalators are common, but you'll do a fair amount of walking up and down stairs and along corridors. Neighbourhood maps, including ones with digital touch screens, inside the stations help you figure out which of the subway exits to take. The closest station and exit number is provided for all listings.

Taxi

Regular orange or grey taxis are a good deal for short trips. The flagfall for 2km is ₩3000 and rises ₩100 for every 144m or 35 seconds after that if the taxi is travelling below 15km/h. A 20% surcharge is levied between midnight and 4am. Deluxe taxis are black and cost ₩5000 for the first 3km and ₩200 for every 164m or 39 seconds, but they don't have a late-night surcharge.

Few taxi drivers speak English, but most taxis have a free interpretation service whereby an interpreter talks to the taxi driver and to you by phone. Orange **International Taxi** (☎02-1644 2255; www.internationaltaxi.co.kr) has English-speaking drivers; these can be reserved in advance for 20% extra on the regular fare and can be chartered on an hourly or daily basis for longer journeys. All taxis are metered, tipping is not required.

Directory A–Z

Customs Regulations

Visitors must declare all plants, fresh fruit, vegetables and dairy products that they bring into South Korea. Meat is not allowed without a certificate. Log on to www.customs.go.kr for further information. Antiques of national importance are banned from export.

Discount Cards

Korea Pass (www.lottecard.co.kr/app/html/koreapass/IHKPAZZ_V100.jsp) is a prepaid card, available in denominations from ₩50,000 to ₩500,000, that provides discounts on a range of goods and services. It can be bought at Lotte Mart and 7-Eleven branches in Seoul as well as at the A'REX booth at Incheon International Airport.

Embassies

Australian Embassy (☎02-2003 0100; www.southkorea.embassy.gov.au; 19th fl, Kyobo Bldg, 1 Jong-ro, Jongno-gu; S Line 5 to Gwanghwamun, Exit 4)

Canadian Embassy (☎02-3783 6000; www.canadainternational.gc.ca/korea-coree; 21 Jeong-dong-gil, Jung-gu; S Line 5 to Seodaemun, Exit 5)

Chinese Embassy (☎02-738 1038; www.chinaemb.or.kr; 27 Myeong-dong 2-gil, Jung-gu; S Line 4 to Myeong-dong, Exit 5)

French Embassy (☎02-3149 4300; www.ambafrance-kr.org; 43-12 Seosomun-ro, Seodaemun-gu; S Line 2 or 5 to Chungjeongno, Exit 3)

German Embassy (☎02-748 4114; www.seoul.diplo.de; Seoul Sq, 8th fl, 416 Hangang-daero, Jung-gu; S Line 1 or 4 to Seoul station, Exit 8)

Irish Embassy (☎02-721 7200; www.embassyofireland.or.kr; 13th fl, Leema Bldg, 2 Jong-ro 1-gil, Jongno-gu; S Line 5 to Gwanghwamun, Exit 2)

Japanese Embassy (☎02-765 3011; www.kr.emb-japan.go.jp; 64 Yulgok-ro, Jongno-gu; S Line 3 to Anguk, Exit 6)

Netherlands Embassy (☎02-311 8600; http://southkorea.nlembassy.org; 10th fl, Jeongdong Bldg, 21-15 Jeongdong-gil, Jung-gu; S Line 5 to Seodaemun, Exit 5)

New Zealand Embassy (☎02-3701 7700; www.nzembassy.com/korea; 15th fl, Kyobo Bldg, Jongno 1-ga, Jongno-gu; S Line 5 to Gwanghwamun, Exit 4)

UK Embassy (☎02-3210 5500; www.gov.uk/government/world/organisations/british-embassy-seoul; 24 Sejong-daero 19-gil, Jung-gu; S Line 1 or 2 to City Hall, Exit 3)

US Embassy (☎02-397 4114; http://seoul.usembassy.gov; 188 Sejong-daero, Jongno-gu; S Line 5 to Gwanghwamun, Exit 2)

Emergencies

If no English-speaking staff are available, ring the 24-hour tourist information and help line ☎1330.

Ambulance (☎119)

Fire Brigade (☎119)

Police (☎112)

Gay & Lesbian Travellers

Korea is a sexually conservative society and although the country has never outlawed homosexuality, this shouldn't be taken as a sign of tolerance or acceptance. Attitudes are changing, especially among young people, but virtually all of the local gay population (called *ivan* in Korean) chooses to stay firmly in closet.

Gay and lesbian travellers who publicise their sexual orientation should be prepared for some less-than-positive reactions.

In mid-June, Seoul pins up its rainbow colours for the **Korea Queer Festival** (www.kqcf.org).

Useful resources:

Chungusai (Between Friends; ☎02-745 7942; chingusai.net) Korean LGBTIQ human-rights group.

Utopia (www.utopia-asia.com) Check the Korea section for maps and reviews of gay bars, clubs and services.

Electricity

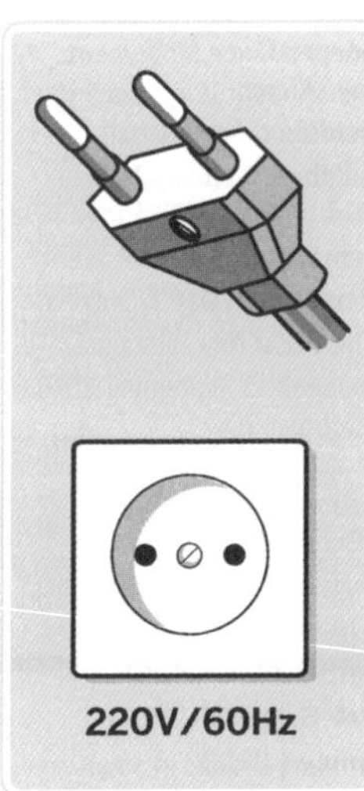

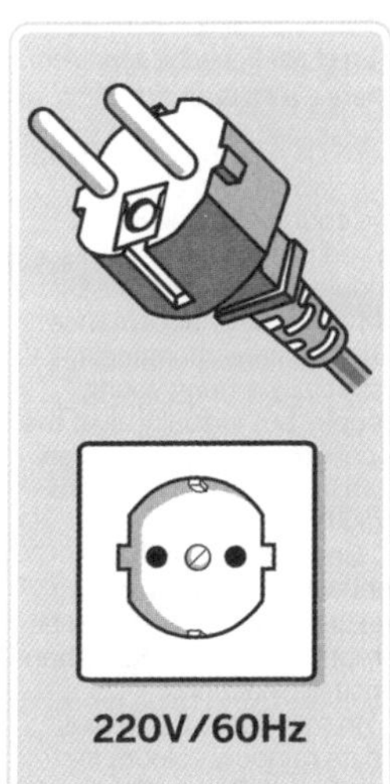

Health

➡ There are no special vaccination requirements for visiting Korea, but you should consider vaccination against hepatitis A and B. Most people don't drink the tap water, but those who do seem to come to no harm. Filtered or bottled water is served free in most restaurants.

➡ The **World Health Organization** (www.who.int/ith) publishes the annually revised booklet *International Travel & Health*, available free online.

Internet Access

➡ Wi-fi is universal and commonly free. Nearly all hotels offer it, too, for free, except a handful of top-end hotels which may charge ₩30,000 per day.

➡ If you need a computer, look for places with a 'PC 방' sign, which charge around ₩2000 per hour and are invariably packed with teenaged online gamers.

➡ The major phone companies offer USB dongle devices to rent, in the same way as mobile phones, to connect to the internet anywhere around Korea.

Maps

The Korean Tourism Organization (KTO) and Seoul Metropolitan Government publish numerous free brochures and maps of Seoul, which are fine for most purposes. **Chungang Atlas** (98 Sambong-ro, Jongno-gu; ⏰9am-6pm Mon-Fri, to 4pm Sat; ⓈLine 1 to Jonggak, Exit 2) has some hiking maps with a bit of English.

Medical Services

Seoul has medical-care standards equal to those of other developed countries. You need a doctor's prescription to buy most medications, and it may be difficult to find the exact medication you use at home, so take extra. A letter from your physician outlining your medical condition and a list of your medications (using generic names) could be useful.

Hospitals normally require cash upfront, which you should be able to claim back from your insurance company, if you have appropriate cover.

Clinics

Asan Medical Center (☎02-3010 5100; http://eng.amc.seoul.kr; 88 Olympic-ro 43-gil, Songpa-gu; ⏰international clinic 8.30am-5.30pm Mon-Fri; ⓈLine 2 to Seongnae, Exit 1) A 10-minute walk from the subway exit.

International Clinic (☎02-790 0857; www.internationalclinic.co.kr; 211 Itaewon-ro, Yongsan-gu; ⏰9am-6.30pm Mon-Wed & Fri, to 4pm Sat; ⓈLine 6 to Itaewon, Exit 2) Appointments are a must.

Severance Hospital (☎02-2228 5800; www.yuhs.or.kr; 50-1 Yonsei-ro, Seodaemun-gu; ⏰international clinic 9.30-11.30am & 2-4.30pm Mon-Fri, 9.30am-noon Sat; ⓈLine 2 to Sinchon, Exit 3) A 15-minute walk from the subway exit.

Pharmacies

Almost all pharmacies stock at least some Western medicines. Pharmacists often know some English but it may help them if you write down your symptoms or the medicine you want on a piece of paper. If you have a language problem and a mobile phone, dial ☎1330, explain what you want in English, and ask the interpreter to explain in Korean to the pharmacist.

Sudo Pharmacy (☎02-732 3336; 40 Insadong-gi, Jongno-gu; ⏰8.30am-7.45pm Mon-Sat, noon-7pm Sun; SLine 3 to Anguk, Exit 6) You'll find English-speaking staff here who can advise on both Western-style medicines and natural Eastern ones.

Money

The South Korean unit of currency is the won (₩), with ₩10, ₩50, ₩100 and ₩500 coins. Notes come in denominations of ₩1000, ₩5000, ₩10,000 and ₩50,000.

ATMs

ATMs that accept foreign cards are common: look for one that has a 'Global' sign or the logo of your credit-card company. ATMs often operate only from 7am to 11pm, but some are open 24 hours. Restrictions on the amount you can withdraw vary. It can be as low as ₩100,000 per day.

Changing Money

Many banks in Seoul offer a foreign-exchange service. There are also licensed money changers, particularly in Itaewon, that keep longer hours than the banks and provide a faster service, but may only exchange US dollars cash.

Credit Cards

Hotels, shops and restaurants accept foreign credit cards, but plenty of places, including budget accommodation and stalls, require cash.

Opening Hours

Banks 9am to 4pm Monday to Friday, ATMs 7am to 11pm

Bars 6pm to 1am, longer hours Friday and Saturday

Cafes 7am to 10pm

Post offices 9am to 6pm Monday to Friday

Restaurants 11am to 10pm

Shops 10am to 8pm

Postal Services

For postal rates refer to the website of **Korea Post** (www.koreapost.go.kr). Offices are fairly common and have a red/orange sign.

Central Post Office
(02-6450 1114; 70 Sogong-ro, Myeong-dong; 9am-8pm Mon-Fri, to 1pm Sat & Sun; SLine 4 to Myeongdong, Exit 5) This basement post office sells train tickets and offers free internet.

Public Holidays

Eight Korean public holidays are set according to the solar calendar and three according to the lunar calendar, meaning that they fall on different days each year. Restaurants, shops and tourist sights stay open during most holidays, but may close over the three-day Lunar New Year and Chuseok (harvest-festival) holidays. School holidays mean that beaches and resort areas are busy in August.

New Year's Day 1 January

Lunar New Year 18 February 2016, 28 January 2017, 16 February 2018

Independence Movement Day 1 March

Children's Day 5 May

Buddha's Birthday 14 May 2016, 3 May 2017, 22 May 2018

Memorial Day 6 June

Constitution Day 17 July

Liberation Day 15 August

Chuseok 15 September 2016, 4 October 2017, 24 September 2018

National Foundation Day 3 October

Christmas Day 25 December

Safe Travel

Drinking Drunks in Seoul are better behaved than in the West, so walking around at 3am shouldn't pose a problem. There's always an exception, of course, and as always it's best

FINDING AN ADDRESS

Most listings in this guidebook use Korea's new address system (in full operation since 2014) that has sequentially numbered buildings on named streets (*daero* for eight-plus lane roads; *ro* for seven- to two-lane roads; and *gil* for one-lane roads) within one of Seoul's 25 districts (*gu*, eg Jongno-gu). Odd numbers are on the left side of the street, even numbers on the right. All official street signs and house numbers are written in *hangeul* and English.

However, many businesses still use name cards and have websites listing their old addresses based on the subdistricts (*dong*, eg Insa-dong) and the age of the building within that subdistrict. Even though you are highly unlikely to find these old addresses marked on buildings or street signs, the public (including taxi drivers) tend to be more familiar with the old addresses than the new.

If you need to work out where exactly a place is, then use http://eng.juso.go.kr/openEngPage.do; type the old address in the search bar to find the new address.

not to antagonise people who have been drinking.

Protests Police in full riot gear, carrying large shields and long batons, are a common sight in downtown Seoul. Student, trade-union, anti-American, environmental and other protests occasionally turn violent. Keep well out of the way of any confrontations that may occur.

Roads Seoul is a safe city, except when it comes to traffic. Drivers tend to be impatient; many routinely go through red lights. For those on foot, don't be the first or last person to cross over any pedestrian crossing and don't expect any vehicles to stop for you. Watch out for motorcyclists who routinely speed along pavements and across pedestrian crossings.

PRACTICALITIES

➡ **Daily Newspapers** Read English versions of the *Korea Times* (www.koreatimes.co.kr), *Korea Herald* (www.koreaherald.com) and *Korea JoongAng Daily* (http://koreajoongangdaily.joins.com).

➡ **Monthly Magazines** Print magazines in English include *Seoul Magazine* (http://magazine.seoulselection.com), *10 Magazine* (www.10mag.com) and *Groove Korea* (groovekorea.com).

➡ **TV & Radio** TV programmes in English are aired on **Arirang** (www.arirang.co.kr). **KBS World Radio** (http://world.kbs.co.kr) broadcasts news and features programmes in English as does **TBS** (http://tbsefm.seoul.kr) which also features music.

Telephone

Mobile Phones

Korea uses the CDMA network system, which few other countries use, so you may have to rent a mobile (cell) phone while you're in Seoul. You can also rent or buy a SIM card for use in smartphones.

➡ Mobile-phone and SIM hire is available from KT Olleh, SK Telecom and LGU+, all of which all have counters at Incheon International Airport arrivals floor and branches throughout the city: for details see www.airport.kr/airport/facility/efalicityInfo.iia?carId=26. SIM cards are also available from **Evergreen Mobile** (www.egsimcard.co.kr/ENG) and **SIMCard Korea** (www.simcardkorea.com).

➡ Each company offers similar, but not identical schemes so compare before buying or signing a rental contract if cost is an issue. Prepaid SIMs are also available from Evergreen Mobile, SIMCard Korea and vendors in Itaewon.

➡ Korean mobile-phone numbers have three-digit initial codes, always beginning with 01, eg ☎011 1234 5678. You'll also come across Internet phone numbers (also known as VoIP) which begin with ☎070. When you make a call from your mobile phone you always input these initial or area codes, even if you're in the city you're trying to reach. For example, in Seoul when calling a local Seoul number you would dial ☎02-123 4567.

Phone Codes

Gyeonggi-do Code (☎031) This province surrounds Seoul.

Incheon city and airport code (☎032)

International access code KT (☎001)

Seoul code (☎02) Do not dial the zero if calling from outside Korea.

South Korea country code (☎82)

Public Phones & Phonecards

➡ Public payphones are rare; the best place to look are subway stations. Ones accepting coins (₩50 or ₩100) are even rarer.

➡ Telephone cards usually give you a 10% bonus in value and can be bought at convenience stores. There are two types of cards, so if your card does not fit in one type of payphone, try a different-looking one. The more squat payphones accept the thin cards. A few public phones accept credit cards.

➡ Local calls cost ₩70 for three minutes.

Time

South Korea is nine hours ahead of GMT/UTC (London) and does not have daylight saving. When it is noon in Seoul, it's 7pm the previous day in San Francisco, 10pm the previous day in New York and 1pm the same day in Sydney.

Toilets

➡ There are plenty of clean, modern and well-signed *hwajangsil* (public toilets).

➡ Toilet signs read 숙녀 for female; 신사 for male.

➡ Virtually all toilets are free of charge.

➡ There are still a few Asian-style squat toilets around. Face the hooded end when you squat.

➡ Toilet paper is usually outside the cubicles, but it's wise to

TRANSLATION & COUNSELLING SERVICES

Tourist Phone Number (☎1330, or ☎02-1330 from a mobile phone) If you need interpretation help or information on practically any topic, any time of the day or night, you can call this number.

Seoul Global Center (☎02-2075 4180; http://global.seoul.go.kr; 38 Jong-ro, Jongno-gu; ⏲9am-6pm Mon-Fri; Ⓢ Line 1 to Jonggak, Exit 6) This comprehensive support centre for foreign residents in Seoul is also very useful; it has volunteers who speak a range of languages as well as full-time staff who can assist on a range of issues. Language and culture classes are also held here.

carry a stash of toilet tissue around with you just in case.

Tourist Information

There are scores of tourist-information booths around the city. In major tourist areas such as Insa-dong and Namdaemun, look for red-jacketed city tourist guides who can also help with information in various languages.

Cheong-gye-cheon Tourist Information Center (Sejong-daero, Gwanghwamun; ⏲9am-6pm; Ⓢ Line 5 to Gwanghwamun, Exit 5)

Dongdaemun Tourist Information Center (☎02-2236 9135; 247 Jangchungdan-ro, Jung-gu; ⏲10am-1am; Ⓢ Line 2, 4 or 5 to Dongdaemun History & Culture Park, Exit 14)

Gangnam Tourist Information Center (http:// tour.gangnam.go.kr; 161 Apgujeong-ro, Gangnam-gu; ⏲10am-7pm; Ⓢ Line 3 to Apgujeong, Exit 6) A shiny new information centre with helpful staff and a stack of brochures on Gangnam. It also has the K-Pop Experience and the Gangnam Medical Tour Center.

Gyeongbokgung Tourist Information Center (161 Sajik-ro, Jongno-gu; ⏲9am-6pm; Ⓢ Line 3 to Gyeongbokgung, Exit 5)

Insa-dong Tourist Information Center (☎02-734 0222; Insa-dong 11-gil; ⏲10am-10pm; Ⓢ Line 3 to Anguk, Exit 6) Two more centres are at the south and north entrances to Insadong-gil.

Itaewon Subway Tourist Information Center (☎02-3707 9416; Itaewon Station; ⏲9am-10pm; Ⓢ Line 6 to Itaewon) Located beside the gate to subway lines in the station.

KTO Tourist Information Center (☎02-1330; www.visitkorea.or.kr; Cheonggyecheon-ro, Jung-gu; ⏲9am-8pm; Ⓢ Line 1 to Jonggak, Exit 5) The best information centre; knowledgeable staff, free internet and many brochures and maps.

Myeong-dong Tourist Information Center (☎02-778 0333; http://blog.naver.com/mdtic1129; 66, Eulji-ro, Jung-gu; ⏲9am-8pm; Ⓢ Line 2 to Euljiro 1-ga, Exit 6)

Namdaemun Market Tourist Information Center (☎02-752 1913; Gate 5 or 7; ⏲10am-7pm; Ⓢ Line 4 to Hoehyeon, Exit 5) You'll find two info kiosks within the market.

Travellers with Disabilities

Seoul is slowly getting better at catering for disabled people. Many subway stations now have stair lifts and elevators, and toilets for disabled people have been built. A few hotels have specially adapted rooms. Tourist attractions, especially government-run ones, offer generous discounts or even free entry for disabled people and a helper. For more information see http://english.visitkorea.or.kr/enu/GK/GK_EN_2_5_2.jsp.

Visas

Tourist Visas

➡ With a confirmed onward ticket, visitors from the USA, nearly all Western European countries, New Zealand, Australia and around 30 other countries receive 90-day permits on arrival. Visitors from a handful of countries receive 60- or 30-day permits, while Canadians get 180 days.

➡ If you need to apply for a tourist visa, this will allow a stay of 90 days.

➡ As long as it hasn't expired, in some cases it is possible to extend your visa for another 90 days; more info is at www.hikorea.go.kr/pt/main_en.pt.

Work Visas

➡ Applications for a work visa can be made inside South Korea, but you must leave the country to pick up the visa. You can also apply for a one-year work visa before entering South Korea but it can take a few weeks to process. Note that the visa authorities will want to see originals (not photocopies) of your educational qualifications. This a safeguard against fake degree certificates.

➡ You don't need to leave South Korea to renew a work visa as long as you carry on working for the same employer. But if you change employers you must normally apply for a new visa and pick it up outside Korea.

➡ If you are working or studying in South Korea on a long-term visa, it is necessary to apply for an alien registration card (ARC) within 90 days of arrival, which costs ₩10,000. In Seoul this is done at either the **Omokgyo office** (☎02-2650 6212; www.immigration.go.kr/hp/imm80/index.do; 319-2 Sinjeong 6 dong, Yangcheon-gu; ⏲9am-6pm Mon-Fri; ⓈLine 5 to Omokgyo, Exit 7) south of the Han River, or the **Anguk office** (☎02-732-6220; 2nd floor, SK Hub Bldg, 461, Samil-daero, Jongno-gu; ⓈLine 3 to Anguk, Exit 5), north of the river.

➡ **Seoul Global Center** (☎02-2075 4180; global.seoul.go.kr; 38 Jong-ro, Jongno-gu; ⏲9am-6pm Mon-Fri; ⓈLine 1 to Jonggak, Exit 6) can also help with issues related to work visas.

Volunteering

The Seoul Global Center is a good place to start looking for volunteer possibilities.

More charities and organisations with volunteer opportunities include the following:

Amnesty International (http://amnesty.or.kr/english) Works mainly on raising awareness in Korea about international human-rights issues.

Korean Federation for Environmental Movement (KFEM; ☎02-735 7000; http://kfem.or.kr) Offers volunteer opportunities on various environmental projects and campaigns.

Korean Unwed Mothers' Families Association (KUMFA; www.facebook.com/groups/kumfa) Provides support to single mothers.

Korea Women's Hot Line (KWHL; ☎02-3156 5400; http://eng.hotline.or.kr) Nationwide organisation that also runs a shelter for abused women.

Seoul International Women's Association (www.siwapage.com) Organises fundraising events to help charities across Korea.

Seoul Volunteer Center (☎070-8797 1861; http://volunteer.seoul.go.kr) Opportunities to teach language and culture, take part in environmental clean-ups and help out at social-welfare centres.

World Wide Opportunities on Organic Farms (WWOOF; ☎02-723 4458; http://wwoofkorea.org/home) Farms across Korea welcome volunteer workers who provide their labour in exchange for board and lodging.

Work

➡ Although a few other opportunities are available for work (particularly for those with Korean language skills), the biggest demand is for English teachers.

➡ Native English teachers on a one-year contract can expect to earn around ₩2.5 million or more a month, with a furnished apartment, return flights, 50% of medical insurance, 10 days' paid holiday and a one-month completion bonus all included in the package. Income tax is very low (around 4%), although a 4.5% pension contribution (reclaimable by some nationalities) is compulsory.

➡ Most English teachers work in a *hagwon* (private language school) but some are employed by universities or government schools. Company classes, English camps and teaching via the telephone are also possible, as is private tutoring, although this is technically illegal. Teaching hours in a *hagwon* are usually around 30 hours a week and are likely to involve split shifts, and evening and Saturday classes.

➡ A degree in any subject is sufficient as long as English is your native language. However, it's a good idea to obtain some kind of English-teaching qualification before you arrive, as this increases your options and you should be able to find (and do) a better job.

➡ Some *hagwon* owners are less than ideal employers and don't pay all that they promise. Ask any prospective employer for the email addresses of foreign English teachers working at the *hagwon*, and contact them for their opinion and advice. One important point to keep in mind is that if you change employers, you will usually need to obtain a new work visa, which requires you to leave the country to pick up your new visa. Your new employer may pick up all or at least part of the tab for this.

➡ The best starting point for finding out more about the English-teaching scene is the **Korea Association of Teachers of English** (KATE; www.kate.or.kr).

Language

Korean belongs to the Ural-Altaic language family and is spoken by around 80 million people in the world. The standard language of South Korea is based on the dialect of Seoul.

Korean script, Hangul, is simple and accessible, as each character represents a sound of its own. There are a number of competing Romanisation systems in use today for Hangul. Since 2000, the government has been changing road signs to reflect the 'new' Romanisation system, so you may encounter signs, maps and tourist literature with at least two different Romanisation systems.

Korean pronunciation should be pretty straightforward for English speakers, as most sounds are also found in English or have a close approximation. If you follow the coloured pronunciation guides we provide, you'll be understood. Korean distinguishes between aspirated consonants (formed by making a puff of air as they're pronounced) and unaspirated ones (pronounced without a puff of air). In our pronunciation guides, aspirated consonants (except for s and h) are immediately followed by an apostrophe ('). Syllables are pronounced with fairly even emphasis in Korean.

BASICS

Hello. 안녕하세요. an·nyŏng ha·se·yo

Goodbye. (when leaving/ staying) 안녕히 계세요/ 가세요. an·nyŏng·hi kye·se·yo/ ka·se·yo

Yes./No. 네./아니요. né/a·ni·yo

WANT MORE?

For in-depth language information and handy phrases, check out Lonely Planet's *Korean phrasebook*. You'll find it at **shop.lonelyplanet.com**, or you can buy Lonely Planet's iPhone phrasebooks at the Apple App Store.

Excuse me. 실례합니다. shil·lé ham·ni·da

Sorry. 죄송합니다. choé·song ham·ni·da

Thank you. 고맙습니다./ 감사합니다. ko·map·sŭm·ni·da/ kam·sa·ham·ni·da

How are you?
안녕하세요? an·nyŏng ha·se·yo

Fine, thanks. And you?
네. 안녕하세요? ne an·nyŏng ha·se·yo

What is your name?
성함을 여쭤봐도 될까요? sŏng·ha·mŭl yŏ·tchŏ·bwa·do doélk·ka·yo

My name is ...
제 이름은 ...입니다. che i·rŭ·mŭn ...·im·ni·da

Do you speak English?
영어 하실 줄 아시나요? yŏng·ŏ ha·shil·jul a·shi·na·yo

I don't understand.
못 알아 들었어요. mot a·ra·dŭ·rŏss·ŏ·yo

ACCOMMODATION

Do you have a ... room? ... 룸 있나요? ... rum in·na·yo

single	싱글	shing·gŭl
double	더블	tŏ·bŭl

How much per ...? ...에 얼마예요? ...·é ŏl·ma·ye·yo

night	하룻밤	ha·rup·pam
person	한 명	han·myŏng

air-con	냉방	naeng·bang
bathroom	욕실	yok·shil
toilet	화장실	hwa·jang·shil
window	창문	ch'ang·mun

Is breakfast included?
아침 포함인가요? a·ch'im p'o·ha·min·ga·yo

DIRECTIONS

Where's a/the ...?
... 어디 있나요? ... ŏ·di in·na·yo

What's the address?
주소가 뭐예요? chu·so·ga mwŏ·ye·yo

Could you please write it down?
적어 주시겠어요? chŏ·gŏ ju·shi·gess·ŏ·yo

Please show me (on the map).
(지도에서) 어디인지 가르쳐 주세요. (chi·do·e·sŏ) ŏ·di·in·ji ka·rŭ·ch'ŏ ju·se·yo

EATING & DRINKING

Can we see the menu?
메뉴 볼 수 있나요? me·nyu bol·su in·na·yo

What would you recommend?
추천 해 주시겠어요? ch'u·ch'ŏn hae·ju·shi·gess·ŏ·yo

Do you have any vegetarian dishes?
채식주의 음식 있나요? ch'ae·shik·chu·i ŭm·shik in·na·yo

I'd like ..., please.
... 주세요. ... ju·se·yo

Cheers!
건배! kŏn·bae

That was delicious!
맛있었어요! ma·shiss·ŏss·ŏ·yo

Please bring the bill.
계산서 가져다 주세요. kye·san·sŏ ka·jŏ·da ju·se·yo

I'd like to reserve a table for ...	... 테이블 예약해 주세요.	... t'e·i·bŭl ye·ya·k'ae ju·se·yo
(eight) o'clock	(여덟) 시	(yŏ·dŏl)·shi
(two) people	(두) 명	(tu)·myŏng

EMERGENCIES

Help!	도와주세요!	to·wa·ju·se·yo
Go away!	저리 가세요!	chŏ·ri ka·se·yo

Call ...!	... 불러주세요!	... pul·lŏ·ju·se·yo
a doctor	의사	ŭi·sa
the police	경찰	kyŏng·ch'al

I'm lost.
길을 잃었어요. ki·rŭl i·rŏss·ŏ·yo

Where's the toilet?
화장실이 어디예요? hwa·jang·shi·ri ŏ·di·ye·yo

I'm sick.
전 아파요. chŏn a·p'a·yo

It hurts here.
여기가 아파요. yŏ·gi·ga a·p'a·yo

I'm allergic to ...
전 ...에 알레르기가 있어요. chŏn ...·é al·le·rŭ·gi·ga iss·ŏ·yo

KEY PATTERNS

To get by in Korean, mix and match these simple patterns with words of your choice:

When's (the next bus)?
(다음 버스) 언제 있나요? (ta·ŭm bŏ·sŭ) ŏn·jé in·na·yo

Where's (the train/subway station)?
(역) 어디예요? (yŏk) ŏ·di·ye·yo

I'm looking for (a hotel).
(호텔) 찾고 있어요. (ho·t'el) ch'ak·ko iss·ŏ·yo

Do you have (a map)?
(지도) 가지고 계신가요? (chi·do) ka·ji·go kye·shin·ga·yo

Is there (a toilet)?
(화장실) 있나요? (hwa·jang·shil) in·na·yo

I'd like (the menu).
(메뉴) 주세요. (me·nyu) ju·se·yo

I'd like to (hire a car).
(차 빌리고) 싶어요. (ch'a pil·li·go) shi·p'ŏ·yo

Could you please (help me)?
(저를 도와) 주시겠어요? (chŏ·rŭl to·wa) ju·shi·gess·ŏ·yo

How much is (a room)?
(방) 얼마예요? (pang) ŏl·ma·ye·yo

Do I need (a visa)?
(비자) 필요한가요? (pi·ja) p'i·ryo·han·ga·yo

SHOPPING & SERVICES

I'm just looking.
그냥 구경할게요. kŭ·nyang ku·gyŏng halk·ke·yo

Do you have (tissues)?
(휴지) 있나요? (hyu·ji) in·na·yo

How much is it?
얼마예요? ŏl·ma·ye·yo

Can you write down the price?
가격을 써 주시겠어요? ka·gyŏ·gŭl ssŏ ju·shi·gess·ŏ·yo

Can I look at it?
보여 주시겠어요? po·yŏ ju·shi·gess·ŏ·yo

Do you have any others?
다른 건 없나요? ta·rŭn·gŏn ŏm·na·yo

That's too expensive.
너무 비싸요. nŏ·mu piss·a·yo

Please give me a discount.
깎아 주세요. ggak·ka·ju·se·yo

There's a mistake in the bill.
계산서가 이상해요. kye·san·sŏ i·sang·hae·yo

ATM	현금인출기	hyŏn·gŭ·min·ch'ul·gi
internet cafe	PC방	p'i·shi·bang

Signs

영업 중	Open
휴무	Closed
입구	Entrance
출구	Exit
... 금지	... Prohibited
금연 구역	No Smoking Area
화장실	Toilets
신사용	Men
숙녀용	Women

post office	우체국	u·ch'e·guk
tourist office	관광안내소	kwan·gwang an·nae·so

TIME & DATES

What time is it?
몇 시예요? myŏs·shi·ye·yo

It's (two) o'clock.
(두) 시요. (tu)·shi·yo

Half past (two).
(두) 시 삼십 분이요. (tu)·shi sam·ship·pu·ni·yo

morning	아침	a·ch'im
afternoon	오후	o·hu
evening	저녁	chŏ·nyŏk
yesterday	어제	ŏ·jé
today	오늘	o·nŭl
tomorrow	내일	nae·il

Monday	월요일	wŏ·ryo·il
Tuesday	화요일	hwa·yo·il
Wednesday	수요일	su·yo·il
Thursday	목요일	mo·gyo·il
Friday	금요일	kŭ·myo·il
Saturday	토요일	t'o·yo·il
Sunday	일요일	i·ryo·il

TRANSPORT

A ... ticket (to Daegu), please.	(대구 가는) ... 표 주세요.	(tae·gu ka·nŭn) ... p'yo chu·se·yo
1st-class	일등석	il·dŭng·sŏk
one-way	편도	p'yŏn·do
return	왕복	wang·bok
standard class	일반석	il·ban·sŏk
standing room	입석	ip·sŏk

Which ... goes to (Myeongdong)?	어느 ...이/가 (명동)에 가나요?	ŏ·nŭ ...·i/·ga (myŏng·dong)·é ka·na·yo
boat	배	pae
bus	버스	bŏ·sŭ
metro line	지하철 노선	chi·ha·ch'ŏl no·sŏn
train	기차	ki·ch'a

When's the ... (bus)?	... (버스) 언제 있나요?	... (bŏ·sŭ) ŏn·jé in·na·yo
first	첫	ch'ŏt
last	마지막	ma·ji·mak

platform	타는 곳	t'a·nŭn·got
ticket machine	표 자판기	p'yo cha·pan·gi
timetable display	시간표	shi·gan·p'yo
transportation card	교통카드	kyo·t'ong k'a·dŭ

At what time does it get to (Busan)?
(부산)에 언제 도착하나요? (pu·san)·é ŏn·jé to·ch'a·k'a·na·yo

Does it stop at (Gyeongju)?
(경주) 가나요? (kyŏng·ju) ka·na·yo

Please tell me when we get to (Daejeon).
(대전)에 도착하면 좀 알려주세요. (tae·jŏn)·é to·ch'a·k'a·myŏn chom al·lyŏ·ju·se·yo

Please take me to (Insa-dong).
(인사동)으로 가 주세요. (in·sa·dong)·ŭ·ro ka·ju·se·yo

Numbers

Use pure Korean numbers (first option below) for hours when telling the time, for counting objects and people, and for your age. Use Sino-Korean numbers (second option below) for minutes when telling the time, for dates and months, and for addresses, phone numbers, money and floors of a building.

1	하나/일	ha·na/il
2	둘/이	tul/i
3	셋/삼	set/sam
4	넷/사	net/sa
5	다섯/오	ta·sŏt/o
6	여섯/육	yŏ·sŏt/yuk
7	일곱/칠	il·gop/ch'il
8	여덟/팔	yŏ·dŏl/p'al
9	아홉/구	a·hop/ku
10	열/십	yŏl/ship

GLOSSARY

-am – monastery
anju – bar snacks
banchan – side dishes
bang – room
buk – north
cheon – stream
Chuseok – Thanksgiving holiday
-daero – major road, boulevard
DMZ – the Demilitarized Zone that separates North and South Korea
-do – province
do – island
-dong – ward, subdivision of a *gu*
dong – east
DVD bang – minicinemas that show DVDs
-eup – town
-ga – section of a long street
gang – river
geobukseon – 'turtle ships'; iron-clad warships
-gil – small street
-gu – urban district
gugak – traditional Korean music
-gun – county
gung – palace
gwageo – Joseon-era civil-service examination
hae – sea
hagwon – private schools where students study after school or work
hanbok – traditional Korean clothing
hangeul – Korean phonetic alphabet
hanji – traditional Korean handmade paper
hanok – traditional Korean one-storey wooden house with a tiled roof
hansik – Korean food
ho – lake
hof – bar or pub
insam – ginseng
jaebeol – huge conglomerate business, often family run
jeon – hall of a temple
jeong – pavilion
jjimjil-bang – luxury sauna and spa
KTO – Korea Tourism Organisation
KTX – Korean bullet train
maeul – town
minbak – a private home in the countryside with rooms for rent
mudang – shaman, usually female
mugunghwa – limited-stop express train
mun – gate
-myeon – township
nam – south
neung – tomb
noraebang – karaoke room
ondol – underfloor heating
ondol room – traditional, sleep-on-a-floor-mattress hotel room
pansori – traditional Korean opera with a soloist and a drummer
PC bang – internet cafe
pojangmacha – tent bar on street
pungsu – Korean geomancy or feng shui
ramie – see-through cloth made from pounded bark
-ri – village
-ro (sometimes -no) – large street, boulevard
ROK – Republic of Korea (South Korea)
ru – pavilion
-sa – temple
saemaeul – luxury express train
samullori – farmer's percussion music and dance
-san – mountain
seo – west
Seon – Korean version of Zen Buddhism
si – city
sijo – short, Chinese-style nature poetry
ssireum – Korean-style wrestling
taekwondo – Korean martial arts
tap – pagoda
USO – United Service Organizations; it provides leisure activities for US troops and civilians
yangban – aristocrat
yo – padded quilt or futon mattress for sleeping on the floor

Behind the Scenes

SEND US YOUR FEEDBACK

We love to hear from travellers – your comments keep us on our toes and help make our books better. Our well-travelled team reads every word on what you loved or loathed about this book. Although we cannot reply individually to your submissions, we always guarantee that your feedback goes straight to the appropriate authors, in time for the next edition. Each person who sends us information is thanked in the next edition – the most useful submissions are rewarded with a selection of digital PDF chapters.

Visit **lonelyplanet.com/contact** to submit your updates and suggestions or to ask for help. Our award-winning website also features inspirational travel stories, news and discussions.

Note: We may edit, reproduce and incorporate your comments in Lonely Planet products such as guidebooks, websites and digital products, so let us know if you don't want your comments reproduced or your name acknowledged. For a copy of our privacy policy visit lonelyplanet.com/privacy.

OUR READERS

Many thanks to the travellers who used the last edition and wrote to us with helpful hints, useful advice and interesting anecdotes:

Jimi Kim, Charles LaBelle, Volker Lehman, Petra O'Neill, Oszkár Péter, Jan Pola and Gerhard Schweng.

AUTHOR THANKS

Trent Holden

Thanks first up to Megan Eaves for giving me the opportunity to work on Seoul – a seriously great gig! As well as to my co-author, Simon RIchmond for all the help and tips along the way, as well as Rebecca Milner. Thanks also to Julia Mellor, Daniel Durrance, Shawn Depress, Daniel Lenaghan and the team from Visit Seoul for their invaluable assistance. A special shout out to all the good folk I met along the road and shared a beer with. But as always my biggest thanks goes to my beautiful girlfriend Kate, and my family and friends who I all miss back home in Melbourne.

Simon Richmond

Many thanks to fellow authors Trent Holden and Rebecca Milner, Maureen O'Crowley and Kim Daegeun at Seoul Tourism, Seunghyo Lee, Daniel Durrance, Charles Usher, Alistair Gale, Joshua Hall, Joshua Davies, Joshua Park, David & Jade Kilburn, Robert Koehler, Monica Cha, Becca Baldwin, Daniel Lenaghan and Julia Mellor.

ACKNOWLEDGMENTS

Climate map data adapted from Peel MC, Finlayson BL & McMahon TA (2007) 'Updated World Map of the Köppen-Geiger Climate Classification', *Hydrology and Earth System Sciences*, 11, 1633–44.

Seoul Metro Map © 2015 Seoul Metropolitan Rapid Transit Corp

Cover photograph: Dongdaemun Design Plaza & Park (DDP), Seoul, Inigo Bujedo Aguirre / Alamy

THIS BOOK

This 8th edition of Lonely Planet's *Seoul* guidebook was researched and written by Trent Holden and Simon Richmond. Simon wrote the previous edition and the 6th edition was written by Martin Robinson with assistance from Jason Zahorchak. This guidebook was produced by the following:

Destination Editor Megan Eaves
Coordinating Editor Monique Perrin
Product Editors Kate Chapman, Anne Mason
Senior Cartographer Corey Hutchison
Book Designer Wibowo Rusli
Senior Editors Andi Jones, Claire Naylor, Karyn Noble
Assisting Editors Lauren O'Connell, Charlotte Orr, Susan Paterson, Amanda Williamson
Cover Researcher Campbell McKenzie
Thanks to Dan Corbett, Ryan Evans, Andi Jones, Anne Mason, Claire Murphy, Wayne Murphy, Claire Naylor, Karyn Noble, Martine Power, Samantha Russell-Tulip, Diana Saengkham, Jaeyoon Shin, Vicky Smith, Lyahna Spencer, Angela Tinson, Lauren Wellicome

See also separate subindexes for:
- EATING P203
- DRINKING & NIGHTLIFE P204
- ENTERTAINMENT P204
- SHOPPING P205
- SPORTS & ACTIVITIES P205
- SLEEPING P205

Index

Sights 000
Map Pages **000**
Photo Pages **000**

Sights 000
Map Pages **000**
Photo Pages **000**

EATING

SHOPPING

SPORTS & ACTIVITIES

SLEEPING

Seoul Maps

Sights
- Beach
- Bird Sanctuary
- Buddhist
- Castle/Palace
- Christian
- Confucian
- Hindu
- Islamic
- Jain
- Jewish
- Monument
- Museum/Gallery/Historic Building
- Ruin
- Shinto
- Sikh
- Taoist
- Winery/Vineyard
- Zoo/Wildlife Sanctuary
- Other Sight

Activities, Courses & Tours
- Bodysurfing
- Diving
- Canoeing/Kayaking
- Course/Tour
- Sento Hot Baths/Onsen
- Skiing
- Snorkelling
- Surfing
- Swimming/Pool
- Walking
- Windsurfing
- Other Activity

Sleeping
- Sleeping
- Camping

Eating
- Eating

Drinking & Nightlife
- Drinking & Nightlife
- Cafe

Entertainment
- Entertainment

Shopping
- Shopping

Information
- Bank
- Embassy/Consulate
- Hospital/Medical
- Internet
- Police
- Post Office
- Telephone
- Toilet
- Tourist Information
- Other Information

Geographic
- Beach
- Gate
- Hut/Shelter
- Lighthouse
- Lookout
- Mountain/Volcano
- Oasis
- Park
- Pass
- Picnic Area
- Waterfall

Population
- Capital (National)
- Capital (State/Province)
- City/Large Town
- Town/Village

Transport
- Airport
- Border crossing
- Bus
- Cable car/Funicular
- Cycling
- Ferry
- Metro/MTR/MRT station
- Monorail
- Parking
- Petrol station
- Skytrain/Subway station
- Taxi
- Train station/Railway
- Tram
- Underground station
- Other Transport

Note: Not all symbols displayed above appear on the maps in this book

Routes
- Tollway
- Freeway
- Primary
- Secondary
- Tertiary
- Lane
- Unsealed road
- Road under construction
- Plaza/Mall
- Steps
- Tunnel
- Pedestrian overpass
- Walking Tour
- Walking Tour detour
- Path/Walking Trail

Boundaries
- International
- State/Province
- Disputed
- Regional/Suburb
- Marine Park
- Cliff
- Wall

Hydrography
- River, Creek
- Intermittent River
- Canal
- Water
- Dry/Salt/Intermittent Lake
- Reef

Areas
- Airport/Runway
- Beach/Desert
- Cemetery (Christian)
- Cemetery (Other)
- Glacier
- Mudflat
- Park/Forest
- Sight (Building)
- Sportsground
- Swamp/Mangrove

MAP INDEX

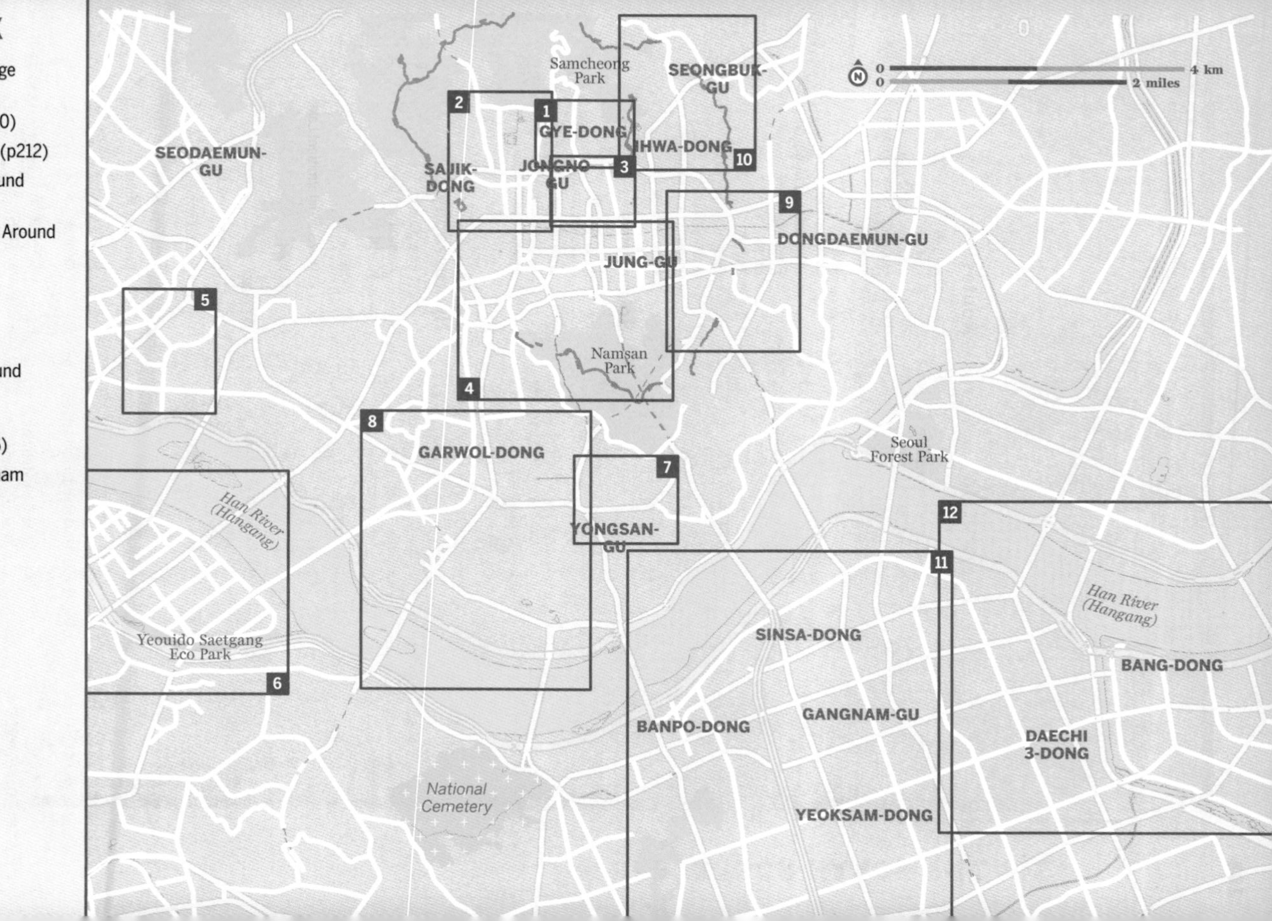

0 4 km
0 2 miles
SEODAEMUN-GU
Samcheong Park
SEONGBUK-GU
GYE-DONG
IHWA-DONG
SAJIK-DONG
JONGNO-GU
DONGDAEMUN-GU
JUNG-GU
Namsan Park
GARWOL-DONG
YONGSAN-GU
Seoul Forest Park
Han River (Hangang)
Yeouido Saetgang Eco Park
SINSA-DONG
BANG-DONG
BANPO-DONG
GANGNAM-GU
DAECHI 3-DONG
National Cemetery
YEOKSAM-DONG
1
2
3
4
5
6
7
8
9
10
11
12

BUKCHON HANOK VILLAGE

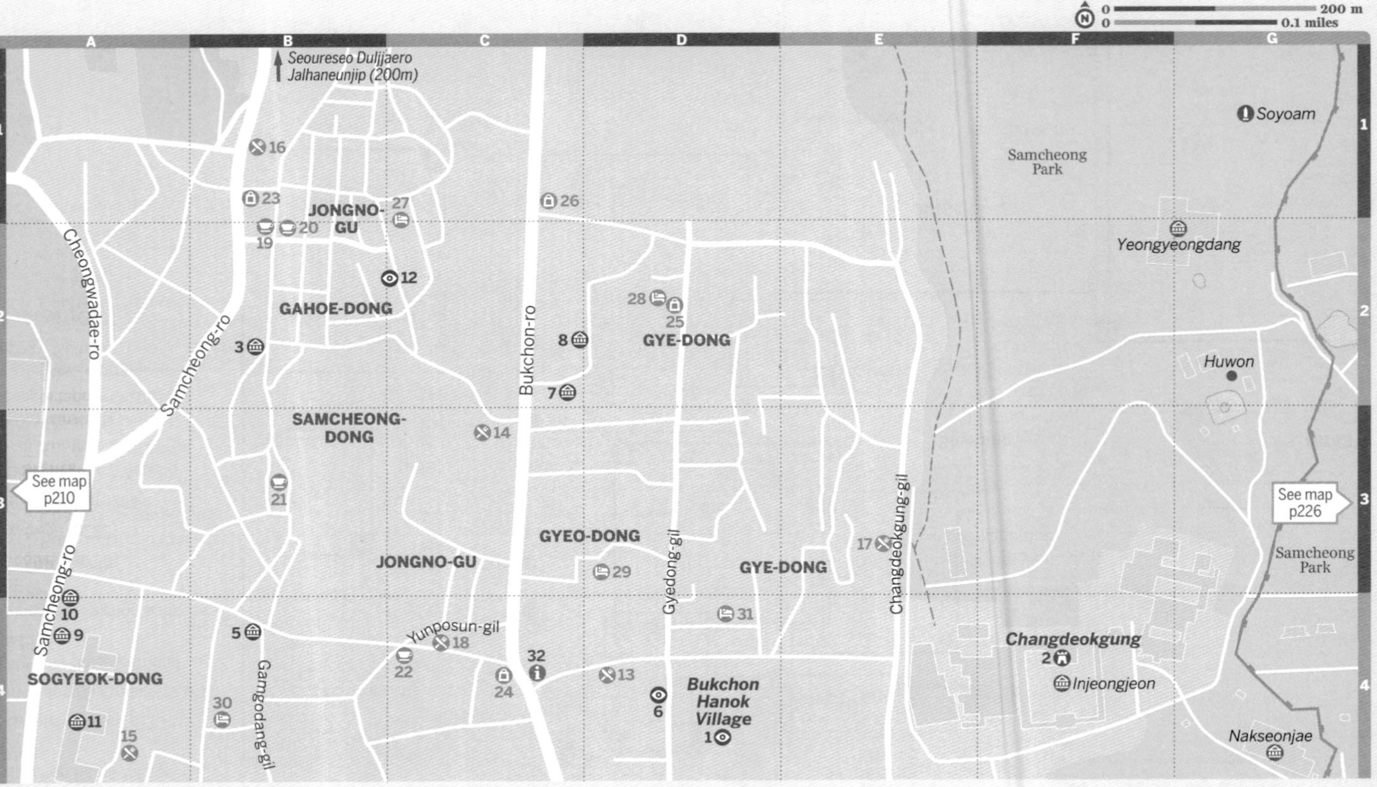

BUKCHON HANOK VILLAGE

ANGUK-DONG
Yunposun-gil
Bukchon-ro
Anguk
See map p212
4
UNNI-DONG
Yulgok-ro
Donhwamun
Changdeokgung Ticket Booth
Jongmyo Park

Top Sights **(p52)**

1 Bukchon Hanok Village D4
2 Changdeokgung F4

Sights **(p59)**

3 Another Way of Seeing B2
4 Arario Museum in SPACE E5
5 Artsonje Center B4
6 Bukchon Traditional Culture Center D4
7 Dong-Lim Knot Workshop C2
8 Gahoe Minhwa Workshop C2
9 Hakgojae A4
10 Kukje A4
11 MMCA Seoul A4
12 Simsimheon C2

Eating **(p64)**

13 2046 Pansteak D4
14 Dejangjangi HwadeogPijajip C3
15 Joseon Gimbap A4
16 Solmoe-maeul B1
17 Tea Museum E3
18 Wood and Brick C4

Drinking & Nightlife **(p66)**

19 Café Yeon B2
20 Cha Masineun Tteul B2
21 Kopi Bangasgan B3
22 Tea Therapy C4

Shopping **(p69)**

Gallery Art Zone .... (see 11)

23 Jilkyungyee B1
24 Jonginamoo C4
25 Mik D2
26 Yido C1

Sleeping **(p148)**

27 Chi-Woon-Jung C1
28 Doo Guesthouse D2
29 Rak-Ko-Jae D3
30 Sophia Guest House B4
31 Wwoof Korea Guesthouse D4

Information

32 Bukchon Tourist Information Center C4

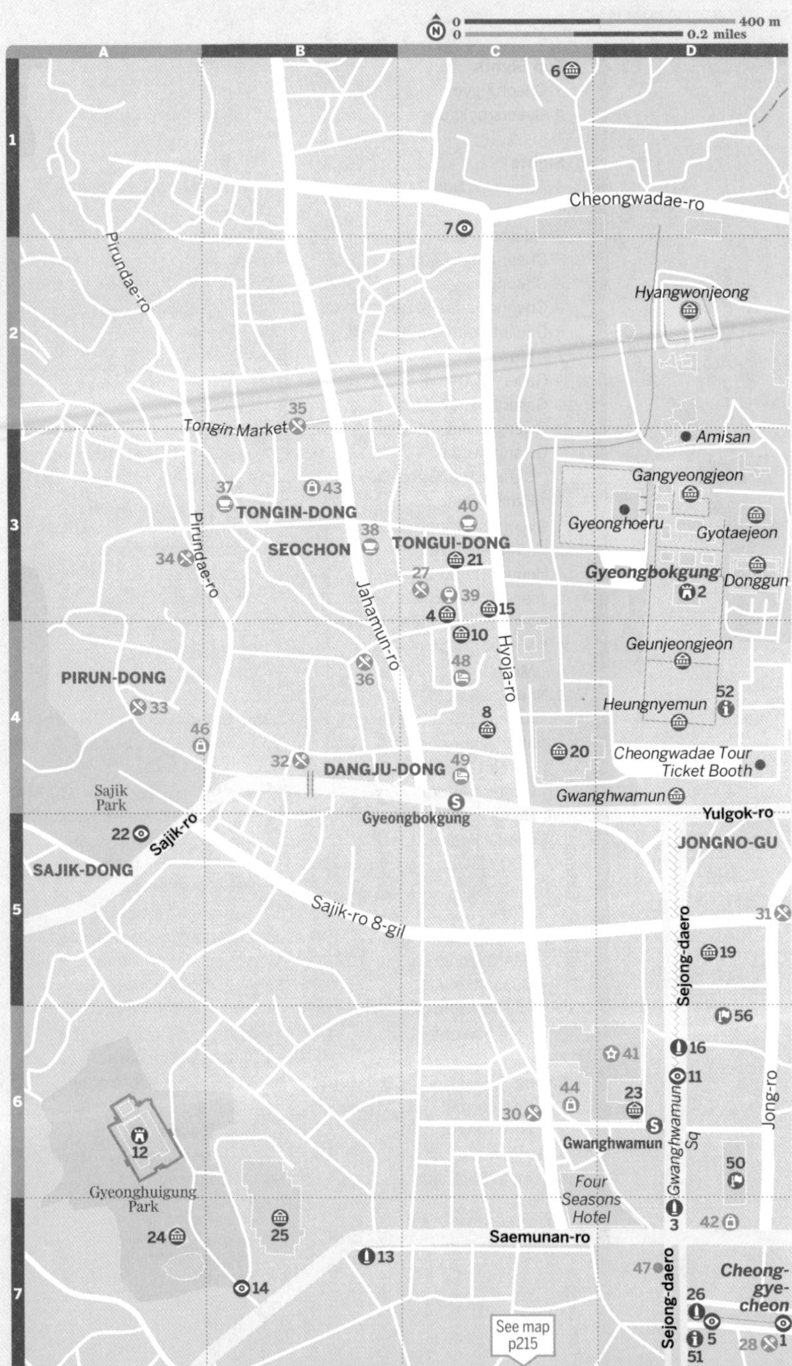
0 400 m
0 0.2 miles
A
B
C
D
1
2
3
4
5
6
7
Cheongwadae-ro
Pirundae-ro
Hyangwonjeong
Tongin Market
Amisan
Gangyeongjeon
TONGIN-DONG
Gyeonghoeru
Gyotaejeon
SEOCHON
TONGUI-DONG
Gyeongbokgung
Donggun
Jahamun-ro
Hyoja-ro
Geunjeongjeon
PIRUN-DONG
Heungnyemun
Cheongwadae Tour Ticket Booth
DANGJU-DONG
Sajik Park
Gwanghwamun
Gyeongbokgung
Yulgok-ro
Sajik-ro
JONGNO-GU
SAJIK-DONG
Sajik-ro 8-gil
Sejong-daero
Jong-ro
Gwanghwamun
Gwanghwamun Sq
Four Seasons Hotel
Gyeonghuigung Park
Saemunan-ro
Cheong-gye-cheon
See map p215
6
7
35
37
43
40
38
21
34
27
39
15
4
10
36
48
52
33
46
8
20
32
49
22
31
19
56
16
41
11
44
23
30
12
50
3
42
24
25
13
47
14
26
5
28
1
51

Top Sights (p50)
1 Cheong-gye-cheon D7
2 Gyeongbokgung D3

Sights (p56)
3 Admiral Yi Sun-Sin's Statue D7
4 Artside C3
5 Cheong-gye Plaza D7
6 Cheongwadae C1
7 Cheongwadae Sarangchae.. C1
8 Daelim Contemporary Art Museum C4
9 Gallery Hyundai E4
10 Gallery Simon C4
11 Gwanghwamun Square....... D6
Gwanghwamun Square Underground Exhibition .... (see 16)
12 Gyeonghuigung A6
13 Hammering Man B7
14 Heunghwamun B7
15 Jean Art Gallery C3
16 King Sejong Statue D6
17 National Children's Museum E2
18 National Folk Museum of Korea E2
19 National Museum of Korean Contemporary History D5
20 National Palace Museum of Korea C4
21 Ryugaheon C3
22 Sajikdan A5
23 Sejong Gallery D6
24 SeMA Gyeonghuigung Museum of Art A7
25 Seoul Museum of History ... B7
26 Spring Sculpture D7

Eating (p63)
Euro Gourmet .... (see 27)
27 GastroTong C3
28 Hanmiri D7
29 Jongno Sarangga E6
30 Ogawa C6
31 OKitchen D5
32 Potato Passion B4
33 Rogpa Tea Stall A4
34 Song's Kitchen A3
35 Tongin Market Box Lunch Cafe B2
36 Tosokchon B4

Drinking & Nightlife (p66)
37 Daeo Sochom B3
38 et M'amie B3
39 Hopscotch C3
40 MK2 .... C3

Entertainment (p68)
41 Sejong Center for the Performing Arts D6

Shopping (p68)
42 Kyobo Bookshop D7
43 Market m* B3
Mono Collection .... (see 40)
44 Sejong Art Market SoSo C6
45 Seoul Selection E4
46 Yuimaru A4

Sports & Activities (p27)
47 Seoul City Tour Bus D7

Sleeping (p148)
48 Hide & Seek Guesthouse C4
49 Inn Daewon C4

Information
50 Australian Embassy D6
51 Cheong-gye-cheon Tourist Information Center D7
52 Gyeongbokgung Tourist Information Center D4
53 Irish Embassy E5
54 Japanese Embassy E5
55 KTO Tourist Information Center E7
New Zealand Embassy .... (see 50)
56 US Embassy D6

Key on p214

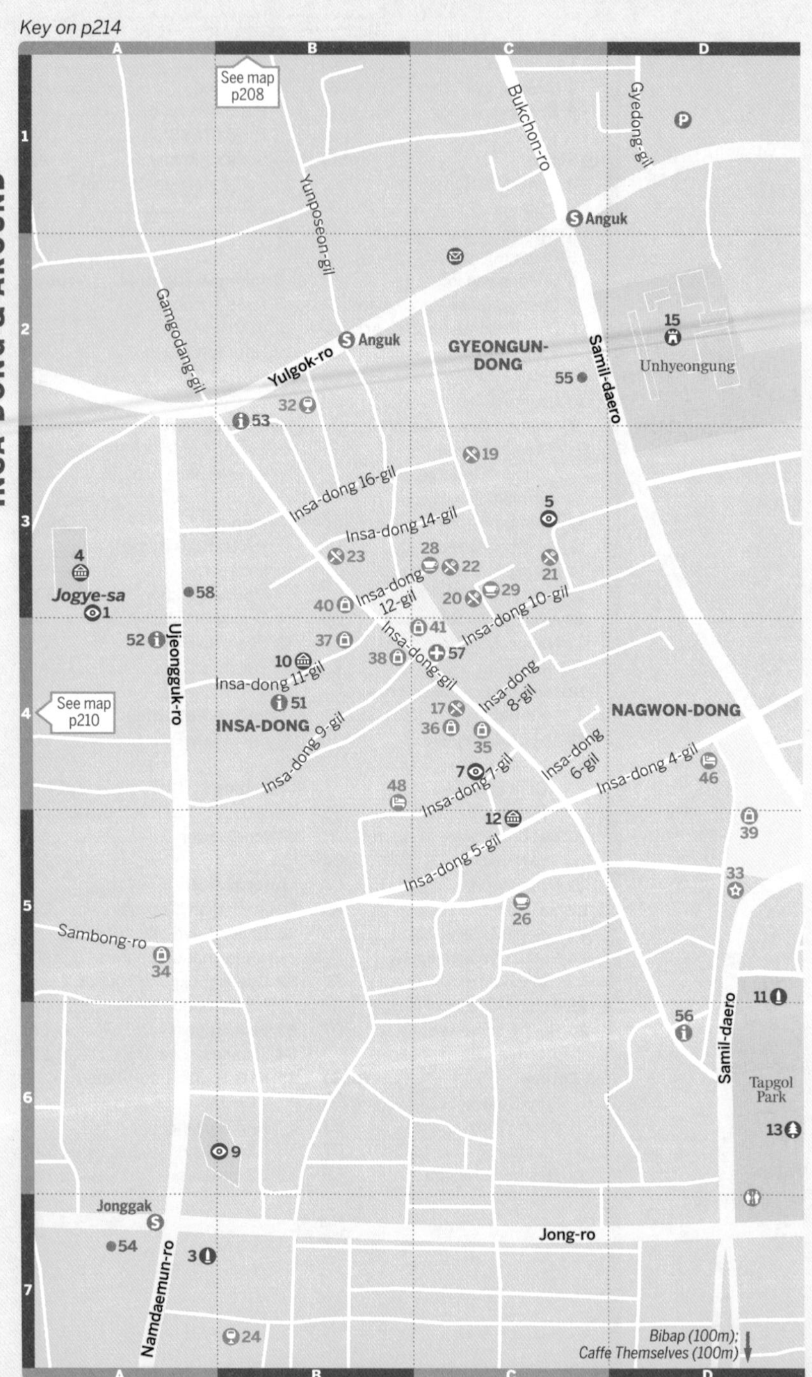
See map p208
See map p210
Gyedong-gil
Bukchon-ro
Yunposeon-gil
Anguk
Gamgodang-gil
Yulgok-ro
GYEONGUN-DONG
Samil-daero
Unhyeongung
Insa-dong 16-gil
Insa-dong 14-gil
Insa-dong 12-gil
Insa-dong 10-gil
Insa-dong-gil
Insa-dong 11-gil
Insa-dong 9-gil
Insa-dong 8-gil
Insa-dong 7-gil
Insa-dong 6-gil
Insa-dong 5-gil
Insa-dong 4-gil
INSA-DONG
NAGWON-DONG
Jogye-sa
Ujeongguk-ro
Sambong-ro
Tapgol Park
Jonggak
Jong-ro
Namdaemun-ro
Bibap (100m);
Caffe Themselves (100m)

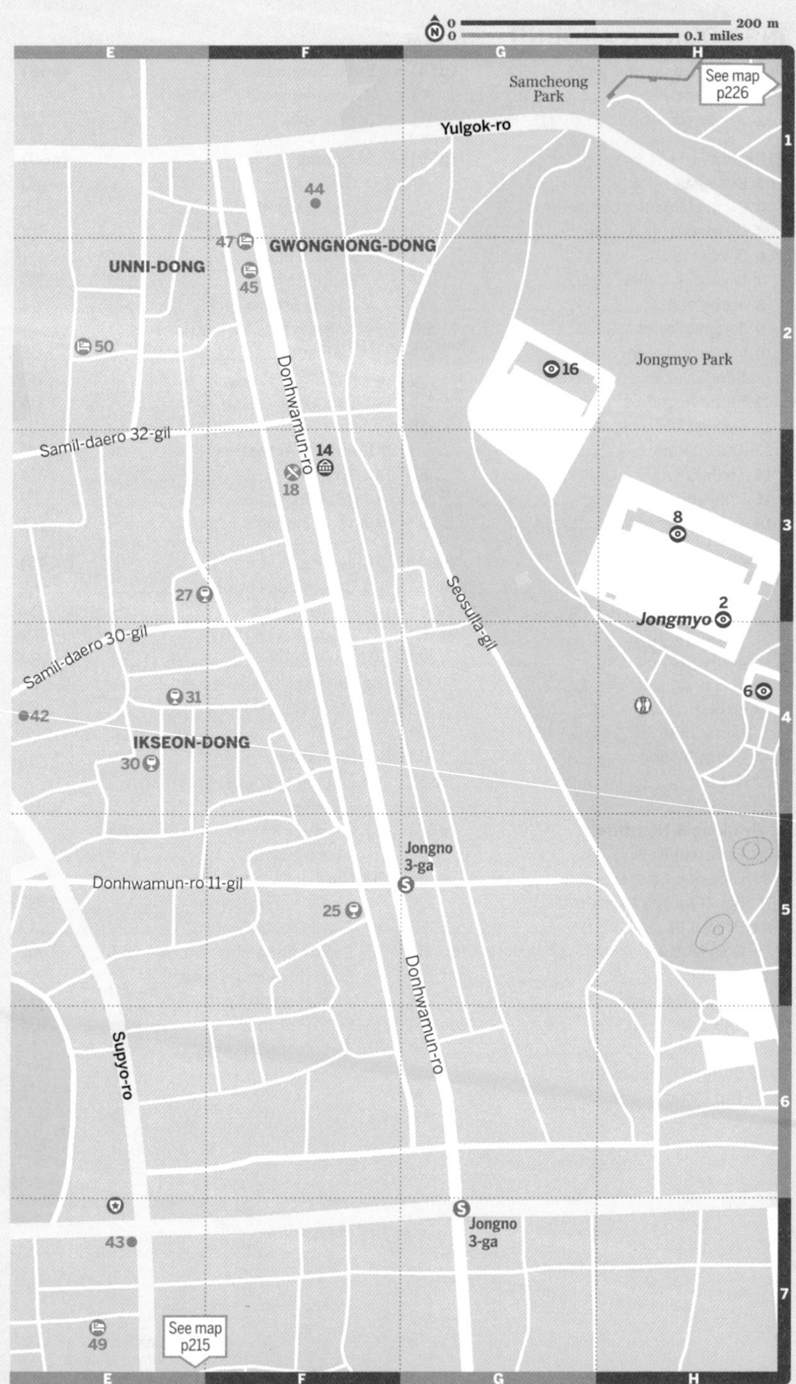
0 200 m
0 0.1 miles
E
F
G
H
Samcheong Park
See map p226
Yulgok-ro
44
47
GWONGNONG-DONG
UNNI-DONG
45
50
Jongmyo Park
16
Donhwamun-ro
Samil-daero 32-gil
14
18
8
27
Seosulla-gil
2
Jongmyo
Samil-daero 30-gil
31
6
42
IKSEON-DONG
30
Jongno 3-ga
Donhwamun-ro 11-gil
25
Donhwamun-ro
Supyo-ro
Jongno 3-ga
43
49
See map p215
1
2
3
4
5
6
7

INSA-DONG & AROUND *Map on p212*

MYEONG-DONG & AROUND *Map on p216*

Top Sights (p73)
1 City Hall C2
2 Deoksugung B2
3 N Seoul Tower & Namsan E6
4 Namdaemun Market C3

Sights (p77)
5 Agriculture Museum A2
6 Ahn Jung-geun Memorial Hall C6
7 Bank of Korea Money Museum D3
8 Bongsudae E6
Citizens Hall ......(see 1)
9 Culture Station Seoul 284 ......A5
Daehan Empire History Museum (see 18)
Gungisi Relics Exhibition Hall ......(see 1)
10 Hamnyeongjeon B2
11 Jeonggwanheon B2
12 Junghwajeon B2
13 MMCA Deoksugung B2
14 Myeong-dong Catholic Cathedral E3
15 Namsan Park F6
16 Namsangol Hanok Village G4
17 PLATEAU B3
18 Seokjojeon B2
19 Seoul Animation Center E4
Seoul Metropolitan Library ......(see 1)
20 Seoul Museum of Art ...C2
21 Seoul Plaza C2
22 Skygarden A5
23 Sungnyemun B4
24 Waryongmyo E5

Eating (p78)
25 A Person C2
26 Baekje Samgyetang D3
27 Cheolcheol Bokjip D1
28 Congdu B1
29 Gogung E3
30 Gosang E1
31 Hadongkwan E2
32 Korea House G3
33 Mokmyeoksanbang E5
34 Myeong-dong Gyoja E3
N.Grill ......(see 3)
Pierre Gagnaire à Séoul ......(see 68)
35 Potala E3
36 Sinseon Seolnongtang E2
37 Soo:P Coffee Flower C3
38 Wangbijip E2

Drinking & Nightlife (p81)
39 Cafe the Story F4
40 Cat Cafe D3
Coffee Libre ......(see 14)
41 Craftworks F2
Davansa Teahouse ......(see 49)
42 Neurin Maeul E1
43 Walkabout E4

Entertainment (p81)
44 Jeongdong Theater B2
45 Jump A1
46 Myeongdong Theater ...D2
47 Nanta Theatre Jung-gu D3
48 National Theater of Korea H6
49 Seoul Namsan Gugakdang G4

Shopping (p82)
50 Åland D3
51 Joongang Building C and D C3
52 Lab 5 ......D3
53 Lotte Department Store D2
54 Migliore Mall E3
55 Primera D3
56 Samho Woojoo C3
57 Shinsegae D3

Sports & Activities (p83)
58 Chunjiyun Spa E3
59 Kimchi Academy House E3
60 Korea Whal Culture Association G6
61 Outdoor Gym H6
62 Seoul Global Cultural Center E3
Seoul Plaza Ice Skating Rink ......(see 21)
63 Silloam Sauna A4

Sleeping (p149)
64 Banyan Tree Club & Spa H7
65 Crib49 ......E5
66 Global Hostel E4
67 Hotel Prince E3
68 Lotte Hotel Seoul D2
69 Metro Hotel D2
70 Myeongdong Tomato Guesthouse E4
71 Namsan Guesthouse E4
72 Namsan Guesthouse 2 ......E4
73 Nine Tree Hotel Myeong-dong E3
74 Oriens Hotel & Residences F4
75 Pacific Hotel E4
76 Plaza C2
77 Small House Big Door .. D1
78 Westin Chosun Seoul ...D2
79 Zaza Backpackers E4

Information
80 Canadian Embassy A1
81 Chinese Embassy D3
82 Deoksugung Ticket Office C2
83 German Embassy B5
84 Myeong-dong Tourist Information Center E2
85 Namdaemun Market Tourist Information Center C3
Netherlands Embassy ......(see 80)
86 UK Embassy C1

Transport
City Airport Terminal ......(see 88)
87 N Seoul Tower Cable Car D5
88 Seoul Station A5

Key on p215

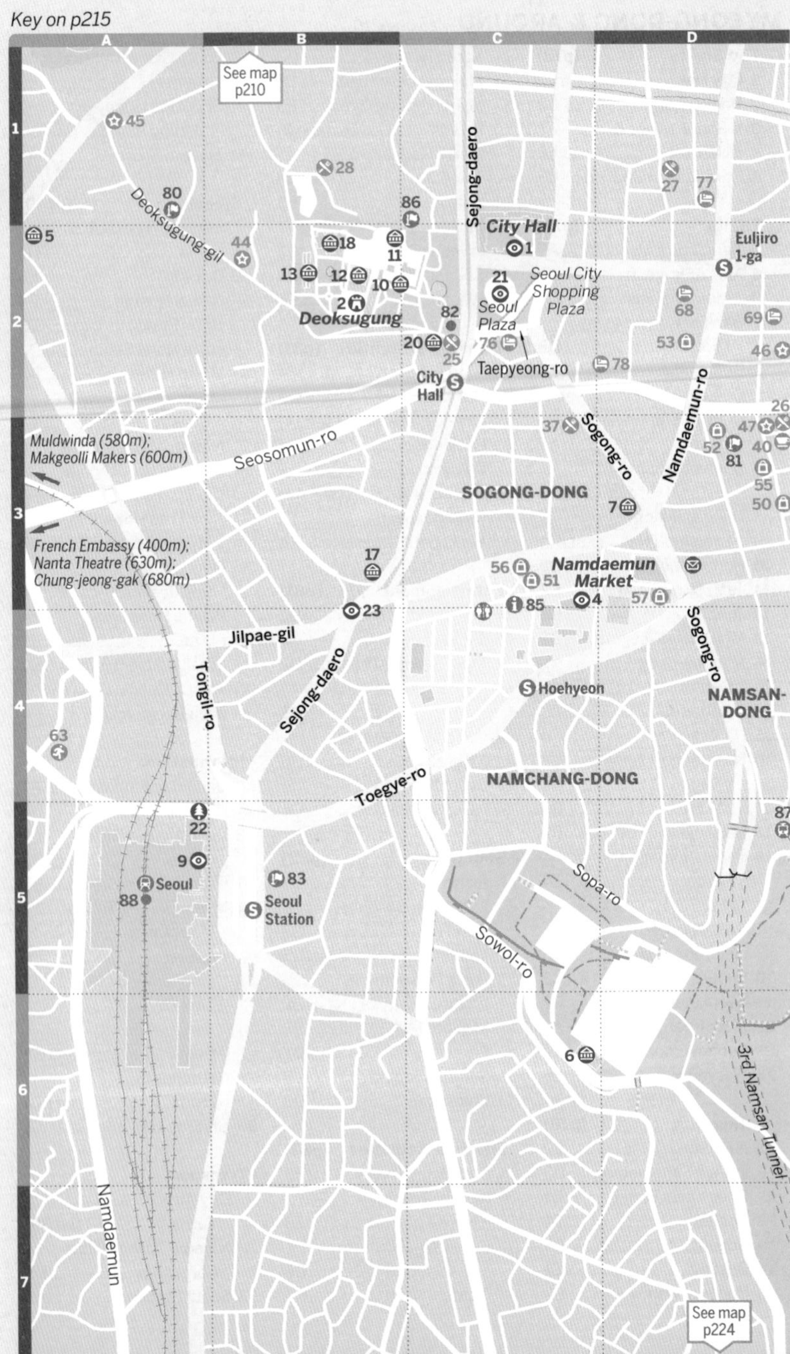

See map p210
City Hall
Seoul City Shopping Plaza
Seoul Plaza
Taepyeong-ro
Deoksugung
Deoksugung-gil
Sejong-daero
City Hall
Euljiro 1-ga
Seosomun-ro
Muldwinda (580m); Makgeolli Makers (600m)
French Embassy (400m); Nanta Theatre (630m); Chung-jeong-gak (680m)
SOGONG-DONG
Sogong-ro
Namdaemun-ro
Namdaemun Market
Jilpae-gil
Tongil-ro
Sejong-daero
Hoehyeon
NAMSAN-DONG
NAMCHANG-DONG
Toegye-ro
Seoul
Seoul Station
Sopa-ro
Sowol-ro
3rd Namsan Tunnel
Namdaemun
See map p224

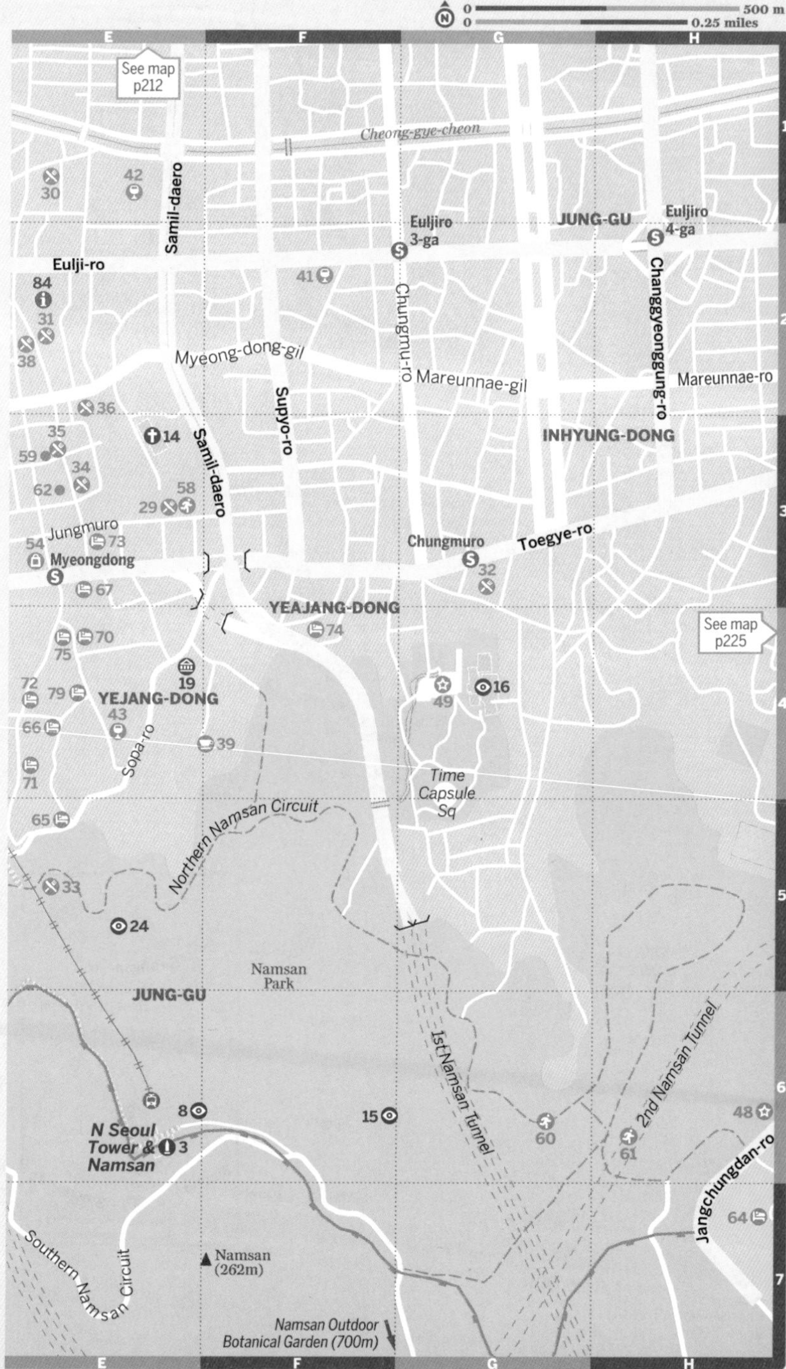

0 500 m
0 0.25 miles
E
F
G
H
See map p212
Cheong-gye-cheon
Samil-daero
Euljiro 3-ga
JUNG-GU
Euljiro 4-ga
Eulji-ro
Chungmu-ro
Changgyeonggung-ro
Myeong-dong-gil
Mareunnae-gil
Mareunnae-ro
Supyo-ro
Samil-daero
INHYUNG-DONG
Jungmuro
Myeongdong
Chungmuro
Toegye-ro
YEAJANG-DONG
See map p225
YEJANG-DONG
Sopa-ro
Time Capsule Sq
Northern Namsan Circuit
Namsan Park
JUNG-GU
1st Namsan Tunnel
2nd Namsan Tunnel
N Seoul Tower & Namsan
Jangchungdan-ro
Southern Namsan Circuit
Namsan (262m)
Namsan Outdoor Botanical Garden (700m)

HONGDAE, SINCHON & AROUND

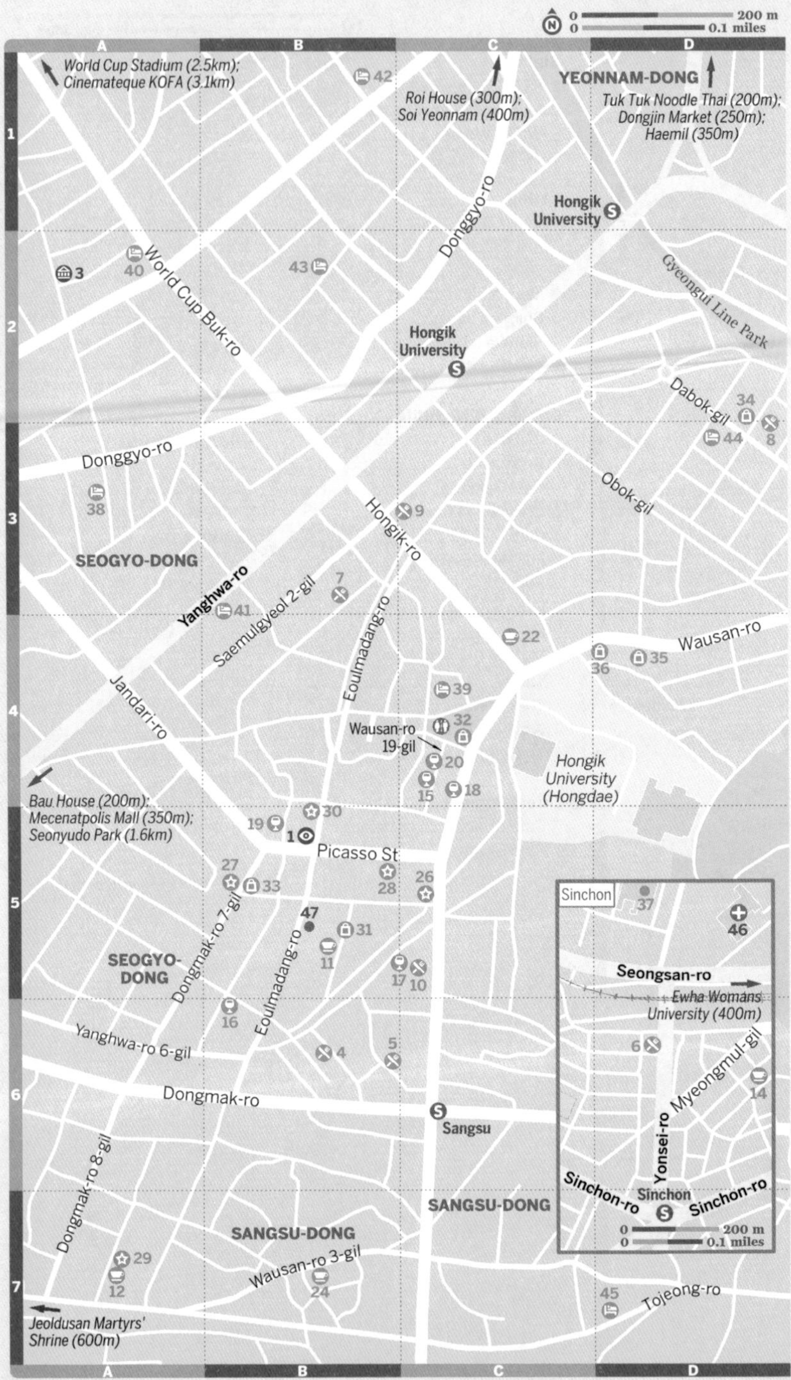

World Cup Stadium (2.5km); Cinemateque KOFA (3.1km)
Roi House (300m); Soi Yeonnam (400m)
YEONNAM-DONG
Tuk Tuk Noodle Thai (200m); Dongjin Market (250m); Haemil (350m)
Hongik University
Donggyo-ro
World Cup Buk-ro
Gyeongui Line Park
Hongik University
Dabok-gil
Donggyo-ro
Obok-gil
Hongik-ro
SEOGYO-DONG
Yanghwa-ro
Saemulgyeol 2-gil
Eoulmadang-ro
Wausan-ro
Jandari-ro
Wausan-ro 19-gil
Hongik University (Hongdae)
Bau House (200m); Mecenatpolis Mall (350m); Seonyudo Park (1.6km)
Picasso St
SEOGYO-DONG
Dongmak-ro 7-gil
Eoulmadang-ro
Yanghwa-ro 6-gil
Dongmak-ro
Sangsu
Dongmak-ro 8-gil
SANGSU-DONG
SANGSU-DONG
Wausan-ro 3-gil
Tojeong-ro
Jeoldusan Martyrs' Shrine (600m)
Sinchon
Seongsan-ro
Ewha Womans University (400m)
Myeongmul-gil
Yonsei-ro
Sinchon-ro
Sinchon
Sinchon-ro
200 m
0.1 miles

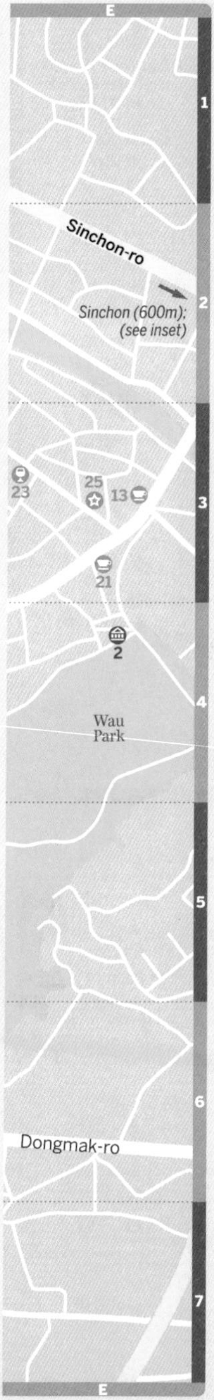

E

Sinchon-ro

Sinchon (600m); (see inset)

23 25 13 21 2

Wau Park

Dongmak-ro

E

Sights (p86)
1 KT&G SangsangMadang B5
2 Modern Design Museum......E4
3 War & Women's Human Rights Museum................. A2

Eating (p89)
4 Ciuri Ciuri B6
5 Fell & Cole B6
6 Loving Hut........................... D6
7 Menya Sandaime................ B3
8 Shim's Tapas D3
9 Slobbie C3
10 Taverna de Portugal........... C5

Drinking & Nightlife (p91)
11 aA Café B5
12 Anthracite A7
13 Café Sukkara E3
14 Chloris Tea Garden D6
15 Club MWG C4
16 Fox Wine Bistro................... B6
17 Keg B B5
18 Labris.................................... C4
19 M2... B5
20 Magpie Brewing Co. C4
21 TableA E3
22 Thanks Nature Cafe C4
23 Wolhyang E3
24 Yri Cafe................................ B7

Entertainment (p93)
25 Café BBang E3
26 Club Evans C5
Club Ta ....(see 28)
27 DGBD.................................... B5
28 FF B5
29 Mudaeruk............................. A7
30 Su Noraebang...................... B5

Shopping (p93)
31 Åland After Åland B5
32 Free Market......................... C4
33 Gentle Monster B5
34 Key.. D2
35 Little Farmers D4
36 Object Recycle..................... D4

Sports & Activities (p27)
37 Yonsei University................. D5

Sleeping (p150)
38 Blu: Home Guest House A3
39 Come Inn.............................. C4
40 Lee Kang Ga......................... A2
41 Marigold Hotel B3
42 Studio 41st B1
43 Travelers Planet Hostel B2
44 Urbanwood Guesthouse....................... D3
45 V Mansion D7

Information
46 Severance Hospital D5
47 XIndie Ticket Lounge B5

YEOUIDO

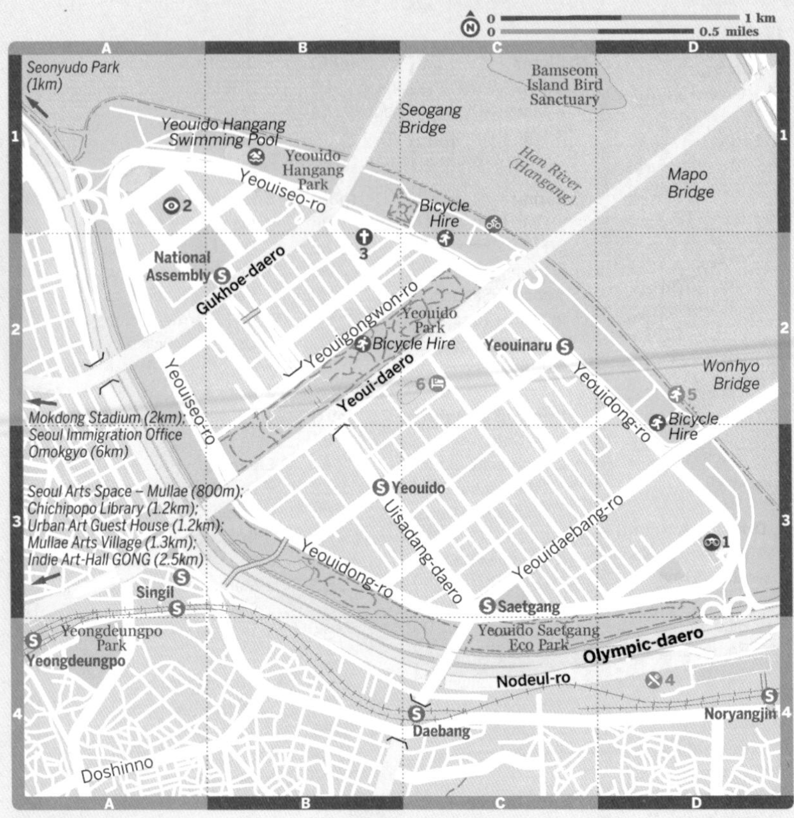

Sights (p88)
- 63 Seaworld (see 1)
- 63 Sky Art Gallery (see 1)
- 1 63 Square D3
- 63 Wax Museum (see 1)
- 2 National Assembly A1
- 3 Yeouido Full Gospel Church B2

Eating (p91)
- 63 Buffet Pavilion (see 1)
- Busan Ilbeonji (see 4)
- 4 Noryangjin Fish Market D4

Entertainment (p88)
- 63 Art Hall (see 1)

Sports & Activities (p94)
- 5 Eland Cruises D2

Sleeping (p151)
- 6 Conrad Seoul C2

ITAEWON *Map on p222*

Top Sights (p99)
1 Leeum Samsung Museum of Art G3

Eating (p99)
2 Atelier du Saint-Ex D4
3 Baker's Table A1
4 Bloc Party F6
5 Bua D5
6 Coreanos Kitchen A5
7 HBC Gogitjip A1
8 Linus' BBQ B5
9 Lobster Bar B5
10 Passion 5 .... H2
11 PLANT C5
12 Suji's B5
13 Tartine D5
14 Vatos B5
15 Zelen D4

Drinking & Nightlife (p101)
16 Against the Machine H3
17 Always Homme E5
18 B1 .... D4
19 Blue 55 .... D5
20 Booth A2
21 Booth Mansion D4
22 Burn A2
Cakeshop .... (see 12)
23 Craftworks F5
24 Craftworks Taphouse A2
25 Damotori A1
26 Flower Gin A1
27 Four Seasons D5
28 G'Day A3
29 Grand Ole Opry F5
30 Lovibond B5
31 Made in Pong Dang A2
32 Magpie Brewing Co. A2
33 Miracle F5
34 Mowmow D4
35 Pet Sounds B2
36 Prost D4
37 Queen E5
38 Rose & Crown C5
39 Soho E5
40 Southside Parlor A3
41 Takeout Drawing G4
42 Takeout Drawing A2
43 Trance E5
44 Venue/ D5
45 Ways of Seeing G4
46 White Rabbit A1
47 Why Not E5
48 Wolhyang H3

Entertainment (p104)
49 All that Jazz E4
50 Rocky Mountain Tavern F5
51 Thunderhorse Tavern A3

Shopping (p104)
52 Ando D6
53 Comme des Garcons H2
54 Dynasty Tailor B5
55 Eelskin Shop C5
56 Hamilton Shirts C5
57 Millimetre Milligram G4
Post Poetics .... (see 57)
58 Steve J & Yoni P G4
59 What the Book C5

Sports & Activities (p105)
60 Itaewonland F5

Sleeping (p152)
61 Grand Hyatt Seoul F2
62 Guesthouse Yacht C4
63 Hotel D'Oro E5
64 IP Boutique Hotel F4
65 Itaewon G Guest House E5
66 Itaewon Hostel & Inn D5
67 POP@Itaewon Guesthouse B5
68 SP@Itaewon Guesthouse C4

Information
69 International Clinic F5
70 Itaewon Subway Tourist Information Center D5
71 Itaewon Tourist Information Center G4

Key on p221

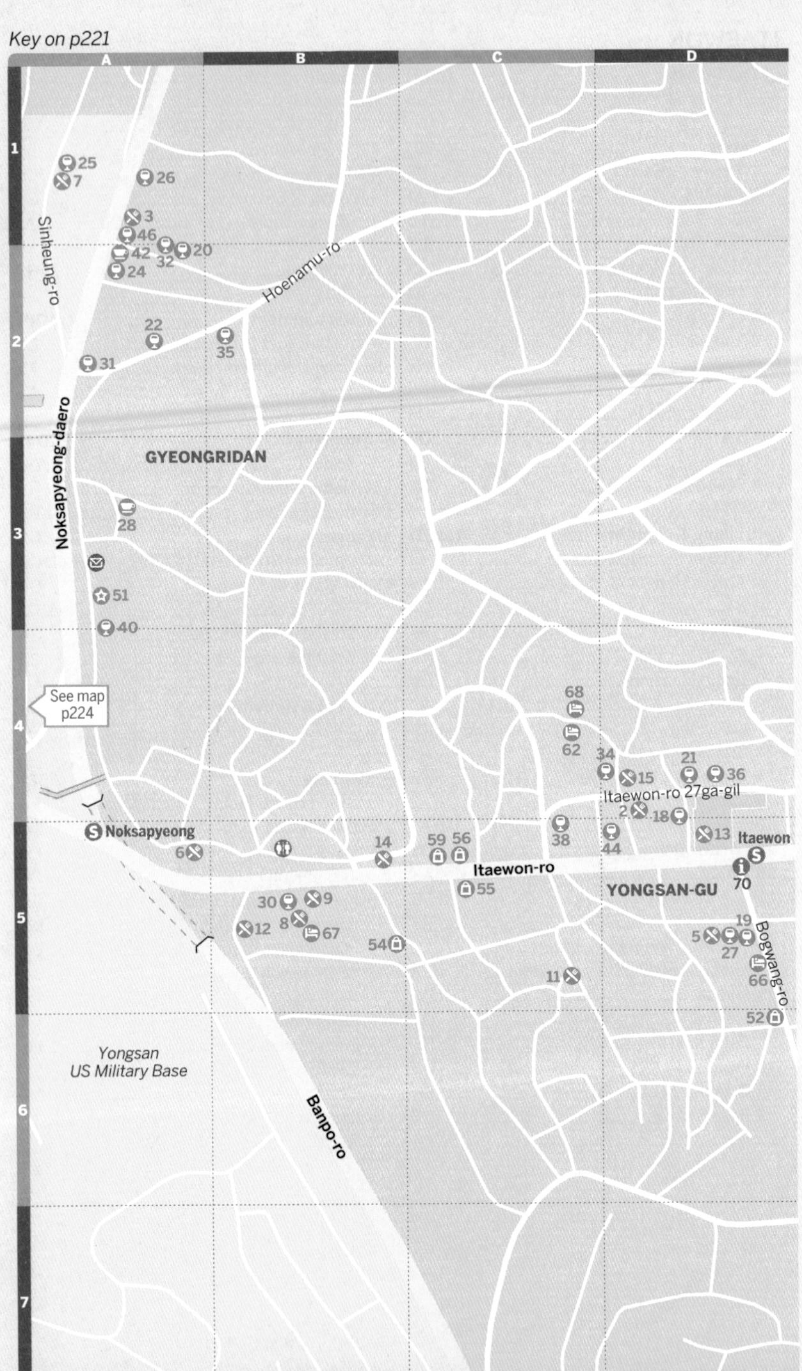
ITAEWON
A
B
C
D
1
2
3
4
5
6
7
Sinheung-ro
Hoenamu-ro
Noksapyeong-daero
GYEONGRIDAN
See map p224
Noksapyeong
Itaewon-ro
Itaewon-ro 27ga-gil
Itaewon
YONGSAN-GU
Bogwang-ro
Banpo-ro
Yongsan US Military Base

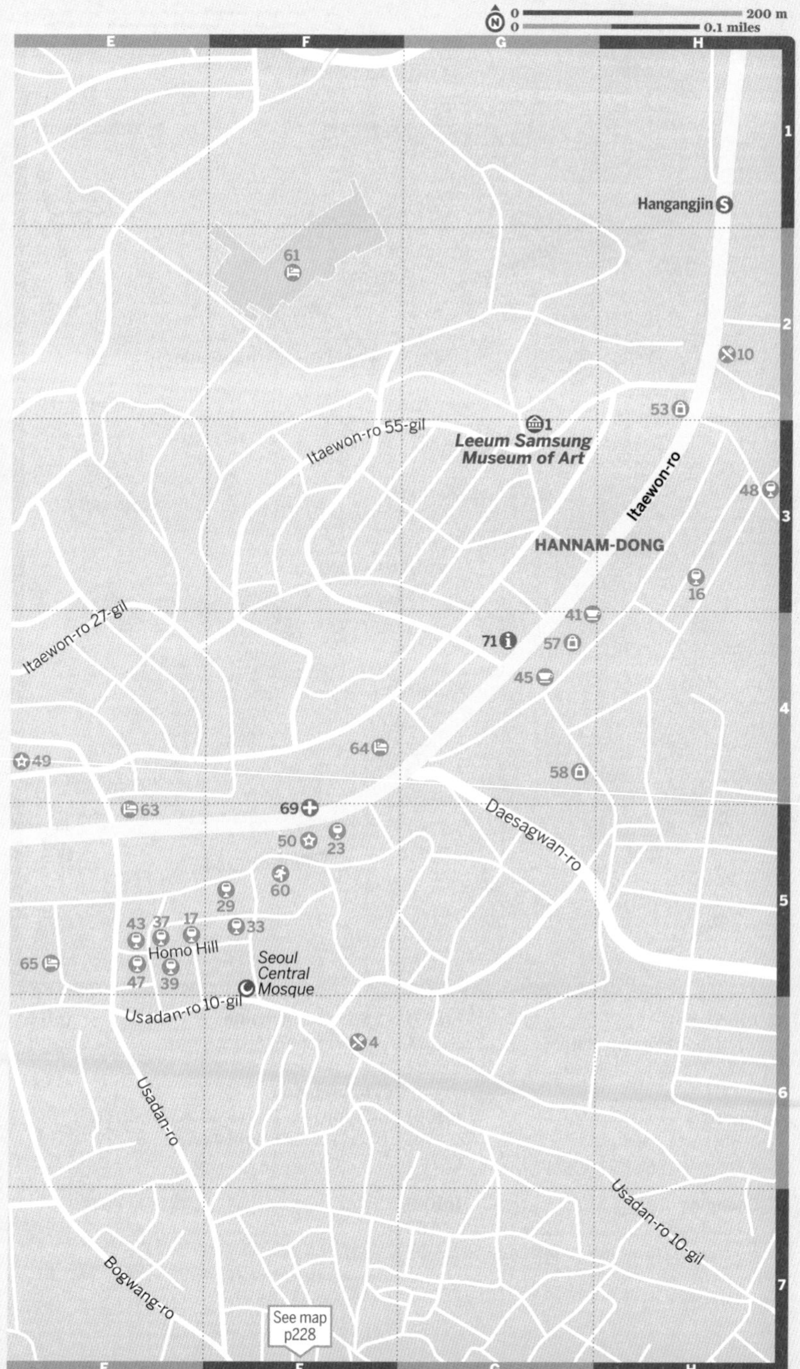

ITAEWON
0 200 m
0 0.1 miles
E
F
G
H
1
2
3
4
5
6
7
Hangangjin
61
10
53
1
Leeum Samsung Museum of Art
Itaewon-ro 55-gil
Itaewon-ro
48
HANNAM-DONG
16
41
71
57
45
Itaewon-ro 27-gil
64
49
58
63
69
Daesagwan-ro
50
23
60
29
43
37
17
33
Homo Hill
65
47
39
Seoul Central Mosque
Usadan-ro 10-gil
4
Usadan-ro
Usadan-ro 10-gil
Bogwang-ro
See map p228

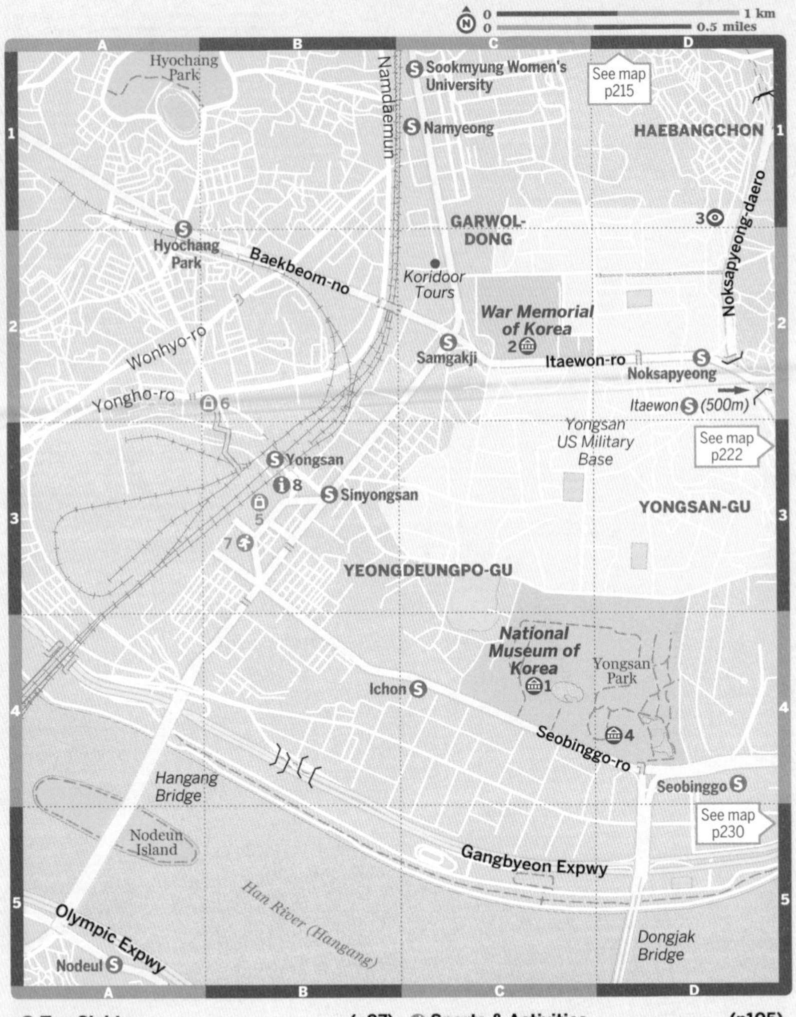

0 1 km
0 0.5 miles
Hyochang Park
Sookmyung Women's University
See map p215
Namdaemun
Namyeong
HAEBANGCHON
Noksapyeong-daero
GARWOL-DONG
Hyochang Park
Baekbeom-no
Koridoor Tours
War Memorial of Korea
Samgakji
Itaewon-ro
Noksapyeong
Wonhyo-ro
Yongho-ro
Itaewon (500m)
Yongsan US Military Base
See map p222
Yongsan
Sinyongsan
YONGSAN-GU
YEONGDEUNGPO-GU
National Museum of Korea
Yongsan Park
Ichon
Seobinggo-ro
Seobinggo
Hangang Bridge
See map p230
Nodeul Island
Gangbyeon Expwy
Han River (Hangang)
Dongjak Bridge
Olympic Expwy
Nodeul

DONGDAEMUN & AROUND

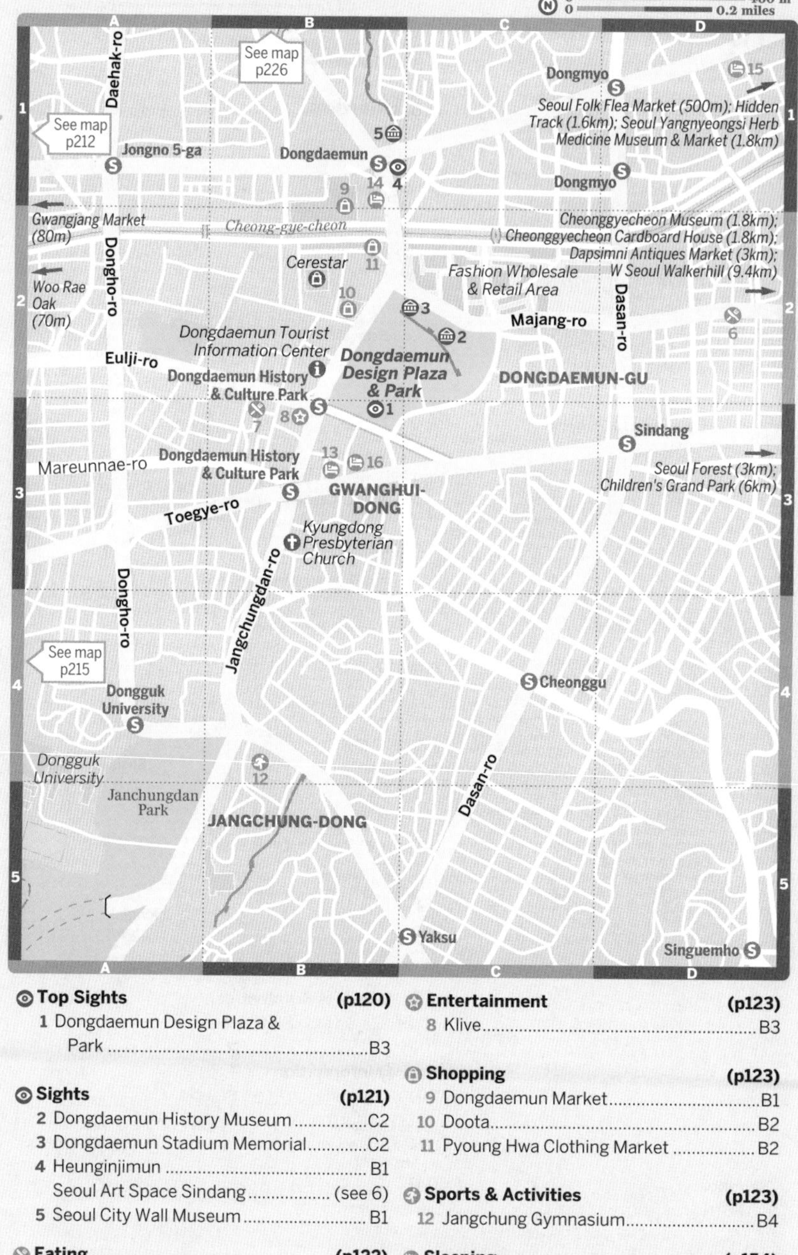

Top Sights (p120)
1 Dongdaemun Design Plaza & Park ... B3

Sights (p121)
2 Dongdaemun History Museum ... C2
3 Dongdaemun Stadium Memorial ... C2
4 Heunginjimun ... B1
Seoul Art Space Sindang ... (see 6)
5 Seoul City Wall Museum ... B1

Eating (p122)
Dongdaemun Market ... (see 9)
6 Jungang Market ... D2
7 Samarkand ... B3

Entertainment (p123)
8 Klive ... B3

Shopping (p123)
9 Dongdaemun Market ... B1
10 Doota ... B2
11 Pyoung Hwa Clothing Market ... B2

Sports & Activities (p123)
12 Jangchung Gymnasium ... B4

Sleeping (p154)
13 Dongdaemun Hostel & Inn ... B3
14 JW Marriott Dongdaemun Square ... B1
15 K Hostel ... D1
16 Toyoko Inn Seoul Dongdaemun ... B3

DAEHANGNO & SEONGBUK-DONG

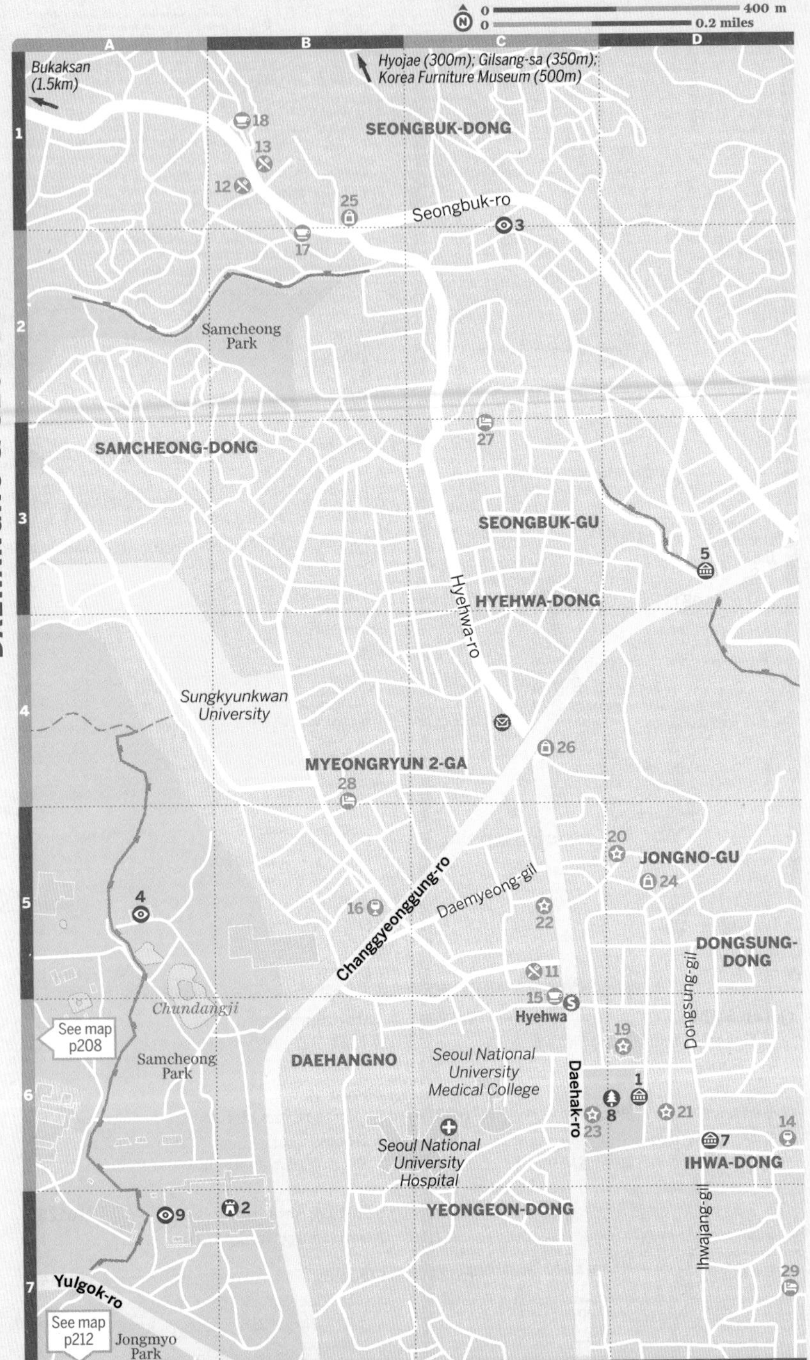

0 400 m
0 0.2 miles
Bukaksan (1.5km)
Hyojae (300m); Gilsang-sa (350m); Korea Furniture Museum (500m)
SEONGBUK-DONG
Seongbuk-ro
Samcheong Park
SAMCHEONG-DONG
SEONGBUK-GU
HYEHWA-DONG
Hyehwa-ro
Sungkyunkwan University
MYEONGRYUN 2-GA
JONGNO-GU
Daemyeong-gil
Changgyeonggung-ro
DONGSUNG-DONG
Dongsung-gil
Chundangji
See map p208
Samcheong Park
DAEHANGNO
Seoul National University Medical College
Hyehwa
Daehak-ro
Seoul National University Hospital
IHWA-DONG
Ihwajang-gil
YEONGEON-DONG
Yulgok-ro
See map p212
Jongmyo Park

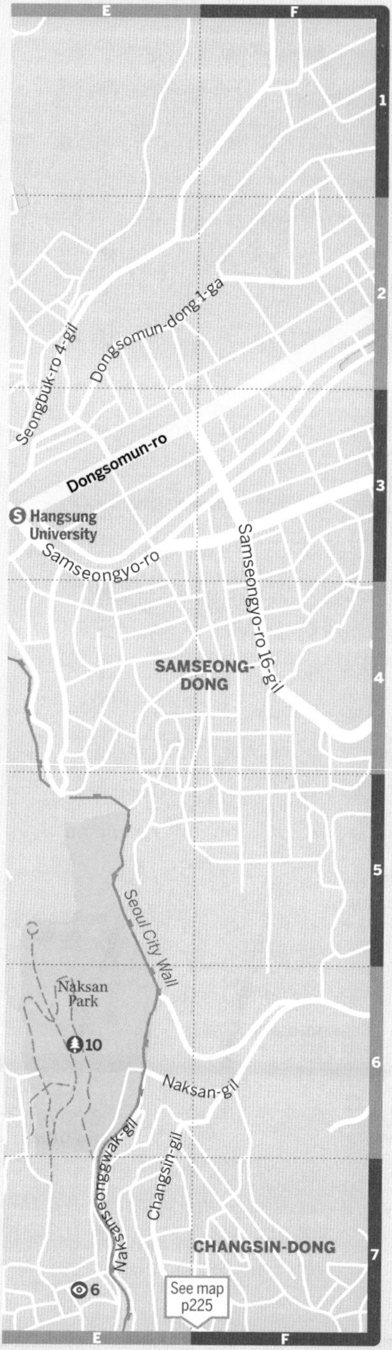

E F

1 2 3 4 5 6 7

Dongsomun-dong 1-ga
Seongbuk-ro 4-gil
Dongsomun-ro
Hangsung University
Samseongyo-ro
Samseongyo-ro 16-gil
SAMSEONG-DONG
Seoul City Wall
Naksan Park
10
Naksan-gil
Naksanseonggwak-gil
Changsin-gil
CHANGSIN-DONG
6

See map p225

E F

Sights (p127)

1 Arko Art Center D6
2 Changgyeonggung B7
3 Choi Sunu House C1
4 Great Greenhouse A5
5 Hyehwamun D3
6 Ihwa Maeul E7
7 Lock Museum D6
8 Marronnier Park D6
9 Myeongjeongjeon A7
10 Naksan Park E6

Eating (p130)

11 Deongjang Yesool C5
12 Serious Deli B1
13 Wood and Brick B1

Drinking & Nightlife (p131)

14 Dallyeora Gaemi 1 .... D6
15 Hakrim C6
16 Mix & Malt B5
On the Hill Cafe .... (see 6)
17 Slow Garden B2
18 Suyeon Sanbang B1

Entertainment (p131)

19 ArkoPAC D6
20 Dongsoong Arts Center D5
21 Jazz Story D6
22 Seoul Theater Center C5
23 Theatre Ticket Office C6

Shopping (p132)

24 10X10 .... D5
25 Baek Baek B1
26 Filipino Sunday Market C4

Sleeping (p154)

27 Eugene's House C3
28 Inside Backpackers B4
29 Minari House D7

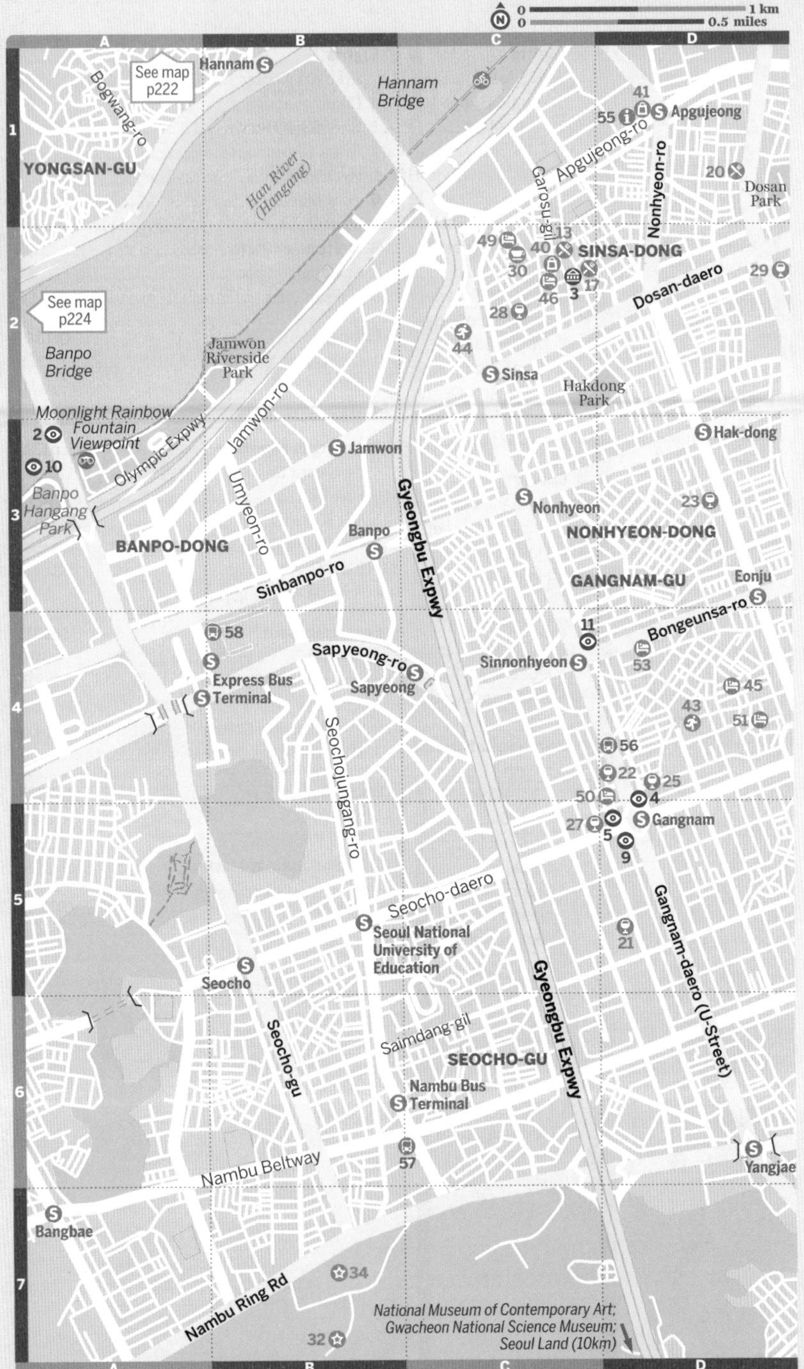
APGUJEONG & GANGNAM
0 1 km
0 0.5 miles
See map p222
See map p224
Hannam
Hannam Bridge
Bogwang-ro
YONGSAN-GU
Han River (Hangang)
Apgujeong
Apgujeong-ro
Garosu-gil
Nonhyeon-ro
Dosan Park
SINSA-DONG
Dosan-daero
Banpo Bridge
Jamwon Riverside Park
Sinsa
Hakdong Park
Moonlight Rainbow Fountain Viewpoint
Jamwon-ro
Olympic Expwy
Jamwon
Hak-dong
Banpo Hangang Park
Umyeon-ro
Gyeongbu Expwy
Nonhyeon
NONHYEON-DONG
BANPO-DONG
Banpo
GANGNAM-GU
Eonju
Sinbanpo-ro
Bongeunsa-ro
Sapyeong-ro
Sinnonhyeon
Sapyeong
Express Bus Terminal
Seochojungang-ro
Gangnam
Seocho-daero
Seoul National University of Education
Gangnam-daero (U-Street)
Seocho
Saimdang-gil
SEOCHO-GU
Seocho-gu
Nambu Bus Terminal
Yangjae
Nambu Beltway
Bangbae
Nambu Ring Rd
National Museum of Contemporary Art; Gwacheon National Science Museum; Seoul Land (10km)

See map p230

Sights (p110)

1 313 Art Project E1
2 Banpo Bridge Rainbow Fountain A3
3 Fifty Fifty C2
4 Gangnam Style 'Horse Dance' Stage D4
5 GT Tower East D5
6 Horim Museum E1
7 K-Star Road E1
K-Wave Experience .... (see 55)
Museum of Gugak .... (see 32)
8 Opera Gallery E2
9 Samsung D'Light D5
Seoul Arts Center .... (see 34)
10 Some Sevit A3
11 Urban Hive C4

Eating (p113)

12 Coreanos Kitchen E1
13 Gilbert's Burgers & Fries C2
14 Ha Jun Min E1
15 Hanmiri E4
16 Jungsik E1
17 Lay Bricks C2
18 Nonhyeon Samgyetang E2
19 Queens Park E1
20 Samwon Garden D1

Drinking & Nightlife (p114)

21 Booth D5
22 Club Mass D4
23 Club Octagon D3
24 Greenmile Coffee E2
25 Meakjugo D4
26 Moon Jar E1
27 Neurin Maeul C5
Oktoberfest .... (see 27)
28 Pongdang C2
29 SJ Kunsthalle D2
30 Steamers Coffee Factory C2
Take Urban .... (see 11)

Entertainment (p115)

31 LG Arts Center E4
32 National Gugak Center B7
33 Once in a Blue Moon E1
34 Seoul Arts Center B7

Shopping (p116)

35 10 Corso Como Seoul E1
36 Boon the Shop E1
37 Boon the Shop (Men's) E1
38 Boy+ by Supermarket E1
39 Galleria E1
40 Garosu-Gil C2
41 Hyundai Department Store D1
42 Pungwoldang E1

Sports & Activities (p117)

43 Kukkiwon D4
44 Spa Lei C2

Sleeping (p152)

45 24 Guesthouse Gangnam Center D4
46 24 Guesthouse Garosu-gil C2
47 H Avenue Hotel E4
48 Kimchee Gangnam Guesthouse E2
49 La Casa C2
50 M Chereville D4
51 Mercure Seoul Ambassador Gangnam Sodowe D4
52 Princess Hotel E1
53 Ritz-Carlton Seoul D4
54 Tria Hotel E4

Information

55 Gangnam Tourist Information Center D1

Transport

56 Bus Stop for Everland Amusement Park D4
57 Nambu Bus Terminal C6
58 Seoul Express Bus Station B4

JAMSIL

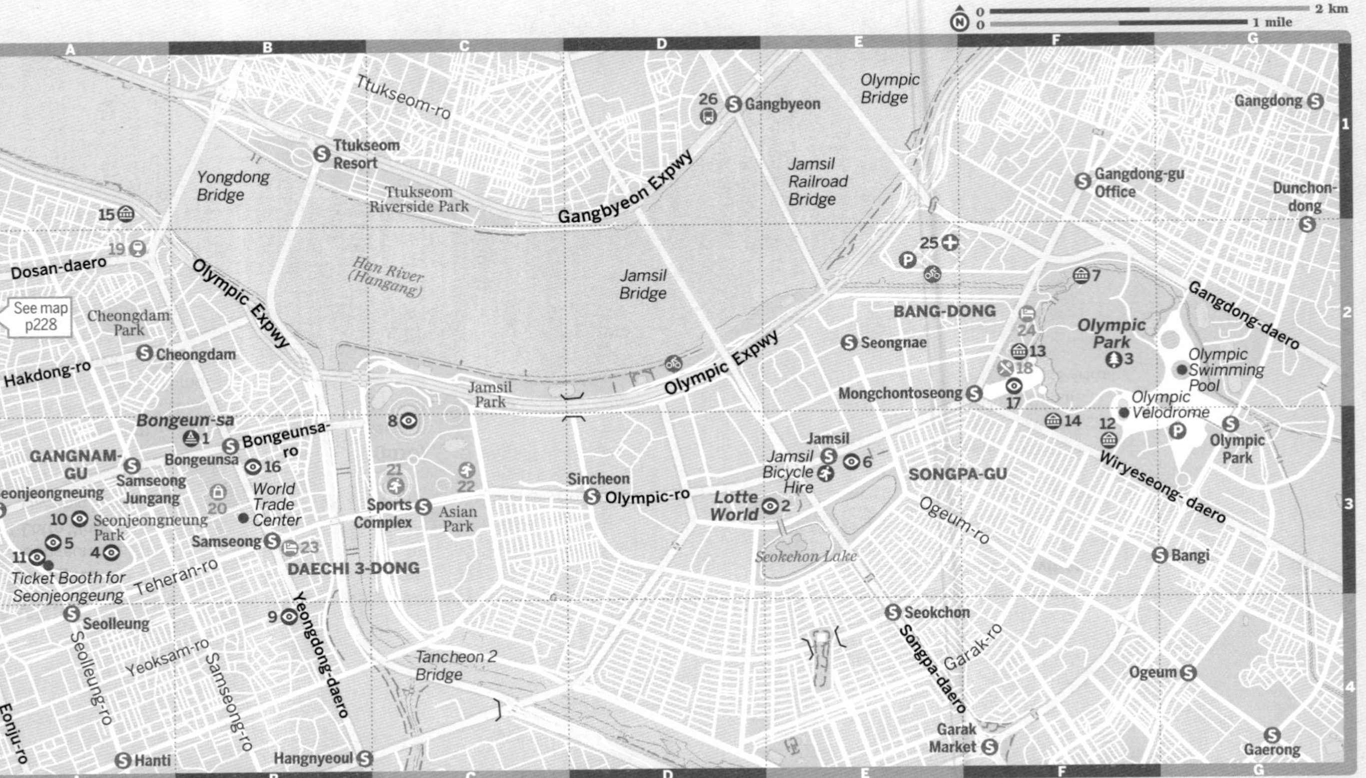
0 2 km
0 1 mile
Ttukseom-ro
Gangbyeon
Olympic Bridge
Gangdong
Ttukseom Resort
Yongdong Bridge
Ttukseom Riverside Park
Gangbyeon Expwy
Jamsil Railroad Bridge
Gangdong-gu Office
Dunchon-dong
Dosan-daero
Olympic Expwy
Han River (Hangang)
Jamsil Bridge
See map p228
Cheongdam Park
Cheongdam
BANG-DONG
Olympic Park
Gangdong-daero
Seongnae
Olympic Swimming Pool
Hakdong-ro
Jamsil Park
Olympic Expwy
Mongchontoseong
Olympic Velodrome
Bongeun-sa
Bongeunsa-ro
Jamsil
Olympic Park
GANGNAM-GU
Bongeunsa
Jamsil Bicycle Hire
SONGPA-GU
Wiryeseong- daero
Samseong Jungang
World Trade Center
Seonjeongneung
Sincheon
Olympic-ro
Lotte World
Sports Complex
Asian Park
Seonjeongneung Park
Ogeum-ro
Samseong
Seokchon Lake
Bangi
DAECHI 3-DONG
Ticket Booth for Seonjeongeung
Teheran-ro
Seokchon
Seolleung
Yeongdong-daero
Songpa-daero
Tancheon 2 Bridge
Garak-ro
Yeoksam-ro
Seolleung-ro
Samseong-ro
Ogeum
Eonju-ro
Garak Market
Gaerong
Hanti
Hangnyeoul

JAMSIL

Top Sights **(p108)**
1 Bongeun-sa ... B3
2 Lotte World ... E3
3 Olympic Park ... F2

Sights **(p110)**
COEX Aquarium ... (see 20)
Folk Museum ... (see 2)
4 King Jeongjong's Tomb ... A3
5 King Seongjong's Tomb ... A3
6 Lotte World Tower ... E3
7 Mongchon Museum ... F2
8 Olympic Stadium ... C3
9 Prugio Valley ... B4
10 Queen Jeonghyeon Wanghu's Tomb ... A3
11 Seonjeongneung ... A3
12 Seoul Baekje Museum ... F3
13 Seoul Olympic Museum ... F2
14 SOMA ... F3
15 SongEun ArtSpace ... A1
16 Tangent ... B3
17 World Peace Gate ... F2

Eating **(p113)**
18 Seasons Table ... F2

Drinking & Nightlife **(p114)**
19 Ellui ... A2

Shopping **(p116)**
20 COEX Mall ... B3
Lotte World Mall ... (see 6)

Sports & Activities **(p117)**
21 Jamsil Baseball Stadium ... C3
Lotte World Ice Skating Rink ... (see 2)
22 Seoul Sports Complex ... C3

Sleeping **(p152)**
Lotte Hotel World ... (see 2)
23 Park Hyatt Seoul ... B3
24 Seoul Olympic Parktel ... F2

Information
25 Asan Medical Center ... E2

Transport
CALT ... (see 20)
26 Dong-Seoul Bus Terminal ... D1

Our Story

A beat-up old car, a few dollars in the pocket and a sense of adventure. In 1972 that's all Tony and Maureen Wheeler needed for the trip of a lifetime – across Europe and Asia overland to Australia. It took several months, and at the end – broke but inspired – they sat at their kitchen table writing and stapling together their first travel guide, *Across Asia on the Cheap*. Within a week they'd sold 1500 copies. Lonely Planet was born.

Today, Lonely Planet has offices in Franklin, London, Melbourne, Oakland, Beijing and Delhi, with more than 600 staff and writers. We share Tony's belief that 'a great guidebook should do three things: inform, educate and amuse'.

Our Writers

Trent Holden

Coordinating Author; Myeong-dong & Jung-gu; Itaewon & Around; Gangnam & South of the Han River; Dongdaemun & Eastern Seoul; Day Trips; Sleeping Having covered the length of the peninsula on other writing assignments – including a piece on the North for BBC Travel – this is Trent's first gig working on the Seoul book for Lonely Planet. He had the not so shabby task of checking out its stunning mix of Joseon-era and modern architecture, world-class museums and galleries, countless bars and way too much good food. Trent has written 20-odd books for Lonely Planet, covering mainly Asia and Africa titles. You can catch him on twitter @hombreholden.

Simon Richmond

Gwanghwamun & Jongno-gu; Western Seoul; Northern Seoul; Sleeping UK-born writer and photographer Simon first coordinated Lonely Planet's *Korea* guide in 2009 when he explored Seoul and its surroundings over several weeks. He liked the place so much that his next visit, to update the 7th edition of *Seoul*, saw him spend over two months living in Seoul and getting to know it even better. For this edition, Simon covered central, northern and western areas of Seoul; he also hiked around the old city walls on a beautiful spring day and had an enjoyable but messy time learning to make *magkeolli*. Follow him on Twitter, Instagram and at www.simonrichmond.com.

Read more about Simon at:
http://auth.lonelyplanet.com/profiles/simonrichmond

Published by Lonely Planet Publications Pty Ltd
ABN 36 005 607 983
8th edition – January 2016
ISBN 978 1 74321 002 4

10 9 8 7 6 5 4 3 2 1
Printed in China